# World Wisdom
# The Library of Perennial Philosophy

The Library of Perennial Philosophy is dedicated to the exposition of the timeless Truth underlying the diverse religions. This Truth, often referred to as the *Sophia Perennis*—or Perennial Wisdom—finds its expression in the revealed Scriptures as well as the writings of the great sages and the artistic creations of the traditional worlds.

The Perennial Philosophy provides the intellectual principles capable of explaining both the formal contradictions and the transcendent unity of the great religions.

Ranging from the writings of the great sages of the past, to the perennialist authors of our time, each series of our Library has a different focus. As a whole, they express the inner unanimity, transforming radiance, and irreplaceable values of the great spiritual traditions.

*Paths to Transcendence: According to Shankara, Ibn Arabi, and Meister Eckhart* appears as one of our selections in the Spiritual Masters: East and West series.

# Spiritual Masters: East and West Series

This series presents the writings of great spiritual masters of the past and present from both East and West. Carefully selected essential writings of these sages are combined with biographical information, glossaries of technical terms, historical maps, and pictorial and photographic art in order to communicate a sense of their respective spiritual climates.

# PATHS TO TRANSCENDENCE

## According to Shankara, Ibn Arabi, and Meister Eckhart

REZA SHAH-KAZEMI

World Wisdom

Paths to Transcendence:
According to Shankara, Ibn Arabi, and Meister Eckhart
© 2006 World Wisdom, Inc.

Library of Congress Cataloging-in-Publication Data

Shah-Kazemi, Reza.
  Paths to transcendence : according to Shankara, Ibn Arabi, and Meister Eckhart / Reza
Shah-Kazemi.
    p. cm. -- (Spiritual masters. East and West series)
  Includes bibliographical references and index.
  ISBN-13: 978-0-941532-97-6 (pbk. : alk. paper)
  ISBN-10: 0-941532-97-6 (pbk. : alk. paper)  1. Transcendence of God. 2. Sankaracarya. 3.
Ibn al-'Arabi, 1165-1240. 4. Eckhart, Meister, d. 1327.  I. Title. II. Series.
  BL205.S24 2006
  204'.2--dc22

                                                              2005033670

Printed on acid-free paper in Canada.

For information address World Wisdom, Inc.
P.O. Box 2682, Bloomington, Indiana 47402-2682
www.worldwisdom.com

Dedicated to the memory of

FRITHJOF SCHUON

# CONTENTS

# PREFACE

The present book is based upon a doctoral thesis that was submitted to the University of Kent at Canterbury in 1994. The central chapters and conclusions remain fundamentally the same, but I have placed some of the material that formed part of the original work at the back of the present book, in the form of an appendix, entitled "Against the Reduction of Transcendence." Here, the focus is on recent important academic attempts to situate and explain mystical experience; the perspectives associated with Steven Katz, Robert Forman, W.T. Stace, R.C. Zaehner, Ninian Smart, and Fritz Staal are all critically examined. The common element uniting all these approaches can be expressed by the phrase "the reduction of transcendence," inasmuch as they all, in different ways, fail to do justice to the summit of mystical realization. The reductionism—implicit or explicit—of these perspectives is thrown into sharper relief by the conclusions of this study.

Grateful acknowledgment of the support I received while conducting the doctoral research that forms the basis of this book is due, above all others, to two people: my supervisor, Dr. Peter Moore, of the University of Kent at Canterbury, whose initial advice led to the conception of this research; and to Ghazi bin Mohammed, without whose generous assistance, from 1991 to 1993, the research could not have been so swiftly completed. I am also profoundly grateful to Antony Alston for the many illuminating hours spent discussing Shankara's doctrines, which he so graciously accorded me. Finally, I cannot sufficiently thank Dr. Martin Lings for reading the present text in its entirety, for making many valuable suggestions, and, most of all, for providing me with a living embodiment of many of the principles, themes, and mysteries explored in this book.

# INTRODUCTION

The aim of this book is to contribute to the elucidation of an important but much neglected theme in comparative religion and mysticism: that of transcendence. More specifically, we intend to shed light on the meaning of transcendence both in itself and as the summit of spiritual realization; thus, both as a metaphysical principle and as a mystical attainment, our principal concern being with the concrete dimensions of the spiritual paths leading to what we shall be calling here "transcendent realization." What we wish to offer is an interpretive essay on this theme, taking as our starting point what three of the world's greatest mystics have said or written on this subject.

Numerous studies have been made on mysticism in general, but this category embraces such a wide range of phenomena—from the psychic to the imaginal, from visionary experience to prophecy, from transient ecstatic states to permanent transformations of consciousness—that the principal aspects of transcendence, in relation to phenomenal descriptions of mystical experience, have been largely overlooked. It is all too easy to mistake the outward phenomena of mysticism for its goal; when the transcendent summit is understood, on the other hand, mystical phenomena can be properly situated in relation to it. It may strike many as presumptuous to put forward any definitive and exclusive notion of what this transcendent summit is; and this would be true were it to be a notion based entirely upon philosophical speculation. The meanings and implications of transcendence elaborated in this study, however, are based on the doctrines and pronouncements of spiritual authorities of the highest rank, that is, sages who, whilst not being prophets in the strict sense, can be said to have realized the ultimate degree of spirituality enshrined within their respective religious traditions.

Shankara, Ibn Arabi, and Meister Eckhart have been chosen as appropriate subjects for this study inasmuch as both the conceptual and experiential aspects of transcendence figure prominently in their articulated writings and discourses; each one has, moreover, expressed himself in a manner that is at once authoritative—bearing witness to his personal realization—and detailed, thus allowing for extensive analytical treatment of these aspects of transcendence. Given the immense importance of these figures within their respective traditions, close scrutiny of their perspectives should yield valuable insights into the ultimate spiritual attainments conceived and realized in the Hindu, Muslim, and Christian traditions.[1]

---

[1] For a good translation of a classic biography of Shankara, see Swami Tapasyananda, *The Sankara dig-vijaya of Madhara Vidyaranya*, Ramakrishna Mission, Madras, 1983; for an excellent spiritual biography of Ibn Arabi, see Claude Addas, *Quest for the Red Sulphur: The Life of Ibn Arabi*, Islamic Texts Society, Cambridge, UK, 1993; and for a good concise overview of Eckhart in his context see Oliver Davies, *Meister Eckhart: Mystical Theologian*, SPCK, London, 1991.

In adopting this approach, we are following the comparative model employed by Toshihiko Izutsu in his work, *Sufism and Taoism*.[2] There, central philosophical concepts of Ibn Arabi are compared with those of Lao Tzu and Chuang Tzu; the key feature of the work which commends itself for this study is the depth with which the two perspectives are dealt with in their own terms; and this forms the basis for entering into the final comparative chapter. This approach stands in stark contrast both to comparative analyses of mysticism taking key mystics as points of departure, such as Rudolph Otto's *Mysticism East and West*,[3] and those analyses which are based on selected quotations from various sources, such as R.C. Zaehner's *Mysticism: Sacred and Profane*,[4] and D.T. Suzuki's *Mysticism: Christian and Buddhist*.[5] While illuminating parallels may emerge through the juxtaposition of selected passages from different mystics, what is lacking is an analysis of each of the perspectives in its own terms as a basis for meaningful comparison. Moreover, there has been no effort to expound rigorously the notion of transcendence in relation to spiritual consciousness.

The concern here is with the vital connection between the awareness of transcendence as a notion, concept, idea, or principle, on the one hand, and the concrete modalities of spiritual attainment on the other. Our aim, then, is not so much to unearth new or hitherto undiscovered material—we shall be confining ourselves to existing translations of the primary sources; nor do we claim to be representing in any exhaustive fashion the doctrines of the three mystics. Rather, the intention is to focus upon, and elucidate, the most essential aspects of the teachings of the three mystics insofar as the highest metaphysical doctrine and the deepest spiritual realization is concerned.

The meaning of transcendent realization will be explored, then, according to each of the three mystics. As for the term "transcendent realization" itself, by it is meant the summit of spiritual attainment, "realization" here intended in the sense of "making real," on the basis of direct experience and personal assimilation; and by "transcendent" is meant that which relates to the ultimate aims of religion insofar as the individual is concerned *hic et nunc*, as opposed to salvation in the Hereafter, without implying thereby any essential incompatibility between the two aims.

The discussion will be closely tied to the major texts and discourses of the three mystics selected for study. This work of interpretive analysis is based on important recent advances in the field of translation: in particular, the efforts of Antony Alston in respect of Shankara's works, William Chittick's contribution to the translation of Ibn Arabi's voluminous writings, and the translation of Meister Eckhart's sermons by Maurice O'Connell Walshe.

There will be little reference to secondary sources in the three main chapters dealing with each of the three mystics in turn, the aim here being to allow the

[2] T. Izutsu, *Sufism and Taoism*, University of California Press, Berkeley, 1983.

[3] R. Otto, *Mysticism East and West*, Macmillan, New York, 1960.

[4] R.C. Zaehner, *Mysticism: Sacred and Profane*, Oxford University Press, 1961.

[5] D.T. Suzuki, *Mysticism: Christian and Buddhist*, George Allen & Unwin, London, 1979.

subjects to speak for themselves as far as possible, and basing philosophical reflection on this data itself rather than on the numerous hypotheses and speculations in the secondary literature. The intention is to study carefully the most essential teachings of the three mystics and to extract therefrom those elements pertaining to transcendence, on both the doctrinal and experiential planes; on the basis of these extracts a mode of evaluation will be used which is partly exegetical—in the sense of explication of, and comment upon, what is expressed—and partly analytical, in that discussion of particular themes, concepts, and relationships will take on a more discursive and comparative nature.

Each of the three substantive chapters is intended to be a case-study in its own right, with discussion crystallizing around the following three basic themes of transcendence:

1. Doctrinal dimensions of transcendence: how the transcendent Absolute is conceived and designated; what it is that constitutes the ultimate Reality or Being; ontological distinctions and relationships between the Transcendent and the non-transcendent. Discussion in this part of each chapter will serve as the conceptual or theoretical background against which the following two parts, concerned with concrete aspects of realization, will be more clearly appreciated.

2. The "ascent" of consciousness in its assimilation of this transcendentally conceived Absolute: what is implied by this transcendent realization, what its preconditions are, what it is that is transcended, and in what ways; the role of the ego, the intellect, the divine "Other" and the divine "Self" in the process or act of transcendence. The precise meaning of what is uncritically referred to as the state of "mystical union" will figure prominently in this section, along with discussion of the disjuncture between the state as such and those aspects of the state that are communicable.

3. The existential "return" to normal awareness within the ontologically diversified realm of the world will then be assessed: how does the realization of the highest state translate into everyday life, what are the cognitive and existential modes of living proper to the "realized" person. In what ways does the "ordinary" world, and life within that world, become transformed within the consciousness of one who has realized transcendence of the world?

Within these broadly defined categories, analysis will be conducted in accordance with the particular emphases found within the respective texts; thus there will be a broad basis for comparison without this entailing any tautologous attempt at forcing the material into preconceived categories. It is for this reason that an additional category will be found in the chapter on Ibn Arabi that is absent in the other two chapters; for the analysis of Ibn Arabi's writings revealed that a key factor relating to transcendence needed to be addressed in its own right: the universality of religious belief. Despite the fact that this element does not figure at all in either Shankara or Meister Eckhart, it is necessary to give it its due within the context of Ibn Arabi's view of transcendence.

Because of the exegetical style of analysis in the three chapters on the mystics, and the dense argumentation which their often elliptical pronouncements requires, an attempt has been made to reduce as far as possible the use of notes at the end of each chapter; for this reason references will be given in the text itself according to a key, found at the beginning of each chapter.

The concluding chapter brings together the central features of transcendence held in common by the three mystics. In the course of this comparative analysis, notable differences between the three mystics will also be evaluated, in an attempt to arrive at an answer to one of the central questions concerning spiritual realization in religion: is the summit of the mystical quest one and the same, or are there as many summits as there are religions? The overriding conclusion is that, based on the pronouncements of the mystics studied here, one can justifiably speak of a single, transcendent essence of spiritual realization, whatever be the religious starting-point. The stress here is on the word "transcendent"; anything short of this level inescapably entails multiplicity and hence differences as well as similarities, but not unity: unity in an absolute sense is only to be found at the level of the Absolute, that is, at the transcendent level, precisely.

It might be objected that the summit of mysticism is not so much something to be analyzed from without, as it is something to be attained from within. This is no doubt true, but the imperative of inward realization does not preclude the right to objective analysis; far from it. For even if the ultimate nature of spiritual realization be ineffable and thus beyond the compass of analysis, volumes have been written by mystics on those aspects of realization that are communicable; and what is communicable is by that very token analyzable, without this in any way detracting from the intrinsic dimension of mystery on which all mystics insist. Also, and more importantly, the initial orientation towards the summit of realization requires conceptual clarity, on pain of falling prey to the most dangerous illusions: *corruptio optimi pessima*. Moreover, given the clear errors that are paraded as spiritual truths in our time, the need for clarity about the meaning of spirituality can hardly be over-emphasized; and the fundamental nature of spirituality is more clearly discernible in the light of what constitutes its ultimate goal. To answer the question of what this goal is, and by means of which paths it can be attained, one can do no better than to examine carefully the teachings of the acknowledged mystical authorities of the world's religious traditions—to try and elucidate the teachings of three of the very greatest authorities on this altogether fundamental question in religion and mysticism— and such is the aim of the present study.

# CHAPTER 1

# SHANKARA: *Tat tvam asi*

This chapter comprises three parts: Part I, entitled "Doctrine of the Transcendent Absolute," will be concerned with the principal conceptual aspects of the transcendent Absolute, the manner in which it can be defined, designated, or envisaged; this will involve discussion of the relationship between the "lesser" and the "greater" Absolute, and correlatively, between "Being" and that which transcends it. These considerations will serve as the analytical complement to the rest of the chapter which will deal with the spiritual attainment or "realization" of that transcendentally conceived Absolute.

Part II, "Spiritual Ascent," comprises six sections, dealing with stages along the path of transcendence, culminating in the attainment of "Liberation," *moksa* or *mukti*; these stages emerge as points of reference from the various writings of Shankara on the question of the "ultimate value" (*nihsreyasa*), referred to also as Enlightenment or simply Knowledge (*jñana*).

Part III, "Existential 'Return,'" will examine the most important aspects of the "return" to normal modes of awareness in the world of phenomena, after the experience of Liberation has been attained by the one now designated *jivan-mukta*—the soul liberated in this life.

The sources used for this chapter consist in translations from the works of Shankara; in selecting the books for this study, priority was given to those works which modern scholarship has established beyond doubt to have been written by Shankara: *The Thousand Teachings* (*Upadesa Sahasri*)—his principal independent doctrinal treatise; translations from his commentaries on the Upanisads, Brahma Sutras and other scriptures, drawing in particular from the excellent and comprehensive set of translations by A.J. Alston in six volumes, *A Samkara Source-Book*. Other works such as *Self-Knowledge* (*Atma-bodha*) and *The Crest Jewel of Discrimination* (*Vivekachudamani*), attributed to Shankara by the Advaitin tradition—but not having the same degree of scholarly authentication—have also been used, insofar as these works form part of the "Shankarian" spiritual legacy within the tradition and, as such, warrant attention from an analysis such as this, which is concerned more with the doctrinal perspective associated with Shankara within Hinduism, than with the historical personage of that name.

For ease of reference, the following system will be used: the book from which the citation is taken will be indicated by a key word in the title, with the page or, where appropriate, the chapter and verse, following it. Full details of the titles are found in the bibliography.

Absolute: *Samkara on the Absolute*. Vol. I of *A Samkara Source-Book*, trans. A.J. Alston.
Atma-bodha (A): *Self-Knowledge* (*Atma-Bodha*), trans. Swami Nikhilananda.

Atma-bodha (B): *Atma-bodha*, trans. "Raphael."

Creation: *Samkara on the Creation.* Vol. II of *A Samkara Source-Book*, trans. A.J. Alston.

Discipleship: *Samkara on Discipleship.* Vol. V of *A Samkara Source-Book*, trans. A.J. Alston.

Enlightenment: *Samkara on Enlightenment.* Vol. VI of *A Samkara Source-Book*, trans. A.J. Alston.

Gita: *The Bhagavad Gita, with the Commentary of Sri Sankaracharya*, trans. Alladi Mahadeva Sastry.

Karika: *The Mandukyopanisad, with Gaudapada's Karika and Sankara's Commentary*, trans. Swami Nikhilananda.

Reality: *Direct Experience of Reality, Verses from Aparokshanubhuti*, trans. Hari Prasad Shastri.

Soul: *Samkara on the Soul.* Vol. III of *A Samkara Source-Book*, trans. A.J. Alston.

Upadesa (A): *The Thousand Teachings* (*Upadesa Sahasri*), trans. A.J. Alston.

Upadesa (B): *A Thousand Teachings—Upadesa Sahasri*, trans. Swami Jagadananda.

Vivekachudamani: *Vivekachudamani*, trans. Swami Madhavananda.

# Part I: Doctrine of the Transcendent Absolute

## 1. Designations and Definitions of the Absolute

The first question that needs to be asked is whether the transcendent Absolute is in any way conceivable, in such a manner that one can speak of the "concept" thereof. If, as is maintained by Shankara, the Absolute is "That from which words fall back," that which ignorance (*avidya*) alone would attempt to define,[1] then what function is served by the variety of names by which the Absolute is referred to—*Brahman, Atman, Om, Turiya*?

Certainly, Shankara asserts that from the viewpoint of ignorance (*avidya*), the Absolute is inexplicable—*anirukta* (Absolute, 177). The attribution of "name and form" (*nama-rupa*) to the Absolute is, likewise, the result of ignorance. Name and form, like the erroneous conception of a snake in place of a rope, are destroyed when knowledge dawns; "hence the Absolute cannot be designated by any name, nor can it assume any form" (Absolute, 87).

Intrinsic knowledge of the Absolute can be acquired, but solely from the *paramarthika* perspective, that is, the viewpoint from the Absolute itself; while from the viewpoint of the relative, the *vyavaharika* perspective, the Absolute can only be viewed under the conditions of name and form. This distinction between the *paramarthika* and the *vyavaharika* perspectives is of the utmost importance, not just in respect of doctrinal formulations, but, as will be seen throughout this chapter, in respect of central ontological aspects of spiritual realization.

---

[1] Shankara cites this text many times; it appears both in the Taittiriya Upanisad, II.4 and in the Brhidaranyaka Upanisad, II.iii.6.

In answer to the question: is the Absolute Self designated by the name *Atman*, Shankara replies:

> No it is not.... When the word *Atman* is used ... to denote the inmost Self (*PratyagAtman*) ... its function is to deny that the body or any other empirically knowable factor is the Self and to designate what is left as real, even though it cannot be expressed in words (Absolute, 144).

This answer points to the apophatic nature of all designations and definitions concerning the Absolute; to "define" something in Hindu logic (as in Western logic) means primarily to mark it off from other objects, thus to isolate it; definition (*laksana*) is thus different from characterization (*visesana*), that is, positively identifying the attributes which characterize a particular object. Thus, to say that the Absolute "is defined as Reality, Knowledge, Infinity" (*Satyam-Jñanam-Anantam*), as it is in the Taittiriya Upanisad on which Shankara comments, means that the adjectives are "being used primarily not to characterize the Absolute positively but simply to mark it off from all else" (Absolute, 178).

Each element negates the non-transcendent dimensions that are implicit or conceivable in one or both of the other elements: to say that the Absolute is "Reality" means that its being "never fails," in contrast to the forms of things which, being modifications, are existent at one time, only to "fail" at some other time; since, however, this may imply that the Absolute is a non-conscious material cause, the term Knowledge is included in the definition and this serves to cancel any such false notion; and then, since Knowledge may be mistaken for an empirical attribute of the intellect, it too needs to be conditioned—*qua* definition—by the term Infinity, as this negates any possibility of that bifurcation into subject and object which constitutes the necessary condition for empirical knowledge. Infinity is said to "characterize the Absolute by negating finitude," whereas "the terms 'Reality' and 'Knowledge' characterize the Absolute (even if inadequately) by investing it with their own positive meanings" (Absolute, 182).

These "positive meanings" must still be understood from an apophatic viewpoint, in accordance with a central dialectical principle concerning knowledge of the Absolute, namely the double negation, *neti, neti*—"not thus, not thus."[2] Shankara illustrates this indirect manner of indicating the nature of the Absolute by means of a story about an idiot who was told that he was not a man; perturbed, he asked someone else the question: "What am I?" This person showed the idiot the classes of different beings, from minerals and plants upwards, explaining that he was none of them, and finally said: "So you are not anything that is not a man": "[T]he Veda proceeds in the same way as the one who showed the idiot that he was not a 'not-man.' It says 'not thus, not thus,' and says no more" (Absolute, 143).

---

[2] This text figures prominently in the Brhidaranyaka Upanisad, at II.iii.6, III.ix.26, IV.ii.4, and IV.iv.22. It should also be noted that we do not follow Alston's translation of *avidya* as "nescience," but rather use the more appropriate English word "ignorance."

For Shankara, communicable meaning is restricted within the following categories: genus, action, quality, and relation. Since the Absolute transcends these categories—it does not belong to any genus, performs no action, has no quality, and enters into no relation with "another" apart from itself—it "cannot be expressed by any word":

> [T]he Absolute is artificially referred to with the help of superimposed name, form, and action, and spoken of in exactly the way we refer to objects of perception.... But if the desire is to express the true nature of the Absolute, void of all external adjuncts and particularities, then it cannot be described by any positive means whatever. The only possible procedure then is to refer to it through a comprehensive denial of whatever positive characteristics have been attributed to it in previous teachings and to say "not thus, not thus" (Absolute, 141).

Because the Absolute is only indirectly designated by terms that must themselves be negated, it can take on, albeit extrinsically, other "definitions," the most important of these being the well known *Sat-Chit-Ananda*, which has been translated as "Being-Consciousness-Bliss," by Alston, who notes that although this definition is not found in any of the works deemed by modern scholarship to be undeniably by Shankara, it is found in the writings of Suresvara, his direct disciple (Absolute, 170), and figures prominently in two works attributed to Shankara by the tradition of Advaita Vedanta, namely *Atma-bodha* and *Vivekachudamani*.[3] Despite the fact that modern scholarship no longer regards these as authentic works of Shankara, they are so closely woven into the spiritual heritage of Shankara that any analysis of his perspective which fails to consider these works would be incomplete. Moreover, the term *Sat-Chit-Ananda* is so closely identified with his perspective that, in terms of the tradition of Advaita, one cannot pass lightly over this designation of the Absolute.

> That beyond which there is nothing ... the inmost Self of all, free from differentiation . . . the Existence-Knowledge-Bliss Absolute (Vivekachudamani, 263).

> Realize that to be *Brahman* which is Existence-Knowledge-Bliss Absolute, which is non-dual and infinite, eternal and One (Atma-bodha (A), 56).

The apophatic logic of the double negation must now be applied to the term. Firstly, to say *Sat*, Being or Reality, is to refer to That which is not non-being or nothingness, on the one hand; on the other hand, it designates transcendent Being, "that which is" as opposed to "things that are." *Chit*, or Consciousness, refers to That which is not non-conscious, on the one hand; and on the other, it designates transcendent Consciousness, as opposed to contents or objects of consciousness; and likewise *Ananda* refers to That which is not susceptible to suffering or deprivation, on the one hand; and on the other, it designates

---

[3] The translators of these works translate the formula as "Existence-Knowledge-Bliss Absolute." This is a less satisfactory translation, for reasons that will be clear from the discussion on Being in the next section.

transcendent Bliss or Bliss as such, as opposed to such and such an experience of bliss; to Bliss which cannot not be, as opposed to blissful experience that is contingent on worldly circumstances.

In this application of the double negation, the first *neti* operates so as to negate the direct opposite of the term, thereby indicating in a relatively direct manner the intrinsic nature or quality intended by it; whilst the second *neti* acts as the denial of any commensurability with what appears, from the viewpoint of *avidya*, to be similar to that quality, thereby indicating indirectly the transcendent degree proper to the quality here in question. Therefore the first negation is intended to direct awareness towards these three internal "modes" of the Absolute, whilst the second negation eliminates any traces of relativity that may appear to pertain to these modes when conceived on the plane of differentiated existence; thus, while a relative subject has the property of empirical awareness and enjoys an object of experience that is blissful, the Absolute Subject is at once transcendent Being-Consciousness-Bliss, in absolute non-differentiation, indivisibility, and non-duality.

The notion of the Absolute as *Sat* will be discussed further in the next section, which deals with Being in more detail; at this point the concern is to probe further into the manner of indicating or designating provisionally the nature of the Absolute.

To say, then, that the Absolute is Being-Consciousness-Bliss gives some provisional idea of the nature of the Absolute even while indicating the incommensurability between that idea and the reality alluded to. It can readily be seen that the principal purpose of the negation is to eliminate those attributes that have been superimposed upon the Absolute; the superimposition (*adhyaropa*) itself is seen to be a necessary starting point for thought on the Absolute, since, by means of endowing it with concrete characteristics, awareness is oriented towards something which truly "is," however faulty may be the initial conception thereof. Only subsequently is this being revealed in its true light, divested of all limitative attributes. At first, the sacred texts speak of the "false form" of the Absolute, "set up by adjuncts and fancifully referred to as if it had knowable qualities, in the words, 'with hands and feet everywhere.' For there is the saying of those who know the tradition (*sampradaya-vid*), 'That which cannot be expressed is expressed through false attribution and subsequent denial (*adhyaropa-apavada*)'" (Absolute, 147-148).

All attributes and names of the Absolute, then, are so many symbols, with the character of an *upaya*, a "saving stratagem" or a provisional means of "conveying the symbolized" (Absolute, 145). When, for example, the Absolute is endowed with the attribute of spatial location, as when scripture refers to the "place" of *Brahman*, Shankara writes that the implicit purpose behind such an *upaya* can be formulated thus: "First let me put them on the right path, and then I will gradually be able to bring them round to the final truth afterwards" (Enlightenment, 22).

It is important at this point to dwell a little on the term *upadhi*, the "particular limiting adjunct." It refers to that through which any determinate name, form, attribute, or conception is applied to the Absolute; it is said to be "set up by ignorance," because it depends upon an initial differentiation, and thus implicitly negates all that which is not encompassed by the particular adjunct in question; an adjunct which is thus to be clearly distinguished from the non-dual Reality.

Strictly speaking it is an illusory limitation superimposed on the object which it is supposed to reveal. It is therefore to be negated by *neti, neti*, in order to make possible the revelation of the real underlying substratum—that on which the superimposition takes place. The *upadhi*, according to one revealing etymology is "that which, standing near (*upa*) anything, imparts (*adhadati*) to it (the appearance of) its own qualities" (Creation, 3). This brings out clearly the distinction between the pure Absolute and all distinct attributes of the Absolute: the attribute as such is not only "other" than the object of the attribution, but it also "colors" that object according to the nature of the attribute; thus, anything that is objectively attributed to the Absolute is both a means of indicating the reality of the Absolute and simultaneously a veil over its true nature:

> In so far as the Self has an element of "this" (objective characteristic) it is different from itself, and a characteristic of itself. . . . It is as in the case of the man with the cow (Upadesa (A), II, 6.5).

The man who possesses a cow may be distinguished as "such and such, possessor of the cow," but the cow serves only to indicate the particular man in question, it does not define the man's essential nature: the man is utterly other than that possession which identifies him as a particular man. Analogously, no aspect of the Absolute that is definable and distinguishable in objective terms can be equated with the Absolute; the very act of positing a "this" involves an irreducible alterity: "this" is a distinguishing feature of the object to be known, and thus "other than" it. In reality, "nothing different from Me can exist so as to belong to Me" (Upadesa (A), II, 8.4).[4]

To speak of *Brahman* as possessing the attributes of "Lordship," such as omnipotence, justice, omniscience, and so on, is both true and false: true if what is in question is the "lower" or "lesser" Absolute, *Apara Brahman*, but false if it is the "higher" Absolute, *Para Brahman* (Enlightenment, 61-62); this same distinction is found expressed as *Brahma saguna* and *Brahma nirguna*, the first relating to the Absolute as endowed with qualities, the second relating to the Absolute insofar as it transcends all qualities. When the Absolute is spoken of as being the "performer of all actions" and as knowing all things, "we are speaking of it as associated with adjuncts. In its true state without adjuncts it is indescribable, partless, pure, and without empirical attributes" (Upadesa (A), II, 15.29).

It may be objected here that the Advaita principle is violated: there is one Absolute that is associated with relativity and another that is not. But this objection would be valid only if it were established that the Absolute undergoes real modification by virtue of its "association" with the adjuncts; only then

---

[4] This is Shankara "speaking" from the perspective of the Self, a mode of expression assuming the *paramarthika* perspective, and employed frequently by Shankara throughout his writings, doctrinal as well as exegetical.

would there be a fundamental dualism constituted by the adjunctless Absolute, on the one hand, and the Absolute associated with adjuncts, on the other. Such a dualism, however, is precluded for Shankara by the fact that no such modification takes place in reality, since the "association" in question is but an appearance, an illusory projection of the Real which cannot, *qua* illusion, constitute any element or "pole," such as could allow of an irreducible duo-dimensionality of the Absolute:

> [T]he Lordship, omniscience, and omnipotence of the Lord exist relative to the limitations and distinctions of ignorance only, and in reality there can be no practice of rulership or omniscience on the part of the Self, in which all distinctions remain eternally negated in knowledge (Creation, 66).

This does not deny the relative reality of the divine attributes themselves nor does it deny that the attributes do indeed pertain to the One Absolute; that the Absolute is the omnipotent Creator and the omniscient Witness is affirmed as a reality that is mediated through the *upadhi*s and received by all created beings. These attributes are the forms in which the One relates to the world, and for as long as worldly experience holds; what Shankara does deny is the ultimate metaphysical reality of this whole domain of relations and distinctions, "set up by ignorance": the One appears as many in relation to a world that is itself illusory. Thus:

> [N]on-duality which is the Supreme reality appears manifold through *Maya*, like the one moon appearing as many to one with defective eye-sight. . . . This manifold is not real, for *Atman* is without any part. . . . (It) cannot in any manner admit of distinction excepting through *Maya* (Karika, III, 19).

This *Maya-sakti*, or power of illusion, is the "seed of the production of the world" (Creation, 65); now the Lord, as *Brahma saguna* or *Apara Brahma* is at one and the same time the source of *Maya* and also included within it. Thus we have Shankara distinguishing the lesser Absolute by reference to its relationship with the *vasana*s, residual impressions deriving from past action:

> In so far as it consists of impressions arising from activity amongst the elements, it is omniscient and omnipotent and open to conception by the mind. Being here of the nature of action, its factors and results, it is the basis of all activity and experience (Absolute, 148-149).

This seems to make, not only the subjective conception of the Lord, but also its objective being, subject to the rhythms of samsaric existence; but this is only true "in so far as it consists of" *vasana*s: the truth is that the reality of the Lord is not exhausted by that dimension in which it participates in *samsara*; therefore its omniscience and omnipotence, while exercised in the world, also and necessarily transcend the world, even if it is to the "lesser" Absolute that these attributes, affirmed as such, pertain.

The reason for asserting that the Lord is both engaged within *Maya* and transcendent vis-à-vis *Maya* is twofold: firstly, as implied in the discussion above, the Lord *qua* Creator is, intrinsically and by virtue of its essential substance, nothing other than the Absolute; it is the Absolute and nothing else that extrinsically takes on the appearance of relativity in order to rule over it, as Lord, precisely: "That which we designate as the Creator of the Universe *is the Absolute* . . ." (Creation, 7, emphasis added).

The second reason for saying that the Lord is both in *Maya* and transcendent vis-à-vis *Maya* is the following: the Lord is referred to as the "Inner Controller" of the Cosmos, and, more significantly, as the conscious agent responsible not just for purposefully creating the visible and invisible worlds, but also for distributing the "fruits" of all action, karmic and ritual; Shankara emphatically opposes the idea of the Purva-Mimamsakas that action carries the principle of the distribution of its fruit within itself, without any need for an external controlling agency. In a colorful, descriptive passage that reminds one of the teleological argument for the existence of God in scholastic theology, he asserts:

> This world could never have been fashioned even by the cleverest of human artificers. It includes gods, celestial musicians, . . . demons, departed spirits, goblins, and other strange beings. It includes the heavens, the sky and the earth, the sun, the moon, the planets and the stars, abodes and materials for the widest imaginable range of living beings. . . . It could only proceed under the control of one who knew the merit and demerit of all the experiencers in all their variety. Hence we conclude that it must have some conscious artificer, just as we do in the case of houses, palaces, chariots, couches, and the like (Creation, 49).

In other words, the Lord is not simply a subjective construct of the individual sunk in ignorance, even though it is only through ignorance that the Absolute is viewed in its *Apara* form. The Lord exists fully and really only as the Absolute, *nirguna*; but as *saguna*, He is also an objective reality vis-à-vis the world over which He rules, a reality which is conditioned extrinsically by this very relationship and thus by the "dream" which this world is. But this dream is not crudely equatable with the imagination of the individual: "The Self . . . Himself imagines Himself in Himself as having the distinctions to be described below (i.e., the cosmic elements)" (Creation, 223). Whatever the individual proceeds to imagine about the nature of the Absolute can only take place because, "First of all the Lord imagines the individual soul" (Creation, 225).

Further considerations on the relationships between the individual, the Lord, and the Self will be forthcoming in the next part of this chapter. At present, further elaboration on the distinction between the lesser and higher Absolute is necessary, and the following section addresses this question in the light of the mode of Being proper to the transcendent Absolute.

## 2. Being and Transcendence

> The Absolute is first known as Being when apprehended through the (provisional) notion of Being set up by its external adjuncts, and is afterwards known as (pure) Being in its capacity as the Self, void of external adjuncts. . . . It is only to one who has already apprehended it in the form of Being that the Self manifests in its true transcendent form (Absolute 130) [parentheses by the translator, Alston].

One can understand more clearly the relativity of this "form of Being" in contradistinction to That which transcends it and which may be provisionally referred to as "Beyond-Being," by dialectically applying the tool of the double negation to this mode of thinking about the Absolute. Firstly, one cannot say that the "transcendent form" of the Absolute, *Brahma nirguna*, is deprived of being or reality: it is therefore "not nothing," this constituting the first *neti*. The second *neti* consists in the denial that it can be regarded as identical with Being when Being is conceived as the unmanifest Principle of all manifested beings.

Regarding the first negation, in terms of which *Brahma nirguna* must be seen as positively endowed with being, it should be noted that the positive attribution of being to the Self, however metaphysically inadequate this may be in the first instance, is the necessary prerequisite for grasping the Absolute in its "transcendent form" as Beyond-Being, this being an instance of the principle of *adhyaropa-apavada*, noted above.

The Absolute, then, must be understood to be real—and thus to "be"—even while it is divested of the relativity entailed by the attribution of Being to it, remembering that whatever is an attribute of the Absolute is not the Absolute, and that, by being attributed to it, Being necessarily constitutes an attribute of it. One now needs to understand more clearly the notion of the relativity of Being.

Commenting on the text "All this was *Sat* in the beginning," Shankara writes that the Being in question is

> ... that which contains within it the seed or cause (of creation). ... [T]he *Brahman* that is indicated by the words *Sat* and *Prana* is not the one who is free from its attribute of being the seed or cause of all beings. ... [T]he Sruti also declares, "It is neither *Sat* nor *Asat* (non-being)." ... [T]he Absolute *Brahman*, dissociated from its causal attribute, has been indicated in such Sruti passages as, "It is beyond the unmanifested, which is higher than the manifested." "He is causeless and is the substratum of the external (effect) and the internal (cause)" (Karika, I, 6[2]).

*Sat* can but be *Brahman* inasmuch as no element in the causal chain of being can be divorced from the one Reality, that of *Brahman*; but the converse does not hold: *Brahman* is not reducible to *Sat*. Only when associated with the "attribute of being the seed or cause of all beings" can one equate *Brahman* with Being; the same *Brahman*, when "dissociated from its causal attribute" is beyond the relativity of Being, also referred to here as the Unmanifest; this Unmanifest, though "higher than the manifested" is nonetheless a relativity as it is conditioned by the fact that it stands in a relationship of causality in relation to the domain of manifestation. To cause something to exist necessarily entails sharing with that thing a common attribute, namely, existence itself: "If the Self were affirmed to exist, such existence would be transient, as it would not be different in kind from the existence of a pot" (Absolute, 134).

This is why *Brahman* is declared to be neither Being nor non-Being: it is "beyond" Being, this term indicating in a paradoxical fashion that transcendent non-causal Reality which, encompassing all things by virtue of containing within itself the ultimate cause of all beings, is nonetheless not identifiable with that cause or its effects, but stands unsullied by any "trace of the development of manifestation (*prapañcha-upasama*)."[5]

Another significant aspect of the relativity of Being lies in its relationship with action: "*Karya* or effect is that which is done . . . which has the characteristic of result. *Karana* or the cause, is that which acts, i.e., it is the state in which the effect remains latent" (Karika, I, 7[11]). Despite the fact that Being is immutable relative to its manifested effects, it is in turn the first "actor" insofar as it is the immediate cause of those things which are "done," that is, its manifested effects; Being is therefore tantamount to act, movement, change, hence to relativity, when considered in relation to the non-causal and non-acting "Beyond-Being," *Brahma nirguna*. Constituting the ontological basis for the process of cosmic deployment, Being is also the first, necessary step in the unfolding of *Maya-sakti*, the power of illusion that simultaneously manifests and veils the Real. Elsewhere, Shankara refers to Being "as associated with action" in contrast to the pure Absolute which is *nirbija-rupa*, the "seedless form," the seed in question being that of action (Soul, 161).

The spiritual dynamics by which the world is reduced to being "not other than *Brahman*" will be addressed in Part III; at this point, it is important to clarify the doctrinal perspective on the world as illusion, as corollary to the principle that the Absolute alone is real, and to expand on the question of what is meant by saying that the world is "unreal."

> Though it is experienced, and though it is serviceable in relativity, this world, which contradicts itself in successive moments is unreal like a dream (Reality, 56).

The fact of ordinary experience in the world is not denied; it does possess a degree of reality, albeit relative, but for which it would not be "serviceable"; this experience, however, is inextricably bound up with a world that is said to contradict itself in successive moments, by which is meant: it is continuously changing, perpetually in motion, each moment's particular concatenation of circumstances differing from, and thus "contradicting," that of the next moment. That which is of a permanently self-contradictory nature cannot be said to truly exist: as soon as existence is ascribed to "it" the entity in question has changed, "contradicting" itself, so undermining that (apparent) existence which formerly obtained; this process repeating itself indefinitely, it becomes absurd to talk of the real existence of such an entity.

Instead, the ontological status of worldly experience is likened to that of the dream-world: it appears to be real for as long as one is dreaming, but, upon awakening, it is grasped in its true nature as "appearance"; the dream-world dissolves and, from the perspective of the waking subject, never "was," in reality. Thus, this world with all its manifold contents appears to be real only from the *vyavaharika* perspective, which is itself proportioned to the relative degree of reality proper to the world, and this degree in turn is conditioned, on the one

---

[5] Mandukya Upanisad, sruti 7.

hand by *avidya*, and on the other, by the very finitude and finality of the world, which not only contradicts itself in successive moments but also comes to a definitive end: like a dream, the world is doomed to extinction, to "be" no more, and whatever is not existent at one time cannot be said to be truly existent at any other: "That which is non-existent at the beginning and in the end is necessarily so in the middle" (Karika, II, 6).

Two further angles of vision from which the world is grasped as illusory may now be explored: those opened up by the "rope-snake" and the "jar-clay" analogies. In Advaita Vedanta, the rope-snake analogy is one of the most frequently employed means of pointing to the exclusive reality of the Absolute, non-dual *Brahman* in contrast to the illusory nature of the manifold phenomena of the world.

> This manifold, being only a false imagination, like the snake in the rope, does not really exist. . . . The snake imagined in the rope . . . does not really exist and therefore does not disappear through correct understanding (Karika, II, 7[17]).

When a rope in the dark is mistaken for a snake, there is a real object that is present and an imagined object that is absent: the snake as such is absent, but "it" is present insofar as it is in truth a rope: that object to which the name and form of a snake are ascribed is in reality a rope. When the rope is perceived, no formerly existent entity, "snake," can be said to have ceased to exist: only the erroneous perception ceases, the illusion disappears; the substratum on which the conception of "snakehood" was imposed stands self-evident. Likewise, the world of multiplicity is an illusion, deriving from ignorance; it is superimposed upon the Absolute, veiling its true nature for so long as it, in the manner of an *upadhi*, imparts the quality of its own nature to that on which it is superimposed, whereas in reality it is that substratum that provides the ontological foundation for the superimposition, thus imparting to it whatever "reality" it can be said to possess; only when it is "seen through," can it be assimilated to its substance.[6] Thus: "the snake imagined in the rope is real when seen as the rope" (Karika, III, 29).

But to see through the world thus and grasp its substratum, one must first be able to distinguish the one from the other:

> [W]hen the rope and the snake for which it was formerly mistaken in the dark have once been distinguished, the snake disappears into the rope and . . . never again emerges (Soul, 167).

Discrimination between the world and *Brahman*, between the relative and the Absolute, between the phenomenal many and the transcendent One—this discrimination, despite being itself a mode of distinction, is the prerequisite for overcoming all distinction; for no sooner is the rope distinguished from the snake, than the snake "disappears into the rope," the superimposed image is

---

[6] It is useful to recall here the etymology of the word "substance": that which "stands below."

reduced to its substratum; the world is grasped as being "non-different" from *Brahman*, one understands that "all is *Atman*." These points will be elaborated further in Parts II and III, dealing with the realization of transcendence.

Another key image which is used to help in the understanding of the relation between the Real and the illusory is that of the jar-clay relationship; it should be noted, however, that such a relationship subsists, or appears to exist, only from the viewpoint of ignorance, the Real being devoid of relations, since there is no "other" to which it could possibly relate.

When the true nature of clay is known, a jar does not exist apart from the clay (Karika, IV, 25).

[E]very effect is unreal because it is not perceived as distinct from its cause (Gita, II, 16).

Because the effects are in truth not distinct from their cause, they cannot be real as effects, but can be called real exclusively insofar as they are that cause; the jar as such is a modification of clay in both nominal and existential terms, in other words, it is clay taking on a particular *nama-rupa*, name and form. One cannot perceive any jar without at the same time perceiving clay, so that the jar has no reality without clay; it possesses no distinct reality on its own account. It is this ultimate absence of distinction that establishes, in doctrinal terms at least, the illusory nature of the world considered in itself: whatever is distinct from the non-dual Absolute must be an illusion, since reality is the exclusive preserve of the Absolute. On the other hand, from an inclusive point of view, non-duality also means that the world, albeit multiple in appearance, must also be that same non-dual Reality, insofar as it is absolutely non-distinguishable from its substratum: in the measure that it is so distinguished, by means of *nama-rupa*, in that very measure it is illusory.

The final unifying vision consists in seeing all things "in" the transcendent One, and that One in all things; it is realized fully only by the *jivan-mukta*, the one "delivered in this life," "who sees Me . . . in all beings, and who sees Brahma the Creator and all other beings in Me" (Gita, VI, 30). It is to the realization of this vision, its requirements, modalities, and consequences, that Part II is addressed.

## Part II: The Spiritual Ascent

This part of the chapter will address the process by which the consciousness within the *jivatman* (individual soul) realizes its true identity as *Brahman*, the realization of this identity constituting *mukti*, or *moksa*—"Liberation," the highest attainment possible to man in this world; this is the *Nihsreyasa*, the supreme value, upon realization of which, all that needs to be done has been done (*krta-krtya*).

Before examining the nature of this transcendent attainment, it is important to establish certain non-transcendent points of reference in order that one can situate the transcendence *a contrario*, as it were; the understanding of what constitutes transcendent realization requires one to know what it is that is being transcended. This epistemological approach, proceeding on the assumption of an experiential ascent from the lower degrees of being and consciousness to the transcendent level, accords with the basic ontological structure envisioned by Shankara:

> All this world consists of a hierarchy of more and more subtle and comprehensive effects which stand as the material causes of whatever is grosser. And knowledge of this hierarchy leads to the notion of Being as its support (Absolute, 129).

Whatever is closer to the material pole is less subtle and comprehensive than its principial cause; and the closer this cause is to the summit of the hierarchy, the more consciousness and reality it possesses—the summit itself, the Absolute, being unconditioned Consciousness and Reality.

The process of realization can thus be analyzed in terms of a mirror-image of this ontology: what is objectively conceived as "higher" in the ontological chain of causality will be seen subjectively as "deeper" in the process of realization of the Self. However, Shankara does affirm that in principle no such ascent in stages is necessary for supreme realization. It can take place instantaneously on the basis of just one hearing of the sacred texts affirming the identity between the essence of the soul and the Absolute. For this reason one should begin with an examination of the role of Scripture in the realization of the Self and then proceed with an assessment of the hierarchical stages along the path to that realization. After the section on Scripture will come five sections dealing with: action, ritual, meditation, concentration, and Liberation.

## 1. The Role of Scripture

Given the fact that the Absolute is "that from which words fall back," it may seem strange to observe the importance Shankara gives to the part played by Scripture—a set of "words," at first sight—in relation to realization of the Absolute. Bearing in mind that for Shankara this realization consists in knowledge of the Absolute and nothing else—leaving aside for now the nature and ontological degree of that knowledge—the following assertion shows how central a role Shankara ascribes to Scripture: the Absolute, he says, "can only be known through the authority of Revelation" (Absolute, 146).

What this means is that not only does Scripture provide the only objective means for supplying valid doctrinal knowledge of the Absolute, but also that key sentences of Scripture have the capacity to impart immediate enlightenment, this being conditional upon the readiness of the hearer. In the view of the non-dualist, the primary purpose of the Veda is to "put an end to the distinctions imagined through ignorance" (Enlightenment, 96), this being the manner in which it can be said to "communicate" that which is strictly inexpressible. All the Upanisadic texts without exception are deemed to be concerned, directly or indirectly, with the establishment of one truth, namely, "That thou art" (*Tat tvam asi*); and the function of this cardinal text, in turn, is "to end the conviction that one is the individual soul, competent for agency and empirical experience in the realm of illusory modifications" (Enlightenment, 110).

In answer to the question of how an abstract sentence, addressed to the mind, hence the not-self, could result in "concrete" Self-realization, Shankara says that, while it is true that all sentences regarding the "not-self" yield only abstract knowledge, "it is not so with sentences about the inmost Self, for there are exceptions, as in the case of the man who realized he was the tenth" (Upadesa (A), II, 18.202).

We shall see the relevance of this reference to the "tenth" in a moment. The impact of sentences affirming the Self is infinitely greater than that of any sentences relating to the not-self, because knowledge of the Self preexists any accidental vehicle by which this knowledge may be extrinsically communicated; this knowledge is one with the very being of the individual soul, who is in reality nothing but the indivisible Self; but it is a knowledge which has become hidden by the veil of individuality, and thus by the "mutual super-imposition of the Self and the not-self called ignorance" (Absolute, 95).

This mutual superimposition can be summed up as follows: first the Self is superimposed on the not-self, that is, the individual mind, senses, and body, so that this compound of relativities is falsely regarded as "myself"; then this compound is imposed on the Self, so that the unique and universal Subject is falsely regarded as having the objective characteristics of a particular individual and relative subject with a body and soul, resulting in an anthropomorphic conception of the Absolute.

The sentence affirming the true nature of the Self, by dispelling this mutual superimposition born of ignorance, awakens the *jiva* to his true identity as the Self, knowledge of which he is not so much taught as reminded. This is the meaning of the reference to the "tenth": the man who counted only nine others, and was perplexed because there were originally ten in the group, instantaneously realizes, upon being reminded, that he is himself the tenth.

Analogously, in the last analysis, it is preexisting knowledge of the Self that constitutes the basis for the revelatory power of Scripture; it is not the case that Scripture imparts or teaches a truth of which one is *a priori* ignorant. Thus one finds Shankara asserting:

> Indeed the Self is unknown (*aprasiddha*) to nobody. And the Scripture which is the final authority gains its authoritativeness regarding the Self as serving only to eliminate the super-imposition of the attributes alien to Him, but not as revealing what has been altogether unknown (Gita, II, 18).

If it is the true aim and transcendent function of Scripture to eliminate all false notions of alterity and differentiation, Shankara has to account for the existence of so many references in the texts to the different worlds in which rebirth takes place, according to degrees of merit and different kinds of ritual activity, all of which appears bound up with diversity, and thus with the non-self. If the Self is alone worthy of realization, and if all other aspirations are necessarily directed to transient states and "perishable regions," why does Scripture appear to encourage these aspirations?

The question is put by the disciple to the teacher in the first part of the *Upadesa Sahasri*, and the following answer is given:

> The Veda removes gradually the ignorance of him who does not know how to obtain what he desires and prevent what he does not desire. . . . Then afterwards it eradicates ignorance proper, which is vision of difference and which is the source of transmigratory life (Upadesa (A) I, 1.42).

What Shankara appears to be saying here is that the individual who is plunged in ignorance, seeking to avoid the painful and to enjoy the pleasurable, and doing so on the plane of outward manifestation—such a person would not be able to immediately grasp either the truth or the relevance of the doctrine of the Self. In seeking the desirable, however, he is in fact seeking the absolute bliss of the Self, and to the extent that he avoids the undesirable, he distances himself from the more painful illusions attendant upon identification with the not-self. Therefore Scripture, in the manner of an *upaya*, operates within a framework that is immediately intelligible for such an individual, and orients his mode of consciousness and being in an upward direction in such wise that the goal which was previously regarded as absolutely desirable in itself gradually comes to be seen as a stage on the path leading to the highest goal—realization of the Self.

This "gradual removal" of ignorance can thus be seen as a response to the need to compromise with the limited conceptions of the average individual, for whom the world and the ego appear as concrete and real, whilst the supra-individual, unconditioned Self appears as an abstraction. To invert this picture immediately—so Shankara seems implicitly to be saying—would be ineffective; rather, emphasis should in the first instance be placed upon a diverse conception of the posthumous states—reducible in fact to a duality, the desirable and undesirable—which, while illusory from the viewpoint of the Self, nonetheless corresponds to a lived reality for those bound by relativity.

It is therefore legitimate to speak of an ascending hierarchy of "degrees," within the realm of illusion, leading up to, and being finally consummated by, the reality of supreme Self-consciousness; the outward aspect of the degree in question being the particular "abode" within the heavenly pleroma, and its internal counterpart corresponding to the "weakening of ignorance" in such a manner that, as he approaches the inward reality of consciousness of the Self, the individual can figuratively be said to "enter" a more elevated world.

This application of eschatological doctrine to states of consciousness on the earthly plane does not deny the objective posthumous reality of these "abodes," but rather assimilates the principles in question according to the perspective implied by Shankara in the above quotation: "transmigration" is just as real now as it is after human death, being constituted by the very diversity of means and ends, in contrast to that which transcends all transmigratory existence, the immutable Self.

As seen above, such an evaluative framework in regard to Scripture is only partially founded upon the scriptural elements themselves; since the Self as one's immanent reality is already known "ontologically," even if obscured existentially, once this knowledge has been awoken, one is in a position to evaluate and interpret Scripture on the basis of a recognition of those essential elements which accord with consciousness of the Self, realization of which constitutes the highest aim of Scripture.

It is clear from this that Scripture alone is not adduced in support of this evaluation of Scripture: rather, it is consciousness of the Self, the very source and end of Scripture, that sheds light both upon the direct references to the nature of the Self, and those indirect references, in which a diversity of means and ends are mentioned, apparently contradicting the unity of the Self, but which in reality have realization of the Self as the ultimate aim; and it is this aim or summit which confers value on all that which leads to it.

Turning now to focus more directly on the cardinal text, "That is the Absolute; That thou art," one hearing of this sentence, as mentioned earlier, is deemed sufficient in principle to enlighten the fully prepared disciple who is able to "attain immediate experience of the fact that his Self is the Absolute" (Enlightenment, 114). This "immediate experience" arises only in the case of those whose spiritual receptivity is perfect, such that there is no barrier either in the intelligence or the character that impedes the dawn of Self-realization or Liberation, *moksa*:

> [T]hose gifted persons who are not afflicted by any ignorance, doubt, or erroneous knowledge to obstruct the comprehension of the meaning of the words can have direct knowledge of the meaning of the sentence when it is heard only once (Enlightenment, 115-116).

Such disciples have the "immediate experience," and not just the conceptual understanding, that the word "That" refers to the transcendent Absolute, *Brahma nirguna*, which is designated provisionally as "the Real, Knowledge, the Infinite, . . . Consciousness, and Bliss" (Enlightenment, 114); and that the "thou" refers to the inmost Self "that which is distinguishable from all other elements in the empirical personality, from the body onward . . . discovered to be pure Consciousness" (Enlightenment, 115).

The sentence that expresses the real identity between the transcendentally conceived Absolute and the immanently realized Self is endowed with a realizatory power not simply because of its theurgic power, divine origin, and sacramental nature, but also because of the relationship between its meaning and the very being of the soul who hears it: it directly expresses the highest truth, which is consubstantial with the deepest ontological dimension of the *jiva*. Just as it was seen earlier that the Absolute comprises within itself the elements Being and Consciousness in an absolutely undifferentiated manner, each element being distinguishable from the other only on the plane of relativity, so these two elements of the soul are indistinguishable at its inmost center, and are bifurcated in appearance only at the surface, that is, at the level of its phenomenal mode of existence. The truth expressed by the sentence is thus one with the innermost identity of the soul, and has the power to actualize the virtual consciousness of this identity, for those souls in the requisite state of spiritual receptivity.

Since, however, the overwhelming majority of those seeking enlightenment do not have the capacity to realize the Self upon the first hearing of the text, the question of the spiritual discipline required for enhancing receptivity to this realization assumes great importance. It is to this discipline that the analysis now proceeds, beginning with the realm of action.

## 2. Action

Realization of the Self is attained through knowledge, and this strictly implies the transcending of action and the realm within which it operates. One can identify an objective and a subjective reason for this being the case in Shankara's perspective. Objectively, action must be transcended because of the definitive conditions proper to its functioning, and subjectively, it must be transcended because it constitutes the dynamic by which ignorance is perpetuated through the vicious cycle of *karma*.

As regards the objective factor, an examination of the basis of action indicates that it consists in the triad of "knowledge-knower-known"; the knower in question is by definition the false self, the empirical ego, the agent setting in motion the intelligential and sensible instruments of knowledge, the knowledge registered by these instruments being thus wholly relative; the known is the object desired, to which the action is oriented. The "factors" of action are: the agent; the body; the organs; the vital energy; and the divine power over them (Discipleship, 3-8).

Action thus defined can in no wise result in transcendent knowledge; built into action is an insurmountable barrier to realization, a barrier constituted by the very prerequisites for action itself. It is evident from this summary that the category "action" covers more than simply physical movement; it is intimately related to cognition and it is this link which reveals the subjective dimension of the limitations of action: "Action is incompatible with metaphysical knowledge since it occurs to the accompaniment of ego-feeling" (Upadesa (A), II, 1.12).

According to Shankara, action fosters the twin-illusion that "I am the one doing the action" and "let this be mine"; the first entrenches the false idea that one's identity resides in the empirical agent, this being a manner of intensifying the superimposition of the Self onto the not-self, while the second, by ascribing to the Self empirical attributes, superimposes the not-self onto the Self, which is thus subject to qualifications, and is thereby reduced to the "lesser Absolute," or "Absolute with qualities," *Brahma saguna* as opposed to the Absolute that transcends all qualities, *Brahma nirguna*.

The Self, then, is not subject to modification; once the nature of the Self is understood, and is identified as one's own identity, the limitative notion of individual agency is eliminated once and for all; now, it is from the perspective of this realization that Shankara is able to relegate the whole realm of action to illusion: if Self-realization entails the transcending of action, then the renunciation of action must be a prerequisite for that realization:

> [H]ow can there be the notions "agent" and "enjoyer" again when once there is the realization "I am the real"? Therefore metaphysical knowledge cannot require or receive support from action (Upadesa (A), II, 1.20).

Since realization—which means in this context "making real" or effective the fact that "I am the real"—eliminates the basis on which the individual is bound by the illusion of being an active agent, it naturally follows that action cannot be a means of realization; action cannot, in other words, lead to the attainment of a state that reveals action to be illusory; just as in the snake-rope image, one cannot attain to the knowledge of the reality of the rope by continuing to act on the basis of the fear of its being a snake.

Realization of the Self is described as "deliverance" or "liberation"; it must be stressed here that it is from the realm of *samsara*—of indefinite births, deaths, and rebirths—that the *jivan-mukta* is delivered, in this life. Samsaric existence is woven out of ignorance, the false identification with the body-mind complex; those who persist in this error, and who take their finite selves as well as the outside world to which these selves relate, as the sole reality, denying "the existence of a world beyond," are said to be "born again and again, and come again and again into my power, into the power of death":

> That is, they remain involved in the unbroken chain of suffering constituted by birth, death, and the other hardships of transmigratory existence. That is exactly the condition of the very great majority of the people (Discipleship, 11-12).

Transmigration is said to be beginningless, it cannot be said to have begun at any particular point in time because that point must have been the result of the fruition of the *karma* that preceded it, and so on; the fruits of *karma* in the form of merit and demerit are earned through action—taken in its widest sense, including cognition, as seen above—and this action *qua* bondage arises on the basis of the false identification with the body-mind complex.

> And this shows that the total cessation of transmigratory existence can only occur through devotion to the path of knowledge, associated with the renunciation of all action (Discipleship, 8).

It is only knowledge that liberates one from the chains of *samsara*, of conditioned existence, but the knowledge in question is of a completely different order from what is conventionally regarded as knowledge:

> A cognition of the mind is an act that can be referred to by a verb and is characterized by change. It is referred to metaphorically as "knowledge" because it ends with an apparent manifestation of knowledge as its result (Upadesa (A) I, 2.77).

In other words, no cognition, insofar as it can be characterized as an act, can be equated with real knowledge, but only with an apparent manifestation thereof; ignorance may be weakened by certain types of action, as will be seen below, but they cannot eradicate it, since ignorance is itself the result of previous merit and demerit arising out of action. To say "action" is thus to say "perpetuation of ignorance."

> Work leads to purification of the mind, not to perception of the Reality. The realization of Truth is brought about by discrimination and not by ten millions of acts (Vivekachudamani, 11).

Deliverance or Liberation cannot be reduced to being an effect of an act since action is a mode of conditioned existence: the freedom from conditioned existence implied by Deliverance would then become dependent on a mode of that very level of existence for its own attainment.

The emphasis placed on the liberating power of transcendent knowledge by Shankara leads to the expression of certain antinomian ideas, the intention behind which is to establish, with the utmost rigor, the incommensurability between the realm of action—involving change, alterity, transience, and illusion—and the realization of the Self, immutable, non-dual, eternal, and unconditionally real. An example of this antinomianism is the following, from his commentary on the Bhagavad Gita:

> Even *dharma* is a sin—in the case of him who seeks liberation—inasmuch as it causes bondage (Gita, IV, 21).

The double qualification here is important: only for the *mumuksu*, the one seeking liberation, can *dharma* ever constitute a sin—and this, only in the measure that it causes bondage to action and not insofar as *dharma* is performed in a disinterested manner. Only in relation to the quest for the highest realization can any lesser goal be regarded as a sin.

There is a distinction here between those who perform their duty in a spirit of renunciation and those who do so in a spirit of attachment. But within the first category there is a further division: there is the one who renounces action because he "sees inaction in action," being disinterested in the whole realm of action, knowing it as illusion; this type of renunciate is "higher" in relation to the renunciate who

> offers all actions to Isvara in the faith that "I act for His sake". . . . The result of actions so done is only purity of mind and nothing else (Gita, V, 10).

This may be interpreted as follows: to act for the sake of the Lord, conceived as the "other" may be a selfless mode of action, but insofar as it is still invested with significance by the agent, and inasmuch as it is conditioned by its reference to the acting Lord, thus *Brahma saguna* and not the actionless *Brahma nirguna*— for these two reasons such action still pertains to the realm of the not-self. It may be "self-less," taking the relative ego as the self in question, but it still falls short of the requirements for the path of supreme Self-realization.

However, the attainment of "purity of mind," despite being the highest result of action, can also be said to constitute a prerequisite for pursuing the path of transcendence; therefore one must take into account that inward quality pertaining to outward action which leads to and cultivates purity of mind, namely virtue.

Shankara makes it abundantly clear that without virtue, liberating knowledge cannot be realized. The very first sutra of the *Atma-bodha* makes it clear that a high degree of virtue is the prerequisite even for receiving the doctrine of the Self: "This *Atmabodha* is being composed for those who, seeking Liberation, have been purified from evil by constant austerities and have reached calm and peacefulness" (Atma-bodha (B), 1). This emphasis upon virtue—being purified from evil—is repeated in the *Upadesa Sahasri*, where Shankara writes that the knowledge of *Brahman* should only be given to "him whose mind has been pacified, who has controlled his senses and is freed from all defects, who has practiced the duties enjoined by the scriptures and is possessed of good qualities, who is always obedient to the teacher and aspires after Liberation and nothing else" (Upadesa (B), II, 16.72).

The essential virtues must already be present in the soul of the disciple, in some degree at least, as a prior condition for the teaching of the higher knowledge. But the teacher must continue to give, as part of the spiritual discipline, "sound instruction" on the central virtues, which are laid down at Bhagavad Gita, XIII, 7-12, and among which one can identify as essentially moral conditions, as opposed to intellectual conditions, the following: humility, modesty, innocence, patience, uprightness, service of the teacher, purity, steadfastness, self-control, detachment, absence of egoism, equanimity, and devotion to the Lord. Commenting on Krishna's phrase "this is declared to be knowledge" (where "this" refers to all the preceding qualities), Shankara writes:

> These attributes . . . are declared to be knowledge because they are conducive to knowledge. What is opposed to this—viz. pride, hypocrisy, cruelty, impatience, insincerity and the like—is ignorance, which should be known and avoided as tending to the perpetuation of *samsara* (Gita, XIII, 11).

One can see that for Shankara morality cannot be divorced from the highest truth, even if the two elements pertain to incommensurable orders of reality. Knowledge relating to the Self infinitely transcends the domain within which morality operates, that is, the outward world on the one hand, and the relative self, the *jivatman*, on the other; but there is nevertheless a crucial relationship between knowledge and virtue: not only is virtue a necessary condition for receiving doctrinal instruction, it is also described as a means to the attainment of knowledge: the teacher "should thoroughly impress upon the disciple qualities like humility, which are *the means of knowledge*" (Upadesa (B), I, 1.5, emphasis added).

The slightest trace of pride—attachment to the illusory ego—not only "perpetuates *samsara*," it is also a form of ignorance, vice being understood here not just as an evil in its own right, but also as a veil over the truth; pride is not simply immoral, it is also an intellectual dysfunction. The virtue of humility, on the other hand, is not exhausted by its purely moral dimension; it has in addition and above all a truly intellectual function. Humility can thus be understood as a moral quality which prefigures that total extinction of the individual that is entailed by realization of the Self; it is a manner of being that conforms with the highest truth, and which, for that very reason, enhances receptivity to it. Moreover, without humility, there is the ever-present danger that knowledge will be misappropriated by the individual, rather than serving to reveal the supra-individual Self:

> He who knows that the Consciousness of the Self never ceases to exist, and that It is never an agent, and also gives up the egoism that he is a Knower of *Brahman*, is a (real) Knower of the Self. Others are not so (Upadesa (B) II, 12.13).

In other words, true consciousness of the Self demands that the ego must not take pride in this knowledge, for the knowledge in question is thereby undermined by the very illusion which it is supposed to eradicate, namely, the ego as a self-subsistent entity; further, it is an absurdity for the ego to pride itself upon knowing "something," as it were outside itself, for then that very duality belies the claim to unitive consciousness; it is only the Self that knows itself. The highest attainment for the ego, in relation to the "experience" of the Self, is extinction in the very bosom of unitive consciousness (a subject to be addressed below). This extinction is prefigured in all the essential virtues, which are also regarded as, on the one hand, preparations and preconditions for this consciousness, and on the other hand, as guarantees that the doctrine will not lead to pride—the intensification of illusory existence apart from the Self—but will rather serve to loosen the hold of the ego upon consciousness and thus assist in the effective assimilation of liberating knowledge.

While humility thus clearly emerges as a key virtue in the pursuit of liberating knowledge, the other virtues mentioned are also indispensable; although Shankara does not elaborate on them individually, the intellectual perspective on pride and humility outlined above can be applied to the other virtues.

Even at this non-transcendent level of the soul, then, the question of "knowing" cannot be isolated from the dimension of "being," which on this level is identified with virtuous being. This may be seen as a reflection of the transcendent realization of the Self, in which pure Consciousness is indistinguishable from unconditioned Being. The soul's knowledge of the Truth must be accompanied by living the Truth, that is, according to impeccable virtue.

The positive aspect, then, of virtuous action is that it is not only an essential precondition for receiving the doctrine, but also a means of purifying the mind and thus preparing the way for the assimilation of liberating knowledge; but, being a means and not the end, it must be transcended. The next section examines the degree to which ritual assists in this process of transcendence.

### 3. Rites and Knowledge
Shankara gives a nuanced answer to the question of the relationship between the performance of rituals and the rise of liberating knowledge, an answer which is in essence the same as that given to the question of the nature and function of action and virtue. On the one hand, there is a disjuncture between ritual and knowledge, and from this point of view one seeking enlightenment must transcend both ritual activity and renounce the rewards proportioned thereto; on the other hand, one can only effect this transcendence insofar as one has attained that degree of receptivity which is required for the reception of the highest knowledge.

Taking first the latter point of view, Shankara asserts that the performance of ritual can be described as a "cause" of knowledge insofar as it "is instrumental in extinguishing that demerit arising out of past sins which obstructs knowledge of the Absolute" (Discipleship, 89). Ritual activity is said therefore to "co-operate" with the knowledge of the Absolute, but it is stressed that this function is contingent upon the discipline of "hearing the metaphysical texts of the

Upanisads, cogitating over them, and meditating on them persistently [*sravana-manana-nididhyasana*] along with faith, singleness of purpose, and other necessary psychological qualities" (Discipleship, 89).

The efficacy of this triple discipline of *sravana-manana-nididhyasana*, then, presupposes, on the one hand, faith, and on the other hand, "necessary psychological qualities" which can be understood as referring to the virtues noted in the previous section, and also to the traditional Vedantin series of virtues, known as the "six treasures" (*satsampatti*).[7]

It is important in this connection to underline Shankara's insistence on faith; without the correct relationship between the *jivatman* and *Isvara*, not only is enlightenment impossible, but all other virtues are also, from a realizatory point of view, invalidated. The soul must be fully aware of its existential subordination to the Lord, to whom is due an attitude of reverent devotion; after specifying that the highest knowledge should only be taught to him who is "devoted to the Lord," Shankara adds:

> The teaching should not be given to anyone who is not obedient or devoted, even if he be a man of self-discipline or intelligent. If a person feels resentment against the Lord, he should not receive the teaching, even if he has all the other virtues under the sun (Discipleship, 278-279).

The question of the ontological status of this devotion will be examined later, in the light of the discussion on Self-realization; it should be noted at this point, however, that the yearning for Deliverance which implies transcending the ontological limitations of the "lesser" Absolute, that is, the Lord, by no means negates faith and devotion to Him; rather, this faith in the Lord is stressed as an essential precondition for the integrity of the aspiration to transcend the Lord, whose limitation is apparent exclusively from the *paramarthika* point of view, that is, from the point of view bestowed by realization of *Brahma nirguna*. The aspiration that focuses on this "higher" Absolute thus coexists with devotion to the "lesser" Absolute: aspiration and devotion may pertain to incommensurable planes, but there is no contradiction between the two attitudes. Aspiration for the Self and devotion to the Lord are not only perfectly compatible, but each in fact enhances the other; and this in the very measure that it is grasped that the Lord is none other than the Self—there are not two Absolutes, but one, each dimension of which must be given its due if the soul as a whole—and not some abstracted element thereof—is to be integrated into the consciousness of the Absolute. Faith in the Lord and identity with the Self are thus in perfect harmony. Thus one finds Shankara, in the opening verse of his Thousand Teachings, explaining that his teaching is imparted for the sake of "those who deeply desire liberation *and* who are possessed of faith" (Upadesa, (A), I.1, emphasis added)

---

[7] These are traditionally given as: *sama*—calm (restraint of the mind); *dama*—self-control (restraint of the senses); *uparati*—self-settledness; *titiksa*—forbearance, fortitude, impassibility in adversity; *samadhana*—concentration; *sraddha*—faith (Atma-bodha (A), 43-45).

Moreover, faith has an intrinsically enlightening function. There is an intellective quality flowing from faith which conduces to the comprehension of metaphysical principles; commenting on why the teacher in the Chandogya Upanisad says, "Have faith," Shankara writes:

> When there is faith, the mind can be concentrated on the point one wishes to know about, and this enables one eventually to know it (Discipleship, 147).

When faith and the other conditions described above are thus present, the rituals can be regarded as "remote auxiliaries" to knowledge (*arad upakaraka*). They can be harnessed to the pursuit of knowledge by means of the gradual elimination of ignorance resulting from previous demerit; and they assist in the progressive purification of the mind, thus serving the function of "auxiliaries" to knowledge; but their aspect of "remoteness" must also be understood, and this leads to the first aspect of the relationship between ritual and knowledge distinguished above, that of disjuncture.

As seen earlier, even *dharma* is considered sinful insofar as it leads to bondage; this is to be understood in the light of the principle that everything but the supreme realization is a relativity and consequently a kind of evil in relation to it:

> When the Self has once been known, everything else is seen as evil (Discipleship, 62).

This being the case, one who yearns for Deliverance from *samsara* must cultivate a "disgust" for those higher worlds which are promised as the fruit of ritualistically earned merit (Discipleship, 70). If the intention of the individual is Liberation, then any inclination towards lesser goals—however elevated and desirable they may be in themselves—must be firmly eliminated, in order that all one's efforts and attention be focused on the highest aspiration; therefore, one must be detached from the rituals that are related to these non-transcendent rewards.

Although Shankara is not rigid regarding the necessity of outwardly renouncing and abstaining from all ritual action, it is clear that he regards this as the most appropriate way to proceed for one whose intention is realization of the Absolute. Just as it is proper for one desirous of the three "external worlds" (*bhur, bhuvah, svah*—this world, that of the ancestors, and that of heaven)[8] to perform rituals related to these worlds, so "those who want the Self as their world must definitely renounce the world as wandering monks. . . . [W]andering forth from one's house as a homeless monk (*parivrajya*), being the renunciation of all means to (ritualistic) action, is implicitly enjoined as part of the discipline" (Discipleship, 114, 115).

---

[8] This is also known as *svarga, satya-loka*, and *Brahma-loka*, which will be mentioned below as the heaven in which the *krama-mukta* resides prior to final reabsorption in the Self at the end of the cycle.

The fact that this renunciation is only implicitly enjoined means that it is not a *conditio sine qua non* for the discipline; in practice, it is most likely to have been what Shankara would insist upon, while admitting that householders performing rituals can also, exceptionally, pursue and realize Deliverance, instances of this being found in the Veda itself. As a rule, however, the true *mumuksu*, seeking Liberation in this life, is one who would "normally give up all connection with ritual whatever and any form of permanent residence, . . . wandering the earth as an ascetic with a single staff, a monk of the *paramahamsa* order" (Enlightenment, 31-32).

Having seen the limitations as well as the importance of action and ritual, we can address the next identifiable stage in the hierarchy of realization: meditation.

## 4. Meditation

According to Shankara, meditation involves "mental action" and "results from the free working of the human mind" (Enlightenment, 4). It combines will with thought, hence it can either be done or not be done, this contingency marking it off from Knowledge which is "not anything which can be done or not done" and which "is conditioned neither by a command nor by human will but by the nature of an already existent reality" (Enlightenment, 4-5).

Whilst meditation stems from, and is thus conditioned by, the relative subject, Knowledge of the Self is "conditioned by the nature of the Real and not by the action of the subject" (Enlightenment, 139). Nonetheless, the Veda is replete with injunctions to meditate on the Self; and Shankara explains this with reference to a tripartite division of the souls "treading the spiritual path": those of excellent, middling, and weak powers of intelligence; the injunctions to meditate relate only to the two lower categories. This implies that there must also be different types of meditation, as indeed there are; but given the complexity of the forms of meditation and their relationships with various elements of ritual and symbolism, and given also the fact that the intention here is to focus on transcendence, this complexity can be reduced in accordance with the meditative principles corresponding to two degrees of *mukti*: the first is deliverance in this life—which pertains to the *jivan-mukta*; and the second is "deferred" or gradual release—pertaining to the *krama-mukta*, who attains to union with *Brahma nirguna* only after death, at the end of the world-period, having been delivered from the samsaric realm of rebirth, and inhabiting, prior to final union, the Paradisal domain of *Brahma-loka*, the "place" of *Brahman*. This attainment is called "conditioned" immortality and constitutes the highest goal for those who have meditated on the Absolute as associated with finite form, in conjunction with the performance of all due Vedic rites.

This form of meditation in the context of the rites is called *upasana* and is to be distinguished from the higher type of meditation, called *dhyana*, by virtue of the fact that *dhyana* is not so much a meditation on the Absolute as "other"—conceived in the form of some attribute of the Absolute or of some particular deity—but is more of an assimilation of the individual to his true Self. Thus, Shankara defines *dhyana* as:

[T]he withdrawal of the outward-going perception of the senses into the mind, and the one-pointed focusing of the mind on the source of its consciousness (Enlightenment, 137).

Before looking at the forms taken by this transcendent mode of meditation, it must first be situated in reference to the lower mode which it transcends.

In this lower mode the meditator takes an entity like the sun or lightning as a symbol of the Absolute and meditates thereupon. Shankara has to explain how this type of meditation is valuable, given the Vedic rule that only meditation on the Absolute yields fruit, and given the obvious fact that such finite entities are distinguishable from the Absolute. He resolves the paradox by saying that, while it is illegitimate to regard *Brahman* as identical with these finite objects, it is not illegitimate to regard them as identical with it, inasmuch as the lesser can be treated as if it were the higher, while the higher must never be treated as if it were the lower; "the charioteer may on certain occasions be treated like the king," but nothing good can come from "treating the king like the charioteer and thereby demeaning him" (Enlightenment, 13).

So, by meditating on the sun as if it were *Brahman*, one is superimposing the notion of *Brahman* onto the sun, which serves as its symbol; therefore the reward for such meditation is derived from that principle which is superimposed, the Absolute itself, and not from the limited properties of the object serving as the symbolic support for the Absolute:

The Absolute is itself the object of meditation in these cases, to the extent that the idea of the Absolute has to be projected onto a symbol, as one projects the idea of Vishnu onto a stone image (Enlightenment, 15).

When meditation takes a particular deity for object, the aim is to identify with that deity to the point where one's own identity is extinguished in and by that of the deity, the result of which is a conviction of one's identity with the deity, a conviction "as powerful as one's (previous) conviction of identity with one's individual personality" (Enlightenment, 8).

However exalted such a state may be, it cannot be of a fully transcendent order, given the fact that whatever deity be in question, it is, as such, distinct from the Self, identity with which alone constitutes unconditional transcendence.

It is important to note that it is on this, the "indirect" path of Deliverance, involving identification with the deities, that superhuman powers arise, whereas on the direct path, that of the *jivan-mukta*, involving nothing but identification with the Self, they do not (Enlightenment, 65-66).

In the case of the one who realizes identity with the Lord, certain powers do arise, such as making oneself minute in form, or projecting oneself into several bodies; such a person is said to "attain to the Lord of the mind" thus becoming "lord of speech, lord of hearing, lord of understanding" (Enlightenment, 67). Now, it is important that Shankara clearly distinguishes the individual soul from the personal Lord: the identification in question is by no means a complete identity of essence, but rather an attainment of a transient nature, in contrast to the realization of the Self as one's "true transcendent state" (*kaivalya*). This is clear from the following assertion:

> [T]he Lord of all minds is He who was ordained before them (individual souls), the Lord, and the soul attains to Him (Enlightenment, 67).

Not only is the relativity of the "attainment" of the Lord evident here in the light of the ontological priority accorded to the Lord in relation to individual souls, it is also underlined by the fact that both entities involved are themselves relative: the soul is "ordained" after the Lord has been "ordained"—the Lord's ontological precedence notwithstanding, it, too, is a relativity as it is subordinated to That which is not "ordained" and which is the ultimate source of all ordainment, namely *Brahma nirguna*.

The impossibility of an unconditional identity between the individual and the Lord is proven not just by this ontological distinction, but also by the fact that, whatever superhuman powers the individual may acquire by virtue of his identification with the Lord, these never include the powers of "creation, maintenance, and dissolution of the universe": "Only the Supreme Lord has the right to govern the universe . . ." (Enlightenment, 66-67).

As seen in Part I, one of the key distinguishing features of *Brahma nirguna* is *prapañcha-upasama*—its being without any trace of the development of manifestation. This means that whenever there is consideration of divine attributes relating to manifestation, it is always the lesser Absolute that is in question; and the only relationship that the individual can have with the lesser Absolute or the Lord, is existential subordination, even, as seen in the above quotation, when the individual is said to have "attained" to the Lord: the unconditional omnipotence of the Lord infinitely surpasses the acquired powers of the individual who must therefore remain in an immutable position of inferiority in relation to the Lord.

There is thus always and inescapably a distinction between the soul and the Lord, even in the very bosom of this exalted state of identity; and it is this very distinction—implying alterity, duality, and thus illusion—that situates the metaphysical relativity of this attainment in contrast with the realization of the Self. Furthermore, any object that is to be "attained" is, by that very token, radically other than the subject in question, who therefore can never fully "become" it; whereas the Self is said to be unattainable precisely because it is *nitya-siddha*—the "eternally true fact," thus, ever-attained, never non-attained:

> When there is a difference between a meditator and that on which he meditates, the meditator may change into the object of his meditation. But no action on one's own Self is possible or necessary in order to change into one's own Self. . . . If it were thought that anything were needed to become one's own Self, it would not be one's true Self that one was aiming at (Upadesa (A), II, 15.14).

The difference here being emphasized is that between meditation on an object conceived as "other," and concentration on the Subject, grasped as one's Self. The latter entails an experience of infinitude proper to one's own inmost being, while the former entails only a change of degree within the framework of the finite, an upward and inward transformation in the direction of the Real, but always falling short thereof, and thus constituting but a change of state within the realm of *Maya*.

One of the ways in which this kind of meditation can be transcended is by adopting Shankara's apophatic discipline; this is like a reflection, within the realm of spiritual practice, of his doctrinal perspective on the transcendence of the Absolute. Rather than this or that object determining the orientation of consciousness, each and every object that is susceptible of determinate conception is eliminated by the double negation, *neti, neti.* This is a key component of *vichara*, the way of enquiry, discernment.

> By a process of negation of all conditionings through the axiom "not this, not this" come to understand . . . the oneness of the individual soul with the Supreme Self (Atma-bodha (B), 30).

It should be strongly emphasized here that the individual soul itself is to be eliminated by the negation before identity with the Self can be realized; this is because it, too, constitutes, on the plane of its separative manifestation, a conditioning or an "object," as it will be described below, before the unique reality of the Subject. The *neti* is here applied subjectively: one negates that which one is not.

This process of negation perforce operates on a limited and conditioned plane of being inasmuch as it presupposes determinate properties susceptible of negation; this means that negation is tied to relativity, and has no meaning or function at the transcendent level of the Self which is unconditioned Being, or as seen earlier, "Beyond" Being:

> Because the Self cannot be negated, it is that which remains after the practice of saying *neti neti* to all else. It is directly apprehended through the practice of saying "I am not this, I am not this." The ego-notion arises from the notion that the Self is a "this" (Absolute, 152).

All trace of "this" must be discarded; that is, the non-dual Self as infinite Subject must be shorn of all objectively determinate qualities in order that it may be "directly apprehended"; in the very measure that the Self is regarded as an object, the ego-notion binds the consciousness of the individual soul to the limited dimensions proper to the ego: attribution of objective alterity to the Self inescapably entails imprisonment within the subjective particularity of the ego. The *neti, neti* is to operate, then, in such wise as to negate the ego, which must be radically objectivized: instead of being the source of limited subjectivity—hence bondage—it must be regarded as an insignificant and ultimately unreal modification of the Self, from the perspective of which it is an outward object:

> The Self Itself is not qualified by an arm which has been cut off and thrown away. . . .
> The ego, the object portion, is also like the part of the body cut off. . . . As it is not the
> Self, the object portion in the consciousness "I" should be renounced by the wise. As

It was mixed with egoism previously, the remaining (non-object) portion is implied by the word "I" in the sentence, "I am *Brahman*" (Upadesa (B), II, 6.1, 4, 6).

Just as an arm is non-conscious and exists for the sake of a conscious agent, so the ego is, relative to the Self, non-conscious and exists only by virtue of the illumination it receives from the consciousness of the Self; when the ego-notion is once fully and effectively eliminated through spiritual discrimination and methodic negation, "The immediate experience that ensues is the Supreme Self" (Upadesa (A), II, 5.5).

This "immediate experience"—*anubhava*—in terms of which the transcendent Absolute is "known" to be one's own true Self, constitutes the veritable summit of spiritual experience, an experience that is not "of" the Self, but, as seen in the last quotation, *it is the Self*; this means that there is no question of a subject, an object, and an experience linking the one to the other; the word "experience" is thus employed elliptically, the intention being to underline the disjuncture between a mere mental, and thus outward, knowledge of the reality of the Self, on the one hand, and the plenary realization of infinite Selfhood, on the other. In this "experience," further aspects of which will be treated below, there can be no dichotomy between knowledge and being; rather, a complete identification between the two is realized, so that each is absolutely the other; it is only within the matrix of the ego that the two elements can subsist as distinct poles.

This *via negativa* is one way which Shankara proposes as a means of transcending the limitations of the lower forms of meditation, arriving thereby at the supreme realization. But this negative path is not the only transcendent mode of meditation; there is also the higher form of meditation, *dhyana*, mentioned earlier, in which consciousness is focused in a positive way, not on something extrinsic, but on the very source of consciousness itself; and there is also that form of positive meditation or, more accurately, concentration upon and invocation of the highest symbolic expression of the Absolute, the holy syllable *Om*. The following section deals with these transcendent forms of meditation.

## 5. Concentration and Interiorization

### (i) *OM*

In Part I of the chapter emphasis was put on the transcendence of the Absolute in relation to all names referring to it; at this point it is necessary to stress the complementary dimension of immanence, in terms of which the pure Absolute is present not only in all that exists, but more importantly, from the point of view of method, in the name which sacramentally designates it. When dealing with the spiritual discipline by means of which the Absolute is realized, it is this operative dimension, deriving from the aspect of immanence, that takes precedence over the doctrinal comprehension of the aspect of transcendence, it being understood that the latter is an essential condition for engaging with the former.

This shift of emphasis must not, however, compromise the principle of *advaita*: the transcendent is at the same time the immanent, and vice versa; there is but one Absolute in question, the different aspects of which are distinguishable only from the viewpoint of the relative, whether the perspective be of a doctrinal nature or, as now, of an operative or "realizational" order.

In this context, the name which is considered most appropriate for the purposes of unitive concentration is *Om*. Shankara writes, in conformity with Scripture, that everything is *Om*: the world, the Vedas, even the Absolute itself.

Regarding the first of these three, the things that make up the world are reducible to the names that designate them, which in turn are modalities of the primordial "sound-universal," the material cause of sound; and this in turn is a modification of *Om* (Creation, 143-145).

Regarding the identity between *Om* and the Vedas:

> This *Om* is the Veda because whatever has to be known is known through this *Om*, which is thus the Veda. On this *Om* depends the Vedahood even of the other Veda! This *Om* being something so magnificent, it should definitely be adopted as an instrument of approach to the Absolute (Enlightenment, 161).

The word *Om* is regarded as both a name of the Absolute and as an "instrument of approach" to it; this is for two reasons: the name is regarded as identical to the Absolute, and it also contains a liberating "grace."

Turning to the first, the name is identified with the named: it is not just a reference to *Brahma saguna*, which is regarded as susceptible of determinate conception and thus designation as the "lesser" Absolute, but is seen as identical with *Brahma nirguna*, which is not so regarded. Though *Brahman* and *Atman* are names of the Absolute, Shankara says that *Om* is the name which "fits closest," thus rendering it the "chief instrument in the apprehension of the Absolute" (Enlightenment, 159-160). Going further, Shankara asserts that "even the Absolute in its highest form is the syllable *Om*" (Creation, 144).

The Absolute can be conceived as truly "existent" or real, even if the true nature of that reality is strictly ungraspable by the mind; and it is that nature which is realized by means of methodic concentration on the name, which, on the one hand, designates that which is conceivable, but which on the other, cannot exhaustively encapsulate within its own nature *qua* name, the nature of the named. In other words there is a relationship of inner identity between the name and the named, by virtue of which the former leads to the latter; but there is also a relationship of difference, failing which one could not make the conceptual distinction between the two. Thus one finds Shankara writing:

> And the purpose of knowing the identity of the name and the named is to enable oneself to dismiss name and named altogether and realize the Absolute, which is quite different from either (Creation, 144).

That the Absolute is "different" from the name is clearly discernible, but the question may be asked: how is it different from the named? Two answers may be proposed: first, the identity of the name and the named can be conceived in terms of a transcendent essence which surpasses both of these elements taken distinctively as correlates; this identity, then, is That which, in its intrinsic reality

*29*

cannot be designated either as "name" or as "named," both of which imply, *a priori*, an object, hence something "quite different" from the Absolute.

Second, to say that the name is the named means: the symbol is not other than the symbolized; but insofar as the symbolized, the named, is viewed as the counterpart to its symbol, a particular form, it is endowed with a degree of relativity, viz., the relativity of constituting one pole in a dualistic relationship, name-named: both the name and the named are *Brahman*, but *Brahman* transcends that trace of relativity entailed by the very opposition that is conceivable between the two elements. It should be stressed that this opposition, or mutual conditioning, exists only in respect of that external "conceivable" dimension in which the difference between the two is manifest: the name as such is finite and formal inasmuch as it is determinate, while the named is infinite and supra-formal in its essential non-determinable reality. It is precisely because this extrinsic opposition is subordinated to the intrinsic identity between the name and the named, that the emphasis, in the first instance—that of methodic concentration on the name—is placed on the inner reality that the name is the named; only upon realization of the Absolute can one "dismiss name and named altogether," doing so on account of the dimension of extrinsic relativity pertaining to the relationship between the two, a relationship which can be conceived by the intellect, even though the dimension of metaphysical identity takes precedence over that of conceivable distinctiveness, this identity pertaining to what is strictly inconceivable, even while being realizable.

Turning now to examine "grace," the second of the reasons proposed above for why *Om* is considered the best instrument of approach to the Absolute, one is struck by an apparent contradiction. It is said by Shankara that: "The syllable *Om* is the most distinctive and intimate name for the supreme Self. When it is used, the Self tends to pour out grace" (Enlightenment, 161).

It is further specified that, despite the fact that the unconditioned Absolute cannot be indicated by sound, when the syllable *Om* is in question there is a major difference from all other sounds: "When it is meditated on as the Absolute with deep reverence, the latter manifests 'grace' and reveals itself to the meditator. This is so in the case of the unconditioned Absolute and it also holds true of the conditioned Absolute" (Enlightenment, 170).

One may ask here: how can the unconditioned Absolute manifest "grace," when it is expressly stated that any relationship with manifestation pertains only to the conditioned Absolute? The "actionless" Self, it would seem, cannot manifest grace or anything at all, on pain of becoming "lesser" (*apara*).

To resolve this problem one must have recourse to the principle of the identity between the name and the named: just as the outwardly finite nature of the name does not nullify the fact that in its inward reality it is nothing but the infinite nature of the named, in the same way, the extrinsically relative operation of grace—which presupposes two relativities: a recipient and a benefactor—does not nullify the fact that the origin and consummation of the operation is absolute, inasmuch as the supreme Self is revealed thereby.

In other words, both the element of grace and the Lord presupposed by its very "activity," can be assimilated to the Self inasmuch as the Lord cannot be other than the Self, even though, from a different angle, the Self transcends the limitations of the Lord. It is also important to bear in mind that, even if the immediate source of grace be the lesser Absolute—or the Lord—the Self as the higher Absolute is the "eternally-known fact" (*nitya-siddha*), and so requires only the elimination of ignorance to be "known" as such. Thus, there is no contradiction between saying, on the one hand, that grace relates in the first instance to the lesser Absolute, and on the other, that the higher Absolute stands self-revealed upon the elimination of ignorance, an elimination brought about by the grace of the Lord which is present in and actualized by the name *Om*.

This line of interpretation accords with the point made earlier: an essential condition for even receiving, let alone realizing, the doctrine of the Self is faith in the Lord: one cannot bypass the Lord in a spirit of what Shankara called "resentment," in an effort to realize the Self that transcends the Lord. Furthermore, this spiritual discipline of meditation on *Om* will be fruitless unless it be accomplished in the framework of the essential virtues, including therein all the rules of ascetic life (Enlightenment, 169).

The supra-personal Self is thus realized through concentration on *Om*, only on the basis of the following eminently "personal" conditions: the grace of the "personal" Lord on the one hand, and the faith and virtue of the individual person, on the other, however paradoxical this may appear, given the fact that both these "persons" are rendered illusory before the unique reality of the Self that is to be realized. This shows, again, the importance of understanding the distinction between the *paramarthika* and the *vyavaharika* perspectives: from the point of view of relativity—the human starting-point of the process of realization—relative conditions must be fulfilled; from the absolute viewpoint, as will be seen below, such conditions presupposing alterity are illusory.

(ii) Interiorization and the Intellect

The other higher form of meditation that we need to examine is that found in the context of *adhyatma-yoga*, a *yoga* or spiritual discipline that is centered on *Atman*.[9] This form of meditation is in fact a discipline of interiorizing concentration, having no "thing" as object of meditation other than the very source of consciousness itself. This interiorization involves a progressive "dissolution" or reabsorption of the outward faculties of knowledge within the inner faculties; these faculties, in turn, are to be dissolved into the highest— which is at the same time the inmost—principle of consciousness.

In order fully to appreciate the principle underlying this method, it is necessary to situate these faculties of knowledge in their hierarchical context, focusing in particular on the intellect (*buddhi*), and to show how these differentiated faculties can be reconciled with the existence of one sole consciousness, that of the Self—the oneness of consciousness constituting a key postulate of the Advaita perspective.

---

[9] This is not to be confused with the *raja-yoga* of Patanjali, which is subjected to a rigorous critique by Shankara.

The hierarchy of the cognitive faculties is ordered according to interiority: any given faculty is "higher" in the measure that it is more "inward"; thus one finds the intellect at the top, because it is most inward:

> The intellect (*buddhi*) receives a reflection of the light of the Self as pure consciousness first, since it is transparent and stands in immediate proximity to the Self. . . . Consciousness next illumines the lower mind (*manas*) as the next inmost principle, mediately through its contact with the intellect. Next it illumines the sense organs mediately through its contact with the mind, and next the body through its contact with the sense-organs (Soul, 54).

It is thus the unique light of the consciousness of the Self that is refracted through successive degrees of relative awareness, having first been reflected in the intellect. Thus, all awareness, from bodily to sensible, mental, and intelligible, is at one and the same time both the absolute consciousness of the Self—in its essential nature—and also relative knowledge, in the measure that it is identified with its particular faculty, that which determines its mode of refraction:

> The knowledge produced by an evidence does not differ in its essential nature whether one calls it eternal or transitory. Knowledge (even though) produced by an evidence, is nothing other than knowledge (Upadesa (B) I, 2.103).

In response to the objection that knowledge cannot be regarded simultaneously as the result of evidences and of a changeless, eternal, and self-evident nature, Shankara replies:

> It is a result in a secondary sense: though changeless and eternal, It is noticed in the presence of mental modifications called sense-perceptions, etc., as they are instrumental in making It manifest. It appears to be transitory, as mental modifications called sense-perceptions . . . are so (Upadesa (B), I, 2.108).

Both knowledge arrived at by discursive thought and knowledge derived from sense-impressions are seen as pertaining to knowledge or Consciousness as such—even if vehicled by means which are transitory; since the "mental modifications" are transient, the knowledge acquired by their means appears to take on the same nature; to say that the light of pure Consciousness is "noticed" in the presence of the modifications means simply that the modifications cannot function except in the light of Consciousness: it is "noticed" in their presence because they cannot be alienated from its presence:

> Just as in the presence of sunlight, colors such as red, etc., are manifested in a jewel, so all objects are seen in the intellect in My Presence. All things are, therefore, illumined by Me like sun-light (Upadesa (B), II, 7.4).

Just as inert objects require illumination from some external luminous source in order to be perceived, so the mental modifications require the light of the Self in order to perceive external or internal phenomena: without this light of the Self, the "jewel" of the intellect will not contain the different colors.

The absoluteness of supreme Knowledge thus implies that it necessarily comprises all relative knowledge, without becoming relativized by this internal dimension of its own immutable nature; any relative form of knowledge must therefore be subsumed by the very principle by which it operates if it is to be assimilated to what Shankara above calls its "essential nature." The intrinsic value of all forms of knowledge thus derives ultimately from the extent to which they contribute to an awareness of this "essential nature," which is one with supreme Self-consciousness; this transcendent Knowledge is therefore "in-tended"— even if this be unconscious—by all lower level cognitions, which can thus be assimilated to the ultimately "in-tended" object.

It should be noted that the intellect in Shankara's perspective is not only regarded as the key faculty for apprehending transcendent realities, it is also seen as the source of suffering for the individual; in other words, it is in relation to the intellect that one can speak either of liberation or bondage, occupying as it does a position intermediary between the unconditioned Self and the empirical ego; whether the intellective consciousness experiences the one or the other depends upon its fundamental orientation, and therefore upon its content: outward manifestation or inward principle.

To turn first to the negative aspect of the intellect, Shankara writes:

> Attachment, desire, pleasure, and sorrow, etc. arise with the presence of *buddhi*; in deep sleep, when the *buddhi* is not in existence, they too disappear; therefore they belong to the *buddhi* and not to the Self (Atma-bodha (B), 23).

If the intellect identifies itself exclusively with external phenomena, it will experience the corresponding instability of successive, determinate, subjective states—which can be characterized as "suffering," despite the mention of "pleasure" in the above quotation, since whatever pleasure may be experienced is of a transient rather than eternal nature. Suffering is thus equated with delusion, the false attribution of reality to manifested phenomena, which then imprison the intellect within their own limitations: "Bondage is nothing but a delusion of the intellect; the removal of this delusion is liberation" (Upadesa (B) II, 16.59).

Penetrating deeper into the source of this delusion, Shankara asserts that it resides in the belief that the intellect is itself conscious, whereas in reality it is but the medium through which the pure consciousness of the Self is refracted, acquiring its capacity of illumination exclusively from that source: "Just as a man looks upon his body placed in the sun as having the property of light in it, so, he looks upon the intellect pervaded by the reflection of Pure Consciousness as the Self" (Upadesa (B), II, 12.1).

If the individual intellect is falsely taken to be the conscious Self, then the resultant mode of awareness will of necessity be determined by outward phenomena and their subjective counterparts, experienced in the form of multiple attachment. Thus, a kind of symbiotic relationship can be seen to subsist whereby the intellect appears to illumine forms, and these in turn feed the delusion of the intellect that it is the consciousness which illumines them, such consciousness possessing in reality a secondary and derivative nature, assuming the character of the forms it illumines: "[J]ust as light, the revealer, assumes the forms of the objects revealed by it, so the intellect looks like all things inasmuch as it reveals them" (Upadesa (B), II, 14.4). Whereas, as seen above, the intellect itself receives its light from the Self.

Turning now to its positive aspect, the intellect occupies a privileged position in relation to the Self, because it receives the light of pure consciousness in a more integral manner than any other modality of the Self:

> (Although) all-pervading, the Self does not shine in everything: It shines only in the intellect, like a reflection in a clear (mirror) (Atma-bodha (B), 17).

The mirror analogy is particularly revealing when considered in connection with the reflection of the sun in water:

> The Self which has for Its adjuncts the intellect and the vital force is reflected in the modifications of the intellect and in the senses like the sun reflected in water. The Self is free and pure by nature (Upadesa (B), II, 14.33).

While the light of the sun is uninterrupted, pure, and constant, its reflected image in the water—the reflection of the Self in the intellect—is subject to distortion, the "moving" water serving as a vivid image of the intellect distracted and deluded by changing configurations of subjective states and external phenomena. However, if the intellect can be stilled, and concentrated on its source, then it will faithfully reflect the Self. If, on the one hand, the reflection is not the object reflected, on the other hand, it cannot be said to possess any reality apart from that of the same object; in this respect it is identical with the object.

This view of the immanence of the object in the reflection thereof contains an important key for understanding the methodic or operative import of the discipline of interiorizing concentration central to *adhyatma-yoga*. While, as seen above, it is the immanence of the Self in the intellect which is accentuated in the domain of method, this stress is legitimate only in the measure that, conceptually, one has grasped the transcendence of the Self in relation to the intellect. Taking the dimension of transcendence first, Shankara writes:

> An ignorant person mistakes the intellect with the reflection of Pure Consciousness in it for the Self, when there is the reflection of the Self in the intellect like that of a face in a mirror (Upadesa (B), II, 12.6).

On the other hand, the essential identity between the reflection—that which is the "content" of the faculty of the intellect—and the Self is affirmed in accordance with the dimension of immanence:

> Just as the reflection of a face which makes a mirror appear like it is the face itself, so, the reflection of the Self in the mirror of the ego making it appear like the Self (is the Self). So the meaning of the sentence "I am *Brahman*" is reasonable. . . . It is only in this way and in no other that one knows that one is *Brahman*. Otherwise the teaching "Thou art That" becomes useless in the absence of a medium (Upadesa (B), II, 18.109-110).

In other words, the Self is seen to transcend the faculty of the intellect, in one respect, even though, in another respect, it constitutes the immanent reality of the intellect, directly reflected therein when the faculty is oriented towards its luminous source and inward principle, and indirectly reflected in, or "noticed in the presence of," the mental modifications which assimilate manifested phenomena, inasmuch as these modifications can only function in the light of the Self.

It is important here to note the difference between the lower mind (*manas*), and the intellect or the higher mind (*buddhi*):

> What belong to the lower mind and the higher mind are thought and knowledge respectively (Soul, 44).

"Thought" can be identified with the individual as such—it is pure Consciousness particularized—whereas knowledge pertains to that Consciousness in itself.

From another angle Shankara says that the different names given to this "inner organ" are the result of the quality of awareness in question; this inner organ "is called mind (*manas*) when doubt, etc., are in play but intellect (*buddhi*) when fixed determination etc. arise" (Soul, 29).

This determination can be equated with firm aspiration and one-pointed concentration; the intellect, the point of contact between the vertical ray of the Self and the horizontal plane of the ego, is thus true to its properly transcendent function only when oriented towards its source, and is relativized in the measure that it allows itself to be determined by the discursive mind, that to which individual thought and its inescapable concomitant, doubt, pertain.

To the extent that the individual mind appropriates the light of the intellect and harnesses its luminous capacity to the pursuit of determinate, relative, and individual aims, then the same consciousness which, in its essential nature, is at one with the Self, acquires the appearance of transience; it becomes falsely regarded as an appendage of the mind, and therefore beneath the individual ego which directs it, instead of being seen as that faculty by means of which alone individuality is transcended. It is thus that one can see the compatibility between, on the one hand, Shankara's assertion that "bondage is nothing other than a delusion of the intellect," and on the other hand, that the Self "shines only in the intellect."

Turning now to the process by which consciousness is to be interiorized according to the spiritual discipline of *adhyatma-yoga*, this is based on the progressive "dissolution" of outward modes of consciousness. The means of effecting this dissolution is abstention: by stilling the functions of the outward faculties, these faculties are absorbed into their subtle cause, which, being itself the relatively gross effect of an anterior and interior subtler cause, must likewise be stilled so as to become reabsorbed within its cause. This process culminates finally in the realization of "the Self that is pure peace," called by Shankara "the highest possible summit of human experience" (Enlightenment, 86).

This process of spiritual ascent is described as follows: all sense-activities are to be dissolved in the mind (*manas*); the mind dissolves into its "luminous principle," the intellect (*buddhi*); the intellect is then to be dissolved within the *Hiranyagarbha*, identified with the universal intellect, the "first-born," and this in turn is to be dissolved into the Absolute, "the true Self, that is pure peace, void of all distinctions, without modifications, existent within all" (Enlightenment, 85).

The operative principle here is that abstention from all exteriorizing tendencies of consciousness, from sensible to intelligible, constitutes what might be called the "shadow" of positive, one-pointed concentration on the inmost source of consciousness; it is only because the light of pure Consciousness runs through all these faculties, like a luminous axis, that abstention from exteriorizing thought, together with concentration on the source of awareness, eventually culminates in the realization of pure Consciousness. Thus it can be said that this consciousness, whilst being the immanent or inmost substance of all modes of awareness, is also the "highest" or transcendent mode of consciousness, in accordance with the previously noted identity between the dimensions of height and depth.

Having realized one's true "oneself" as the Self of all, there can be no question of abstention, just as earlier it was seen that the *neti, neti* ceases to operate at the highest level, the Self not being susceptible to negation. Furthermore, there is no longer any question, at this stage, of an individual agent capable either of abstention or action, as the consciousness of the *jivatman* has now been fully and indistinguishably identified with That on which concentrated consciousness was formerly focused, its own inner principle; this is the consummation of the spiritual ascent by means of concentration and is the highest instance of the following universal principle: "Whatever a man thinks of steadfastly and with unshakeable conviction that he soon becomes" (Reality, 140).

It should be clear that the very realization, by means of the intellect, of this transcendent mode of consciousness necessarily implies the transcending of the intellect itself, considered in its relation with the individual; the very "success" of the intellect in reflecting the Self must involve the disappearance of the intellect as a faculty or medium of consciousness:

> The intellect knew the non-existence of the supreme *Brahman* before the discrimination between the Self and the non-Self. But after the discrimination, there is no individual self different from *Brahman*, nor the intellect itself (Upadesa (B), II, 7.6).

In other words, there can no longer be awareness of the intellect as an entity apart from that which it reflects; the consciousness of the individual must be completely dissolved into Consciousness as such—only then can it be properly characterized as transcendent, unitive, and infinite, all other forms of consciousness being limited, extrinsically, by duality and therefore finitude and relativity. Such Consciousness is synonymous with *mukti* or *moksa*; the next section will examine the meaning of this Liberation, or Deliverance.

### 6. *Moksa*

(i) Bliss and States of Consciousness
In relation to the unitive state, or the consummation of the discipline of interiorizing concentration, the question of bliss or ecstasy acquires considerable importance. As seen earlier, since *Brahman* has been provisionally designated as

*Sat-Chit-Ananda*, realization of identity with *Brahman* must entail bliss as an inseparable concomitant. However, Shankara firmly establishes the transcendent status of this bliss by rejecting all empirical "experience" of bliss that may arise on the meditative path.

First of all, it must be understood that all experience of joy in the world is the result of "a fragment of the Bliss of the Absolute"; this bliss, in essence, is eternal and infinite, but in the measure that ignorance predominates over knowledge, it becomes subject to the appearance of transience and limitation. Nonetheless, worldly joy, which "only blossoms when the inner and outer conditions for it are present," does offer some provisional idea of the "utter joy and beatitude" that comes to the *jivan-mukta*. The intensity of the experience of beatitude increases in proportion to the elimination of ignorance, such that one rises in knowledge and happiness, "until the bliss of *Hiranyagarbha* is reached at the top of the scale. But when the distinction set up by ignorance between subject and object has been abolished through knowledge, then what remains is the natural infinite Bliss alone, one without a second" (Absolute, 223-224).

Tying this in to the interiorization process described above, it could be said that as one approaches the Self, the five "sheaths" (*kosas*) in which the Self is apparently enwrapped, are transcended, surpassed—but in the dimension of inner depth: the *kosas*, made up of the material body, vital breath, mind, knowledge,[10] and finally bliss, are so many relativities, each standing as the subtle, inner principle of what is more outward and gross than it, while being itself the outward effect of what is more inward and subtle than it. It can thus be seen that the macrocosmic principle of *Hiranyagarbha* corresponds outwardly or in "height" to the "bliss-sheath," or "bliss-self," inwardly and in "depth"; both represent the penultimate stage of bliss, the first being transcended by *Brahman*, and the second by the unconditioned *Atman*, identity between these two constituting transcendent realization, and in consequence, the highest bliss. However great may be the bliss experienced at the penultimate stage, it must not be mistaken for the bliss of the Self:

> But the Absolute is superior to the bliss-self which, if one compares it with the concrete realization of the Absolute, the final reality, is something that is seen to increase by stages (Soul, 40).

There is no common measure between an experience of bliss that can be increased or decreased by contingent circumstances, and that bliss which is infinite, immutable, and thus not subject to such modifications; human language cannot adequately express the transcendent nature of this beatitude: Shankara calls it "unutterable joy" (Absolute, 226). The question arises, however: how is one to discriminate between an intense experience of bliss and the bliss that is entailed by realization of the Self?

---

[10] This is *vijñanamaya-kosa*, referring to discursive or distinctive knowledge as opposed to pure *jñana*, or *chit*, the undifferentiated essence of knowledge or consciousness as such.

The answer to this is forthcoming in a passage where Shankara describes the state of the Yogi who is "on the point of acquiring" the unitive experience of *samadhi*:

> [G]reat joy comes to him, but he should not pause to savor it. He should not develop attachment for it. He should practice intellectual discrimination and avoid all desires and constantly revolve in his mind the idea that whatever joy comes to him is a fantasy of ignorance and quite unreal. . . . That is, he should reduce all to pure Being, to Consciousness in its true form (Enlightenment, 92).

Lest this intellectual "reduction" of joyful experience to Being and Consciousness be misconstrued as something contrary to joy, it should be stressed that it is the relative experience of joy that is to be transcended, and this, for the sake of that infinite joy which is inseparable from realization of pure Being, "Consciousness in its true form," the Self.

In his commentary on Gaudapada's *Karika*, from which the translator took the above quotation, Shankara comments on this highest bliss:

> It is all peace . . . liberation. It is indescribable . . . for it is totally different from all objects. This ultimate bliss is directly realized by the Yogis. It is unborn because it is not produced like anything resulting from empirical perceptions (Karika, III, 47).

This extract helps to locate the lower form of bliss, that which *is* experienced: it is an "object," distinct from the subject that has the "experience" of it; this lower form of bliss is "born," or produced like an "empirical perception," again implying an irreducible duality, and hence is "a fantasy of ignorance and quite unreal." One sees the importance of the maintenance of discrimination even in these higher states of spiritual experience: the aspirant is not to be allowed the luxury of becoming attached to the experience of bliss, for upon full realization, there will be a complete identity with that bliss which is the very essence of the Self; that bliss will no longer be the object of the experience of the individual subject, but will be inseparable from the very being of the universal—and unique—Subject, the Self. Thus, to say that one has an "experience" of the Real is, strictly speaking, a contradiction in terms: to say "experience" is immediately to set up a distinction between subject and object, a distinction which has no place in the Real; to "experience" the Real is thus to remain distinct from it, while to be identified absolutely with the Real is true realization.

It is because of this absence of any experience involving individual agency and empirical content that Shankara uses, as a point of reference for understanding the nature of realized consciousness, the state of deep sleep. In the Mandukya Upanisad, the states of wake, dream, and dreamless sleep are posited as principles of spiritual states, being identified respectively with *vaisvanara* ("common to all men"), *taijasa* ("composed of light"), and *prajña* ("undifferentiated wisdom"). Of the three, it is the state of deep sleep that most closely approximates the nature of the consciousness proper to *Atman*. Shankara demonstrates the similarity between the two apparently different states of consciousness by showing that in deep sleep one enjoys a state which is a prefiguration of permanent, unitive consciousness; in contrast, the consciousness ordinarily experienced by the ego in the waking or dream state is ever-changing and dualistic, subject to the separative distinction between knowing subject and object known. Consciousness that is linked with the changing world of phenomenal existence is thus contrasted with consciousness that is at one with transcendent and immutable Being. Thus, the waking and dream states, the teacher tells his disciple,

> are not your own nature inasmuch as they are non-persistent like clothes and other things. For what is one's own nature is never seen to cease to persist while one is persisting. But waking and dream cease to persist while Pure Consciousness, the Self, persisting in deep sleep, whatever is non-persisting (at that time) is either destroyed or negated inasmuch as adventitious things, never the properties of one's own nature, are found to possess these characteristics (Upadesa (B), I, 2.89).

To the obvious objection that in deep sleep one is conscious of nothing, Shankara replies that pure, eternal, and transcendent consciousness is of an entirely self-evident nature, requiring no extraneous object to "prove" its nature or existence to itself; therefore, being conscious of nothing is in reality being conscious of "no thing" apart from the very nature of consciousness itself:

> The Consciousness owing to whose presence you deny (things in deep sleep) by saying "I was conscious of nothing" is the Knowledge, the Consciousness which is your Self. As It never ceases to exist, Its eternal immutability is self-evident and does not depend on any evidence; for an object of knowledge different from the self-evident knower depends on evidence in order to be known (Upadesa (B), I, 2.93).

To be conscious of nothing does not negate consciousness; rather, it is an affirmation of unconditioned consciousness, unsullied by contingent content, although, as will be seen shortly, to be conscious of nothing does not on its own suffice to attain to pure Consciousness.

Shankara goes on to compare consciousness to the sun: just as the sun does not depend on any object for its light, but rather illumines those objects such as stones, which are non-luminous, so consciousness cannot require any non-conscious object to provide evidence for its existence, since it constitutes that very "evidence" or "evident-ness" by means of which the non-conscious object is grasped aright. It is in its light that other things are seen; it is not seen on account of other things.

Shankara elsewhere describes what takes place in the deep sleep state by means of the mirror analogy, which will figure prominently in the discussion below: when the mirror is taken away, "the reflection of the man that it contained goes back to the man himself":

> And in the same way, when the mind and the other senses cease to function in dreamless sleep, the supreme deity that has entered the mind, as the individual soul, in the form of a reflection of consciousness . . . returns to its own nature, abandoning its form as the soul (Soul, 130).

39

However, one does not attain realization simply by falling into dreamless sleep; this state is what might be called an unconscious mode of deliverance from limited consciousness, and is thus somewhat similar to the lower form of enstasis, called *sambija samadhi*, that is, a state of consciousness which transcends ordinary modes of awareness but which nonetheless retains intact the "seeds" of ignorance.[11]

To have a state of consciousness wherein the mental functions have been suspended, and the mind is free of content, is by no means to be simplistically identified as a state of realization of the Self; what the two states of deep sleep and *sambija samadhi* have in common is that, although the state of absolute indistinction proper to the Self has been attained,

> because wrong knowledge has not been altogether eradicated, when one awakens from dreamless sleep or from deep meditative concentration (*samadhi*), there are distinctions just as before (Soul, 138-139).

On the other hand, when there has been an "awakening" to the Real, the stilling of the mind that may be experienced as a "state" is an effect of that awakening, which burns up all the seeds of ignorance in the fire of knowledge:

> In dreamless sleep it (the mind) is swallowed up in the darkness and delusion of ignorance. It is dissolved into seed-form, retaining the latent impressions of evil and activity. In its stilled state, on the other hand, the seeds of ignorance, evil, and activity have been burnt in the fire of the awakening to the sole reality of the Self (Soul, 139-140).

One has to distinguish, then, between an apparently "stilled" state of mind that in fact contains the seeds of ignorance and thus remains distinct from transcendent realization, and a properly "stilled" state in which, the Self having been realized, there are no such seeds; it should be stressed that it is the "awakening to the sole reality of the Self" that constitutes the criterion of realization, and not any phenomenally defined state of the mind—a point to which we will return below.

The metaphysical awakening here in question is to be strictly distinguished from the ordinary state of wake, one of the three relative conditions of consciousness. Shankara in fact defines all but this transcendent "wakefulness" as a form of sleep: "Sleep, defined as 'not-being-awake-to-reality' is present in the mental modifications of waking and dream" (Soul, 151).

The positive aspect of deep sleep as an undifferentiated state of consciousness is distinct from this negative aspect of sleep, defined in terms of not being awake to reality; but this negative aspect is also present, implicitly, or in "seed" form, within the state of deep sleep, since the man ignorant of the Real remains such upon returning to the normal state of wake. Thus the deep sleep state is likened to an "indiscriminate mass":

---

[11] This is contrasted with *nirbija samadhi*, "seedless" enstasis, identified also with *nirvikalpa samadhi*, which will be examined further below.

> [W]ith all its differentiations intact, (it) becomes an undifferentiated unity like the day swallowed up by the darkness of night (Soul, 151).

This may be related to the degree of Being, in contrast with what was designated as "Beyond-Being" in Part I of this chapter. In deep sleep, a *de facto* union is consummated with "Being-as-associated-with-seeds-of-action," so that the emergence from that state into dream or wake constitutes the fruition of the karmic seeds that had remained intact during deep sleep. Full realization of the Self, on the other hand, pertains to the domain of Beyond-Being, or *Turiya,* the "Fourth," beyond the three states of wake, dream, and deep sleep. Therefore this *Turiya* is not to be identified as a particular state, one among four, but is the Reality which is only apparently modified by the three illusory states that are superimposed on it. It is realized neither through cognition nor through the simple cessation of cognition, but rather, through a flash of spiritual intuition which, it must be stressed, cannot in any way be reduced to or equated with mental cognition. That which is intuited as the transcendent Reality is grasped, once and for all, as one's true Self; and a concomitant of this realized identity is omniscience:

> That which has finally to be known through spiritual intuition is . . . the final reality, called the Fourth, the Self as metaphysical principle, non-dual, unborn. . . . When this occurs, that man of great intellect, being now himself the Self, attains to omniscience here in this very world (Soul, 168-169).

It should be noted that the meaning of the "omniscience" in question is clarified by Shankara immediately: the consciousness of the delivered one "transcends all empirical knowledge," therefore it is a form of supra-empirical knowledge "which never leaves him." Omniscience, then, is not to be equated with an exhaustive knowledge, within the domain of manifestation, of the data pertaining to all empirically knowable phenomena; rather, it is knowledge of a completely different order, grasping all things in their transcendent source, wherein they abide in undifferentiated form, exalted above any "trace of the development of manifestation" (*prapañcha-upasama*); it is precisely because this knowledge is supra-empirical that it "never leaves him," that is, it is not susceptible to cancellation like an empirical datum that is at one time present to consciousness and at another time absent.

This spiritual intuition that attains to the "omniscience" of the Self, and thus constitutes realization of the Self, is also called *pramana,* authoritative cognition, which must not be confused with individual, non-authoritative cognition or thought in the ordinary sense; it is also referred to as *anubhava*—direct or immediate experience. In the light of the above considerations on "experience" and "thought," the provisional and approximate nature of these designations will be clear.

Turning first to *pramana,* it is said by Shankara that, with its rise, all plurality is eliminated instantaneously, this extinction of differentiation being the shadow, as it were, of the inclusive plenitude of the simple, undifferentiated Self. The *pramana* that negates the notion that the Self really undergoes the three successive states of wake, dream, and deep sleep, also has the result that "one simultaneously achieves the cessation of the notion of plurality in the Self" (Soul, 155).

It is on the instantaneity of the realization that attention should focus here; as seen above, the notion of "awakening" is much emphasized, and Shankara likens the state of identification with the individual psycho-physical complex to a bad dream, from which one awakens upon the establishment of one's true identity as the Self:

> Just as all the pain pertaining to a dream ceases on waking, so the notion that one's Self is the sufferer ceases for ever through the knowledge that one is the inmost Self (Upadesa (A), II, 18.193).

One should recall in this connection the snake-rope image: the change in perception that results from correct discrimination of the rope in the dark is instant: suddenly the "snake" is no more and the rope is grasped not only as truly present, but as having been there all along, as that which was mistaken for the snake. Likewise, the story of the man who was himself the "tenth" but had forgotten to count himself: upon being told of this simple fact, the realization that ensues is immediate. These examples assist in the comprehension of that instantaneous enlightenment attained by the disciple of "high intellect" upon the first hearing of the words *tat tvam asi*, "That thou art." In the present context, the receptivity of the disciple, having been enhanced by the different stages of the discipline, is precipitated in a moment's plenary awareness of the Self. It is realization in a "blessed moment" (Vivekachudamani, 479).

(ii) *Samadhi* and Liberation

Given this emphasis on the "momentary" nature of the enlightenment experience, it will appear surprising to see Shankara positing as a *conditio sine qua non* for realization of the Self, the state of *nirvikalpa samadhi*:

> By the *Nirvikalpa Samadhi* the truth of *Brahman* is clearly and definitely realized, but not otherwise (Vivekachudamani, 365).

Insofar as this type of *samadhi* consists in a particular psycho-physical state wherein breathing is stilled, consciousness of the outer world is suspended, and all mental functions cease for the duration of the state, it cannot be regarded as a prerequisite for liberating knowledge; this is because, among other reasons, such knowledge can arise spontaneously, as noted earlier, in the case of the highest class of aspirant, without any need for meditation, let alone the consummation of meditation which *samadhi* constitutes. Rather, in the light of Shankara's repeated insistence that it is knowledge, alone, which liberates, one is compelled to interpret the above statement on *samadhi* in the sense indicated by the following comment of Shankara on Gaudapada's assertion that *Atman* is attainable by "concentrated understanding," this being another meaning of *samadhi*:

The *Atman* is denoted by the word "*samadhi*" as it can be realized only by the knowledge arising out of the deepest concentration (Karika, III, 37).

In other words, within the framework of a spiritual discipline centered on the practice of interiorizing concentration, *samadhi,* understood as the deepest mode of concentration, is the prerequisite for the rise of liberating knowledge; but this by no means denies the possibility of the same knowledge arising, outside this framework, without the experience of *samadhi,* defined as a particular psycho-physical state; one example seen already is the case of the highest aspirants, to whom Shankara does not attribute the need for any discipline whatsoever, other than the hearing of the sacred texts which identify the essence of the *jivatman* with the Absolute.

Insofar as *samadhi,* like deep sleep, constitutes a break in the continuity of the illusory notions identifying the Self with the non-self, it can indeed be said to extinguish *samsara,* albeit temporarily; if the *samadhi* in question be preceded, accompanied, or consummated by effective knowledge of the Self, then it is qualified as *nirbija* or *nirvikalpa;* but it is this knowledge and not the state that is the *conditio sine qua non* for transcendent realization. Since, as seen above, the "awakening" is a flash of spiritual intuition, it cannot depend on any particular state situated in the phenomenal matrices of time, space, and the other existential categories, since this whole framework arises only on a plane that is rendered illusory by the awakening in question.

Applying Shankara's metaphysical criteria to the question of *samadhi* as prerequisite for the highest realization, the following observations may be proffered: realization of the Self, being im-mediate, strictly speaking transcends time, arriving like a flash of all-illuminating light: the question of how much time is spent in that state of enlightenment is immaterial; whether or not one has a "state" of *samadhi* lasting hours or minutes is of no consequence; if importance is given to such a question, this would be to judge the eternal and supra-phenomenal in terms of temporality and phenomenality: the transcending of relativity cannot depend on relative conditions for its realization.

Even to say that the flash of intuition takes place in a "moment" or an "instant" is, strictly speaking, inaccurate, for these notions are still related to duration, which is unreal from the viewpoint of the Absolute: what is revealed in that "moment" is that there was no "time" when the Self was not immutably and infinitely itself, above and beyond time—and all other conditions for phenomenal existence.

From the viewpoint of the individual, however, it is possible to "locate" in temporal and spatial terms, the experience of enlightenment, even if the content of the enlightenment or the "authoritative cognition," extinguishes forever all notion of individual experience and its existential concomitants, just as correct perception of the rope extinguishes definitively the false perception of the snake. To clarify the distinction between the state of *samadhi* and the moment of "immediate experience" (*anubhava*) wherein the Self is realized through "spiritual intuition," the following point may be considered. *Samadhi* as a particular state is a break in the continuity of the samsaric dream which *may* yield knowledge of the Real, while *anubhava* does not require as precondition any phenomenal break in the dream, since the dream and its apparent continuity are known to be illusory; one cannot require a "break" in the unreal in order for the Real to be attained, for, from the standpoint of the Self, such a break is of the same nature as that which is "broken": both pertain to the level of the non-self, as there can be no break in the Self, no lack of continuity, or change of state. Upon enlightenment the unreal is transcended inasmuch as its phenomenality is "seen through"; the unreal is not necessarily "seen through" simply by a phenomenal break in its continuity such as is constituted by a loss of consciousness of the outer world.

All this is not to say that ordinary perception persists in the moment of enlightenment: all particular contents of consciousness are necessarily absent in respect of their distinctive nature, while being no less necessarily present in their undifferentiated essence, that is, in the all-inclusive nature of pure consciousness:

> [I]n the realm of enlightenment, the particularized consciousness associated with sight and the other sense-faculties does not exist (Soul, 60).

> On enlightenment, perception and the other empirical means of knowledge cease. . . . [T]he Veda itself disappears on enlightenment (Soul, 78).

The Veda is said to "disappear" insofar as it consists in objective data which require an individual mind to assimilate them: this mode of cognition and the duality presupposed by it are no longer operative in the moment of enlightenment. The point here to be emphasized is that the moment of Liberation, of positive realization of the Self, excludes phenomenal awareness because all distinctions born of ignorance are eliminated through knowledge: it is not because of the exclusion of phenomenal awareness that transcendent realization is attained; rather, it is because of this very realization that phenomenal awareness "disappears."

The next question that arises is: what is it that actually experiences Liberation, given the fact that the Self is ever-free by nature, and the human ego is revealed as illusory? This and the allied question of what the individual as such can know of the content of liberation will now be addressed.

## (iii) Individual Experience and Knowledge of Liberation

It has been seen that Liberation transcends the realm wherein experience, defined in relation to individual agency and object of experience, has any meaning: what, then, can constitute the agent in the experience of Liberation? Likewise: Liberation strictly precludes individual modes of cognition; what, then, can the individual as such know of the "experience" of Liberation?

The two questions are closely related, as they impinge on the subtle relationship between the consciousness of the Self and that of the human ego, a relationship that is both real and illusory, depending on the angle of vision.

The simple and, metaphysically, most rigorous answer to the first question is that nobody or nothing experiences Liberation but an illusion: the Self, being eternally free by nature cannot "experience" anything other than what it immutably is; and anything other than the Self is by definition illusory in the measure that it is distinct from the Self. However, from the viewpoint of the *jivatman* within the realm of illusion, the experience of Liberation is not only "not unreal" but is the very means by which the absolute reality of the Self is realized as one's own true being, and this realization is always accompanied by absolute consciousness and absolute bliss.

Therefore there is a certain relative reality that pertains to the world of illusion for one situated in that world—just as there is a certain reality to the dream for as long as one is dreaming; and the flight from this relative reality to absolute reality is the "experience" of Liberation. It is thus legitimate to speak of the "experience" of Liberation from the unreal to the Real, but only from the viewpoint of the individual, and however paradoxical this may be, given the immutability of the Real.

It is not, however, permissible to speak of the individual ego as having been liberated:

> It is not to the ego as agent that the experience of liberation falls, for freedom from pleasure and pain is impossible in the case of the ego as agent (Discipleship, 208).

The ego is ever bound by nature, its very existence as such presupposing the realm of relativity from which Liberation is attained; it experiences only the oscillations of contingent existence—here summed up in the phrase "pleasure and pain," implying thereby that whatever pleasure may be experienced by the ego is always susceptible to negation by its contrary, whereas the bliss of the Self, being infinite, cannot be limited, let alone annulled, by anything save illusion.

The ego, then, is an illusory superimposition which cannot "become" the Self, just as the snake cannot "become" the rope. However, it is also true that the ego is non-different from the Self: the snake, in reality, is the rope, it does not become it. Shankara affirms that while the ego is non-different from the Self, the Self is not non-different from the ego; this non-reciprocal relationship, called *tadatmya* (Upadesa (A), II, 18.81), can also be expressed by saying that the drop is water but water is not the drop: the Self infinitely transcends the ego, but whatever reality the ego possesses can only be that of the Self, which is alone real.

This principle of *tadatmya* highlights the fact that the ego cannot experience Liberation; the ego has two incommensurable dimensions: one, eternally free, deriving from its identity with—or "non-difference" from—the Self; in its other dimension it is eternally bound, insofar as it is distinct from the Self, this resulting necessarily from the fact that the Self is not non-different from the ego. Thus there can be no possible relation between these two dimensions, and if there is no relation, there can be no movement or "flight" from the one to the other, and thus no Liberation.

The possibility of Liberation rests not on relationship, but on identity: the identity between the essence of the ego and that of the Self; this is likened to the identity between the space enclosed in a jar and space in its unlimited extension:

> As, when a jar is broken, the space enclosed by it becomes palpably the limitless space, so when the apparent limitations are destroyed, the knower of *Brahman* verily becomes *Brahman* Itself (Vivekachudamani, 565).

Otherwise put, it is the consciousness that is immanent within the ego that is one with the consciousness of the Self:

> [C]onsciousness is not different in the individual soul and the Lord, just as heat is identical in fire and sparks (Soul, 69).

One sees again the principle of *tadatmya*: the spark is not the fire, but the heat of the spark cannot be conceived as something other than that of the fire whence the spark springs. This analogy is referred to elsewhere in relation to the knowledge by which *Brahman* is "known":

> The knowledge of which *Brahman* is the object is non-different from *Brahman* as is the heat from the fire. The essence of the Self, which is the object of knowledge, verily knows itself by means of unborn knowledge, which is of the very nature of *Atman* (Karika, III, 33).

This establishes that from the highest point of view—the *paramarthika* perspective—the Self is both subject and object of knowledge, in that its immutable Self-knowledge is inseparable from its very being, as heat is inseparable from the fire whence it radiates; for the individual who comes to "know" the Self through spiritual intuition, this knowledge is in truth identical with that very knowledge by means of which the Self knows itself; thus it is also "unborn," that is, of an order which transcends individual thought, which is "born" or relative. When it is said, therefore, that the individual "knows" the Self this can only mean that the Self knows itself by means of that transcendent knowledge with which the individual's consciousness has become indistinguishably merged; it can only be on the basis of the identity between the consciousness of the individual and the consciousness of the Self that the former is able to participate in this transcendent knowledge and be "liberated" from the illusory cage of individuality.

This identity between the consciousness of the ego and that of the Self is still problematic, however, from the point of view of Liberation: for identity is not "relationship": there must be something "other" to take cognizance of or "realize" the identity in question, in other words, to experience Liberation.

Could it then be said that it is the intellect, vehicle of knowledge for the individual, that experiences Liberation? Earlier it was noted that both Liberation and bondage pertain to the intellect, but this must be interpreted according to the fact that the intellect is a faculty and not an agent. When it was said that suffering depended upon the existence of the intellect, it is clear that it is the individual ego that is the agent of this suffering and not the intellect as such. In the present context, the intellect may well be the instrument by means of which Liberation is attained, but cannot be the agent that experiences Liberation.

The answer given by Shankara to this problem can be extrapolated from his concept of *abhasa*, the theory of the "reflection of consciousness." It is the existence of a reflection of the consciousness of the Self in the ego that accounts for the fact that the word "thou" (*tvam*) in the sentence "that thou art" designates the ego directly and the Self indirectly; that it pertains directly to the ego is clear, but it can only relate implicitly to the Self because the Self is reflected in the ego which is directly addressed (Upadesa (A), II, 18.50).

To the extent that Liberation is actually experienced as such, it must pertain to this reflection of consciousness which is like a bridge connecting the ego and the Self, as will be seen shortly. But it must first be understood that this reflection is unreal.

According to Shankara there is, on the analogy of a face reflected in a mirror "a Self, a reflection thereof, and a receptacle for that reflection," but he adds immediately that the reflection is "unreal" (Upadesa (A), II, 18.43).

The reflection of consciousness that returns to its source, as seen earlier, is the graphic way in which the moment of enlightenment was described; the ego, constituting the mirror in this analogy, is extinguished, and it is this which accounts for the fact that the reflection ceases to be a reflection and can only be "found" as the very face itself. For this reason Shankara affirms the unreality of the reflection. The reflection is a property neither of the mirror nor of the face: "[I]f it were a property of either of them, it would persist in one or other of them when the two were parted" (Upadesa (A), II, 18.37).

The reflection ceases to exist in the mirror when the face and the mirror are parted; likewise it ceases to exist "in" the face for it is no longer distinguishable *qua* reflection, from the face. It is thus a reality that is contingent upon the confrontation of the face and a mirror, possessing no intrinsic reality on its own account; hence it is "unreal" in itself.

To the extent, however, that it is endowed with an apparent reality, it is this reflection of consciousness that is the transmigrant (insofar as the illusory realm of *samsara* is concerned) and also the agent in the experience of enlightenment or Liberation: when the mirror of the ego is operative as such, the reflection of consciousness in the intellect and other cognitive faculties will register and experience the varied contents of the samsaric realm; but when, by means of the interiorizing discipline of concentration described above, this reflection is redirected to the object it reflects, and the plane of the ego is surpassed and thus abandoned, the result is that the reflected ray of consciousness is no longer distinguishable from the Self whence it was projected; the "moment" in which the reflection returns to its source is the moment of Liberation, and it is this reflection which "experiences" Liberation, insofar as it can be said that any agent has experience of it.

But can one speak convincingly of a reflection—with its impersonal connotation—actually being an agent in the enlightenment/Liberation experience? On the one hand the answer must be yes, and on the other, no. It is yes, firstly, by default: no other entity can possibly be the agent, neither the eternally bound ego nor the eternally free Self. Secondly, since the Self is infinite subjectivity, a reflection of the Self *can* be regarded as possessing the property of finite, but nonetheless relatively real, subjectivity. The positive aspect of the reflection of consciousness consists, then, in the fact that it possesses a degree of subjectivity; the negative aspect derives from two factors: the reflection is distinct from its source, and, on the analogy of terrestrial reflection, also constitutes an inversion with respect to the object reflected. This negative aspect, then, consists in the fact that the degree of subjectivity proper to the reflection will be finite, and therefore, from the transcendent perspective alone, illusory. But it is this very limitation which allows of the possibility of experiencing anything at all; therefore the reflection can legitimately be accorded the status of agency in the experience of Liberation.

But the answer is also no, in that the illusory nature of the experience of Liberation itself renders illusory the agent of that experience:

> Bondage and Liberation, which are conjured up by *Maya*, do not really exist in the *Atman*, one's Reality, as the appearance and exit of the snake do not abide in the rope, which suffers no change (Vivekachudamani, 569).

The paradox of the metaphysical unreality of Liberation coexisting with the personal experience of Liberation can only be resolved through an understanding of the angles of vision bearing upon this experience. From the viewpoint of ignorance, Liberation is not simply real, but is said to constitute the only experience which is ultimately worth striving for, and is indeed the only experience that is authentic, in the last analysis: the "immediate experience" (*anubhava*) that one is the Self is, alone, real:

> And all other experience is false. . . . [W]e do not admit the existence of any experience apart from that (*anubhava*) (Absolute, 159).

From the viewpoint of the Self, however, the experience of Liberation is illusory, as it can only be the immutable and unfailing reality of the Self that is true reality. In other words, that which is revealed through Liberation is real; but, in the light of that very Reality, Liberation as a particular experience appears unreal.

Another key reason why the Liberation experience must be regarded as illusory is that the very experience presupposes both the state of ignorance—that from which Liberation is attained—and the state of knowledge, into which finite consciousness is reabsorbed; since ignorance is itself of an illusory nature, the experience of Liberation which implies this illusion must itself partake of the same nature, *qua* experience, even if that transcendent reality, grasped in depth as one's own being, could not have been realized as such without the occurrence of this experience. Shankara writes that the Self is inexplicable (*anirukta*) from the vantage point of ignorance (Absolute, 177); at this point one could add that the experience of Liberation—both real and illusory—is likewise inexplicable from the vantage point of logical analysis. Just as it is spiritual intuition that produces enlightenment, so a degree of intuition is necessary for the unenlightened even to comprehend the process of enlightenment.

These considerations lead to the second question posited above: what is it that the individual as such can know of the liberating moment of enlightenment?

The answer to this question again involves the "reflection" theory.

First of all, if the "fruit" of Liberation is said to accrue to the Self, as it is in the Advaitin tradition, the individual can have no knowledge whatsoever of that transcendence of the bounds of individuality which Liberation implies. But Shankara understands such a notion as figurative only:

> [B]ecause the two active causes of the fruit of liberation—the preliminary mental activity and the ensuing cognition in its empirical aspect—are not of the nature of the fruit, it is but right to attribute it to the Immutable, just as victory is fitly attributed to a king (Upadesa (A), II, 18.108).

The cognition that one is the Self thus has an empirical aspect and a supra-empirical aspect; there is no common measure between the first, which is proper to the individual, and the second, which pertains to realization of the Self which transcends the individual; therefore, the "fruit" of Liberation cannot be said to accrue to the individual, and must by default accrue to the Self. On the other hand, the Self, being actionless and immutable, cannot in truth receive any such fruit, so the attribution is figurative only: although his servants actually fought and won the battle, the victory is "fitly attributed to the king" who did no fighting.

This means that, despite the impossibility of the individual having a complete cognitive awareness of Liberation, he nonetheless, as a *jivan-mukta*, is the immediate beneficiary of the Liberation in question; furthermore, inasmuch as something of the Self—its reflected consciousness, precisely—must pervade the cognitions of the individual for these to be endowed with any consciousness whatsoever, it is this same reflection of consciousness that can know, to some degree, what was revealed in the liberating experience. This principle is clearly formulated in the following:

> [W]hen the mind, which is not itself conscious, shines with reflected consciousness, its ideas shine with reflected consciousness too, as the sparks emerging from a burning iron shine like the fire within it (Upadesa (A), II, 18.83).

Something of the transcendent can be known by the mind, without that knowledge encompassing the content of the realization of transcendence, just as sparks are something of the fire, and can convey something of its nature, without ever being able to encompass the full nature of the fire. This analogy helps one to understand the state of mind of one who has experienced Liberation and attempts to describe it. Shankara writes of the bewilderment that coexists with liberating knowledge, by describing the state of the disciple who, having been instructed in the highest Truth, realizes it "at a blessed moment" and then speaks as follows:

> My mind has vanished, and all its activities have melted, by realizing the identity of the Self and *Brahman*; I do not know either this or not-this; nor what or how much the boundless Bliss is! (Vivekachudamani, 481).

The dimension of subjectivity in question here can only be the empirical mind, reflecting on what was revealed in the moment of realization: in that moment, all activities of the mind had melted; outside that moment, in the framework of the mental functions, it cannot gauge the bliss of that state. The mind is aware, now, that in that state it had "vanished"; it is also mysteriously aware of its own illusory nature *qua* mind, since only that which was realized in such a state is fully real, and is one's own true being. The reflection of consciousness in the intellect is the locus of actual consciousness in these thoughts, but as it is identifying with its source, and no longer with the plane of its refraction—that is, the mind—it can see the mind as absolutely "other." Because of the positive aspect of the reflection, the mind can know that boundless Bliss was attained, and that this pertained to the immutably real Self, but it also knows that, *qua* mind, it cannot measure or truly encompass that Bliss in its fullness, this incapacity deriving from the negative aspect of reflected consciousness, that is, the finitude attendant upon the reflection insofar as it is an inversion: the finite cannot know and still less be, the infinite.

This is why Shankara says that only he "knows" the Absolute who gives up the notion that he is a "knower of the Absolute," adding:

> [T]he mind's discriminating cognition, "I am the knower, unknowable, pure, eternally liberated," is itself transitory, from the very fact that it is an object (Upadesa (A) II, 12.14).

Here again one sees the empirical aspect of the liberating cognition being distinguished rigorously from that which is realized through supra-empirical or spiritual intuition. Both the mind and its cognitions are "objects," that is, they are outward and non-conscious when considered in relation to the supreme Subject or Witness. To directly experience the Witness in an indescribable *anubhava* is truly to be the Witness, but the mental affirmation of the knowledge that this Witness is one's true reality is but a transitory and extrinsic modality—an "object," precisely—of the uninterrupted consciousness of the Witness.

The *jivan-mukta*, then, is not so much a "knower of the Absolute": he is one in whom the identity of being and knowledge has been realized, and this at a degree which strictly precludes his own finite individuality, and, with it, all cognitions that are conditioned by that individuality.

These considerations show that all of Shankara's statements affirming his identity with the Self are to be understood as ellipses: they omit to indicate the ontological degree of the "I" in question, and, as affirmations, they are always transcended by what they affirm. In this light, one can appreciate what Shankara means when he writes, in apparent contrast to the above quotations, that the Absolute "can be apprehended by a modification of the mind as the Witness of the mind, distinct from it" (Discipleship, 195-196).

The kind of "apprehension" here is quite different from direct, unmediated knowledge of the Absolute; rather, it must refer to the individual's awareness of an inner Witness, totally other than itself, and yet more truly "its Self" than that modification by means of which the awareness in question is mediated. Since the Self cannot be the object of the mind, the nature of the awareness in question here is totally different from that which pertains to ordinary objects susceptible of determinate conception; the mind can be aware of the existence of the inner Witness, but can never know, exhaustively, that Witness:

> The lower empirical vision, itself an object for the Seer, cannot aspire to see the Seer who sees it (Discipleship, 198).

The Self is said to be "known" when the *jivan-mukta* has realized that his true Self "alone truly exists"; he also knows that, as the Self cannot be known by anything but itself, it is unknowable: "[H]ence it is 'known' and 'unknowable' without there being the slightest contradiction" (Absolute, 125-126).

The *jivan-mukta* is thus not only the one who, by transcending the bounds of his own individuality, has realized and "known" the Self, but he also knows, as a necessary concomitant of this very realization, that he as an individual cannot know the Knower of knowledge:

> He only is a knower of the Self who is aware of himself as unbroken light, void of agency, and who has lost the feeling, "I am the Absolute" (Absolute, 159).

> Those who think "I am the Absolute and I am also the one who undergoes individual experiences" are ruined both by their knowledge and by their action (Upadesa (A), II, 11.8).

The feeling or cognition, "I am the Absolute" must be freed from its association with relativity; the *jivan-mukta* no longer has this thought because the very conditions that define the thought as such—individual agency, empirical cognition, fundamental dualism and hence alterity—contradict the reality that one's true—supra-individual—being is the Absolute.

On the other hand, there can—and must—be something more profound than a "thought" or "feeling" that one is the Absolute; the *jivan-mukta* has an absolute certitude not only that he is nothing but the Absolute, but also that he is animating an individual existence, without there being the slightest contradiction:

> For if a person . . . has the conviction in his own heart that he has direct knowledge of the Absolute and is also supporting a physical body at the same time, how can anyone else cause him to deviate from that conviction? (Enlightenment, 228).

The "knower" of the Absolute has a conviction in depth—the "heart"—that he is simultaneously the Absolute—hence a non-agent—and the animator of the body—hence an agent; the first aspect of the conviction pertains to the vantage point of the Real and the second, to that of the illusory. There are two subjectivities only when the point of view—and thus the domain—of cosmic illusion is assumed; in reality there is but one Subject, void of agency and thus of individual experiences. One again observes the importance of the distinction between the *paramarthika* and *vyavaharika* perspectives.

The existence of this conviction by no means contradicts the point that one cannot have the "thought" or "feeling" that one is the Absolute: to think that one is in reality the Absolute and the individual at the same time is to be conceptually and existentially bound by a contradiction pure and simple; thus one is "ruined" in terms of both "knowledge" and "action." But to have the conviction in the heart, not a thought of the mind, that one's true Self is the Absolute, while one's empirical experiences pertain to the non-self—such a conviction is both authentic and unshakeable in the measure that realization is direct and total, rather than simply mental and fragmentary. It is a question of realizing in depth that which appears on the surface as a paradox; a paradox which, insofar as it is viewed from the mental plane alone—and hence from the viewpoint of ignorance—is nothing but a contradiction. This further underlines the difference between a mental cognition and the plenary realization of the content of that cognition; as such, the cognition itself remains always a determinate conception, and hence a limitation, of the nature of ignorance, and must in its turn be transcended.

These considerations may be aptly drawn to a close by referring to Shankara's criticism of those who "dabble" in metaphysics, mistaking their purely mental comprehension of the highest truths for realization thereof:

> Those alone are free from the bondage of transmigration who, attaining *Samadhi*, have merged the objective world, the sense organs, the mind, nay the very ego in the *Atman* . . . and none else, who but dabble in second-hand talks (Vivekachudamani, 356).

## (iv) Grace and Realization

A final question remains to be considered in regard to the "ascent": how can one explain the attainment or realization of transcendence by the individual, when the individual is of a strictly non-transcendent nature? In other words: how can the efforts of the individual—meditation, concentration, and so on—have as result a supra-individual attainment? How is it that such efforts are not vitiated in advance by the non-transcendent source of those efforts?

The answer to these questions is implicit in the preceding section: just as it is the Self alone that can know the Self, so the efforts of the individual which apparently result in enlightenment are in reality derived not from the individual but from the transcendent source of the individuality, the Self.

No hard and fast distinction between individual effort and supra-individual or divine "grace" is tenable, given that the Lord is described by Shankara as the "source" of the individual's intelligence which in turn directs the effort of the will. Thus:

> [L]iberation of the soul can come only through knowledge proceeding from His grace (*anugraha*) (Soul, 67).

Earlier it was seen that in the invocation of *Om*, realization of the Self occurs as a result of the grace of the Lord, immanent within the syllable, being attracted by the invocation and revealing the Self to the invoker; this underlying principle can be seen at work not just in regard to invocation but in all paths of realization. Thus, whenever Shankara appears to attribute enlightenment to the conscious efforts of the aspirant, to his receptivity, "high intellect," or powers of concentration, it must not be forgotten that, insofar as all of these factors are governed by the intelligence, and this in turn is derived from the Self, all efforts made by the individual are in fact modes of grace emanating first and foremost from the Self. When these efforts meet with success, a further grace is involved: for insofar as concentration, meditation, and invocation are still actions of the individual—despite being simultaneously modes of the supra-individual grace whence they stem—they cannot on their own account result in anything that transcends the individuality; hence the final consummation of these efforts is always a grace from the Self, a grace that is attracted by the efforts in question, but which is by no means reducible to them. Thus the realization of identity between the individual and *Brahman* is said by Shankara to be attained "through the grace of the Supreme Lord in the case of one or two perfect souls only, those who meditate on the Lord and who make great efforts to throw off their ignorance" (Soul, 75-76).

This grace is elsewhere referred to as the *Sakti* or dynamic power proper to *Brahman*, which is identical with *Brahman* itself, as "Sakti cannot be distinct from the one in whom it inheres" (Gita, XIV, 27).

The relationship between devotion to knowledge and realization through grace is expressed by Shankara in the following image:

> I am like fire: just as fire does not ward off cold from those who are at a distance, and wards it off from those who go near it, so I bestow My grace on My devotees, not on others (Gita, IX, 29).[12]

The aspirant must then do all that is in his power to approach the "fire" of liberating knowledge, knowing all the while that his vision of the fire—that is, his theoretical awareness that this knowledge is liberating—as well as his capacity to approach it—that is, the will by which his efforts are galvanized in the spiritual discipline—are in truth so many effects of grace; they prefigure that final grace which is incommensurable with the efforts that apparently led to or resulted in realization: if the individual in the above image can in one sense be said to have "approached" the fire by means of his own efforts, he cannot in any sense be said to have generated the heat of the fire that "wards off" the cold, the transcendent knowledge, that is, which burns up ignorance.

The individual, then, participates in the process whereby knowledge of the Self is attained and identity with the Self is realized; but that mode of participation is precluded by the final consummation of the process which, being of a strictly supra-individual nature, can no longer fall within the domain of the individual, and therefore can only be referred to as a "grace."

## Part III: Existential "Return"

This final part of the chapter deals with the "return" of the *jivan-mukta* to the world of phenomena, that is, to the existential domain, that of outward being,

---

[12] This is Shankara "speaking" again from the perspective of the Self, in his commentary on the Bhagavad Gita.

after having realized the Self, at the supra-ontological degree, "Beyond-Being."

Discussion will center on four key elements that emerge from the writings of Shankara on the state of awareness and being proper to the one who has attained liberation in this life.

The four elements are: the view of the mind in the light of the supra-mental realization; the ontological status of the world in the light of the realized vision of "all is *Brahman*"; the significance of residual *karma* for the *jivan-mukta*; and the question of whether the *jivan-mukta* is susceptible to suffering.

## 1. The Mind

A key distinction between transcendent realization of the Self and a transitory state of apparent union with the Self such as is experienced in the lower form of *samadhi*, is that outside this state, the individual feels that the return to "normal" consciousness entails a loss of consciousness of identity with and as the Self; whereas in full realization of the Self, such a "return" does not entail a definitive rupture of this consciousness, as the non-dual nature of the Real is known—in depth—to persist even while the individual is apparently engaged in the world of duality. Thus, even while the mind is perceiving phenomena, the knowledge of the One that has been realized ensures that neither the objective world of phenomena outwardly perceived, nor the subjective locus of phenomenal awareness—the perceiving mind—can veil the true nature of the Self which is the only reality underlying both poles of illusion. Regarding the lower Yogi, who may have transitory moments of what appears to be union, Shankara writes:

> When his mind is concentrated he sometimes thinks he is happy and one with the Self. He declares, "Oh, I am now one with the essence of Truth." When he falls from this state, he declares, "Oh, I am now fallen from the knowledge of the Self" (Karika, II, 38).

The true knower of the Self, however, never experiences such a fall:

> As it is impossible for *Atman* to deviate from its own nature, the consciousness that "I am Brahman" never leaves him. He never loses the consciousness regarding the essence of the Self (Karika, II, 38).

The fluctuating states of mind no longer affect the consciousness of the Self, now the realized locus of awareness for the *jivan-mukta*, even after the enlightenment "experience"; that consciousness is independent of the mind, persisting as its underlying reality, in which light the mind itself loses its opacity, that is, its aspect of limitation or not-self. This means that the mind is "seen through" insofar as it is distinct from the Self, or else it is grasped as the Self in respect of the awareness which it refracts; the important point is that this understanding of the mind as a limitation, an "object," or not-self, can take place not only from the perspective of the supra-individual Self, realized in a flash in the enlightenment experience, but also persists even in the framework of multiplicity: the viewpoint of the Self, in other words, is somehow maintained even while the not-self, that is, the limited mind, is operative.

One way of understanding this subtle point is to recall the distinction made earlier between the certitude proper to the heart, and thinking proper to the mind. The consciousness that one is the Self can only pertain to the Self, but the mind has indirect access to this consciousness in the sense that it may register the reflection of this consciousness that resides in the heart: thus one can explain the paradox that the mind can be understood as an object even while the mind is functioning as subject. Even after the supra-mental moment of realization, then, the mind is viewed from the vantage point of the Self, the content of that realization: having realized identity with and as the Self, transcending the mind, the *jivan-mukta* continues to identify with the Self—and its vantage point—even when the mind is functioning, because he intuits—with the "heart," thus the core of his being—that the mind, along with the world proportioned to it, is of a dream-like nature. It is from this point of view that one can appreciate how it is that Shankara engages in a conversation with his own mind, in his *Thousand Teachings*:

> O my mind . . . thou art of the nature of non-existence. . . . The real cannot be destroyed and neither can the unreal be born. Thou art both born and destroyed. Therefore thou art non-existent (Upadesa (A) II, 19.8).

Even though such a statement and the idea it expresses are mediated by the mind, their source cannot be located in the mind itself; Shankara is able to make of his own mind a medium for the expression of a truth which renders illusory that very mind; and this is only conceivable in the light of a realized locus of consciousness that is of a strictly transcendent and necessarily supra-mental order.

It should be noted that, while the *jivan-mukta* possesses the supra-mental vantage point continuously, it is the mark of the lower class of Yogis that they need to subject the mind to various disciplines in order to arrive at the same vantage point; and then, as seen above, this perspective is attained only momentarily, or for as long as the particular "state" of identity lasts. For such Yogis, the mind is incorrectly seen, on the one hand, as something separate from, but related to, the Self—when the mind is functioning normally—and on the other hand, as one with the Self only in the supra-phenomenal state wherein it is extinguished *qua* mind.

On the other hand, knowledge of the Self having once been realized, the true knowers of the Self depend on no further mechanical efforts of the mind in order to acquire identity with the Self, as they "spontaneously enjoy, as quite natural to them, fearlessness and eternal peace, known as freedom." This is contrasted with those other Yogis "who are also traversing the path, but who possess inferior or middling understanding, and who look upon the mind as separate from but related to *Atman*" (Karika, III, 40).

The *jivan-mukta*, then, knows that the mind—whether in or out of the state of *samadhi*—cannot be described as "separate from but related to *Atman*"; rather, the mind is understood to be either an illusion or the Self. Insofar as it is viewed in its aspect of limitation or modification of consciousness, and thus as an entity distinct from the Self, it is illusory; but insofar as it is viewed in respect of the consciousness of the Self which is refracted by it, the mind is seen to be not other than its real substratum, the Self which imparts to the superimposition constituted by the mind its very capacity for consciousness:

> As the snake imagined in the rope is real when seen as the rope, so also the mind, from the standpoint of the knowledge of the ultimate Reality, is seen to be identical with *Atman* (Karika, III, 29).

In other words, only when the mind is seen through to its substratum—when the snake is grasped as the rope—can it be assimilated to *Atman*. The mind is *Atman* only in respect of its transparency, and not in respect of the particular attributes that characterize it as mind; that is, the mind/snake is only "real" when it is understood to be an illusion and hence "seen through," to reveal rather than veil its real substratum.

These points will be seen to apply also, in certain key respects, to the question of the ontological status of the world from the viewpoint of the *jivan-mukta*.

## 2. "All is *Brahman*"

Despite the unreality or "non-existence" of the mind in respect of its separative affirmation, the positive aspect of the mind—deriving from the fact that its awareness cannot be other than that of the Self—allows for the continued consciousness of the Self even while the multiple phenomena of the world are being cognitively registered. This is possible since those phenomena in turn are reducible to their ontological substratum, the Self. In other words there are two key factors involved in the realization of the vision "all is *Brahman*": a subjective factor, centering on the immanence of the Self in all cognitions, and an objective factor relating to the ontological root of the world in the Self.

Taking first the subjective factor:

> The Self, which takes all mental ideas for its object, illumines all cognitions. . . . It is revealed by the cognitions as that which is non-different in each. There is no other way to have knowledge of the inmost Self but this (Discipleship, 205).

There is no other way, that is, within the framework of the world and in respect of the functioning of the cognitive faculties; this, in contrast to the unmediated knowledge of the Self that is realized on the plane that transcends mental cognition. Insofar as the knower of the Self is conditioned—albeit in appearance only—by the adjunct of individuality, and is engaged in the multiple perceptions of the phenomenal domain, he can only know—or rather, intuit—the Self as that light by means of which, and in which, all cognitions stand illumined: he knows the Self, not by means of cognition, but "*through* every cognition" (Discipleship, 204, emphasis added).

That is, the principle of cognition, pure awareness, is not veiled by the multiple specific instances of cognition springing therefrom; rather, that principle is grasped, with the "spiritual" intuition and thus supra-cognitively, through each and every cognition; for these cognitions have now lost their ability to veil the Self and instead, for the *jivan-mukta*, reveal the Self, becoming transparent to the light of their source, the light by which they subsist, "that which is non-different in each."

Turning now to the objective side: the world of phenomena is itself grasped as *Brahman*, insofar as it cannot exist apart from its material cause, which is *Brahman*; the example given by Shankara to illustrate this point is the relationship between clay in itself and pots, buckets, plates, etc., made out of clay: "The truth is there is only clay" (Creation, 39-40).

Another illustration is the image of water: foam, ripples, waves, and bubbles are distinct from each other, while remaining in reality nothing but transient modifications of water, and thus reducible in principle to it. Thus:

> [T]he experiencer and the objects of his experience need not be mutually identical though they remain non-different from the Absolute (Creation, 39).

To reconcile this view of the positive ontological root of the world in *Brahman* as its material cause, with the view of the world as illusory, based on the rope-snake image, it could be said that the rope stands as the "material cause" of the snake exclusively from the vantage point established by the initial perception of the snake. In other words, the snake can only be said to have a material cause in the framework of the illusion that accords to it an apparent reality; in actual fact it does not exist, and thus any material cause of the non-existent must likewise share in that non-existence. *Brahman* is "cause" only in relation to an "effect," which, for its part, is reducible to illusion; in itself *Brahman* is, as seen in Part I of this chapter, not conditioned by the fact of standing in a causal relationship with anything whatsoever. This is why Shankara, following Gaudapada, is so strict in upholding the theory that there is in reality no creation (Karika I, 6[7]). According to the theory of *ajati*, the creation is akin to a magician's trick: he appears to climb a rope, disappear, fall in fragments to the ground, reassemble, and climb up the rope again; but in reality he never leaves the ground.[13]

Another useful image that reconciles the two apparently contradictory views of the world is that of the torch making circles of fire in the air: one imagines that there are real circles of fire when in fact only the torch exists, just as one imagines the world of multiplicity when in truth non-duality is alone real (Upadesa (A), II, 19.10).

However, in order to accord fully with Shankara's perspective, this analogy must be qualified by the principle of *tadatmya*: the world *qua* effect has the nature of its material cause, *Brahman*, but *Brahman* does not have the nature of its effect, the world. The immanence of *Brahman* in the world by no means diminishes the transcendence of *Brahman* above the world. In other words, although *Brahman* in a certain sense imparts to the world its ontological substance, this does not mean that the world, in its existential multiplicity, can be crudely equated with *Brahman*:

---

[13] This does not prevent Shankara from proffering a theistic interpretation of creation as seen earlier; without an understanding of the distinction between the *paramarthika* and *vyavaharika* perspectives, such metaphysical suppleness would appear to be nothing more than a contradiction pure and simple.

[N]on-duality which is the Supreme Reality appears manifold through *Maya*. . . . This manifold is not real. . . . [T]he changeless *Atman* which is without part cannot admit of distinction excepting through *Maya* (Karika, III, 19).

The unreality of the manifold does not negate the empirical perceptions that are proportioned thereto, even in the case of the *jivan-mukta*; he continues to perceive multiple phenomena, but is not deluded into attributing to the objects of his perception any final ontological status:

> The enlightened one, having thus beheld that attributeless One . . . who no longer beholds the attributes of the world, does not fall into delusion, being relieved of the fault of taking his perceptions for real (Upadesa (A), II, 19.26).

There is here an important distinction between beholding the attributes of the world and the perceiving of the world: the *jivan-mukta* will continue to perceive things in the world but he will not behold them as attributes of the world; that is, having once known the non-dual Self transcending all attributes, it becomes impossible to ascribe attributes—in an ultimate manner—to any object whatsoever: "attribute" or quality loses its distinctive character, and is sublimated as an undifferentiable element of the non-dual Subject. To "see *Brahman* everywhere," then, comes to mean, not that the objects of one's perceptions in the world are distinctively grasped as *Brahman*—this would mean that *Brahman* consisted in parts—rather, it refers to the capacity to reduce all objects to their pure ontological substance, to the Subject, that is, which imparts to them their very capacity for apparent existence; to the Subject which has been realized as the very Self of the *jivan-mukta*. This reduction, then, far from equating empirical perceptions on the plane of phenomena with *Brahman*, on the contrary, allows of the continuous vision of *Brahman* exclusively on the basis of the negation of the final reality of these perceptions; thus, the *jivan-mukta* does not fall into the delusion of taking "his perceptions for real." This point is succinctly made by Shankara: "negate the world and know it" (Reality, 64).

In this light one understands better what Shankara means when he says that the enlightened man "though seeing duality, does not see it" (Enlightenment, 146): he sees duality in one respect, but does not see it in another; he sees, that is to say, nothing but *Brahman*; for such a man "all is *Brahman*":

> All this universe . . . is nothing but Brahman; there is nothing besides Brahman. . . . Are the pitcher, jug, jar, etc. known to be distinct from the clay of which they are composed? (Vivekachudamani, 391).

It may be answered that there is no distinction between these objects in respect of their fundamental substance, but the objects are distinct both from each other and from clay in respect of their name and form. To "see" non-distinction means, then, not to pretend that the distinctions born of *nama-rupa* are empirically unreal, but rather that they are metaphysically unreal; it implies the capacity to grasp the ultimately unreal nature of the entire sphere within which such empirical distinctions exist.

To sum up this discussion: to see a clay cup is to see an apparent modification of clay; to see the world is to see an apparent modification of the Self; the modification will reveal that substance which it apparently modifies, but only in the measure that its accidental properties—making for its empirical distinctiveness—are rendered transparent, thus revealing rather than veiling its underlying substance.

Finally it should be emphasized that this capacity for "seeing through" things arises, not from any dialectical or purely conceptual operations, but flows from, and indeed is partly constitutive of, realization of the Self: having once "beheld that attributeless One," the *jivan-mukta* is no longer deluded by the phenomenal limitations of his own perceptions, but rather "sees through" the objects of his perception by means of a spiritual vision which necessarily transcends the domain of ordinary perception; this vision of the One in the world can be regarded as a fruit of the vision of the One beyond the world, bearing in mind Shankara's understanding of such a vision:

> [H]aving seen the Supreme Reality, . . . [the aspirant] thinks "I am myself That"; that is to say, his perception of sensuous objects becomes seedless, has lost all germ of evil (Gita, II, 59).

This "germ of evil" is the karmic seed of ignorance that is "burnt up" in the fire of knowledge of the Self; but the fact that the *jivan-mukta* persists as an individual means that some *karma* must remain. This question is addressed in the following section, in the light of the relationship between the *jivan-mukta* and action in general.

### 3. Action and *Prarabdha Karma*

Although the *jivan-mukta* acts, he is said to be actionless. This is because he acts in a manner proper to the one who has transcended the three cosmic tendencies, the *guna*s, thus earning the title *Trigunatita* (Gita, XIV, 25).

This means that he may indeed act, but such action has no binding effect, no further karmic "fruit"; such action that may be performed, ritual or otherwise, is done either for the sake of setting an example to others, or else it consists exclusively in that action necessary for the physical maintenance of the body. But, always, it is action that is not performed for the sake of the fruits of the action; it is always detached action:

> For want of egoism these actions do not pollute Me . . . nor have I a desire for the fruits of these actions (Gita, IV, 14).

Though expressed by Krishna, through the paraphrase of Shankara, this attitude pertains to the *jivan-mukta*. It was seen earlier that detachment from action and its results was posited as a *sine qua non* for progress along the path of transcendence; at this point it should be observed that detachment is not so much a quality to be cultivated as it is an effect or constitutive element of plenary realization; that is, detachment is something which cannot but arise as a direct consequence of Liberation. Indeed it could even be said that perfect detachment can *only* be attained as an effect of Liberation, and will perforce remain imperfect or virtual—as opposed to actual—until Liberation is attained: for while the abstemious man finds that he is detached from objects, he will not be fully detached from desire for those objects until realization of the Self is attained:

> Objects withdraw from an abstinent man, but not the taste. On seeing the Supreme, his taste, too, ceases (Bhagavad Gita, II, 59).

Another way of putting this is that there can be no desires left in the soul of one whose every desire is satisfied; and this is what happens—precisely and exclusively—when the Self is realized:

> How does one become free from desires? By realizing them; but this can only be achieved when one's desire is for the Self alone. . . . Only that which is thought of as other than oneself can be an object of desire, and in the case of the enlightened man . . . . no such thing exists (Enlightenment, 207).

The *jivan-mukta*, then, knows that all possible desire is eternally consummated in his own true Self; there is then nothing existent that could constitute an object of desire; and when no such object exists, no action rooted in desire can take place; hence it is said that the *jivan-mukta* acts while being actionless.

His actions do not cling to him, they no longer give rise to karmic forces (*vasanas*, *samskaras*) which generate further samsaric action, as the inner nexus between action and desire has been eliminated, that nexus which consists of ignorance.

But Shankara introduces a nuance into this picture by saying that there is a stock of *karma*, called *prarabdha*, that is not burnt up in the fire of knowledge, but which gives forth its fruit, even though the *jivan-mukta* is not bound to the samsaric realm by this fruit; nor is his realization contradicted by this fructification of past action. In response to the question: what actions are "burnt in the fire of knowledge," Shankara replies, specifying the following three types of action: all acts committed in the present birth, prior to the enlightenment of the *jivan-mukta*; all acts committed in the life of the *jivan-mukta* subsequent to his enlightenment; and all acts committed in all past births—except the *prarabdha-karma*, that is, the particular portion of karmic "fruit," taken from the total stock of accumulated *karma* that is responsible for initiating the present life of the individual (Discipleship, 277).

The total stock of *karma*, called *samcita-karma*, consists in the accumulated merit/demerit of all past action, the fruits of which have not begun to manifest; in contrast to the *prarabdha-karma*, which, having begun to fructify, must continue to do so until this particular causal mass is exhausted. It is only because of this unexhausted portion of *karma* that the bodily existence of the *jivan-mukta* is maintained subsequent to Liberation:

> Final peace comes at the fall of the body. If it were not for the distinction between action the effects of which have begun to fructify, and action the effects of

which have not . . . all action without exception would be destroyed by knowledge of the Absolute. And in that case there would be nothing further that could sustain the empirical existence of the enlightened man, and he would enter the final peace forthwith (Enlightenment, 227).

It is the continuing fructification of the *prarabdha-karma* which accounts not just for the fact of the continued empirical existence of the *jivan-mukta*, but also for the fact that he continues to act; to this extent he will then appear to be bound by his previous actions, but one must stress the word "appear": for, unlike the unenlightened man, the *jivan-mukta* acts out his *karma* in the full knowledge that this "acting out" no longer entails further *karma* to which he is bound, but simply exhausts that karmic stock that gave rise to his present birth. He thus sees such action that flows from him as pertaining to the not-self, and hence of an illusory character. Thus, his action is "apparent" in contrast to the reality of the action of the unenlightened man: "reality" here pertaining not to the ontological degree of the action in question, but to the subjective experience of bondage to action that is felt by the unenlightened man.

A useful image of this unspent *karma* is given by Shankara: that of the potter's wheel which revolves for some time even after the cessation of the action that set it in motion: "Hence one has to wait until the energy of the action is exhausted" (Enlightenment, 227). The very fact of the experience of enlightenment implies a prior state of ignorance, which in turn can only be the fruit of past action:

[T]he rise of knowledge presupposes a fund of action, the effects of which have begun to manifest (Enlightenment, 227).

Enlightenment, though not constituting a change of state from the viewpoint of the Self, is a change of state from the perspective of the empirical subject, who is the embodiment of the *prarabdha-karma* that must be exhausted. It is important to emphasize here that though the "final peace" is only attained at the death of the body when this karmic force is spent, this peace is known by the *jivan-mukta* to be the eternally real and immutably omnipresent peace that can never be absent, but only appear such: just as his own actions pertain to the level of appearances only, so too is the non-attainment of the "final peace" but an appearance. Thus, the capacity to see through the mirage of action and alterity, even while empirically engaged in that mirage, is a central distinguishing feature of the *jivan-mukta*.

However, there is an important qualification to this on-going vision of the Self: even if in principle the *jivan-mukta* cannot fall prey to illusion, in practice he may be subject to a certain momentary loss of total knowledge, and this, by virtue of the particular nature of his *prarabdha-karma*, which "will overpower the knowledge of the Real that you have, and produce its results. Totally unobstructed metaphysical knowledge will finally supervene when the merit and demerit that produced the body come to an end" (Upadesa (A), II, 4.3).

It may be objected that if "final peace" and "unobstructed knowledge" come only upon physical death, it is incorrect to speak of either Liberation or omniscience as attainable in this life. This objection can be answered by Shankara's assertion that those who have realized the Self "are not associated with the suspicion of a defect, as they do not identify themselves with the psycho-physical complex" (Enlightenment, 283).

In other words: it is always possible that the *jivan-mukta* may err in the world as a result of his *prarabdha-karma*, but such error will always be superficial and insignificant, therefore in no wise detracting from the actual knowledge of the Self fully realized—this realization pertaining to a transpersonal depth to which the individual psycho-physical complex has no access. It is precisely his awareness of the illusory nature of the psycho-physical complex that not only renders him immune from false identification with that complex, but also ensures that any errors arising within that complex cannot significantly modify or relativize his state of realization. Thus, Shankara says that the *jivan-mukta* who may find his knowledge of the Real temporarily overcome by the effects of his *prarabdha-karma* is like one who "inexplicably loses his sense of direction momentarily, although really in possession of it" (Enlightenment, 221).

The *jivan-mukta*, then, is simultaneously the agent experiencing the effects of unspent *karma* and the one "liberated in life" from the bondage of all *karma*. The paradox is resolvable only in the light of the understanding that, for the *jivan-mukta*, the realm of empirical experience is illusory whilst the liberation attained pertains to a Reality that can be contradicted in appearance only; thus, for such a one, "the existence of *prarabdha* work is meaningless, like the question of a man who has awakened from sleep having any connection with the objects seen in the dream-state" (Vivekachudamani, 454).

From this quotation can be inferred both the possibility of the enduring influence of illusion and the transcendence of the consequences flowing from that possibility: having awoken from a dream, one may continue to dwell upon the objects of which one was dreaming—and thus in some sense be "connected" to those objects—even while knowing that there can be no objective connection between oneself and those non-existent objects. Thus, while the "existence" of *prarabdha* is "meaningless" for the *jivan-mukta*—that is, it is devoid of real substance—its effects will still be experienced on the empirical plane proper to them; the point here is that those effects are transcended by the very knowledge of their illusory nature: in this respect the *jivan-mukta* is like the one who acts in a dream while knowing that it is a dream. Inversely, he is also like the one in deep sleep—the state of virtual Self-realization to which all have access—wherein the differentiated world is absent, except that for him, this absence is sustained even in the very bosom of its apparent manifestation. Thus he is one who "acts" but is "actionless."

To sum up: it is the very disjuncture between the individual as such and the Self—stemming from the fact that, though the self is non-different from the Self, the Self is not non-different from the self—which explains the possibility of the *jivan-mukta* being subject to the unfolding of unspent karmic energy, and, with it, the susceptibility to momentary breaks in the continuity of his consciousness of the Self: insofar as the *jivan-mukta* remains a *jiva*, a relative being, this susceptibility is a contingent possibility, but insofar as his essential defining quality is *mukti*, and thus the Self, there is no question of being affected by the vicissitudes of outward existence; any susceptibility to contingency can only relate to that which is itself a contingency, the ego which is "ever bound." It is not the ego or the empirical self that can be said to have realized transcendence: only the Self can know the Self—it is this immutable Self-knowledge that the *jivan-mukta* realizes, and this, at a transpersonal depth to which the relativities attendant upon the outward existence of the relative self have no access.

The *jivan-mukta*, then, maintains an attitude of indifference towards the fruits of his *prarabdha-karma*, that is, his empirical experience in the world. It remains to be seen whether this indifference operates even in relation to that most intense kind of human experience: pain and suffering.

## 4. Suffering and the *Jivan-Mukta*

The key to understanding Shankara's position on suffering is the notion of objectivity. This may seem surprising, given the degree of emphasis on the subjective nature of the Self; but in fact the two aspects, transcendent subjectivity and radical objectivity, go hand in hand: as seen earlier, to realize the Self as true subject is also and necessarily to regard the ego and all its adjuncts as "objects"; it is thus to be perfectly objective with regard to the not-self, a perspective which is possible only from the vantage point of the Self, or, derivatively, from that of the reflection of the Self in the individual.

What is most important to note here is that the awareness of the *jivan-mukta* participates in that transcendent perspective even in the context of empirical existence, and is not identified with that perspective only in the supra-empirical moment of enlightenment: rather, a certain awareness of that which is revealed as one's true Self is maintained even outside the moment of revelation, which thus becomes no longer momentary, but permanent; and, in line with the considerations noted above, such an awareness may be termed a "reflection" of the consciousness of the Self within the individual, and thus an awareness surpassing the limitations of the individual.

In the measure that identification with the Self is ceaseless, pain and suffering will be seen to pertain to something "other," that is, to the not-self. This, as will be seen, does not negate the reality of suffering on its own plane, but it does negate the possibility that the Self is subject to suffering, and it is this awareness, along with the full identification with the Self whence flows this operative—in contrast to merely theoretical—awareness, that makes it possible to say, elliptically, that in the experience of suffering, the *jivan-mukta* does not suffer.

The degree of objectivity attained in relation to one's own body as a result of realizing the true locus of subjectivity, is neatly summed up by Shankara thus:

> Just as one does not identify oneself with the body of another, so does one not identify oneself with one's own body after vision of the Supreme (Upadesa (A), II, 16.73).

Just as the unenlightened person possesses a concrete sense of identification with his own body and a correspondingly concrete non-identification with the body of anyone else, so the *jivan-mukta* fully and effectively identifies himself with the Self, this identification entailing, inversely, the concrete non-identification with his own body, now correctly grasped as composed of the very stuff of ignorance. The subjective experience of pain flows from the absence of this knowledge:

> [E]xperience of pain is not real in the highest sense. . . . The soul experiences the pain arising from cuts and burns in its body through identifying itself with them in error. And it experiences the pains of sons and friends and the like in the same way through identifying itself with them (Soul, 71).

The individual's identification with the body-mind complex prior to enlightenment is likened by Shankara to the false notion, on the part of one who wears ear-rings, that his essential defining characteristic is to wear ear-rings; when the ear-rings are once removed, "the notion 'I am the one with the ear-rings' is permanently cancelled" (Upadesa (A), II, 18.161). Likewise, the false self-identification with the individual body-mind complex is permanently effaced through the realization that one is the Self.

What is "permanently cancelled" in the above illustration is the idea that the nature of the individual is essentially defined by the wearing of ear-rings; but this does not preclude the wearing of ear-rings. Analogously, the realized individual will no longer be under the sway of the idea that his true Self suffers, but this does not preclude the existence, and thus objective experience, of suffering in the framework of the individuality.

In another place, Shankara compares the experience of pain in the dream-state to the experience of pain by the individual in the world:

> [W]hen the dream is over the pain is regarded as non-existent now and as being unreal before. For pain and error, once cancelled, do not assert themselves again (Enlightenment, 129).

The *jivan-mukta*, then, having "awoken" to reality, knows—even whilst witnessing the experience of suffering on the part of his own individual being— that it is only an outer empirical "envelope" of his own true Self that is suffering. In terms of the dream analogy, it would be like one who, dreaming that pain is being inflicted upon him, knows that he is dreaming and thus, even while "experiencing" pain in the dream, is aware that the recipient of the painful experience is but a projection of his own imagination: the pain is then not negated on its own level, but it is that very level, along with the sense of agency proportioned to it, that will be concretely grasped as an illusory superimposition on the substratum of the Self, which is immutable beatitude.

However, given the fact that it is possible for the *prarabdha-karma* to operate so as to "overcome the knowledge of the Real," it is necessary to qualify the above points with a *de jure* clause: in principle, the *jivan-mukta* will be capable of transcending all suffering by means of his identification with the Self, while in practice it is possible that such and such an experience of pain, as fruit of the *prarabdha-karma*, will result in the temporary eclipse of knowledge of the Self, and thus in the consequent feeling that "I am the sufferer."

In other words, the notion and the feeling that one is the agent in the experience of suffering is precluded only to the extent that knowledge of the Self is uninterrupted; if this knowledge is susceptible to any momentary lapse, in that measure there will be the possibility of the reemergence of the notion and feeling that one is the sufferer. This important qualification of the immunity from suffering, though not articulated as such by Shankara, is nonetheless implicit in some of his statements, of which the following may be taken as an example:

> Where there is but the one perfectly pure consciousness without a second, there the Mahatmas experience no grief or delusion (Upadesa (A), II, 10.12).

"There" may be taken as referring to the "realm of enlightenment" wherein, as seen in Part II of this chapter, no empirical perceptions exist, as there is no empirical agent; in principle, this is just as much the case within the realm of empirical existence, inasmuch as, once known to be illusory "there," the realm of apparent existence is "cancelled" even "here," that is, in the very bosom of the illusion itself. This is the case in principle and in the very measure that consciousness of the Self remains uninterrupted; but, just as it has been seen that "unobstructed knowledge" and the "final peace" come only with the exhaustion of the *prarabdha karma* and bodily death, so, while still living, the *jivan-mukta* will remain subject in practice to the unfolding of this unspent karmic force, which carries with it the possibility of a momentary lapse of knowledge, and consequently the subjective experience of "grief."

However, it must be stressed, finally, that such an experience does not disprove or qualify the state of transcendent realization attained by the *jivan-mukta*; for the realization in question pertains in the last analysis to the "realm of enlightenment" wherein there is no question of being subject to the vicissitudes of outward existence. It is the in-depth realization, the "making real" of that domain of the Self, that constitutes Liberation or the transcendent attainment, in "this life"; neither the cessation of the objective existence of that relative "life," nor the absolute immunity from suffering, constitute conditions of transcendent realization.

## 5. Devotion

> Even great gods like Brahmà and Indra are pitiable beings in the eyes of that knower of the Self (Upadesa (A), II, 14.27).[14]

It may be thought that personal devotion to a personal God would be precluded by the knowledge that both elements of such a relationship are, in the very

---

[14] It should be noted that the "Brahmà" in question here (male gender) is not *Brahma nirguna* or *saguna*, but one of the "Triple Manifestations" (*Trimurti*) of *Isvara*; it thus occupies an ontological degree which is beneath that of *Isvara*, the Lord.

measure of their distinctive affirmation, unreal and thus "pitiable beings." Anything that can be distinguished from the Self is relative and therefore illusory and "pitiable." But in fact this consciousness by no means entails any diminution in the devotion of the individual to the Lord, and this is for two identifiable reasons: firstly because the Lord, as "lesser" (*apara*) Absolute, is not other than the "higher" (*para*) Absolute, in respect of essential identity, even while being distinguishable from the higher Absolute in respect of ontological determination; secondly, because the individual as such is infinitely surpassed by the Lord, to whom an attitude of humble adoration is consequently due, and this, not only as a prerequisite for adopting the path which transcends the Lord as lesser Absolute, but also even after that transcendence has been realized.

The concluding salutation of Shankara's commentary on Gaudapada's *Karika* is addressed to *Brahman* and then to his own Master: "I bow to that Brahman, destroyer of all fear for those who take shelter under It. . . . I prostrate to the feet of that Great Teacher, the most adored among the adorable . . ." (Karika, IV, conclusion).

This attitude of devotion and humility on the part of the *jivan-mukta* is explained by Shankara in the comment preceding the above, by referring to the possibility of "saluting" that knowledge which liberates:

Having attained this knowledge which is free from multiplicity, having become one with it, we salute it. Though this absolute knowledge cannot be subjected to any relative treatment, yet we view it from the relative standpoint and adore it to the best of our ability (Karika, IV, 100).

This "view" from relativity persists, then, even while being inwardly transcended by the "view" of the Self; but the very fact that the individual continues to exist as such, in the domain of relativity, necessarily entails humble devotion to all that which ontologically or spiritually surpasses him. The devotion offered to *Brahman* is *a priori* addressed to the "lesser" Absolute: the "higher" cannot "be subjected to any relative treatment," since *Brahma nirguna* has no possible relationship with the manifested world; nonetheless, this devotion is implicitly directed to the higher aspect of *Brahman* which in fact constitutes whatever reality the "lesser" aspect may be said to possess.

Transcendent realization, then, does not entail the ontological elevation of the individual above the personal God, the "lesser" Absolute: on the contrary, only when there is awareness of the fact that the individual as such is an illusion, an "object" which can be "cut off like an arm and thrown away"—only then has consciousness been liberated from its illusory limitations, rejoining its immanent and immutable source which is the Self.

As an individual, then, the *jivan-mukta* remains outwardly subject to all that which surpasses him in the ascending hierarchy of Being; this is expressed not just in the reverence noted above, but in the many devotional hymns attributed to Shankara. However, in fulfilling those obligations attendant upon his provisional ontological situation, the *jivan-mukta* at one and the same time sees the illusory nature of the entire plane on which dualistic relationships exist, and also knows concretely that in his very essence—in that Essence to which "his" consciousness in fact "belongs"—he "is" That which is intended by all relationships, actions, thoughts, modes of being, happiness, and consciousness, that which bestows upon them all their value and ultimate significance, the supreme Self "which has no second."

# CHAPTER 2

# IBN ARABI: *La ilaha illa'Llah*

Whereas Shankara's doctrine was seen to flow from the text, "That is the Absolute; That thou art," Ibn Arabi's doctrine of transcendence can be regarded as an elaborate esoteric commentary on the first article of Islamic faith: "There is no divinity except the (one) Divinity." Whilst in the first perspective the all-inclusive nature of the immanent Self is affirmed, in the second, the all-exclusive nature of the transcendent Divinity is affirmed; but this second affirmation also contains an implicit denial of alterity, being centered on the absolute oneness of the Divinity, and thus rejoins the perspective of immanence. One of the key questions in the examination of Ibn Arabi's approach to this identity between the immanent and the transcendent will then be how this "Doctor Maximus" (*al-Shaykh al-Akbar*) of Islamic mysticism expresses the deepest implications of the oneness of being in the context of a theistic and dogmatic faith which emphatically maintains a rigorous distinction between Creator and creature. As will be seen, his doctrines are not put forward in a manner which suggests an individual effort of comprehension, or an attempt to compromise between the dogmatic demands of the exoteric religion and the inner realities unveiled by mystical experience; on the contrary, divine inspiration is explicitly claimed by Ibn Arabi even for the very modalities of conceptual expression of that experience, an experience—or rather, a realization—which nonetheless remains inexpressible insofar as its innermost essence is concerned.

In regard to his monumental writings, two caveats need to be expressed at the outset: firstly, in regard to quantity, only a very small fraction of his work has been translated into western languages, so that no analysis based on this fraction can claim to be comprehensive; secondly, regarding mode of expression, his doctrines are of a highly elliptical nature, and cannot be reduced to a neat system of inter-related concepts which maintain a consistent meaning irrespective of their place within his metaphysical doctrines. Moreover, the concepts employed are most often drawn from Quranic verses, and, in particular, from subtle esoteric interpretations of these verses, so that the complex and multi-faceted ramifications of his doctrine properly call for detailed philological and etymological analyses. This, however, would take us far beyond the bounds of this chapter, not to mention the limits of our own competence; a certain minimum of this type of detail will be unavoidable, but it will be determined by the focus of this analysis, which will be on the highest and most universal aspects of his doctrine. There will therefore be an inevitable sacrifice of breadth—the "horizontal" spread of symbolic and semantic associations—for the sake of height—the most transcendent aspects of doctrine and realization.

Many fundamental aspects of Ibn Arabi's ontology, cosmology, and spiritual psychology will necessarily be either briefly alluded to or omitted; the intention of this chapter is to distill the essence of Ibn Arabi's approach to the meaning and fundamental implications of the ultimate realization, with a view to meaningful comparative analysis in relation to the other mystics dealt with in this study.

The sources used for this chapter consist for the most part in translations of Ibn Arabi's magnum opus, *The Meccan Illuminations* (*al-Futuhat al-Makkiyyah*) and his most commented and studied work, *The Bezels of Wisdom* (*Fusus al-Hikam*), a much shorter book, which summarizes and synthesizes his most essential teachings. The translations used here are taken from the following works, which will be referred to in the chapter by a key word in the title, with the page number following it. In the case of *Les Illuminations de La Mecque*, a most valuable set of translations from the *Futuhat* into French and English (all translations from the French to English are by myself, on the basis of the original Arabic text), the book is edited by Michel Chodkiewicz, but reference will be given to the name of the translator of the text being cited; in the bibliography fuller details will be found under this entry.

Ascension: "The Spiritual Ascension: Ibn Arabi and the *Mi'raj*" (Ch. 367 of the *Futuhat*), James W. Morris, *Journal of the American Oriental Society*, Vol. 108, 1988.

Bezels: *The Bezels of Wisdom* (*Fusus al-Hikam*), trans. Ralph Austin.

Chari'ah: "La notion de *Chari'ah*," trans. Michel Valsan, *Études Traditionnelles*, July-Oct. 1966, Nos. 396-397.

Extinction: *Le Livre de l'Extinction dans la Contemplation*, trans. Michel Valsan.

Hal: "Sur la notion de *Hal*," (Ch. 192 of the *Futuhat*), trans. Michel Valsan, *Études Traditionnelles*, July-October, 1962, Nos. 372-373.

Illuminations: *Les Illuminations de La Mecque*, ed. Michel Chodkiewicz.

Imaginal: *Imaginal Worlds: Ibn al-'Arabi and the Problem of Religious Diversity*, William Chittick.

Imagination: *Creative Imagination in the Sufism of Ibn Arabi*, Henri Corbin.

Journey: *Journey to the Lord of Power*, trans. Rabia T. Harris.

Khalwah: "Sur la notion de *Khalwah*," trans. Michel Valsan, *Études Traditionnelles*, March-June 1969, Nos. 412-413.

Muhyiddin: Roger Boase and Farid Sahnoun, "Excerpts from the Epistle on the Spirit of Holiness (*Risala Ruh al-Quds*)," in S. Hirtenstein and M. Tiernan, eds. *Muhyiddin Ibn 'Arabi: A Commemorative Volume*.

Nom: "Le Livre du Nom de Majesté," trans. Michel Valsan, *Études Traditionnelles*, I: Jan-Feb, 1948, No. 265; II: July-Aug, 1948, No. 268; III: Dec. 1948, No. 272.

Path: *The Sufi Path of Knowledge*, William Chittick.

Quest: *Quest for the Red Sulphur*, Claude Addas.

Sagesse: *La Sagesse des Prophètes* (*Fusus al Hikam*), trans. Titus Burckhardt.

Seal: *Seal of the Saints*, Michel Chodkiewicz.

Self-Disclosure: *The Self-Disclosure of God*, William Chittick.

Sufism: *Sufism and Taoism*, Toshihiko Izutsu.

Tarjuman: *The Tarjuman Al-Ashwaq*, trans. R.A. Nicholson.

# Part I: Doctrine of the Transcendent Absolute

## 1. Doctrine as Seed or Fruit?

Before beginning to evaluate Ibn Arabi's doctrine on the Absolute, it is important to take full cognizance of the fact that this doctrine, rather than acting as a means of preparation for realization, on the contrary crystallized as an effect of this very realization itself, in the form of an extrinsic and provisional expression of the realities apprehended in the highest states of contemplation; his mystical "opening" (*fath*) occurred prior to any methodic spiritual discipline (*riyadah* or *suluk*, the latter bearing the more general meaning of methodic spiritual "traveling," by stages, along the Path); despite being in agreement with the general Sufi tradition on the importance of this preparation, without which the foundations for spiritual "virility" will be lacking, he allows that there can be exceptions to this rule; and affirms that his case was precisely one such exception (Quest, 35). This opening occurred through a particular divine grace, an ecstatic "attraction" (*jadhbah*); this "attraction" came at sunrise, after having entered this, his first spiritual retreat, at first light: "My opening was a single attraction in that moment" (Path, XII).

This opening is also referred to in terms of a vision of the "Face" of God:

> When I kept knocking on God's door, I waited mindfully, not distracted, until there appeared to the eye the glory of His Face and a call to me, nothing else. I encompassed Being in knowledge—nothing is in my heart but God. . . . Everything we have mentioned after that (vision of the glory of God's Face) in all our speech is only the differentiation of the all-inclusive reality which was contained in that look at the One Reality (Path, XIV).

As to the meaning of the "one look," this will be examined in detail in Part II, as will the general conditions for entering the retreat, along with its principal methodic means of concentration; but at this point it suffices to establish that doctrine, "our speech," is the exteriorized expression of the highest realization, rather than being given as an indispensable prerequisite for realization. In recounting his famous meeting, as a "beardless youth," with the already renowned philosopher Ibn Rushd, Ibn Arabi makes this point:

> He (Ibn Rushd) thanked God that in his own time he had seen someone who had entered into the retreat ignorant and had come out like this—without study, discussion, investigation, or reading (Path, XIV).

This highlights not simply the fact that realization may be attained without the need for any preceding study, but also the highly exceptional nature of this possibility, and may rather be seen as an exception that proves the rule, thus at one and the same time affirming the general validity and desirability of the study of doctrine, without attributing to this study an absolute degree of necessity, given the imponderables of divine grace.

In Ibn Arabi's case, this grace operated such that the knowledge of divine reality was attained even though it had not been explicitly sought; referring elsewhere to this same meeting, Ibn Arabi wrote: "He (Ibn Rushd) had seen what God had opened up to me without rational consideration or reading, but through a retreat in which I was alone with God, even though I had not been seeking such knowledge" (Path, 384, n. 13).

The next point that is to be noted is the incommensurability between the doctrine of divine Reality and that Reality as it is in itself; this is referred to when Ibn Arabi says that what had been deposited in each chapter of the voluminous *Futuhat* is but a drop of water compared to the ocean (Path, XII), whilst the *Fusus* contains only "that which he (God) dictated to me, not all I was given, since no book could contain all of it"; this in turn goes back to the fact that a complete "definition of Reality is impossible" (Bezels, 58, 74).

However, the study of doctrine is not deprived of all value because of this inescapable inadequacy; rather, one must search deeper for the meanings and spiritual ramifications implicit in doctrine, just as one must study revealed scripture and probe its deeper allusions and levels of significance:

> It is known that when the Scriptures speak of the Reality,[1] they speak in a way that yields to the generality of men the immediately apparent meaning. The elite, on the other hand, understand all the meanings inherent in that utterance, in whatever terms it is expressed (Bezels, 73).

In the case of Ibn Arabi, there are two strong reasons for taking his doctrines seriously as conceptual starting-points: firstly because, as noted above, they are claimed to be the expression, not of an individual effort at philosophy, but of an enlightenment bestowed upon, and consequently surpassing, the individual as such; secondly, even the process by which the "one look" was differentiated was itself of an inspired nature, as he claims both in regard to the *Fusus* which, as just seen, was "dictated" to him, and in regard to the *Futuhat*: he claims that not a single letter was written without it being divine dictation and "lordly projection" (Seal, 18).

Also, doctrinal conceptions do play a part in fashioning receptivity to types of contemplation and in this sense may be seen as prerequisites for the realization of the corresponding contemplation, so long as it is understood that the degree here envisaged falls short of the transcendent level; moreover, doctrines and beliefs can also be seen as constituting obstacles barring the way to that level, by "binding" the Divine to the particular conceptions posited within these beliefs.[2] This point will be further analyzed both in Part II of this chapter, in relation

---

[1] *Al-Haqq*: Chittick translates this as "the Real." It is an extremely important Divine name, combining the notion of absolute Reality with that of absolute Truth, so that it is often used as a synonym for both the Divine Essence and the name Allah itself: "The Real can be viewed in respect of the Essence or in respect of the name Allah" (Path, 49).

[2] The Arabic word for "belief" ('aqidah) stems from the root meaning "to bind," an association which Ibn Arabi makes much use of in his more antinomian pronouncements. See especially Part IV of this chapter, regarding the necessity of transcending the "god" that is "bound by beliefs."

to the ontological degrees of contemplation, and in Part IV, dealing with the universality of religious belief.

At this juncture, having established the basic character and status of the doctrine, a summary of its essential content in regard to the Absolute will be presented. One may begin with the crucial distinction, within the divine order, between the "Level" (*al-martabah*) or the Divinity (*al-uluhiyyah*), and the Essence (*al-Dhat*).

While all existentiated—hence relative—realities find their immediate principle stemming from the Level of the Divinity, absolute reality pertains exclusively to the Essence, which can only be referred to apophatically, since any positive affirmation would constitute a definition of That which is indefinable: "He who supposes that he has knowledge of positive attributes of the Self has supposed wrongly. For such an attribute would define Him, but His Essence has no definition" (Path, 58).

Despite this aspect of conceptual inaccessibility pertaining to the Real as it is in itself, Reality in respect of its totality can but be one; therefore all relative being, which does accept positive definition and delimitation, cannot be separated, in its essence, from that which does not accept delimitation; this amounts to saying that the non-delimited Real cannot be delimited by its own non-delimitation from assuming delimited being; or again: the very infinitude of Reality implies a dimension of finitude, this dimension constituting a necessary expression of one of the possibilities inherent in infinite possibility, and without which the infinite could not be the infinite, since it would be limited by the absence of the finite; Ibn Arabi makes this very important point in relation to the distinction between God's "incomparability," or non-delimitation, and His "similarity" or delimitation:

> He is not declared incomparable in any manner that will remove Him from similarity, nor is He declared similar in any manner that would remove Him from incomparability. So do not declare Him nondelimited and thus delimited by being distinguished from delimitation! For if He is distinguished then He is delimited by His nondelimitation. And if He is delimited by His nondelimitation, then He is not He (Path, 112).

In other words, both aspects of the Divine must be simultaneously affirmed or, at a more fundamental level, intuited, so that relativity or delimited reality is seen as an intrinsic dimension of absoluteness or the non-delimited Real, this dimension pertaining to "similarity" and ultimately to the immanent ipseity (*huwiyyah*) pervading all that exists and without which nothing could exist; thus, it is the plane of manifestation that is relative and delimited, while the essential reality of that which is manifested as relative is nothing other than the One Absolute, non-delimited Real, whose very non-delimitation or infinitude presupposes the manifestation of delimited realities.

This important metaphysical principle establishes the relationship between the relative and the Absolute in a manner which at once identifies the relative with the Absolute in respect of the essential unity of reality, and clearly distinguishes the relative from the Absolute in respect of the exclusive reality of the Essence.

Put another way, the very perfection of being requires an apparent aspect of imperfection: "part of the perfection of existence is the existence of imperfection within it, since, were there no imperfection, the perfection of existence would be imperfect" (Path, 296).

The translation of *wujud* should strictly be "being" in the above quotation, in order to distinguish between "existence" and "being": that which exists is, in accordance with its etymology, that which "stands apart from" being; and this, moreover, is extremely important in order to highlight the distinction, within the divine nature, between God as the Creator, identifiable with Being and source of all existence, on the one hand, and on the other, God as the Essence, which so far transcends the created cosmos that it cannot be said to have any relationship whatsoever with it: this inaccessibility is described by the notion of *tanzih*, while the complementary dimension, that of relationship and thus "similarity" is referred to as *tashbih*.

In terms of the latter dimension, the Divinity or Level can be identified as Being, which stands as the primordial principle determining and comprising within itself all that comes to possess a degree of being; and it is the creative act of the personal God at this primordial level which existentiates all relative existents; this creative act is the divine address: *Kun!* (Be!) to a possibility which thus acquires existence.[3] The word for cosmos, *al-kawn*, is directly related to this existentiating command: the cosmos is that which has come to exist by virtue of the divine address to it.

Now, just as the existent thing is distinguished from the existentiating command, so the Level of the Divinity upon which the act of creation devolves must be distinguished from the non-acting degree of the Essence: God as personal Creator relates to the Level of Divinity which is the deployment of the Essence with a view to its Self-manifestation; Ibn Arabi expresses this by saying that all the divine names—such as Creator, Judge, etc.—belong to the Level, not to the Essence (Path, 54); so this level of Being must in turn be subordinated to its principle which is the degree of the Essence.

It is not correct for the Real and creation to come together in any mode whatsoever in respect of the Essence, only in respect of the fact that the Essence is described by Divinity (Path, 59).

In other words, only when the Essence is endowed with a degree of form—"Divinity"—can there be any possibility of relationship between the Real and the world: the world is seemingly given a degree of reality and the Real appears to acquire a degree of relativity. Only in and as the Essence can the Real be divested of that relativity entailed by relationship with the multiple world. These points will become clearer in the following discussion of the illusory nature of all multiplicity and the distinction between the oneness of unity and the oneness of multiplicity.

[3] This whole doctrine is rooted in the Quranic account of cosmogony: "His command, when He intendeth a thing, is only that He saith unto it: Be! and it is" (Qur'an, 36, 82).

Insofar as the world is multiply differentiated it is "imagination," "fantasy," or "other than God"; on the other hand, it is said to be real in respect of the existence—which is unique—that is bestowed upon it; in the following extract the relationship between the world and God is compared to that between a shadow and the person projecting it:

> The cosmos is, in relation to the Reality, as a shadow is to that which casts the shadow. . . . The thing on which this divine shadow, called the cosmos, appears is the [eternally latent] essences of contingent beings (Bezels, 123).

The status of the *a'yan* (sing. *'ayn*) in relation to spiritual realization will be more closely examined in the following section, but for now, it suffices to note that they are the immutable essences, archetypes, or "entities" (Chittick's preferred translation), non-manifest in themselves, existing only as purely intelligible possibilities, which determine all the states of the things that are lent existence by Being. It should be emphasized that the shadow of Being, in itself inseparable from Being, and thus real in respect of the source of its projection, assumes a multiple nature as soon as one considers it in relation to the *a'yan* upon which it is cast:

> [T]he shadow is nothing other than He. All we perceive is nothing other than the being of the Reality in the essences of contingent beings. With reference to the Identity[4] of the Reality, it is Its Being, whereas, with reference to the variety of its forms, it is the essences of contingent beings. Just as it is always called a shadow by reason of the variety of forms, so is it always called the Cosmos and "other than the Reality" (Bezels, 124).

Therefore, anything which receives a degree of being—becoming *mawjud* as opposed to being *wujud*—is both real and illusory: real in its inward participation in Being, but illusory both because it is transient and because it is outwardly one among a multiplicity of other forms, and what is multiple is "other than the Reality." It follows naturally that,

> the Cosmos is but a fantasy[5] without any real existence. . . . [K]now that you are an imagination as is all that you regard as other than yourself an imagination. All existence is an imagination within an imagination, the only Reality being God, as Self and Essence, not in respect of His Names (Bezels, 124-125).

## 2. Unity and Multiplicity

These considerations lead us to address the relationship between the One and the many. The key to understanding this relationship is a correct comprehension of the distinction between the Essence and the Divinity: one must look for the source of the "imaginary," relative, finite, and differentiated cosmos in the Divine itself, which means that even within the Divine nature, the plane upon which the Names and Attributes become distinctive and differentiated realities

---

[4] This again refers to *huwiyyah*, which has been rendered above as "immanent ipseity."

[5] Literally: "imagined" (*mutawahham*).

must be distinguished from the Essence, which is the intrinsic reality of those attributes, ineffably comprising them within itself in absolutely undifferentiated mode, while simultaneously transcending them and even—from the strictly metaphysical view—rendering them illusory in respect of their distinctive differentiation:

> The Names in their multiplicity are but relations which are of a non-existent nature (Sufism, 161).

The Names therefore represent specific ways by which the Real enters into relationships with contingent things, and by this very fact, they represent the pathways by which the Real descends into the realm of relativity; each Name is outwardly an aspect of the manifestation of the Real—and to say manifestation is to imply something that is "other than" what is manifested—while inwardly the Name denotes the Real in itself:

> [T]he Names have two connotations; the first connotation is God Himself Who is what is named, the second that by which one Name is distinguished from another. . . . As being essentially the other, the Name is the Reality, while as being not the other, it is the imagined Reality (Bezels, 125).

In other words, each Name is, on the one hand, identified with all the Names by virtue of its essential identity with the Named, the One Essence which is the ultimate source of all the Names, and on the other, it is distinguished from the other Names by virtue of its specific property; now, distinction implies limitation, hence relativity and, ultimately, transience; it is thus that the Name assumes the nature of "imagined Reality."

This plane of plurality within the Divine nature is referred to by Ibn Arabi as the "Unity of the many" (*ahadiyyat al-kathrah*), in contrast to the "Unity of the One" (*ahadiyyat al-ahad*) which pertains exclusively to the Essence:

> In respect of His Self, God possesses the Unity of the One, but in respect of His Names, He possesses the Unity of the many (Path, 337).

The process of universal manifestation requires the "Level" of the Names, which are multiple as a result of their relationship with the diverse possibilities of cosmic phenomena; these possibilities are lent existence by Being and acquire their specific qualities by virtue of their contact with the Names; the Names in turn acquire their distinctive features by virtue of their ruling property over those effects—the cosmos in its entirety—which are thus existentiated. The Names do not possess distinctive ontological entities, since this would undermine the principle of the Oneness of Being by negating the reality that all of the Names are in their essence but the Named; thus one observes degrees within the One Being: all the things of the world are reduced to "effects" of the Names, and the Names in turn are the Named:

> Since the effects belong to the divine names, and the name is the Named, there is nothing in Being/existence (sic) except God (Path, 96).

Therefore the Names constitute an isthmus (*barzakh*) between contingent existence and necessary Being; considered inwardly, they have no separate entities, while outwardly they possess ruling properties over engendered things; now these ruling properties require ruled effects just as the notion of "lord" requires that of "vassal" and that of king, a kingdom; there is, therefore, a mutual dependency between the Names and the contingent things, such that each would be inconceivable without the other. Thus, all the Names which presuppose the world are Names of the "Level" or Divinity and not Names of the Essence:

> The names do not become intelligible unless relationships become intelligible, and relationships do not become intelligible unless the loci of manifestation known as the "cosmos" become intelligible. Hence the relationships are temporally originated through the temporal origination of the loci of manifestation. . . . That which is denoted by the name Allah demands the cosmos and everything within it. So this name is like the name "king" or "sovereign." Hence it is a name of the Level not the Essence (Path, 50).

This shows, in another way, how it is possible to regard the Names as, in one respect, non-real: insofar as they are rendered distinct through their relationship with relative, temporally originated phenomena, they must be attributed an unavoidable degree of relativity, only that which is eternal being absolutely real. These points are illustrated in the form of a dramatic personification in which the contingent possibilities, in their non-manifest latency, ask the Names to render them manifest; the Names in turn seek help from the higher Names (the "Powerful," the "Desiring," etc.) which may be able to initiate the process of manifestation; recourse is had to the "Knowing," who says:

> [W]e have a presence which watches over us, and this is the name Allah. We must all be present with it, since it is the Presence of all-comprehensiveness.

After being addressed by the Names, *Allah* replies:

> I am the name that comprehends your realities and I denote the Named, who is an All-holy Essence described by perfection and incomparability. Stay here while I enter in upon the Object of my denotation.

And finally, the reply of the Essence:

> Go out and tell each one of the names to become connected to what its reality requires among the possible things. For I am One in Myself in respect of Myself. The possible things demand only My Level, and My Level demands them. All the divine names belong to the Level not to Me, except only the name One (*al-wahid*) (Path, 54).

The significance of this Oneness resides in the fact that it comprises both the Unity of the One and the Unity of the many, hence it is the least inappropriate Name of the Essence, and of Being as such; for inasmuch as nothing in existence can be situated in a dimension apart from the One Reality, all cosmic multiplicity must be assimilated to the plane of the Unity of the many, which in turn is assimilated to the Unity of the One; one thus returns to the crucial notion of the absolute Unity of Being, which comprises distinctive levels and degrees, from the relative point of view, whilst from the absolute viewpoint, there is but the undifferentiated nature of Pure Being:

> Naught is except the Essence, which is Elevated in Itself, its elevation being unrelated to any other. Thus, from this standpoint, there is no relative elevation, although in respect of the aspects of existence there is (a certain) differentiation. Relative elevation exists in the Unique Essence only insofar as It is (manifest in) many aspects (Bezels, 85).

To say "Pure" Being is thus implicitly to say Being insofar as this is not limited to the "Level" of the Divinity—that "Presence of All-Comprehensiveness" to which the name *Allah* was seen to refer—but rather opens out onto the Essence which, while comprising within itself this same Presence or Level and all it comprehends, cannot be "tainted" with the relativity implied by being the immediate principle of universal manifestation.

The reason for dwelling at some length on the metaphysical meaning of this oneness is to establish that there is, in Ibn Arabi's perspective, but the One Reality which is relativized—albeit in appearance only—in the very measure that one can speak of distinctive or differentiated realities—whether this multiplicity be in the cosmos or *in divinis*; this needs to be firmly established at the outset of any discussion of Ibn Arabi's position on transcendent realization, given the complexity of the points of view from which he approaches this question.

To conclude this section, it should be emphasized that, although the Essence is in no wise susceptible of determinate conception, it is nonetheless legitimate to conceive of it as That which transcends all determinate conception, failing which it would not be possible to make any reference whatever to it. The Essence is rendered conceivable in positive and distinctive fashion only when "it is described by Divinity": that is, the Essence is the very reality of the Divinity/Level inasmuch as it deploys itself with a view to entering into relationships with those possibilities which are comprised within its own infinitude.

Therefore this Essence is both absent from the world by way of absolute transcendence, and at the same time it is present in the world by virtue of the unavoidable immanence of the One Reality in all that exists; however transient and thus illusory may be the character of its distinctive mode of being, each thing necessarily participates in, and is thus essentially identified with, the Real, of which it is an aspect or locus of manifestation, and without which it could not subsist. Therefore, "the transcendent Reality is the relative creature, even though the creature is distinct from the Creator" (Bezels, 87).

To speak of the distinction between the creature and the Creator is to speak of a real ontological distinction, but this does not preclude the assertion that the entire context in which this and other distinctions are manifested is necessarily relative and ultimately illusory, since the Real in its absoluteness does not admit of differentiation and distinction; this is what Ibn Arabi appears to be intending when he assimilates the creature to the Transcendent: insofar as the creature *is*, and insofar as being is unique, the creature, in its essence, cannot be other than the transcendent One.

This is the metaphysical logic which follows from the principle of the oneness of Being; Part II will proceed to an examination of the way in which this logic is expressed in terms of spiritual realization.

# Part II: The Spiritual Ascent

The ascent to the summit of spiritual realization will be addressed on the basis of the following three themes: (i) the relationship between sanctified and prophetic consciousness, the key question here being which of the two is higher, and in what ways the two types of consciousness are related to the degrees of Being; (ii) the nature and ontological status of the mystical vision of God's theophanic Self-manifestation; (iii) the essential meaning of the state of *fana'* or annihilation from self, the extinctive mode of union with the Real; its requirements—legal, moral, and methodic—and its implications—metaphysical, spiritual, and existential.

## 1. Sainthood and Prophethood

The distinction between the saint and the prophet assumes importance in relation to the question of transcendent realization because, in the context of a prophetic religion such as Islam, it is commonly assumed that the prophets alone have access to the highest realization, and that the saints are necessarily subordinate to the prophets both in personal terms and in respect of the highest content of spiritual realization. If this is the case, then transcendence would be the preserve of prophethood, and one should have to speak of only a relative degree of transcendence as the highest possibility for the rest of humankind.

Ibn Arabi's position on this question is, however, more nuanced; and in the course of presenting this position it will be observed that absolute transcendence is not only the distinguishing feature of sainthood, but also that it critically involves a vantage point whence the relativity of formal revelation—and with it the prophetic function as such—is apparent.

Although the subject of much misinterpretation and scandal, Ibn Arabi's position on the relationship between prophethood and sainthood is clear: while sainthood in itself is superior to prophethood, the source of sainthood for the saint is the sainthood of the prophet. Even though the saint *qua* saint is superior to the prophet *qua* prophet, that is, in regard to the respective spheres of consciousness specifically entailed by sainthood and prophecy, the saint is nonetheless existentially subordinated to the prophet in regard to their respective status as persons. As regards the intrinsic superiority of sainthood over prophethood:

> This is because the office of apostle and prophet comes to an end, while sainthood never ceases (Bezels, 66).

The name given to the saint, *wali*,[6] is also a divine Name occurring in the Qur'an, whilst neither *rasul* nor *nabi* are given as divine Names; Ibn Arabi

---

[6] Literally "friend," that is, of God.

emphasizes this, while drawing attention to the fact that sainthood is an all-inclusive and universal function, relating to Reality as such, whereas prophethood is determined by the specific needs and imperatives attendant upon a particular legislative function in respect of a given community; in this sense, the prophets are seen to "conform to the level of their communities." The knowledge with which they have been sent is determined by the "needs of their communities"; this statement follows the general assertion that "every governor is itself governed by that in accordance with which it governs" (Bezels, 165), and can thus be regarded as an illustration of the paradoxical condition of mutual determination within creation, which, as seen earlier, is an important aspect of Ibn Arabi's perspective.

When the prophet expresses realities that fall outside the domain of the Law with which he is sent, then he does so in his capacity as "a saint and a gnostic," and this means that "his station as a knower is more complete and perfect than that as an apostle or lawgiver." Therefore, what is meant by the claim that the saint is superior to the prophet is that "this is so within one person" (Bezels, 169).

The Prophet Muhammad, regarded in the Islamic tradition as the Seal of the Prophets is, in Ibn Arabi's doctrine, also regarded as the Seal of the Saints, but this latter function is hidden by the former, and is manifested more explicitly by Ibn Arabi himself.[7]

The intricacies of the relationships between the different types of Seal and their historical expressions would take us far beyond the scope of this chapter; what should be noted, however, is that the saints derive their sainthood from that of the prophets, and are thus called "inheritors" of the legacy of the prophets. This does not, however, imply that the consciousness of the saint is restricted in its scope to the limitations attendant upon the specific characteristics of any particular revealed Law, even if the saint must submit thereto. This is what is meant by Ibn Arabi's allusion to himself in the symbol of a "silver brick"— signifying submission to the Law—and a "gold brick," signifying his inner, sanctified consciousness (Bezels, 65-66).

These important points are elucidated by Ibn Arabi's description of the "station of nearness" (*maqam al-qurbah*). This station is posited as intermediate between that of "confirmation" (*siddiqiyyah*) and prophecy, which implies that the saint who has attained to proximity reaches a level of consciousness which is not circumscribed by the outward form of prophecy, but is rather more akin to the inner reality of what is hidden within the prophetic consciousness.

Those who are "brought nigh" (*al-muqarrabun*) are situated hierarchically; the highest group is constituted by the Law-bringing messengers, the second by the non-legislating prophets, and the third by the saints (Illuminations (Gril), 337-338).

In other words, if sanctity be the criterion of the hierarchy, it is their degree of sanctity that establishes the superiority of the prophets and not their legislative

---

[7] See the extended discussion on this point in Chodkiewicz, Seal, chapter 9.

function. It remains to be seen in what way this distinction on the basis of sanctity enters into the definition of transcendent realization.

First, however, the nature of this station of "proximity" should be explained. It is referred to somewhat cryptically in a poem which introduces the chapter in the *Futuhat* dealing with this station;[8] it is then elaborated in connection with the Quranic story of the encounter between Moses and the mysterious personage al-Khidr, an encounter frequently referred to in the Sufi tradition as indicative of the confrontation between exoteric/outward knowledge and esoteric/inward science.

Turning first to the poem: he describes a vision of the descent of a gazelle from Paradise; it is destined for him, and he falls in love with it; the face of the beloved is then unveiled and the gazelle stands revealed as the *Laylat al-Qadr*, the Night of Power, that is, the night in which the first revelation of the Qur'an descended: the gazelle is thus a symbol of Revelation. Ibn Arabi then proceeds:

> I prostrated before her through love. Seeing this, I knew that I was not attached to any "other." I glorified God, praising Him for having loved me; it was but the secret of my own being that my appearance had loved. Realizing that I am the very being of that which I love, I no longer fear separation nor do I fear abandonment [by the beloved] (Illuminations (Gril), 340).

The divine revelation which *a priori* descends from above and beyond him is thus transformed into an aspect of his own intimate being, or "secret," revealing itself to itself. One can distinguish two modes of interiorization here: the first is the assimilation of formal revelation to the supra-formal essence of the individual, and the second is the reintegration of universal manifestation within its supra-manifest source. In regard to the first mode, one may cite in support of this interpretation the following clear assertions made by Ibn Arabi:

(i) The culminating revelation to Ibn Arabi, in his spiritual "ascent" (*mi'raj*—to be examined again later in this chapter) was the Quranic verse emphasizing the intrinsic unity of the messages of all the prophets: "Say: we believe in God and that which is revealed unto us and that which was revealed unto Abraham and Ishmael and Isaac and Jacob and the tribes (of Israel) and that which was vouchsafed unto Moses and Jesus and the prophets from their Lord. We make no distinction between any of them, and unto Him we have surrendered" (3, 84). After which Ibn Arabi adds: "Henceforth I knew that I am the totality of those (prophets) who were mentioned to me (in this verse)" (Illuminations (Morris), 379).

That this verse is given as the culminating revelation, and that it is said to be the "key to all knowledge" is highly significant; although it is not to be identified with the transcendent degree of realization—for reasons which will be clear from the discussion below—it is nonetheless an essential element comprised within this degree. Thus, transcendent realization implies, for Ibn Arabi, the assimilation of the principle of the universality of revealed religion: it is understood that there is

[8] The importance of the poem is stressed by Ibn Arabi himself: "Pay attention to what my poem contains."

no distinction between the prophets at the highest level of religion, and also that the respective revelations vouchsafed them are consequently all to be accepted as valid. This principle, inasmuch as it figures so prominently at this high degree of spiritual realization, will be examined more fully in its own right in the final part of this chapter.

(ii) The "totality of the prophets" referred to in the above quotation can also be assimilated to the essence of man or Adam, the first man and the first prophet: in the chapter on Adam in the *Fusus* one finds the following:

He is Man, the transient (in his form), the eternal (in his essence); he is . . . the (at once) discriminating and unifying Word (Bezels, 51).

The "discriminating" aspect of the Word, in one of its significations, refers to the distinctive realities of the different prophets as crystallizations of the Word, whilst the unifying aspect pertains to their inner unity within the Word—the realization of which, alone, can justify Ibn Arabi's claim to "be" the totality of the prophets. Despite the fact that Ibn Arabi was not a prophet, his claim is intelligible in that, as a saint, the essence of his consciousness is one with the intrinsic and undifferentiated Word, which is the source both of sanctity and prophecy.

(iii) In another account of a spiritual ascent, in the treatise called the "Night Journey," one finds Ibn Arabi saying that God bestowed everything upon him and "when He had entrusted me with His Wisdom and made me aware of every inner secret and wisdom, He returned me to myself. And He made what had been (imposed) upon me (to be) from me" (Ascension, 75). Thus, objective revelation from without is transmuted into subjective self-revelation from within.

In regard to the second mode of assimilation, that of the reintegration of universal manifestation, this can be seen as a microcosmic recapitulation of the nature and purpose of manifestation as such, which Ibn Arabi, following the Sufi tradition, refers to in terms of the famous divine utterance transmitted by the Prophet (*hadith qudsi*): "I was a hidden treasure and I loved to be known, so I created." In the chapter on Adam, Ibn Arabi refers implicitly to this principle, by saying that God's purpose in creating man was to see His own Entity "in an all-inclusive object encompassing the whole Command[9] which, qualified by existence, would reveal to Him His own mystery" (Bezels, 50).

Now, on the one hand, this creation, in its highest meaning as divine Self-manifestation in the human form, is beautiful since "this human creation . . . was created by God in His own image" (Bezels, 208); but on the other hand, this manifestation is not identical in every respect with its transcendent source, and this aspect of "otherness" implies imperfection; therefore we find Ibn Arabi saying in the poem: "Through me the Real acquires the perfection of its being, with imperfection . . ." As seen in the last section, just as the infinitude of Reality

[9] The "Command" (*al-'amr*), can here be taken to connote the entire "Divine Order."

implies a necessary dimension of finitude, so the perfection or completeness of Being requires an element of imperfection, without which it would lack totality, being limited by the absence of imperfection.

Therefore the gazelle, an object of beauty, represents not only the manifestation of the "hidden treasure" which desires to be known—the Self-revelation of the Essence—but it also symbolizes formal revelation and indeed manifestation as such; and to say manifestation is to say determination, delimitation, and hence the "imperfection" without which, as the poem says, there would not be perfection; this imperfection is thus assimilated to form as such, or "my appearance," which had made "my secret" (*sirr*)[10] mad with love. This secret or inner essence must in turn be assimilated to the Essence as such, the hidden treasure, which desired to be known through and by creation.

At this point it would be appropriate to support this interpretation by further references to the metaphysical principle of identity between the essence of the creature and the Essence of the Real. (i) In regard to his "corporeal formation" Adam is a creature, but in respect of his "spiritual formation" he is "the Reality" (Bezels, 57); (ii) Adam is further referred to as the prototype which synthesizes all the degrees of the divine Presence and, most significantly, this includes not just the Qualities/Attributes and Actions, but also the Essence (Bezels, 154); (iii) in the chapter on Solomon one reads that, just as each divine Name is outwardly distinct from the other Names and inwardly identical with them by virtue of its identity with the Named, the same is the case with each creature: "Thus the fact that the Identity (or: Ipseity) of God is the essence of (e.g.) Zaid and Amr does not contradict our saying that Zaid is less learned than Amr" (Bezels, 191).

In other words, since man is a microcosmic recapitulation of all the degrees of the divine Nature, the individual process by which man comes to realize his inner essence or *sirr* not only mirrors the universal teleology but, in concrete terms, actually constitutes this teleology itself: spiritual self-realization is thus assimilated to divine Self-realization: the Divine comes to know itself starting from relativity, the apparently "other," this mode of self-knowledge being distinct from its eternal and immutable Self-Consciousness in its own Essence, above and beyond the realm of manifestation:

> For the seeing of a thing, itself by itself, is not the same as its seeing itself in another, as it were in a mirror (Bezels, 50).

Other dimensions of this realization will shortly be addressed, but for now the underlying principle of this station of proximity needs to be further elaborated in order to situate clearly the degree of consciousness which distinguishes sainthood from prophethood.

Returning to the chapter on proximity, the story of Moses' encounter with al-Khidr implicitly conforms to the line of interpretation we are following; for the import of the story is that formal revelation, insofar as it pertains to form,

---

[10] *Sirr* is literally translated as "secret"; this term assumes great significance in the final realization, as will be seen below.

cannot be regarded as exhausting the nature of the Absolute, or the Essence; and that there is a mode of consciousness, or a "station," in which the limitations of all form—including all formal revelation and manifestation—become clear.

In brief, the story is as follows: Moses, in his search for the Waters of Life comes upon al-Khidr, one of "Our slaves, unto whom We had given mercy from Us, and had taught him knowledge from Our presence" (Qur'an, 18, 65); he wishes to accompany this personage in order to learn of this knowledge, and is accepted on condition that he not question any of al-Khidr's actions. After being bewildered by three apparently unjustified and unlawful acts, Moses remonstrates with al-Khidr; Moses is then shown the divine purpose underlying the acts; and by this means, Moses learns the science of hidden realities that lie behind formal appearances. The distinction between esoteric and exoteric science is clearly implied here, but Ibn Arabi draws out two further meanings: firstly, that there is a distinction between the station of "confirmation" (i.e., confirming and submitting to the Law) and that of "proximity" (i.e., knowledge stemming from the divine Source of the Law); secondly, that the two modes of consciousness to which these stations refer can coexist within one individual. In regard to the prophet, this implies that his consciousness as a saint surpasses the level of his consciousness as a prophet; thus the story of Moses and al-Khidr is interpreted microcosmically, as an expression of an inner unfolding within the consciousness of Moses himself, al-Khidr symbolizing a "form" or "state" of Moses' own spiritual realization: "He [al-Khidr] showed him [Moses] nothing but his own form; so it was his own state that he beheld, his own soul with which he remonstrated" (Illuminations (Gril), 342).

In other words, the "al-Khidr" of Moses' being is that element of his own consciousness which transcends the formal limitations attendant upon the specific ordinances of religious law.

Turning now to the application of this principle to the saint, one observes Ibn Arabi referring to Abu Bakr, the first Caliph and successor to the Prophet, from whose title, *al-siddiq*—the truthful, the "confirmer" of truth—the designation *siddiqiyyah* is derived; he is proposed by Ibn Arabi as also personifying the station of proximity; and he illustrates this through citing the famous words uttered by Abu Bakr immediately after the death of the Prophet:

> O people, whoso hath been wont to worship Muhammad—verily Muhammad is dead; and whoso hath been wont to worship God—verily God is Living and dieth not.[11]

This may be taken as an objective expression of the distinction between form and Essence, or between the relative and the Absolute; that this distinction should also apply on the level of consciousness and in relation to formal revelation is made clear by the final words of Ibn Arabi in this chapter, which assert that while Abu Bakr in his capacity as "confirmer," was a "follower" (*tabi'*) of the Law through faith and submission, this mode does not exhaust the content

---

[11] This translation from Martin Lings' *Muhammad*, Islamic Texts Society, Cambridge, UK, 1983, p. 346, conveys more clearly the meaning intended here by Ibn Arabi.

of his consciousness: "He denies that which the one whom he follows denies, approves that which he approves; this behoves the *siddiq qua siddiq*. But there is another station by virtue of which he is not governed by the state of *siddiqiyyah*" (Illuminations (Gril), 347; *Futuhat*, II, 262).

This "other station," thanks to which the sage is not ruled in an exhaustive or exclusive manner by the state of being a follower and confirmer, is precisely the station of proximity, coexisting with this existential state of subordination to the form of revelation, but nonetheless transcending the entire domain of relativity presupposed by formal revelation and manifestation, and thereby rejoining the essence of that which is revealed through form, that which is "intended" by form, and thus that which constitutes the very *raison d'être* of all form.

Those "brought nigh" in the station of proximity include different types and grades of saint, so one needs to ask what significance should be attributed to these distinctions. The answer emerges clearly if one focuses on the highest grade of saint: the "supreme degree" of sainthood is that of the *afrad*, the "solitary ones," also called the *malamiyyah*, the "people of blame," or the "pure slaves," which categories will be addressed shortly. For now, it suffices to note that this degree of sanctified consciousness refers to the essential content of the realization both of the saints, and of the prophets in their capacity as saints; this inner realization, it should be stressed, takes precedence over all cosmic function. It is in relation to this function that distinctions among the saints become manifest: the "Spiritual Pole," his "supports," "deputies," etc., are all included in this highest category of saints—and Ibn Arabi adds that the "supreme head of this world," the Prophet Muhammad, is himself one of them (Seal, 110).

In the *Futuhat* one finds Ibn Arabi making this same point by means of distinguishing between "essential (*dhati*) perfection" and "accidental (*'aradi*) perfection," the first pertaining to pure slavehood, the second to "manliness":

> The degree of the essential perfection is in the Self of the Real, while the degrees of accidental perfection are in the Gardens. . . . Ranking according to excellence (*tafadul*) takes place in accidental perfection, but not in essential perfection (Path, 366).

In other words, accidental perfection pertains to the distinctive existential affirmation of the individual—whether this be in the world or in the heavens—and is thus "manly" in contrast to the ontological effacement of the individual in the highest realization, this effacement being evoked by the term "slave." The different degrees of personal receptivity to this realization and the corresponding extent to which this realization therefore overflows into the personal dimension of the individual, result in the "ranking according to excellence," and consequently to differentiated cosmic function; whilst the essence of this realization, considered in itself and apart from the question of its cosmic—hence "accidental"—application, is undifferentiable.

From this important principle one can deduce the answer to the question raised above: what significance should be attributed to the hierarchical distinctions between the Law-revealing prophet (*rasul*), the non-legislative prophet (*nabi*), and the saint (*wali*)? These distinctions pertain to cosmic function and are "accidental" in relation to the undifferentiable "essential" perfection, which pertains not to the cosmos or the individual's role therein, but to the metacosmic "Self of the Real," where the individual as such is effaced. The nature of this effacement will be further analyzed in section 3; at this point it suffices to note that transcendent, metacosmic perfection is identified with this ontological effacement of the individual, on the one hand, and to the "one degree" which is "in the Self of the Real," on the other.

The distinction between essential and accidental perfection is also useful in clarifying the relationship between the saint and God; the realization of the saint reflects the degrees within the divine nature, for his "accidental" perfection reflects the perfection of the Level of the Divinity, while his essential perfection reflects the perfection of the Essence: once the first perfection is realized, the second follows:

> God calls the servant in his inmost consciousness, a call from His own perfection to the servant's essential perfection. Then the servant declares the essence of Him who brought him into existence incomparable with accidental perfection which is the divine perfection (Path, 367).

This divine perfection consists in the manifestation of the properties of the divine Names, and to this the individual responds by "assuming the divine traits" or the fundamental virtues; it is important to note that essential perfection cannot be realized without accidental perfection having first been realized. In other words, the attainment of the fundamental virtues, which are regarded as the human reflections of the divine traits, is the necessary prerequisite for the transcendent realization called "essential perfection." The "ranking according to excellence" is found in this domain of "accidental perfection," since the plenitude of personal realization of the divine traits will differ from individual to individual, the most exalted individual being the Law-revealing prophet.

However, all such distinctions, along with the quality of accidental perfection itself, are declared incomparable with the Essence, once the "inmost consciousness" of the servant is awakened by the call from the inmost perfection of God, i.e., His own infinite and transcendent Essence.

One clearly observes here that essential perfection is another way of referring to the station of proximity, both of them pertaining to the realization of the content of the highest possible discernment, that between the Absolute and the relative; and, implied within this discernment, the following distinctions: between the Absolute Self and the relative Divinity; and between the supra-formal Essence and its formal expressions—including therein both divine Revelation and universal Manifestation.

Thus, not only is the station of "confirmation" relativized by virtue of its being delimited by a specific religious form, but all distinctive aspects of the individual's relationship with the Divine—that is, all his modes of worship and praise—inasmuch as this concerns forms, are accidental/relative; in possessing "accidental perfection" the servant praises God "with a praise worthy of God, *accident for accident*" (emphasis added); whilst the form of the Divine calls forth formal praise, the Essence, on the contrary, enjoys supra-formal incomparability:

"Nothing is like Him," because of the perfection of the Essence, and "He is the Hearing, the Seeing" ([Qur'an] 42:11) because of the perfection of the Divinity, which demands both the heard and the seen (Path, 367).

Ibn Arabi's comment on this apparently self-contradictory verse—the first statement affirming incomparability (*tanzih*), and the second, comparability (*tashbih*)—derives its explanatory power from the crucial distinction between the supra-formal Essence and the formal Divinity; despite the fact that in one respect there is incommensurability between these two degrees within the divine nature, in another respect there is identity: the Divinity is no other than the "Essence described by Divinity" as it was put earlier. Without the dimension of incommensurability, the Essence would not be incomparable with the world, and without the dimension of identity, there would be not one but two divinities, the Level/Divinity and the Essence.

To conclude this discussion of the relationship between sainthood and prophecy: what should be underlined is that the sanctified consciousness of the prophet must be distinguished from the particular contents of his consciousness *qua* prophet; for while the specific "openings" and "unveilings" related to the prophetic function are the exclusive prerogatives of the prophet, his sanctity is, on the contrary, of a universal nature and hence, in principle, accessible to his "followers" and "confirmers" in the form of the quintessential spiritual heritage bequeathed to his community; hence, as seen above, the designation of "inheritor" given to the saint. Adherence to orthodoxy is maintained by stressing that greater than all of the saints are the prophets, and the greatest of the prophets is the prophet of Islam.

Before directly exploring the essential content of this sanctified consciousness, it is important to address the hypothesis that the ultimate spiritual attainment involves, not the Essence, but the vision of God's *tajalli*, or theophanic Self-revelation.

## 2. Ontological Status of the Vision of God

The claim that, for Ibn Arabi, the highest spiritual attainment cannot go beyond the realm of God's Self-disclosure can be critically addressed by reference to the arguments advanced by Henri Corbin and Toshihiko Izutsu. These arguments can be summed up as follows: since the Absolute is absolutely unknowable in its Essence, the highest possibility for man in his quest of the Absolute is a vision of a particular divine self-manifestation; this vision, moreover, is ultimately determined by the receptivity or preparedness inherent in the individual's immutable entity/archetype.

There are indeed grounds for advancing this claim, for Ibn Arabi in many places does appear to suggest this, but it is nevertheless clear that this mode of realization falls short of the transcendent level, and it is equally clear that Ibn Arabi does not restrict the possibilities of spiritual realization to this particular mode.

First, the claims made by the scholars will be stated, then the grounds for these claims will be examined, before proceeding to the third section where extinctive union (*fana'*) will be presented, instead, as the transcendent mode of spiritual realization.

Turning first to Corbin:

> What a man attains at the summit of his mystic experience is not, and cannot be, the Divine Essence in its undifferentiated unity. And that is why Ibn Arabi rejected the pretension of certain mystics who claimed to "become one with God" (Imagination, 273).

The state of *fana'*, therefore, does not designate the "passage into a mystic state that annuls his (the mystic's) individuality, merging it with the so-called 'universal' or the pure inaccessible Essence" (Imagination, 202).

This denial complements the affirmation that what is encountered in the highest mystical state is the specific divine Name, or "Lord," that serves as the particular celestial source and counterpart of the existentiated individual:

> [W]e rise in equal measure above the empirical self and above collective beliefs to recognize the Self, or rather, experientially, the Figure who represents it in mental vision, as the paredros of the gnostic, his "companion-archetype" that is to say, his eternal hexeity (i.e. his *'ayn thabitah*) invested with a divine Name in the world of Mystery (Imagination, 267).

Likewise, one finds in Izutsu:

> [N]ot only in the normal forms of human cognitive experience . . . but also even in the highest state of mystical experience, there is, according to Ibn Arabi, kept intact the distinction between the one who sees and the object seen. . . . Thus even in the highest degree of mystical experience, that of *unio*, the prime Unity must of necessity break up and turn into diversity. The Absolute on the level of Unity, in other words, remains for ever unknowable (Sufism, 24).

One may respond to this position by accepting that there is, according to Ibn Arabi, an unavoidable duality which inheres in all forms of mystical experience in which the experiencing subject is distinct from the experienced object; however, one needs to examine the arguments carefully in order to discern the purpose of Ibn Arabi's emphasis on the relativity of these forms of mystical vision.

When a given individual experiences the vision of God, what he in fact sees is a divine Self-revelation "which occurs only in a form conforming to the essential predisposition of the recipient of such a revelation. Thus, the recipient sees nothing other than his own form in the mirror of the Reality. He does not see the Reality Itself, which is not possible . . ." (Bezels, 65).

In other words, when one sees God, one is seeing an aspect of one's own eternal receptivity/preparedness; this does not entail a reduction of the divine image to the level of the individuality, but rather the converse: it means raising the individuality to its highest possible expression *qua* individual, that is, to the level at which it most faithfully reflects the highest content of its own *'ayn*, as source or essence of its own specific possibility; and this ineluctably leads back to the divine Consciousness, since the *'ayn* is found therein in its pure immutability, as a supra-manifest possibility of individuation. Moreover, the preparedness of the '*ayn* is itself an aspect of God's self-revelation:

> God has two forms of self-manifestation: one is self-manifestation in the Unseen and the other in the visible world. By the self-manifestation in the Unseen, He gives the "preparedness" which will determine the nature of the heart (in the visible world) (Sufism, 156).

Therefore, if to see God means seeing your own "form," seeing this "form," in turn means seeing God, or: seeing nothing but an immutable possibility inherent in the divine Essence; and, from another point of view, it also means seeing God by virtue of the objective content of the divine manifestation, even if this content conforms to the subjective receptivity of the container: one recalls here the famous utterance of Junayd, that the water takes on the color of the cup, a saying frequently cited by Ibn Arabi.

Despite the divine nature of this vision, however, it is situated only on a relatively transcendent level, since the subject remains distinct from the object; using Ibn Arabi's analogy, the image is seen in the mirror of the Real, but the surface of the mirror, the Real in itself, cannot be seen: that which sees is still distinct from that which is seen; this shows that so long as one speaks of the divine vision in the context of the subsistence of individual consciousness or the '*ayn*—even if this be essentialized—one has not attained to absolutely transcendent consciousness.

At this point, one finds Ibn Arabi appearing to establish this non-transcendent level as the limit of spiritual realization, when he says that, if this vision is experienced,

> you have experienced as much as is possible for a created being, so do not seek nor weary yourself in any attempts to proceed higher than this, for there is nothing higher, nor is there beyond the point you have reached aught except the pure, undetermined, unmanifested (Absolute) (Bezels, 65).

One may distinguish two main reasons why the individual should refrain from seeking anything higher than this level in the context of mystical experience: firstly, from the point of view of the object of vision, it is not possible for the Essence to reveal itself *as Essence* to something other than itself in order to be distinctively apprehended or attained; the Essence must become "described by Divinity" or manifest in a distinct mode of formal self-revelation in order to become the object of mystic vision—and to say "formal" means that which is distinct from, and hence "other than," the Essence; secondly, from the point of view of the subject, it is not possible for the creature *as such* to transcend his own limitations and bypass the duality necessarily implied once one has posited the contingent created being as the subjective agent in any cognitive act or experience. Therefore one must stress Ibn Arabi's use of the term "created being." The phrase in the Arabic is *fi haqqi'l-makhluq*, literally, "according to the right of the created thing," which even more clearly underlines the relativity of the context within which this seeming restriction on spiritual realization is made. In other words, the relative creature cannot seek to surpass his own level and attain the pure Absolute. He should therefore not "weary" himself in the quest for that which is attainable solely as a result of grace; for the individual cannot will his own negation, that negation which, as will be seen shortly, is the price to be paid for the ultimate realization.

This being the case, the creature *qua* creature can never come either to know or, *a fortiori*, to "be" the Absolute; this is the meaning of Ibn Arabi's rejection of the claim of becoming one with God, referred to earlier. Since there is no common measure between the created individual as such and the transcendent Essence of the One, even the individual's worship does not reach the One, but only relates to the personal Divinity. This very important point is made by Ibn Arabi by means of an esoteric interpretation of the following Quranic verse: "Let him not associate (any) one with his Lord's worship" (18, 119). The literal meaning of the verse relates to the prohibition of *shirk* or associating false gods with the true Divinity, but Ibn Arabi makes the "one" in question refer to the Essence, and thus says:

> He is not worshipped in respect of His Unity, since Unity contradicts the existence of the worshipper. It is as if He is saying, "What is worshipped is only the 'Lord' in respect of His Lordship, since the Lord brought you into existence. So connect yourself to Him and make yourself lowly before Him, and do not associate Unity with Lordship in worship. . . . For Unity does not know you and will not accept you" (Path, 244).

This worship, then, connects the servant to the Lord, and is, as seen earlier, "accident for accident"; the corollary of this is that only God can know God, this Knowledge being identical with Being; one now comes closer to understanding the higher, transcendent meaning of "divine vision": "There is no one who sees the Absolute except the Absolute" (Sufism, 76).

This will be more fully investigated in the next section; at this point it is necessary to return to the fundamental principle of metaphysical identity established in Part I and elaborated upon in the discussion of the station of "proximity." This will help to show that what is intended by Ibn Arabi in relativizing all mystical states involving alterity is quite different from that which was extrapolated by the scholars referred to earlier: realization of the Essence must not be denied simply because it is impossible to conceive of this realization in distinctive fashion and in relation to the individual as such, rather: it is impossible to conceive of this realization in distinctive mode precisely because it pertains to Reality as such, which infinitely transcends the individual and permits of no relationship with any distinct "otherness." Conversely, the vision of God which the individual experiences, while being undoubtedly of a divine nature, is nonetheless endowed with a degree of reality commensurate with that which inheres in the individual, which amounts to saying that it, too, ultimately constitutes an "imagined reality"; even if it be admitted that, insofar as this is an object of the imagination of the Real, it necessarily possesses a degree of objective, and divine, reality. To thus possess a degree of reality is, however, to be distinguished from Reality in itself, which is absolutely undifferentiated. While realization of the Essence pertains to this undifferentiated Reality, the vision of

God, on the contrary, has the dual character of being both real and unreal, thus constituting a differentiated reality: that which is seen is both "He" and "not He"—the manifestation of God being both "something of God" at the same time as "other than God." That which sees is likewise both "He/not He"—the creature being outwardly delimited but inwardly not other than the Infinite.

As seen earlier, the moment one establishes distinctiveness—even within the divine Nature—one has entered the realm of relativity, and thus "imagined existence," even if this realm be required by, and an expression of, the infinity of the Absolute. It is therefore impossible for the distinctively determined individual either to see, worship, know, or be the undetermined Essence. This being the case, how is the individual to realize union with that which he knows, metaphysically, is the sole Reality, before which all else—himself included—is strictly illusory?

A clue to the resolution of this dilemma is given by Ibn Arabi's description of the process by which the individual comes to know his own *'ayn* in its supramanifest state within the divine Consciousness:

> When God shows the creature the contents of his own immutable essence—which receives Being directly—this evidently surpasses the faculties of the creature as such; for the creature is incapable of appropriating to itself the divine knowledge which relates to these essences in their state of non-existence. . . . It is in this respect that we say that this identification [with divine knowledge] represents a mode of divine assistance predestined for the particular individual (Sagesse, 43).

It is thus only by means of divine grace that the individual comes to possess objective knowledge of his own immutable archetype/possibility, by virtue of an effective identification of his consciousness with the divine Consciousness which encompasses and comprises all such supra-manifest possibilities.

Therefore, if it be established that the consciousness within the individual can be lifted by grace out of the extrinsic limitations attendant upon individual existence, so that an objective, divine perspective is acquired of one's own immutable archetype, then the same principle should apply in regard to the transcendent level, and thus to the universal Self-realization alluded to in the station of proximity.

This emphasis upon the intervention of divine assistance at one and the same time confirms both the notion that the individual creature cannot attain that which surpasses the ontological degree proper to his own existence, *and* the possibility of realized consciousness surpassing this degree, but then no longer insofar as such consciousness can be qualified as "individual." Corbin and Izutsu therefore attribute to the individual mode of realization an unwarranted exclusivism: it is held to exclude the ultimate degree of realization, in relation to which individuality as such is surpassed.

It is to the implications and nuances of this transcendent realization, beginning with the extinctive state of union, that discussion now turns in the following section.

### 3. *Fana'*

There are two important aspects of the state of *fana'* which should be clearly understood from the outset of the discussion. Firstly, it is a passing "state" and not a permanent "station," which means that the reality revealed or "made real" in that state is necessarily, albeit in appearance only, conditioned by the return of the individual to the phenomenal level of awareness.

Secondly, as mentioned above, such a state cannot be the result of any human effort, but is strictly a divine "bestowal," a pure grace; even if this bestowal be preceded by spiritual practices, these can never be regarded as having caused the bestowal, but at most may be said to have enhanced receptivity to it, while always admitting the possibility of such a grace being bestowed even upon one who has not submitted to such a discipline.

In the *Futuhat*, there is a chapter on the notion of *Hal* or "state," in which Ibn Arabi writes:

> The *hal* is one of the favors which the All-Merciful accords through an act of pure Providence; it is not a personal "acquisition," nor is it the effect of any investigation (Hal, 173).

Likewise: "Every station in the path of God is earned and fixed, while every state is a bestowal, neither earned nor fixed" (Path, 278).

In other words, the individual, one who is *mawjud*, (i.e., rendered "existent" by virtue of the degree of Being lent to him) as opposed to *wujud* (i.e., pure "Being" in itself) does not cease being such after returning to normal consciousness; nor, in terms of outward corporeal existence, does he cease to be such during the state itself, for it is consciousness that transcends the bounds of contingent being, rejoining its immutable source and essential nature during the state of annihilation. In terms of consciousness, then, there is a reabsorption within pure Being; thus one finds, in a formula which closely corresponds to the Vedantin *Sat-Chit-Ananda*, the following expression of the supreme state of spiritual realization: "*wujud* [Being] is finding the Real in ecstasy"[12] (Path, 212).

Here, the emphasis is placed upon the fact that the true nature of Being is revealed only when it is absolutely identical with consciousness ("finding"); the inner content of this experience being the supreme Beatitude proper to the Absolute.

However, this transcendent level strictly excludes the individual, so one must ask: what is the meaning of the statement quoted earlier in this chapter about the "one glance" of Reality that constituted Ibn Arabi's realization; what can "witnessing" or "contemplation" mean in the context of identity, which annuls the distinction between the seer and the seen?

---

[12] In Arabic: *wujud wijdan al-Haqq fi'l wajd*. Ibn Arabi makes use here of the triliteral root W-J-D, which is common to the three words *wujud-wijdan-wajd*.

Ibn Arabi repeatedly emphasizes that there is a strictly inverse relationship between the affirmed reality of the individual as such, and the Real in itself, so that where the first is present, the other must necessarily be absent, or, to speak more metaphysically, hidden. Therefore one reads in the important treatise "Extinction in Contemplation" the following:

> The essence of divine reality is too elevated to be contemplated . . . for as long as there subsists a trace of the condition of the creature in the eye of the contemplator (Extinction, 27-28).

The reason for the incompatibility between the slightest trace of creatureliness and the highest state of "witnessing" is the nature of the "object" witnessed; in elucidating this nature, Ibn Arabi makes use of the saying of the Prophet in which God is referred to as having seventy thousand veils of darkness and light which, if removed, would reveal the "glories of His Face" which would burn everything upon which His Look falls. Ibn Arabi identifies these "glories" with the "lights of Transcendence," the veils being the divine Names which shield existent things from extinction, since, were these veils to be lifted, the Unity of the Essence would appear, before which no *'ayn* could subsist in its existential condition (Nom (III), 334-335, n. 2).

Elsewhere a similar point is made, the *'ayn* this time being referred to as a veil; Ibn Arabi writes that God "obliterates" the individual from himself: "Then you do not halt with the existence of your own entity and the manifestations of its properties" (Path, 176).

What must be underlined here is that transcendent consciousness is attainable only when the individual, along with his immutable entity, is completely annihilated in the unitive state, this being the only conceivable manner in which consciousness—now no longer qualifiable as "individual"—can be said to surpass the level of the individual entity and the "manifestation of its properties."

To establish further this crucial principle, the following extracts may be adduced. Firstly, in the chapter on Ibn Arabi's own spiritual ascent through the heavens, one finds the following dialogue with Moses, in the sixth heaven:

> (I said to him), ". . . you requested the vision (of God), while the Messenger of God (Muhammad) said that 'not one of you will see his Lord until he dies'?" So he said: "And it was just like that: when I asked Him for the vision, He answered me, so that 'I fell down stunned' (Qur'an, 7, 143). Then I saw Him in my (state of) being stunned." I said: "While (you were) dead?" He replied: "While (I was) dead. . . . I did not see God until I had died" (Ascension, 375).

Likewise, in the form of a quotation from Junayd, an early Sufi Master:

> The phenomenal, when it is joined to the Eternal, vanishes and leaves no trace behind. When He is there, thou art not, and if thou art there, He is not (Tarjuman, 90).

As seen earlier, the creature is outwardly "imagination" and other than God, while inwardly being not other than the ipseity of God; therefore the movement towards reality is one of interiorization, and the mutually exclusive poles referred to in the above quotation may be seen to correspond, *a priori*, to the two dimensions of the inward (related to the divine Name *al-Batin*), and the outward (related to the divine Name *al-Zahir*); that this mutual exclusion is only relative becomes clear on the basis of the effective realization of the inward, in the light of which realization the outward is itself spiritually assimilated as a dimension of the One Reality. But first, the apparent alterity of outwardness must be negated:

> The Inward says "no" when the Outward says "I"; and the Outward says "no" when the Inward says "I" (Sagesse, 63).

Likewise, the following, which contains an extremely important principle: When Ibn Arabi wished to enter into the being of the Real, he writes that he had to "disappear" from his own existence, "leaving my place to His reality. His manifestation therefore rests on a disappearance. . . . Thus, the manifestation of *Huwa* [He], who is God, comes about when I am no longer I,[13] since this [I] prevents Him from being Him. . . . If the "I" subsists during the manifestation of Him, one will then have "You" (Nom (III), 343).

This sheds further light on the error of the claim examined in the previous discussion: if it is true that, so long as the "I" subsists, there must be the "Thou" as Divinity, it is no less true that when the indivisible Essence is realized, neither the individual nor the Divinity—insofar as it is defined as such in relation to the cosmos—can subsist, for this indivisibility does not permit the subsistence of distinctive relationships, relationship as such implying relativity, something to be "related" to an-"other"; therefore one speaks in a provisional and approximate manner in saying that man "sees" God or "realizes" the Essence only after being annihilated from himself. For, in reality, none can either know or see God but God, a principle illustrated by Ibn Arabi in commenting upon the famous formulation of an earlier Sufi, Abu Talib al-Makki: None sees Him "to whom nothing is similar" but him "to whom nothing is similar." Ibn Arabi adds that the one who sees is thus identical to the one seen (Nom (II), 214).

Two meanings in particular may be extracted from this short but important statement. Firstly, the human agent can only come to see the uncreated One—to whom nothing is similar—insofar as he, the individual, is himself rendered incomparable with any "thing," that is, any created reality. This implies the withdrawal from the illusion constituted by the cosmos; not simply the objective cosmic illusion outside him, but, more critically, the illusion or, as it was said above, the "veil," that he himself constitutes insofar as he exists or, taking this word in its root-meaning, "stands apart from" the One Being. Therefore a whole program of spiritual discipline, centering on the retreat, is implied here.

---

13 *Huwa* is not to be taken as a simple affirmation of the divine otherness, but of the divine Essence at once transcending the ego in its false sense of subjectivity—the divine "Other" conceived only as pure Object—and the polarity established between the ego and the Divinity/Level relationship alluded to in terms of "accident for accident," as we saw in the first section.

This methodic aspect will be addressed shortly, but the second point should be noted: that the realization of this union rests upon the prior reality that there is something within the individual which already transcends the domain of relativity and duality, in principle if not in fact. This identity has been doctrinally posited in the first section, and, in Ibn Arabi's chapter on the station of proximity, referred to implicitly; but the explicitly experiential realization of this principle, starting from the perspective of the individual, has not yet been addressed.

For this, one may turn to one of Ibn Arabi's descriptions of his spiritual ascent, at the climax of which there is a clear allusion to the transcendence of duality:

> He made His Throne to be a couch for me, the kingdom a servant for me, and the King to be a prince to me. Thus I remained in that (state) unaware of anything comparable to myself among the (eternal individual) entities (*a'yan*) (Ascension, 75).

It is important to note that Ibn Arabi is not made the "King," even though God's Throne and kingdom are subordinated to him, for the King Himself is also subordinated to him: but to "him" precisely insofar as "he" cannot be said to "exist," and thus cannot enter into any relationships implying duality. The "me" to which all is thus subordinated can therefore only be the One Subject, the "Self of the Real" as it was termed earlier; this transcendent subjectivity surpasses all duality, and cannot be regarded as referring to Ibn Arabi's personal individuality, since individuality presupposes ontological duality: so long as there is "I" there must be "Thou." If Ibn Arabi then employs the first person in the above quotation, and simultaneously claims to have transcended duality, then in good metaphysical logic, the "I" in question can only be the divine Self which alone escapes all distinctive ontological differentiation.

Referring back to the ineffable experience in discursive terms thus necessitates this paradoxical mode of expression, so open to misinterpretation; this highlights the incommensurability between the unitive state and verbal allusions thereto; nonetheless, as will be seen later in this discussion, there does exist a less inappropriate mode of expressing the inexpressible.

In this unitive state, then, there is nothing comparable to "him" amongst the *a'yan*, which, as has been shown, constitute those principial possibilities of manifestation upon which the light of Being projects its shadow, resulting in the cosmos; so Ibn Arabi is here asserting the realization of a supra-cosmic reality, that is both prior and posterior to the cosmos, at the same time as immanently pervading it and transcending it at every moment of its "imagined" existence. It is important to establish here the absolutely transcendent level in question; there must be a clear distinction between the level upon which the *a'yan* are distinctively affirmed—albeit in their immutable, supra-manifest state—and the level where they are transcended or reabsorbed into their undifferentiated source in the Essence. It should also be noted that this realization came about strictly as a result of the operation of grace: Ibn Arabi says that "He"—that is, God—"made His Throne a couch for me ...": in other words, it can only be God Himself that actualizes the consciousness of the relativity of God *qua* "Divinity/Level," and by the same token, consciousness of identity with that pure absoluteness of the divine Essence.

This absolutely transcendent level is the "Oneness of the One," beyond any degree of Self-manifestation; the first degree of *tajalli* is the "essential" or "hidden" Self-manifestation referred to earlier, corresponding to the "most holy effusion," and to the "Oneness of the Many," which is also referred to as *wahidiyyah*— inclusive unity—as distinct from *ahadiyyah*—exclusive unity; according to Ibn Arabi's traditional commentator, al-Qashani:

> The essential self-manifestation is the appearance of the Absolute under the form of the permanent archetypes. . . . By this appearance the Absolute descends from the Presence of Unity (*ahadiyyah*) to the Presence of Oneness (*wahidiyyah*) (Sufism, 155).

The location of the *a'yan* on this relatively transcendent plane of inclusive unity is supported by Ibn Arabi's interpretation of the Quranic verse in which a "moment" is referred to when man was "not a thing remembered" (76, 1): this "moment" is not in time, but refers to the ontological degree of *ahadiyyah*, that is, to the pure unity of the Essence, in which the entities of all things are strictly speaking "nothing" (Illuminations, 37).

Ibn Arabi's "state" in which the *a'yan* are transcended can therefore only be a realization of this degree of unconditional unity proper to the Essence alone.

In connection with the realization of this union, the following point should also be carefully noted: Ibn Arabi does not speak of union in relation to the "King," that is, the acting, creating, judging, personal God, for this would necessarily relativize and subvert the union in question, the very notion and reality of the "King" implying and requiring that of a kingdom and subjects over which to rule. Also, as seen in the first section, the whole plane of Divinity, upon which the divine Names are distinguishable, is but a plane of relationships; the Names have no ontological entities, but are distinctively realized only as the correlates of the effects over which they govern: the individual, constituting just such an effect, cannot then be united with that which has no distinctive reality apart from his own existence as an individual. Thus, as Ibn Arabi says, there can be no "mixing" of immutable realities, the Creator always remaining Creator and the creature always remaining creature:

> It is impossible for realities to change, so the servant is servant, and the Lord Lord; the Real is the Real and the creature creature (Path, 312).

To the objection that the "Lord" is comparable to the slave by virtue of the attributes—such as hearing, seeing, and so on—they have in common, Ibn Arabi replies that such attributes do not belong to the slave but are "attributes of Lordship in respect of Its manifestation within the loci of manifestation, not in respect of Its He-ness. . . . Lordship is the relationship of the He-ness to an entity, while the He-ness in Itself does not require relationships" (Path, 312).

Thus it is possible to assert, on the one hand, that the creature is distinct from the Creator, and on the other hand, that the creature manifests—albeit in relative mode—attributes that properly pertain, not to the ipseity of the Essence, but to the Essence insofar as It is related to the creatures by means of the level of the Lordship; this helps to explain many of Ibn Arabi's apparently contradictory—

even blasphemous—statements about God "needing" creatures as creatures need God.[14]

There is another objection that may be raised in relation to the above statement that realities do not change: if the creature cannot become one with the Creator, despite manifesting attributes which properly pertain to the Creator, how is it possible for him to realize absolute union with that Reality with which he has no common measure?

The problem can be usefully addressed in terms of an analogy given by Ibn Arabi; he compares the relationship between nothingness and the Real to that between darkness and light. There is no common measure between the two, such that the one may "become" the other, but this does not prevent light from projecting itself into darkness such that an ambiguous reality is produced, a reality possessing two faces: one turned towards the light, the other turned towards darkness:

> The Real is sheer Light, while the impossible is sheer darkness. Darkness never turns into light nor does light turn into darkness. Creation is the *barzakh* (isthmus) between Light and darkness. . . . In himself, man is neither light nor darkness, since he is neither existent nor non-existent (Path, 362).

Therefore when it is said that man "sees" God and that the nature of this vision is such that the one seen is identical with the seer, this can only mean that the light within man escapes the illusory limitations of individuality—the darkness of non-existence—and rejoins its universal and infinite nature:

> The object of vision, which is the Real, is light, while that through which the perceiver perceives Him is light. Hence light becomes included within light. It is as if it returns to the root from which it became manifest. So nothing sees Him but He. You, in respect of your entity are identical with shadow, not light (Path, 215).

The manner in which the light of Being may be said to reside within the shadow of the existentiated individual is elucidated by Ibn Arabi's description of the relationship between the "permeating" subject, and the "permeated" object:

> Know that whenever something "permeates" another, the first is necessarily contained in the second. The permeater becomes veiled by the permeated, so that the passive one (i.e. the permeated) is the "outward" while the active one (i.e. the permeater) is the "inward" which is invisible (Sufism, 233).

This shows clearly that the inward light of reality which resides in the immanent depths of the exteriorized shadow of imagined existence is veiled by that shadow with which it nonetheless has no common measure: thus it cannot be the individual as such who realizes the Essence, just as darkness can never become light; rather, when the Essence is realized, this must of necessity

---

[14] For example: "He praises me, I praise Him: where then is His Self-sufficiency since I help Him and grant Him bliss?" (Bezels, 95).

imply the absolute annihilation of the individual, the complete disappearance of the shadow, the return of the ray of light to the transcendent source of its projection.

This is summed up in the following words of Ibn Arabi in the above-quoted book of "Extinction in Contemplation"; he refers to the inner reality of this transcendent mode of unitive "vision," where the seer is the seen:

> When that is extinguished which never was—and which is perishing—and there remains that which has never ceased to be—and which is permanent—then there rises the Sun of the decisive proof for the vision through the Self. Thus comes about the absolute sublimation (Extinction, 27-28).

That which is extinguished "never was" from the viewpoint of absolute Reality, and even while it possessed a relative degree of existence, its essential nature was "perishing"; while, again from the absolute viewpoint, That which remains "never was not." Thus, what is realization of union in the state of *fana'* from the human perspective, is no change of state for the Real, but simply the removal of what did not truly exist in the first place:

> Naught save the Reality remains. . . . There is no arriving and no being afar, spiritual vision confirms this, for I have not seen aught but Him, when I looked (Bezels, 108).

Returning now to the human perspective, one must attempt to retrace the process by which consciousness, starting from its apparent encasement within the contingent existence of the individual, ascends to its transcendent source in pure Being.

One should begin by recalling Ibn Arabi's dictum: Pure Being is the finding of the Real in ecstasy; the accent here is on the "finding": consciousness must be rendered identical with unconditional Being, and thus liberated from the boundaries of contingent being, constituted, subjectively, by the conditions of individuality. It is important at this juncture also to recall the metaphysical reduction of the entire cosmos to the status of "imagined" reality; this notion, combined with the inverse relationship between the ephemeral creature and the eternal Real, observed above, results in the spiritual imperative, for man, to effect a contraction (*qabd*) from outward existence, in order to experience a corresponding expansion (*bast*) inwardly, towards the Real:

> The final end and ultimate return of the gnostics . . . is that the Real is identical with them, while they do not exist. . . . Hence they are contracted in the state of their expansion. A gnostic can never be contracted without expansion or expanded without contraction (Path, 375).

The highest knowers must be "contracted" both from the world and from themselves if "expansion" is to occur, this expansion culminating in a spiritual assimilation of true identity with the Real: if "the Real is identical with them while they do not exist," then their apparent existence along with the chimerical identity proportioned thereto, must be annulled.

The chief means of effecting this, as implied earlier, is the spiritual retreat—the *khalwah*, a word deriving from the root-meaning of emptiness; this signifies that the heart, as the inmost seat of consciousness, should be emptied of all cosmic properties in order that it may be filled with the presence of God: "The relationship which the heart has with God rests on the fact that it is made according to the form of God, and that nothing can fill it but Him" (Khalwah, 78).

Man is created according to the "form of God"; the quotation above focuses attention on the quintessential element of man's "form": that receptacle of consciousness, the heart, is so fashioned that it can only be filled with the pure Being/Consciousness of God; all other contents of consciousness only appear to fill the heart with so many "imaginations" or cosmic illusions which veil and thus negate the Real: the negation of the negation means pure affirmation: the removal of illusion results in the self-revelation of the Real.

Turning now to examine the methodic aspects of the retreat, Ibn Arabi stresses the importance of correct preparation before entering the cell. Firstly, it is crucial to have the proper intention: God alone—and not self-glorification, or phenomenal powers and states—must be the object of the aspirant's quest. Secondly, he must strictly observe the external rules of the religion. Thirdly, his imagination must be "under control," and this presupposes the appropriate "spiritual training" (*riyadah*) which means "training of character, abandonment of heedlessness, endurance of indignities" (Journey, 30).

These three elements—on which Ibn Arabi has expounded at length in innumerable treatises—can be related to what earlier was called "assuming the character traits of God" and "accidental perfection"; in other words, the perfection of human virtue is a prerequisite for advancement along the path of transcendence.

The main spiritual practice in the retreat is *dhikr*, the remembrance/invocation of God: "it is your saying 'Allah, Allah,' and nothing beyond 'Allah.'"

Ibn Arabi details numerous stages of realization that are attained by the invoker: paranormal powers of perception; initiation into the secrets of the natural, cosmic, and heavenly realms; acquisition of sciences of spiritual states; perceiving the inner forms of divine mysteries: the throne of Mercy, the Pen, etc.; at each of which he is not to "stop," but to proceed further, persevering with the invocation, his intention riveted on God alone, rather than on His bestowals.

> If you stay with what is offered, He will escape you. But if you attain Him nothing will escape you (Journey, 32).

It is to be noted that, prior to the extinctive state of *fana'*, one of the degrees to be transcended is an experience in which "a great rapture and deep transport of love seizes you, and in it you find bliss with God that you have not known before." But again, the invoker is not to "stop with this" but to proceed on to higher revelations of esoteric science which culminate finally in the extinction of the individual:

And if you do not stop with this, you are eradicated, then withdrawn, then effaced, then crushed, then obliterated (Journey, 48).

Following this, consciousness "returns" to the individual; the manner of this "return" will be examined in Part III of this chapter. For the moment, attention must stay fixed on this final stage of the ascent.

In the treatise summarized above, Ibn Arabi is writing as a master instructing an aspirant in a relatively impersonal manner; in another treatise, he relates a more personal account of the stages of this ascent, centering on his own experience. The degrees leading up to the unitive state are given in a description of the "journey" of the saints to God, in God. In this journey the composite nature of the saint is "dissolved," first through being shown by God the different elements of which his nature is composed, and the respective domains to which they belong; he then abandons each element to its appropriate domain:

> [T]he form of his leaving it behind is that God sends a barrier between that person and that part of himself he left behind in that sort of world, so that he is not aware of it. But he still has the awareness of what remains with him, until eventually he remains with the divine Mystery (*sirr*), which is the "specific aspect"[15] extending from God to him. So when he alone remains, then God removes from him the barrier of the veil and he remains with God, just as everything else in him remained with (the world) corresponding to it (Illuminations (Morris), 362).

The constitutive elements of human nature are, in terms of inward consciousness, "dissolved" through being absorbed by those dimensions of cosmic existence to which they properly pertain, so that consciousness is purified and disentangled from all the gradations of matter and their respective animic prototypes or principles; the consciousness which is said to "remain with God" in the same way that the other elements of human nature "remain" with their respective principles, means that there is no longer any distinction between this essentialized consciousness and pure Being: it is "finding the Real in ecstasy"; the ray of light returns "to the root from which it became manifest." The removal of the "barrier of the veil" can be understood as the elimination of the trace of individuality still attached to consciousness and thus relativizing it, recalling the statement earlier that the individual *'ayn* is but a veil and a shadow; this is the meaning of the statement that the saint "still has the awareness of what remains with him," in other words, he is still aware of himself as the conscious agent; it is this final self-awareness that must be extinguished in order that supreme Self-awareness be realized.

In describing the climax of his own ascent, Ibn Arabi confirms this interpretation; after journeying through the different heavens and receiving

---

[15] *Al-wajh al-khass*: one can understand this term as the divine "ray" that emanates from God to man, which on the one hand furnishes the "secret" identity between the two, but on the other, in respect of its very specificity, presupposes individuality, which is the last "barrier" to be overcome, as the text goes on to describe.

from the prophets different forms of spiritual science, he exclaims:

> "Enough, enough! My bodily elements are filled up, and my place cannot contain me!", and through that, God removed from me my contingent dimension.[16] Thus I attained in this nocturnal journey the inner realities of all the Names and I saw them returning to One Subject and One Entity: that Subject was what I witnessed and that Entity was my Being. For my voyage was only in myself and pointed to myself, and through this I came to know that I was a pure "servant" without a trace of lordship in me at all (Illuminations (Morris), 380).

In regard to bringing out more clearly the meaning of the highly important "return" of the Names to the One Subject and Entity, the translation of Chodkiewicz is preferred: he more literally translates *Musamma* as the "Named," and *'Ayn* in this context as the "Essence," which shows the objective-subjective complementarity between the two poles. Thus one has: "this Named One was the object of my contemplation and this Essence was my own Being" (Seal, 165). The removal of his "contingent dimension" is the essential condition for attaining this realization of transcendent identity: the Named is one with the Essence, and this identity can only be predicated of Ibn Arabi insofar as his contingent particularity is effaced, for it must not be forgotten that the "inner realities of all the Names" return to, and are thus comprised within, the transcendent One, the Essence as such; they cannot in any manner be said to pertain to Ibn Arabi's own individuality, however exalted be his state, or however metaphorically or poetically this individuality be conceived.

In this light, one sees more clearly the connection between this account and the perspective alluded to in the description of the station of proximity: the gazelle, having been there identified with revelation and manifestation, can thus also be symbolically assimilated to the Names which both reveal, and return to, the Named—"the object of my contemplation"—which is ultimately realized as identical with the subject of contemplation; as it was put in the poem: realizing that I am the very being of that which I love, I no longer fear separation. There is thus identity between subject and object at this transcendent degree: the one Essence—the locus of realized consciousness—and the one Named—the transcendent source of all Being—form a unique, inseparable Reality, and are distinct only on the relative plane.

In another account of the extinctive stage of realization, Ibn Arabi says:

> Then ... the even and the odd come together, He is and you are not. .... He sees Himself through Himself (Seal, 169).

Thus, when it is said that none knows the Absolute save the Absolute, it should be clear that what is meant is that only the ipseity of the Absolute, immanently pervading or "permeating" man can be that which "knows"—because it "is"—the

---

[16] *Imkani*: this could also be translated "my possibility"; that, in other words, which makes for his specificity, distinctiveness, and thus relativity.

very Absolute which infinitely transcends man; this ipseity is revealed in its true nature as identical with the Transcendent only when it is dissociated from any trace of the human condition, and hence presupposes the complete extinction of the individual; thus one speaks of the *'arif bi-Llah*, the knower *through* God, not the knower *of* God. Ibn Arabi distinguishes here between two types of gnosis: the first consists in "knowing Him as knowing yourself" whilst the second consists in "knowing Him through you as Him, not as you" (Bezels, 108).

The first type is related to the prophetic utterance: "whoso knoweth himself knoweth his Lord," which Ibn Arabi identifies with the specific Lord or Divine Name which rules over the individual.[17] This is relatively transcendent realization, and is the limit for the human individual as such; the level of absolute transcendence, the second type of gnosis, is only conceivable on the basis of that "aspect" of the individual which is in reality "He," not "you." One employs the term "aspect of the individual" in a wholly provisional manner here, since the individual is himself properly an "aspect" of the universal which he particularizes in "imaginary" mode; the ambiguity of the "specific aspect" should be recalled: in respect of its specificity it is relative, but at the same time it is that through which identity is realizable. Gnosis of the highest kind therefore consists in knowing—concretely, and not just theoretically—precisely who is the true Subject of Knowledge: the absolutely undifferentiated One, before which the individual is strictly nothing.

One is now in a better position to understand the meaning of "extinction in contemplation"; at the very end of the treatise bearing this title, Ibn Arabi conveys the deepest meaning of this type of contemplation by means of an esoteric interpretation of a Prophetic utterance. The saying refers to the meaning of virtue (*ihsan*): "that thou shouldst worship God as if thou sawest Him, and if thou seest Him not, He (nonetheless) seeth thee." The Arabic wording is such that, by effecting a stop in the middle of the phrase "if thou seest Him not" (*in lam takun: tarahu*), the meaning is completely transformed into: "if thou art not, thou seest Him" (Extinction, 48-49).

So "contemplation" here strictly means annihilation of the individuality; there is then no human agent as subject that can "contemplate" anything: the elimination of "that which never was" is tantamount to realization of "that which never ceased to be"; thus, what is meant by "witnessing" the Real is the realization of the absolute Unity of pure Being. This, then, is the "final end and ultimate return of the gnostics": they are identified with the Real, exclusively insofar as "they do not exist." Thus, the gnostic is the one who knows "through God" and not through himself; and he knows that he, as an individual, cannot know the Knower: he can only *be* the Knower, and this strictly implies his own non-existence as an individual. In order for knowledge to be perfect, there must be a perfect identity between knowledge and being: "I encompassed Being in Knowledge" as Ibn Arabi put it earlier, and: Being is the finding of the Real

---

[17] This is what Corbin referred to as "the paredros of the gnostic, his . . . eternal hexeity invested with a divine Name."

in ecstasy. Thus, only when relative consciousness and individual existence are both effectively sublimated and assimilated within absolute Consciousness and pure Being, can there be a perfect identity between knowledge and being: and this no longer has anything to do with the individual.

In this context one should take cognizance of Ibn Arabi's nuance of the famous saying of Abu Bakr, the first Caliph of Islam: to understand that one cannot know Knowledge is a form of knowledge.

> Some of us [Sufis] imply that within their knowledge is ignorance, and cite in this connection the saying: "To understand the inability to understand is understanding" (Sagesse, 46).

One can discern clearly what is intended by this saying: for the individual as such to grasp the reason for his incapacity to "know" the essence of Knowledge, is itself a form of knowledge, one which knows that this essence cannot itself be a distinctive object of knowledge for anything apart from itself.

Ibn Arabi, while obviously understanding this intention, nonetheless reformulates it by replacing the notion of ignorance with that of the inexpressible:

> But there is amongst us one who knows and does not utter these words; his knowledge does not imply an incapacity to know, it implies the inexpressible. It is such a person who realizes the most complete knowledge of God (Sagesse, 46).

Nonetheless, the inexpressible has been expressed, in somewhat problematic terms, by the *shathiyat*—ecstatic utterances—of certain Sufis; Ibn Arabi offers a clue as to the "less inadequate" mode of referring to the Supreme Identity by juxtaposing two Quranic verses, the first, a declaration of Pharaoh: "I know of no god for you apart from me" (28, 38); the second being a verse uttered by the Sufi Abu Yazid, after exclaiming "I am Allah": "There is no god if it be not Me" (21, 25) (Nom, 152).

The first point is that Pharaoh's words were not spoken under the influence of an ecstatic state which transcended his individuality, while Abu Yazid was, on the contrary, not "himself" when this expression of Divinity came from him; it is strictly in the unitive state, or at least from its perspective, that any such expressions of identity may be regarded as legitimate. Secondly, the very words employed indicate different shades of metaphysical meaning in the two statements; Ibn Arabi draws attention to this by making mention of the exclusive aspect of the word *ghayri*—"apart from/except me" in the saying of Pharaoh. Although he does not elaborate, it is clear that what he implies is that the creature cannot express his Divinity in terms of what he excludes—the rest of creation, the Creator, the uncreated Essence—but only in terms of what he includes, or more accurately, what includes him: his transcendent source, the ipseity of the Real immanent within him. Pharaoh's statement thus refers to the creature claiming the status of the Creator, and attempting to deify himself, while Abu Yazid's utterance was in truth that of the Divine, speaking from behind the veil of the creature, as its immanent, essential reality: it is the proclamation, by the all-inclusive immanence of the One, that nothing can be definitively excluded from itself.

Therefore, one understands Abu Yazid's utterance in accordance with a traditional "immanent-al" Sufi interpretation of the first *Shahadah*, "there is no reality if it be not the Real." While the *Shahadah* implicitly expresses both dimensions—transcendence and immanence—the creature can only legitimately attribute his Divinity to the inclusivity pertaining to immanence, not the exclusivity pertaining to transcendence; the moment he claims exclusivity, he thereby inescapably imprisons himself within the narrow confines of his existential individuality; and his claim to transcendence moreover implies distinction—between the non-transcendent creation and the transcendent Creator; and, as established earlier, in terms of this distinction, the creature remains always creature. Thus, to claim transcendent exclusivity is self-contradictory and metaphysically unacceptable.

This amounts to saying that what is realized in the state of union and referred to here as "transcendent" consciousness is more accurately described as being the realization of transcendence insofar as it is immanent in the individual: the transcendent can thus only be regarded as susceptible of realization by way of immanence.

Abu Yazid's utterance is referred to also in the following extract, where Ibn Arabi establishes with indubitable clarity that the identity revealed in the highest state is the true nature of things, "the affair as it is" in reality:

> If He were to lift the veils in the case of the knowers, they would see themselves as identical with Him, and the affair would be one. But He did lift the veils from them, so they saw their essences as one essence. They said what has been recounted from them, such as "I am God" and "Glory be to me." As for the common people, the veils are not lifted from them, so they do not witness the affair as it is (Self-Disclosure, 159).

The important point to stress, finally, is that the expressions of identity, by Abu Yazid, Ibn Arabi, and other mystics, can only be legitimate on the condition that the individual is not the agent of the expression; it can only be God, or the divine element within the soul but infinitely transcending it, that is expressing itself through the effaced soul. Herein lies the danger of asserting that the highest spiritual possibility is the vision of God: for then the expressions deriving from the transcendent realization of identity become either meaningless or blasphemous. While it is evidently true that the beatific vision is the highest possibility for the creature as such—this vision being predicated on an inescapable ontological dualism—this does not preclude the fulfillment of a higher possibility, one that derives from metaphysical unity: this is the possibility of the divine essence of the creature realizing its true identity as the One-and-only Reality, the realization of this identity constituting the ultimate spiritual fruit of the metaphysics of unity.

## Part III: Existential "Return"

### 1. Poverty and Servitude
It is significant that, immediately following his account of the realization of extinctive union, Ibn Arabi should conclude with the words: "I came to know that I was a pure servant." For slavehood appears to be at the very antipodes of that state of absolute freedom implied and realized in the unitive state, being by definition free of all limitations. But this renunciation of freedom is precisely what is required, on the part of the individual, if he is to avoid the greatest of all illusions: mistaking an aspect—however "deep" in relation to surface consciousness—of his individual and relative existence for the Being of the Absolute. For, as has been stated above, despite the fact that Being is One, the intrinsic reality of this unity can only be realized by the individual insofar as he is no longer himself; and outside of this particular state, upon returning to the normal ontological conditions of extrinsically differentiated degrees of Being, the same individual must see not only that, *qua* individual, he has no possible common measure with the Essence, but also that, in his very real relationship with the personal God, he possesses no property apart from essential poverty—*faqr*—and thus can properly be described only as a slave. Individual human existence—irrespective of the "secret" of consciousness comprised therein—therefore necessarily implies ontological poverty, and one does not stop being human after the state of *fana'*:

> It is impossible for you to cease being human, for you are human in your very essence. Though you should become absent from yourself or be annihilated by a state that overcomes you, your human nature subsists in its entity (Path, 176).

Therefore, from the point of view of the individual, even if what is revealed in the state of annihilation is the Real as such, this state nonetheless takes on the nature of a particular relationship with the Real—in respect of its being a "state" and not, it must be stressed, in respect of the intrinsic content of the unitive experience. Seen in this light, such a relationship is of a transient nature, in contrast to the "subsistence" (*baqa'*) of that relationship of slavehood vis-à-vis the Real, which is invariable and inescapable for so long as the individual himself subsists as an individual:

> Subsistence is a relationship that does not disappear or change. Its property is immutably fixed in both the Real and the creature. But annihilation is a relationship that disappears. It is an attribute of engendered existence and does not touch upon the Presence of the Real (Path, 321).

While the Real eternally subsists in its own reality, and cannot therefore experience annihilation from itself, the individual on the contrary, having been existentiated and thus "standing apart" from pure Being, can only be reabsorbed into that Being through the spiritual annihilation of his separate existence. This very change of state explains Ibn Arabi's statement that *fana'* is an "attribute of engendered existence" which does not "touch upon the Presence of the Real": it cannot be identified with the Real because, *qua* transitory state, it is defined both in terms of the engendered existence which it transcends or annihilates, *and* in relation to the Real which is the essential content of the state; the Real in itself, on the other hand, is not in any way conditioned by a relationship with "engendered existence," as seen in the first part of the chapter. One can therefore take the above quotation not so much as a denial of the transcendent content of the state of *fana'*, but as a reminder of the context in which *fana'* occurs, a context to which consciousness returns, that of engendered existence, or more accurately, that contingent dimension of individuality which is the subjective counterpart of objective engendered existence. So when Ibn Arabi says that annihilation is an "attribute" of engendered existence, one may add: and *as such*—"it does not touch upon the Presence of the Real." Only the absolutely unconditioned Real can "touch" the absolutely unconditioned Real: insofar as it is the individual who experiences a state in which this takes place, the relativity of the context of the experience must be taken into account, even while affirming that this context is transcended by the spiritual content of the state, this transcendence consisting in the elimination of the "contingent dimension" of individual existence.

It is strictly in relation to the human, relative context, then, that Ibn Arabi stresses the relativity of the state of annihilation; moreover, its very susceptibility to duration proves its relativity in the face of the eternal Real which can never not be. The "subsistence" of the individual, in contrast to the transience of the state which annihilates the individual, is a subsistence within engendered existence, and whatever subsists within this existence must share with it its fundamental nature: poverty and dependence in regard to unconditioned Being. To exist is therefore to be poor: "The servant's entity subsists in immutability, while his existence is immutable in its servitude" (Path, 321).

Insofar as the state of annihilation is a state, its nature reverts to the being experiencing it as a state, thus it reverts to the individual of which it is akin to a specific modality; it is thus necessarily subordinate to the *essential* or definitive attribute of the individual as such, which is slavehood—despite the fact that what is revealed in the state of annihilation infinitely transcends the plane of duality on which, alone, the relationship slave-Lord has any reality. For so long, therefore, as the individual is affirmed as a subject possessing a *degree* of being, he must be rigorously distinguished from that which constitutes pure Being; he can therefore be characterized as "poor" in relation to that upon which he is totally dependent for his relative being:

> The ultimate illusion is for a person to bring together Lord and servant through *wujud*. . . . For the *wujud* of the Lord is His own Entity, while the *wujud* of the servant is a property which the servant is judged to possess. . . . Since the *wujud* of the servant is not his own entity, and since the *wujud* of the Lord is identical with Himself, the servant should stand in a station from which no whiffs of lordship are smelt from him (Path, 324).

Just as the saint/gnostic knows that his being only apparently pertains to him, so he knows that whatever positive, or "lordly" qualities he manifests cannot be appropriated by his individual entity but must on the contrary be seen as strictly pertaining to the Real, leaving him in an invariably humble and detached state, a state which conforms to the nature of his entity, immutable in its non-existence. The spiritual master or *shaykh* therefore knows that he has nothing "lordly" about his own person or entity: he is but the "locus for the flow of the properties of lordship."

This perfect objectivity in regard to the true source of qualities which the sage may manifest means that he also has perfect objectivity with regard to himself, seeing his own soul as something "other" than himself, not identifying with it, even in the context of its subsistence as an engendered being. Ibn Arabi expresses this important point by referring to an inner dialogue with his own soul. It should be noted carefully that the very fact that he engages with his soul as if it were another itself implicitly expresses the principle established through the dialogue. The dialogue involves two of the greatest saints of Islam, Mansur al-Hallaj and Uways al-Qarani. Ibn Arabi's soul argues that al-Hallaj surpassed the degree of Uways because, while Uways satisfied his own needs before giving away his surplus in charity, al-Hallaj was prepared even to sacrifice his own needs for the sake of others. To this argument of his own soul, Ibn Arabi replies:

> If the gnostic has a spiritual state like al-Hallaj, he differentiates between his soul and that of others: he treats his own soul with severity, coercion, and torture, whereas he treats the souls of others with preference and mercy and tenderness. But if the gnostic were a man of high degree . . . his soul would become a stranger to him: he would no longer differentiate between it and other souls in this world. . . . If the gnostic goes out to give alms, he should offer it to the first Muslim whom he meets. . . . The first soul to meet him is his own soul, not that of another (Muhyiddin (Boase), 56-57).

It is precisely because of the fact that the gnostic does not identify with the ego that he does not appropriate to the ego whatever qualities may be manifested through it, but refers all positive qualities back to their supra-personal source in the Divinity, and from thence to the Essence. To claim lordship, then, does not only mean claiming divine status, but, more subtly, it refers to that tendency of the individual to take pride in whatever positive qualities he may manifest, forgetting his personal nothingness, and that these qualities cannot therefore be attributed to him. The perfect gnostic is the one who most completely realizes his nothingness, not just in the unitive state—wherein his nothingness is concretely negated by Reality—but also outside of this state, in the condition of his affirmed existence and even when manifesting—though in no wise appropriating— "lordly" attributes, such as wisdom, mercy, etc.: "Happy is he who is upon a form which requires such an elevated station and which has no effect upon him and does not bring him out of his servanthood" (Path, 318).

Having concrete knowledge of the true nature of freedom in the unitive state, the gnostic knows that outside of this state there can but be servanthood; he knows that absolute freedom can only pertain to the Absolute, so that the return to the conditions of relativity necessitates the servant's renunciation of freedom; however, he is now fully conscious of the absolute reality of freedom, the freedom of the Real who "never is not," in contrast to the ultimately illusory nature of servanthood, the servanthood of the creature who "never was." Nonetheless he sees that this servanthood is endowed with a concrete—albeit relative—degree of reality for so long as his own dimension of relativity subsists. Therefore freedom can only be a state and not a station so far as the individual is concerned:

> Freedom is a station of the Essence. . . . It cannot be delivered over to the servant absolutely, since he is God's servant through a servanthood that does not accept emancipation (Illuminations (Chittick), 257).

The servant does, however, have access to this station in a relative manner, through his very consciousness that, in reality, he does not exist. That which is not, has no need of liberation:

> So when the servant desires the realization of this station . . . and he considers that this can only come about through the disappearance of the poverty that accompanies him because of his possibility, and he also sees that the Divine Jealousy demands that none be qualified by existence except God . . . he knows through these considerations that the ascription of existence to the possible thing is impossible. . . . Hence he looks at his own entity and sees that it is nonexistent . . . and that nonexistence is its intrinsic attribute. So no thought of existence occurs to him, poverty disappears, and he remains free in the state of possessing nonexistence, like the freedom of the Essence in Its Being (Illuminations (Chittick), 257-258).

In other words, there is realized freedom for the individual only to the extent that he is concretely aware of his own non-existence; servitude and poverty are inescapable concomitants of individual existence. This permanent awareness of one's non-existence may be considered as the complement, in subsistent mode, of that consciousness of pure Being experienced in the unitive state; in other words, it faithfully transcribes, in the realm of differentiated being and relative consciousness, that reality of undifferentiated being and transcendent consciousness attained in annihilation.

To clarify further this important point, it is necessary to introduce the ontological distinction between the entity in its state of immutable non-existence, on the one hand, and its "preparedness"—*isti'dad*—to receive existence on the other:

> [W]hen the possible thing clings to its own entity, it is free, with no servanthood; but when it clings to its preparedness it is a poor servant (Illuminations (Chittick), 259).

It should be remembered that the entity in its immutable state is "existent for God" and not for itself, being a purely intelligible possibility residing in the divine Consciousness; and becoming "visible with Being and disappearing with non-Being" in the words of the commentator al-Kashani (Sufism, 26); when this possibility receives the existentiating command: Be!, what flows forth into existence are the innumerable states of the being inherent in the preparedness of the entity, while the entity in itself remains immutably fixed in its non-existent state, known only by God. Therefore, insofar as the immutable entity can be said to possess any attribute, it can only be that of eternal receptivity. To use the word "eternal" here raises the following difficulty, which must be resolved before proceeding any further: how can the entity be qualified by the term eternal, when only the Real is eternal? The "eternity" of the entity must be sharply distinguished from the eternity of God, not only because, as seen in the last section, it is excluded from the degree of absolute unity proper to the Essence alone, but also because it depends on the orientation towards it of the Divine Name/Word which will existentiate it; this must be understood "so that we realize thereby the secret of their createdness in time and of their eternity, and distinguish their eternity from His eternity" (Illuminations (Chodkiewicz), 38).

In other words, one must distinguish between the eternity pertaining to the immutable non-existence of the entity, and the eternity of immutable Being which pertains to the Real, the eternity of the first being as a non-existent but intelligible shadow of the second, acquiring thereby the qualification of eternity despite its non-existence.

Returning now to the "eternal" receptivity of the entity to the divine command, this can be described as poverty: "Independence from creation belongs to God from eternity without beginning, while poverty toward God in respect of His Independence belongs to the possible thing in the state of its non-existence from eternity without beginning" (Path, 64).

Therefore, if the individual is to live in a manner which is appropriate to his knowledge both of the Being of the Real, and of the non-existence of his entity, he must reflect, even while remaining necessarily himself, a state of quasi-absolute non-existence. And it is this non-existence within existence that Ibn Arabi describes as servitude. The following explanation of why servitude is superior to servanthood will help to illustrate these points:

> Servitude is the ascription of the servant to Allah, not to himself; if he is ascribed to himself, this is servanthood not servitude. So servitude is more complete (Illuminations (Chittick) 555, n. 16).

That is, insofar as servanthood (*'ubudiyyah*) requires the affirmation of the individual, it relates to the affirmation of relative existence before it is subordinated to Being, whilst servitude (*'ubudah*), as a quality which subsumes the individual, pertains directly to subordination to Being, the individual ceasing to be a barrier between the quality of servitude and pure Being. Servitude, therefore, more faithfully reflects the entity in its immutable non-existence, while servanthood relates more to the preparedness of the entity to receive existence, thus pertaining to a more relative degree of being, such preparedness being as the "face" of the entity turned towards existence and thus the dimension open to relativity and change.

The saint who is thus assimilated to the attribute of servitude "sits in the house of his immutability, not in his existence, gazing upon the manner in which God turns him this way and that" (Illuminations (Chittick) 555, n. 16).

The nature of this "turning" will be addressed later in this discussion; for now, this important station of subsistent non-existence in immutable servitude needs more attention.

The underlying principle in question here is illustrated in Ibn Arabi's approach to the relationship between obligatory and supererogatory religious worship. Sufism traditionally ascribes a higher degree to the latter, in accordance with a *hadith qudsi*, a divine utterance often cited by Ibn Arabi:

> My slave draws near to Me through nothing I love more than that which I have made obligatory for him. My slave never ceases to draw near to Me through supererogatory acts until I love him. And when I love him, I am his hearing by which he hears, his sight by which he sees, his hand by which he grasps, and his foot by which he walks.[18]

Ibn Arabi, on the contrary, establishes the superiority of the obligatory works over the supererogatory ones. He does so, firstly, by distinguishing between the "state" of the one and the "station" of the other: "When the Real is the hearing of the servant this is a state of the servant"; whereas in the case of the realization of obligatory works, this is a station in which the servant "becomes" the attributes of the Real, "even while knowing that the Real is he/not he." While the possessor of the "station" is aware of being identical to the Real in one respect and non-existent in another respect, the possessor of the "state" in which God becomes the servant's attributes is only aware of the one dimension, that of identity, and consequently says "I" (Path, 329).

This is a typical feature of Ibn Arabi's dialectic, apparently subverting traditional concepts in order to accentuate a particular relationship or meaning of overriding importance; and it is important to make an effort of creative interpretation in order to bring out the underlying intention here.

Four ways of interpreting this—at first sight puzzling—inversion of the traditional relationship between the two degrees of worship may be suggested:

(i) The permanent station in which one is fully aware both of one's nothingness and of one's identity with the Real is higher than the passing state in which one is only aware of the dimension of identity.

(ii) Insofar as God becomes the faculties of the individual, it is the individual who is affirmed even if it be in divine mode, whereas when the individual is identified with the faculties of God, then it is exclusively God that is affirmed, the individual's existence being extinguished and sublimated in that affirmation.

(iii) Supererogatory works pertain to the lower degree, that of servanthood, since they are works which may or may not be done, and thus involve the free will of the individual, and this free will in turn leads back to the affirmation of the individual. Even if the individual chooses to be a servant, the very operation of his will takes priority, existentially, over the quality of servanthood that is chosen. On the contrary, obligatory works are those in which the individual's free will is overridden by divine necessity, and thus relate to the higher degree, that of servitude. The individual, being effaced by the quality, rather than affirming it, is thereby "ascribed" to God, not to himself.

---

[18] *Sahih al-Bukhari* (Summarized) (Riyad, 1996), no. 2117, p. 992.

(iv) A further line of interpretation opens up in the light of the following extract:

> The Real Himself does not descend to be the "hearing of the servant," because His Majesty does not allow this. Hence He must descend through His attribute. . . . Supererogatory works and clinging fast to them give the servant the properties of the attributes of the Real, while obligatory works give him the fact of being nothing but light. Then he looks through His Essence, not through His attributes, for His Essence is identical to His hearing and His seeing. That is the Real's Being, not the servant's existence (Path, 330-331).

The "upward" identification of the individual with the divine attribute implicitly means identity with the Essence, given the fact that the attribute of the Divine has no specific entity, but is one with the Essence when it is regarded inwardly and retraced to its source; on the other hand, when the Divine "descends" in order to "become" the faculties and attributes of the individual, this can only be in terms of its attributes—outwardly deployed and differentiated, and hence in their aspect of "other than" the Essence. Therefore, in the station of servitude/obligatory works, there is the ongoing extinction of the entity of the individual in the attributes of God, this upward and inward movement tending towards the Essence as source of the divine attributes, while in the station of servanthood/supererogatory works, there is an extinction of the individual's attributes in the divine attributes, an extinction that coexists with the affirmed entity of the individual. On the one hand, this very affirmation relativizes the degree of realization in question, and on the other hand, the outward deployment of the divine attributes implies an ontological degree lower than that of the Essence.

The intention of his dialectic here should be clear: permanent self-effacement is the ontological complement to consciousness of the One indivisible Real.

## 2. "The People of Blame"

This discussion leads us to another aspect of ontological poverty: the highest saint withdraws from all ostentatious behavior, refraining from manifesting supernatural powers—if these have been granted him—knowing that these are strictly irrelevant, from the point of view of the highest realization; he acts conventionally, prefers anonymity. Such a saint belongs to the highest class referred to earlier, the *malamiyyah*, the "people of blame" or the *afrad*, the "solitary ones," among whose number as already noted, is the Prophet Muhammad himself. The people of blame are "those who know and are not known. . . . [T]hey flow with the common people in respect of the outward acts of obedience which the common people perform" (Path, 372). They are protected by God "in the abandonment of freedom and enslavement to that which wisdom demands" (Path, 261).

This wisdom consists in putting each thing in its place, giving each thing its due; the "perfect sage" does not confuse levels of being, he treats outward phenomena according to principles governing those phenomena, even while being inwardly rooted in his identity with the transcendent source of those phenomena: "Transcendence of the customary order will become his secret, so that events beyond the ordinary will accompany him ordinarily" (Path, 60).

When the "ordinary" world is itself assimilated as an aspect of the "extraordinary" beyond, then the divine presence is inalienable at every degree of the cosmos; this is the "stage of divine wisdom appearing within the customary outward principles."

Another aspect of this wisdom is that the realized saint continues to abide by the revealed Law, seeing in it the strongest of all "secondary causes," since it "holds in its grasp the light by which one can be guided in the darknesses of the land and sea of these secondary causes" (Path, 179).

Knowledge of a transcendent nature, far from producing indifference or disdain in regard to all things which are situated beneath this absolute degree of transcendent reality, on the contrary establishes a proper submission of the individual to the revealed Law, which is absolute by virtue of its provenance, even if it be recognized as relative by virtue of the differentiated plane of being upon which it operates. Also, despite his knowledge that the Essence is alone real, the saint, as seen earlier, worships not the One, which remains inaccessible to all worship, but the Divinity/Level, his personal nature coming into contact with the personal God, "accident for accident." This very important aspect of the saint's consciousness is well brought out in the chapter on Job in the *Fusus*.

What must be noted carefully here is the distinction between two viewpoints: first, that pertaining to "reality" and revealed through "spiritual disclosure" (*haqiqatan wa kashfan*); and second, that which stems from "veiled/curtained" awareness (*hijaban wa sitran*) and which relates to relative reality. The two are not contradictory, but complementary, running as it were parallel to each other and deriving from the two dimensions of consciousness, inward and outward. From the viewpoint of unveiled consciousness, "the Reality is the Identity of the cosmos. . . . [A]ll determinations are manifest from Him and in Him, as in the saying 'The whole matter reverts to Him' (Qur'an, 11, 123)" (Bezels, 215).

This means that the saint brings all multiplicity back to the undifferentiated unity of its source and origin, so that outward phenomena lose their distinctive and thus privative character; from this point of view, there can be no privation, hence no suffering, as only the Reality, by definition beatific, can be said to be "real." But this does not exclude the possibility and the necessity of abiding by the Quranic injunction immediately following the above-quoted verse: "Worship Him and trust in Him"—even if this relates to the standpoint of "veiled consciousness." In other words, the saint is not veiled from his existential poverty by his unveiled consciousness which knows that all but the One is illusory.

Therefore, when suffering from an affliction, the saint, like the Prophet Job, humbles himself before God and supplicates Him for help, this in no way detracting either from the saint's virtue of patience, or his acceptance of destiny, or his awareness of the ultimately illusory nature of the affliction. As for this latter quality, it is referred to implicitly by the statement attributed to Job by Ibn Arabi: "That which is far from me is close to me by reason of its power within me" (Bezels, 216). Suffering is that which, objectively and from the viewpoint of unveiled consciousness, is "far from me"; but it appears to be "close to me" from the viewpoint of existential outwardness which is veiled consciousness: the saint is fully aware that his true being is not subject to privation of any kind, even while supplicating God for help in removing the affliction to which his outward existence is subject.

Moreover, in thus praying for help, the saint knows that the reason for being subjected to the trial in the first place is precisely that he should pray for relief, and he also knows that the Helper and the helped are ultimately one and the same:

> What greater hurt is there for Him than that He should try you with some affliction . . . so that you might beg Him to relieve it, when you are heedless of Him? It is better that you approach Him with the sense of indigence, which is your true condition, since by your asking Him to relieve you, the Reality Himself is relieved, you being His outer form (Bezels, 217).

Therefore it is only the saint's outer dimension of existence that experiences trials, his inward dimension of consciousness remaining impassible; nonetheless, putting each thing in its place, he seeks relief for that outer dimension, knowing both that this is required by his ontological poverty and that this dimension is itself but an aspect of the divine dimension referred to as the Outward (*al-Zahir*).

### 3. Theophany: Witnessing God's "Withness"

The contemplation of God within the world is also closely related to poverty: Ibn Arabi emphasizes that if poverty towards God is to be complete, there must also be poverty in regard to His secondary causes: all of those relative, mediate, natural laws of the cosmos through which and in which God as Primary Cause is present and active. The important point here is that the secondary causes are to be regarded as transparent veils over the Real: insofar as they are rendered transparent, they permit the Real to be perceived through them, and insofar as they are veils imagined, willed, and established by the Real, they must be obeyed and respected with that outer dimension of the individual which, likewise, is a veil:

> God established the secondary causes and made them like veils. Hence, the secondary causes take everyone who knows that they are veils back to Him, But they block everyone who takes them as lords (Path, 45).

Therefore, in submitting to the secondary causes as loci for the manifestation of God, one is submitting to God; but submitting to them in their own right is polytheism: "A person's ears must rend all these veils to hear the word 'Be!'" (Path, 45).

Likewise, the "sight" of the individual must see the manifest dimension of God, while his "insight" intuits the non-manifest dimension: "God is the Manifest who is witnessed by the eyes and the Nonmanifest who is witnessed by the intellects"

(Path, 89). In other words, the individual knows the interior aspect of things by means of his interior, and the exterior aspect by his exterior.[19]

What must be stressed here is that, having realized God in supra-manifest mode, the perfect gnostic is one who cannot but see Him continuously through and in all the modalities of manifestation; having "climbed up to the Real" the gnostic comes to know God in His aspect of transcendence, since "the Real discloses Himself to him without any substratum"; then knowledge of Divine immanence in the substrata will flow forth as a natural consequence. He who has "seen" the One *above* all things will see the same One—*mutatis mutandis*— *in* all things:

> When this servant returns from this station to his own world, the world of substrata, the Real's self-disclosure accompanies him. Hence he does not enter a single presence which possesses a property without seeing that the Real has transmuted Himself in keeping with the property of the presence. . . . [A]fter this he is never ignorant of Him or veiled from Him (Path, 185).

This witnessing of God in all things is the positive complement, in terms of consciousness, of the essential poverty of the saint in terms of being: albeit outwardly poor in relation to the secondary causes by which and in which God transmutes Himself, his very consciousness of the reality of God's inescapable presence means that the saint is witness to a perpetual theophany:

> The Real is perpetually in a state of "union" with engendered existence. Through this he is a god. This is indicated by His words, "He is with you wherever you are" (Qur'an, 57, 4); and it is the witnessing of this "withness" that is called "union" (*wasl*), insofar as the gnostic has become joined (*ittisal*) to witnessing the actual situation (Path, 365).

It should be noted here that this mode of union is related to the Divine, not in its Essence, but insofar as it has "descended" as a "god" in the forms of His Self-manifestations, that is, the cosmos in its entirety; "union" upon this plane is thus to be rigorously distinguished from the realization of the supra-manifest Essence, even though this union with the Divine in the very midst of manifestation can only be fully realized on the basis of the realization of that Essence which transcends all relationship with manifestation.

The saint is not only continually aware of this divine "withness" in all things around him, he also knows that the seer is not other than the seen: "He sees only God as being that which he sees, perceiving the seer to be the same as the seen" (Bezels, 235).

In the chapter of the *Fusus* on Elias, from which the above quotation is taken, emphasis is put on the "completeness" of gnosis, which requires that God be known both above and within all things. Those who "return" to phenomenal existence with a transformed awareness thereof, are deemed to possess a greater

---

[19] This is again related to the purpose of God's creation, that he might be "known": that His Inward be known by man's inward, and His Outward by man's outward. See Bezels, p. 65.

plenitude than those who "remain" in the state of ecstatic extinction in God;[20] this is also the message received from Aaron in the fifth heaven: those who remain unaware of the world are said to be "lacking" in respect of the totality of the Real inasmuch as the world—assimilated as an aspect of this very totality—was veiled from them. This is because the world is "precisely the Self-manifestation of the Truly Real, for whoever really knows the Truly Real" (Illuminations (Morris), 374).

This relates to the distinction between *khalwah* and *jalwah*, the first, as seen in the last section, signifying a retreat from the world, the second being a "coming out" into the light of day, a return to the world by the transformed man who sees the phenomena of the world as God's Self-manifestations (*tajalliyat*—a word sharing a common root with the word *jalwah*): the main reason for entering the retreat is not just to realize the Divine in the innermost depths of supra-manifest Reality, but also to recognize the Divine, as inalienable Totality, in the very midst of the manifest world, the "secondary causes." The gnostic, then, is able to "witness Him in his outward dimension within the secondary causes, after having gazed upon Him in his inward dimension" (Path, 158-159).

Again, in describing the purpose of the *mi'raj*, Ibn Arabi stresses that one reason for the ascent is to be shown the divine reality of the "signs" that are the phenomena of the cosmos, the forms of God's Self-expression (Illuminations (Morris), 358).

Elsewhere, Ibn Arabi says that the underlying reason for the *khalwah* is not so much a retreat from engendered things as it is a withdrawal from false conceptions about these things, in which category is preeminently included the agent who undertakes the retreat; referring to his instruction to an aspirant, Ibn Arabi writes:

> Among the things I have taught him is that by being a locus of manifestation he does not acquire existence. So he "withdrew" from this belief, not from acquired existence, since there is none. That is why, in (the discussion of) withdrawal, we have turned away from (the position) that it is withdrawal from acquired existence (Illuminations (Chittick), 277).

In other words, all phenomena, being loci for theophanic revelation, are existent only in terms of this function; they are vessels into which Being is poured: they do not acquire Being so much as delimit and specify it in a manner conforming to their entity, which is non-existent. Thus, phenomena do not "acquire" existence in their own right such that existence, having at one time not been their property now becomes their property. That which apparently comes into existence is destined only to disappear from existence, and thus cannot be said to have acquired Being, whose essential characteristic is immutability. The

---

[20] In Journey, p. 51, Ibn Arabi distinguishes between those "sent back" (*mardudun*) and those "absorbed" or effaced (*mustahlikun*); the former are deemed "more perfect" and are in turn subdivided into those who return only to themselves, and those who return with the mandate to guide others to the Truth, these being the higher of the two.

individual must therefore withdraw from the false conception which assigns an autonomous or an acquired ontological status not only to the phenomena around him, but also to himself: he must see through his illusory self-sufficiency.

## 4. The Heart and Creation

By way of concluding this discussion, the relationship between consciousness and being can be viewed in respect of the "heart" and the perpetual "renewal of creation." The station wherein the subjective pole of the heart and the objective pole of this perpetually renewed existence are in perfect accord is referred to as "no station"; it is a manner of being which transcends the limitative aspect connected with the determinative designation of "station"; this is the "stability in variegation," attained by the "Muhammadan," the saint who is the perfect inheritor of the supreme source of Prophecy and Sainthood:

> The most all-inclusive specification is that a person not be delimited by a station whereby he is distinguished. So the Muhammadan is only distinguished by the fact that he has no station specifically. His station is that of no station. . . . The relationship of the stations to the Muhammadan is the same as the relationship of the names to God. He does not become designated by a station which is attributed to him. On the contrary, in every breath, in every moment, and in every state he takes the form which is required by that breath, moment, and state (Path, 377).

The perpetual renewal of creation in each instant is an ontological reality which can only be apprehended by the "heart" of the Muhammadan; this is because it is only the spiritual faculty, symbolized by the heart, that is capable of conforming to the constant fluctuation and variegation that characterizes the deployment of the innumerable possibilities of being; the very word for heart, *qalb*, suggests this, being etymologically related to the notions of overturning, fluctuation, revolution. Therefore, this constant fluctuation in the heart is the reflection of, and participation in, "the divine self-transmutation in forms" (Path, 112).

Ibn Arabi relates this all-embracing capacity of the heart to the divine utterance: "My earth and My heaven do not contain Me, but the heart of My believing servant does contain Me." One should recall here that in the description of his first "opening," Ibn Arabi said that he "encompassed Being in knowledge." Now, the highest application of this union between Being and Consciousness relates to the extinction of the individual in the transcendent state of *fana'*; and as seen earlier, this degree of pure Being is "the finding of the Real in ecstasy." However, a homologous principle may be seen to apply even within the differentiated degrees of existence in relation to the transformed awareness of the subsistent individual; this amounts to saying that the saint sees God in all things and all things in God, in such a manner that every moment of existence transcribes, in relative mode, that supreme Bliss experienced in the unitive state.

Thus, one finds that there is both inverse analogy and positive analogy as between the saint and the Absolute: while the quasi-absolute poverty of the existent slave is the inverse reflection of the absolute freedom of pure Being, the continual experience of bliss within the saint's inner consciousness is the positive analogue, or prolongation in relative mode, of the absolute bliss proper to the Essence alone. So one sees clearly that the blissful Reality unveiled in the unitive state is both prolonged and delimited by the return to the individual state: prolonged in regard to the essential content of this consciousness, and delimited by virtue of the relative ontological degree within which it is necessarily situated.

This "stability in variegation" is a reflection, within the created realm, of the Essence, which is both One—hence "stable"—and infinite—hence infinitely "varied," without this variation in any way detracting from its unity, just as, in the consciousness of the saint, constant variation does not detract from "stability." The very indefinitude of created things, and the perpetually renewed instants of time in which they occur, transcribes the infinitude and eternity of the Essence; the saint's "return" to creaturely consciousness is thus accompanied by an essential capacity of the heart to be in perpetual contact with the Divine in all the fluctuations inherent in outward existence, these fluctuations being grasped as theophanic Self-revelations of the Divine, and thus as expressions, in finite mode, of the Infinite. One recalls Ibn Arabi's essential metaphysical principle: the very completeness of Being requires incompleteness, since to lack this dimension is itself an incompleteness. This principle also explains why the "returners" are deemed superior to those who "stop" at the stage of extinctive union.

To witness God's "withness" in all things and in every moment means not only being in a state of perpetual union with Him, but it also means being in a permanent condition of inward peace and bliss that is best described as Paradisal: "[T]he folk of the (Celestial) Garden dwell in a bliss that is renewed at each succeeding instant in all their senses, their meanings, and the divine self-disclosures; they are constantly in delight . . ." (Path, 106).

This is the case even in this world, since existence is also being renewed at each instant here and now, and the inner essence of existence is bliss: "But a person who is ignorant does not witness the renewal of bliss so he becomes bored. Were this ignorance to be lifted from him, so also would boredom be lifted. Boredom is the greatest proof that man has remained ignorant of God's preserving his existence and renewing his blessings at each instant" (Path, 106).

To conclude: for the enlightened saint there is no need any longer to look for the "supernatural"; the very substance of all that is "natural" is revealed in its divine aspect; there is no need to search for miracles, since the miracle of existence is perpetually proclaimed by all existent things; he sees the divine substance through the transparent earthly forms, while also seeing the forms as the loci of divine Self-revelation; the veils of the forms are thus not simply rendered transparent for God to be seen through them, but they are also apprehended as divine transmutations themselves, since they constitute the Outward. Therefore, existence is "marvelous," both outwardly, in terms of what it manifests—the *tajalliyat* of God *qua* Divinity—and inwardly, in terms of its non-manifest, transcendent source—God *qua* Essence: "[T]he 'marvelous' (as men usually understand it) is only what breaks with the habitual. But for those who comprehend things from the divine perspective, every thing in this 'habitual' course is itself an object of marvel" (Illuminations (Morris), 146).

The phenomena of creation, although nothing from the point of view of the Essence, are positively assimilated by the saint as so many aspects of the divine totality, so many ways in which the "hidden treasure" loved to be known: what the Infinite loved to be known must be infinitely lovable. Therefore Ibn Arabi proclaims, with the Qur'an: "We created not the heavens and the earth and all that between them is, in play" (21, 116; Path, 134).

## Part IV: Transcendence and Universality

As seen in Part II of this chapter, the universal validity of religion as such was established for Ibn Arabi in his spiritual ascent in a manner which left no doubt as to the significance that is to be attached to this principle: coming just before the final degree of extinctive union, it was referred to as the "key to all knowledge." The fact that this knowledge was attained in the bosom of the highest spiritual realization accords to it an elevated ontological status; the validity of other faiths is not simply a matter of conceptual understanding. It is therefore necessary to examine this principle in its own right.

The discussion on the station of "proximity" revealed that the universality of divine revelation is in fact implied by the distinction between form and essence, since this distinction was seen to apply both to formal manifestation and to religious revelation insofar as the latter necessarily partakes of form: if the absoluteness of a religion resides in its supra-formal, transcendent essence, then, in its formal aspect, the same religion is necessarily relative; and this amounts to saying, on the one hand, that no one religion can lay claim, on the level of form, to absolute Truth, to the exclusion of other religions, and on the other hand, that each religion is true by virtue of the absoluteness of its "intended" essence, which is none other than its divine source.

This implication conforms with what Ibn Arabi explicitly lays down elsewhere. His position on this question may be more clearly appreciated in the light of the following three points: (i) in the context of Islamic revelation, Ibn Arabi makes a distinction between "accidental" and "necessary" aspects of the Word; (ii) on the basis of this distinction one can situate more objectively that substantial element that constitutes religion as such, and which calibrates the distinctions between Islam and the other religions; (iii) from "above," the distinction between divine Essence and religious form reveals the reality that each religion is relative and limited by virtue of what it excludes, and at the same time is absolute by virtue of that which it includes and to which it leads. Each of these points will now be considered in more detail.

(i) The distinction between primary and secondary aspects of the revealed Law of Islam is implicit in many places throughout Ibn Arabi's writings; in terms of explicit references thereto, it suffices to note the following two: firstly, in his discussion of the *Shari'ah* (Ch. 262 of the *Futuhat*), he distinguishes between divine ordinances responding to particular questions within the community, and those dispensations issuing from the Divine in the absence of these particularities (and thus, implicitly, referring to the more essential aspects of the Law). He adds:

> Many of the rulings instituted by the Law have come through questions posed by the community; and without these questions, the respective prescriptions would not have been established (Chari'ah, 209).

Secondly, in discussing the establishment of the five daily prayers, a similar principle of distinction is applied. According to tradition, the first instruction given to the Prophet Muhammad, in his ascension to the Throne of God, was that the Muslims should pray fifty times each day; on his return through the heavens he meets Moses who commends him to return and seek a reduction in the number; this is repeated until the number five is arrived at, and God then proclaims: "They are five and they are fifty: the Word changes not with Me." Ibn Arabi says that by these words Moses understood that there is in the divine Speech that which comprises change and that which does not; on the one hand, there is the "necessary Word/Speech" (*al-qawl al-wajib*) which does not change, and on the other, the "accidental Word/Speech" (*al-qawl al-ma'rud*) which is subject to change (Nom, 345).

Ibn Arabi himself does not elaborate further, but one may interpret this distinction as referring to the divine capacity for changing the "accidental" aspect of the decree without detriment to its necessary or substantial import; hence the prayers are said to be simultaneously five and fifty, the number of prayers relating to the "accidental" Word, and the principle of prayer relating to the "necessary" Word.

It is also possible to apply this principial distinction to other religions: each religion can be regarded as a revealed "Word," which comprises accidental and necessary aspects; thus the formal differences between the religions can be seen as so many outward accidents which do not detract from their unity in terms of inner substance. This leads to the second of the above points.

(ii) The knowledge that all religions are united in their essence was crystallized in Ibn Arabi's consciousness by one of the key Quranic verses proclaiming the message of all the prophets to be one and the same, and asserting that no distinction should be made amongst the prophets (Qur'an, 3, 84); Ibn Arabi adds: "Thus He gave me all the Signs in this Sign" (Illuminations (Morris), 379). Since the word for "sign" is the same as that for "verse" (*ayah*), this can also be taken to mean that all revealed verses are implicitly contained in this verse which establishes the universality and unity of the essence of the religious message, despite the outward differentiation of its formal expression.

This last point is clearly implied in another account of a spiritual ascent, in which Ibn Arabi encountered the Prophet Muhammad amidst a group of other prophets and is asked by him: "What was it that made you consider us as many?" To which Ibn Arabi replies: "Precisely (the different scriptures and teachings) we took (from you)" (Ascension, 75).

Implicit in the Prophet's question is the intrinsic unity of all the revelations. As to the manner in which the extrinsic differences are to be reconciled, one observes in the *Futuhat* a more explicit expression of this principle of inner unity residing at the heart of outward diversity. Ibn Arabi quotes the verse (42, 13) which affirms that the Law with which Muhammad is charged is the same as that with which Noah, Abraham, Moses, and Jesus were charged; then he quotes from another verse, mentioning further prophets, and concluding: "Those are they whom God has guided, so follow their guidance" (6, 90).

Ibn Arabi then adds: "This is the path that brings together every prophet and messenger. It is the performance of religion, scattering not concerning it and coming together in it" (Path, 303).

It would appear that Ibn Arabi is suggesting here a distinction between religion as such, on the one hand, and such and such a religion, on the other; it is religion as such that warrants the definite article (*al-*); and he emphasizes this essential, unifying dimension of religion by referring to, and elaborating on, the orthodox Islamic notion of the oneness of religion, as indicated by the chapter-heading of the most authoritative exoteric source of Prophetic sayings, the collection of Bukhari: this one path, writes Ibn Arabi,

> is that concerning which Bukhari wrote a chapter entitled, "The chapter on what has come concerning the fact that the religions of the prophets is one." He brought the article which makes the word "religion" definite, because all religion comes from God, even if some of the rulings are diverse. Everyone is commanded to perform the religion and to come together in it. . . . As for the rulings which are diverse, that is because of the Law which God assigned to each one of the messengers. He said, "To every one (of the Prophets) We have appointed a Law and a Way; and if God willed, He would have made you one nation" (5, 48). If He had done that, your revealed Laws would not be diverse, just as they are not diverse in the fact that you have been commanded to come together and to perform them (Path, 303).

Thus, on the basis of scriptural and exoteric orthodoxy, Ibn Arabi points to the substantial content of religion which both transcends and legitimizes the various revelations; the key criteria of this substance are centered on two elements: divine command and human response. In other words, however diverse may be the particular rulings pertaining to the different "religions," the substance or principle of these rulings remains the same: to submit to that which has been divinely instituted. The inner reality of religion is thus unfolded for the individual—of whatever religion—in the course of his submission to God and the practice of the worship enjoined upon him. One recalls the saying above: the prayers are five and they are fifty. It is neither the number of prayers nor indeed the form of worship that constitutes the substance of religion, the "necessary Word"; rather, it is the very fact that the worship ordained is of divine origin, and therefore leads to or "in-tends" the divine, that constitutes the essence of religion as such, and cannot therefore be the exclusive prerogative of such and such a religion.

One might add here that Ibn Arabi's conception of the necessary and immutable Word dovetails with the fundamental principle enshrined in the following Quranic verse: "And We never sent a messenger save with the language of his folk, that he might make the message clear for them" (14, 4). The message—the necessary Word—is one; the "languages" are many. Needless to say, the distinction in question is not to be understood as relating to a merely linguistic difference with identical semantic content, but rather, by "language" should be understood the whole gamut of factors—spiritual, psychological, cultural, and linguistic—that go to make the message of the supra-formal Truth intelligible to a given human collectivity. Herein, indeed, lies an important aspect of the message conveyed by Ibn Arabi's *Fusus al-Hikam*: the nature of the jewel (Revelation) is shaped according to the receptivity—conceptual, volitive, affective—of the bezel (*fass*, sing. of *fusus*)—the particular human collectivity addressed by the Revelation.

The very real differences of conception, orientation, and ritual as exist between the religions—taking this word now in its common usage—are not ignored in this perspective; rather, one is urged to submit entirely to the form of one's own religion even while recognizing its inevitable particularity and hence relativity; therefore for Ibn Arabi there is no substantial contradiction between following the dictates of one's own "way"—in terms of which certain things may be forbidden—and accepting the intrinsic validity of another "way" which permits those same things. It is important also to make it clear that recognizing the validity of other ways by no means entails the belief that these ways are equal to the Islamic *Shari'ah*. In many places Ibn Arabi exalts the Quranic revelation above all others, but he does so in a nuanced manner, making it clear that the historical appearance of Islam (or: the final revelation of the one religion, "Islam," in the sense of universal submission) did not nullify the efficacy of the earlier religions (or: the earlier revelations of this one religion); the commonly held view in Islamic exoterism, that Islam "abrogated"—in the sense of annulled or invalidated—all other religions is thus rejected; for him, Islam's "abrogation" (*naskh*) of other religions means that Islam takes precedence over them, it "supersedes" them, in the literal sense of "sitting above" them. And, in a brilliant dialectical stroke, he transforms the whole doctrine of abrogation from being a basis for the rejection of other religions into a decisive argument for the validity of the other religions: the necessity of believing in the validity of pre-Quranic revelations is one of the proofs of the pre-eminence of Islam:

> All the revealed religions [*shara'i'*] are lights. Among these religions, the revealed religion of Muhammad is like the light of the sun among the lights of the stars. When the sun appears, the lights of the stars are hidden, and their lights are included in the light of the sun. Their being hidden is like the abrogation of the other revealed religions that takes place through Muhammad's revealed religion. Nevertheless, they do in fact exist, just as the existence of the lights of the stars is actualized. This explains why we have been required in our all-inclusive religion to have faith in the truth of all the messengers and all the revealed religions. They are not rendered null [*batil*] by abrogation—that is the opinion of the ignorant (Imaginal, 125).

In other words, following the dictates of Islam and believing it to be the most complete religion can coexist with an awareness that the other religions retain their enlightening function and their spiritual efficacy for their adherents. The very real differences of conception, orientation, and ritual as exist between the religions are not ignored in this perspective; rather, one is urged to submit entirely to the form of one's own religion even while recognizing its inevitable particularity and hence relativity; thus for Ibn Arabi there is no substantial contradiction between following the dictates of one's own "way"—in terms of which certain things may be forbidden—and accepting the intrinsic validity of another "way" which permits those same things.

He illustrates this point by way of recounting the Quranic story of how Moses, as a baby, was made by God to refuse the milk of all but his own mother; by this means she was eventually reunited with her son. Ibn Arabi recounts the story, and then adds the above-quoted verse relating to the fact that each community is given a particular path (*shir'a*) and way (*minhaj*) by God. He continues by saying that the milk signifies that "way" which provides the "sustenance for the law-abiding servant, just as the branch of a tree feeds only from its root. Thus, what is forbidden in one Law is permitted in another, from the formal standpoint" (Bezels, 255).

To draw out somewhat the meaning of this imagery: the fact that it was only his mother's milk that could nourish Moses did not signify that the milk of other mothers was not nutritious; so, the fact that one's own "way" satisfies one's own religious needs does not signify that other "ways" are intrinsically incapable of providing for the religious needs of their own respective communities.

Elsewhere, Ibn Arabi writes of the ultimate convergence of the roots of all the revealed religions, despite the fact that rulings of the religions diverge:

> [M]essengers were sent according to the diversity of the times and the variety of the situations. Each of them confirmed the truth of the others. None of them differed whatsoever in the roots by which they were supported and of which they spoke, even if rulings differed. . . . The governing property belonged to the time and the situation, just as God has declared: "To every one of you We have appointed a right way and a revealed law" (5, 48). So the roots coincided, without disagreement on anything (Imaginal, 134).

Even though in this passage the "governing property" of the diversity of revealed religions is said to be "time" and "situation," elsewhere Ibn Arabi gives primacy to the diversity of divine relationships (or Names or Qualities) as being the immediate cause of the diversity of revealed religions. But there is no contradiction here, for each apparent cause—diverse religions, divine relationships, states, times, movements, attentivenesses, goals, self-disclosures—is itself an effect of a prior cause which leads back, finally, to itself again.[21]

Again, one comes back to the essential distinction between what is substantial or necessary, and what is accidental: it is only in relation to particularities—by definition accidental—that differences exist, whilst the substance relates to that process by which those particularities are channeled in the direction of the universal, the intended essence of worship and orientation; or: the process by

---

[21] For this complex circle of interlocking causes and effects that closes in on itself perpetually, see Imaginal, chapter 9, entitled "Diversity of Belief," pp. 137-160.

which the relativities attendant upon human existence are mitigated, overcome, and finally reabsorbed into the absoluteness of pure Being. This leads to the third point.

(iii) The logical concomitant of the view that all religious paths are validated by their divine origin and goal is that this divine element—as Essence—transcends the religious forms emerging therefrom and leading thereto. In other words, the distinction between religious form and divine Essence at one and the same time validates the form as a means of access to the Essence whilst also highlighting the inevitable relativity of all such forms in the face of the Essence.

Such a position flows naturally from the perspective expounded in Part I of the chapter, concerning the absolute transcendence of the Essence and the consequent necessity of referring to it in apophatic terms. It is important to place this discussion in the light of the distinction between the "gold brick" of sanctified, universal consciousness, and the "silver brick" that symbolizes submission to the particular Law: as it was expressed in reference to the station of "proximity," the saint, even while being necessarily a "follower" of a revealed Law, has access to a mode of consciousness that is not bound by the specificity of the Law, a mode of consciousness that flows from the assimilation in depth of the distinction between form and essence. It should not be forgotten that this consciousness is not the prerogative of the saints to the exclusion of the prophets: for, within the very soul of the Prophet, there is a dimension of sanctity which is open to universal Reality, whereas his consciousness *qua* prophet pertains to the particularities of the specific mission with which he is charged. The "Khidr" of Moses' own soul teaches him of the distinction between form and essence, and of the transcendence of the essence of reality over the forms—legal and phenomenal—by which it is at once manifested and veiled. In regard to the overt application of this principle to the religions themselves as so many delimited forms falling short of the undelimited Essence, it is to Ibn Arabi's poetry that one should look in the first instance.

In discussing the nature of essential, divine Truth/Reality, the *haqiqah* personified by the beautiful maiden Nizam, he writes: "She has baffled everyone who is learned in our religion, every student of the Psalms of David, every Jewish doctor, and every Christian priest" (Tarjuman, 49). In the commentary written by himself to reveal the symbolism of his poems—and thereby rebut the charges that they were nothing but scandalous romantic and erotic outpourings—the following explanation is given: "All the sciences comprised in the four Books (Qur'an, Psalms, Torah, and Gospel) point only to the Divine Names and are incapable of solving a question that concerns the Divine Essence" (Tarjuman, 52).

Insofar as the books are divinely revealed, they implicitly contain the Truth, but insofar as they are forms of the Truth, and thus "other than" that of which they are so many projections, they must be distinguished from the supra-formal Essence; and nothing pertaining to the formal order can "solve a question concerning the Divine Essence," because it is only in terms of spiritual realization and the complete identification of knowledge and being, subject and object, that the Essence is attainable, and "questions" concerning it are effectively "solved," inasmuch as all possible mental construction is "dissolved" within pure Being. Any conceptions of the Essence, as already seen, will always remain inadequate to the Essence in itself, because they are incommensurable with it, even if they be rooted in religious doctrine and revealed books: as conceptions they always remain distinct from what is being conceived, the separation between subject and object is maintained, and the Essence thus remains forever unknowable in the framework of this dualism which is inextricably tied up with the domain of form.

While the gnostic grasps the exclusive reality of the Essence, he is nonetheless—or for this very reason—able to say:

> My heart has become capable of every form: it is a pasture for gazelles and a convent for Christian monks,
> And a temple for idols and the pilgrim's Ka'ba and the tables of the Torah and the book of the Koran.
> I follow the religion of Love: whatever way Love's camels take, that is my religion and my faith (Tarjuman, 52).

One is reminded here of the symbolism in the station of proximity, where the gazelle, as a beautiful form, is revealed as a message of love which ultimately is one with the Lover and the Beloved; in the lines above, the religions are likewise seen as so many forms of the supra-formal, whose essential nature is infinite Beatitude; thus, the knowledge that only the Essence is absolutely Real is accompanied by the contemplative appreciation of all sacred forms as aspects or modes of this Essence which both infinitely transcends them—otherwise they would not be differentiable from the Essence or from each other—and immanently pervades them—failing which they would be deprived of all positive quality; they could not be lovable: they could not even exist.

This witnessing of the Divine in the diverse forms of religion can be seen as a fundamental aspect of what was earlier referred to as the heart of the "Muhammadan," which witnesses the Divine "withness" in every moment and in every form. The "Muhammadan" is then not delimited by the terms of any specific revelation, but is receptive to the divine manifestation in all forms of revelation, for he

> gathers together through his level every call that has been dispersed among the messengers. . . . So the Muhammadan friend does not stop with a specific revelation. . . . [T]hose things about which nothing was said, and those things concerning which nothing was sent down in Muhammad's Law indicating that it should be avoided, he does not avoid it if it was brought by any revelation to any of the prophets (Path, 377-378).

Despite being bound by the specific prescriptions of Islamic Law, the consciousness of the "Muhammadan" is not restricted by any specific conceptions of God; rather, seeing all revelations as branches of the one religion—"Islam" as universal "submission" rather than as particular Law—all the diverse conceptions of God posited within these revelations are assimilated as so many self-revelations of God, so many manifestations of the divine Beauty.

Thus he is able to accept aspects of God deriving from other revelations even if these same aspects be absent from the particular spiritual universe disclosed by the narrowly defined "Islamic" revelation. In terms of universally-defined Islam, however, all previous revelations are assimilated as "Islamic"—a position implicitly contained in the Qur'an itself, where pre-Muhammadan prophets are defined as "Muslim." The key criterion here is that the "Muhammadan friend" or perfected saint "does not avoid it if it was brought by any revelation to any of the prophets." In this sense, revelation is conceived as a unique phenomenon comprising multiple facets: underlying Ibn Arabi's position is the idea that one must not be veiled from the unicity of the principle of revelation by the variety of its possible modes; rather, one should recognize God in all revelations and thus give Him "His due," whilst also personally "gathering the fruit" of this knowledge; whence the following recommendation to study other faiths:

> He who counsels his own soul should investigate during his life in this world, all doctrines concerning God. He should learn from whence each possessor of a doctrine affirms the validity of his doctrine. Once its validity has been affirmed for him in the specific mode in which it is correct for him who upholds it, then he should support it in the case of him who believes in it. He should not deny it or reject it, for he will gather its fruit on the Day of Visitation. . . . So turn your attention to what we have mentioned and put it into practice! Then you will give the Divinity its due. . . . For God is exalted high above entering under delimitation. He cannot be tied down by one form rather than another. From here you will come to know the all-inclusiveness of felicity for God's creatures and the all-embracingness of the mercy which covers everything (Path, 355-356).

Two important relationships need to be emphasized here: first the all-embracing Mercy of God is connected with the very diversity of His self-revelation; and second, the capacity to recognize God in these diverse modes is related to the spiritual "fruit" which will be gathered in the Hereafter.

As regards the first point, Ibn Arabi refers to the conception of God as found within the faiths as the "God created in belief" as opposed to the intrinsic reality of the Divine which transcends all conceptual bounds. Despite the inevitable relativity attendant upon the former, one may nonetheless observe both its providential character—being a relativity willed by the Divine—and its merciful nature: being itself the first object of the existentiating Mercy,[22] this "God created in belief" in turn exerts a merciful attraction upon the receptive heart of the believer: "Since God is the root of every diversity in beliefs . . . everyone will end up with mercy. For it is He who created them (the diverse beliefs)" (Path, 388). So the various revelations, along with their respective concomitant beliefs, constitute so many ways by which God invites His creatures to participate in His infinitely merciful nature.

Turning now to the second relationship—concerning the modalities of this participation—the beatific vision experienced by the believer in the Hereafter will conform to the nature of his conception and attitude towards God in the here-

---

[22] "[A]fter the Mercy Itself, 'the god created in belief' is the first recipient of Mercy" (Bezels, pp. 224-225).

below; thus, there is a direct correspondence between the universal recognition of God in all faiths and the experience of paradisal Bliss. This is clearly asserted by Ibn Arabi in the course of describing the "share" accorded to the highest saint: he enjoys the felicity which is the fruit of all forms of belief held by the faithful of the different religions, because he recognized their correspondence to real aspects of the divine nature (Seal, 54). This direct and plenary participation in the felicity that is contained within the forms of beliefs concerning God is thus seen to be a reality already in this life, as a prefiguration of the higher celestial states.

In a famous passage in the *Fusus* Ibn Arabi counsels all believers to guard against particularism, referring to the *hadith* in which the believers, on the Day of Judgment, refuse to acknowledge God except in the form corresponding to their beliefs:

> Beware of being bound up by a particular religion and rejecting others as unbelief! If you do that you will fail to obtain a great benefit. Nay, you will fail to obtain the true knowledge of the reality. Try to make yourself a Prime Matter for all forms of religious belief. God is greater and wider than to be confined to one particular religion to the exclusion of others. For He says: "To whichever direction you turn, there surely is the Face of God" (2, 115) (Sufism, 254).

In this famous passage Ibn Arabi counsels all believers to guard against particularism; it should be noted that this counsel resonates with a Quranic warning to the same effect: "And they say: None entereth Paradise unless he be a Jew or a Christian. These are their own desires. Say: Bring your proof if ye are truthful. Nay, but whosoever surrendereth his purpose to God while doing good, his reward is with his Lord; and there shall be no fear upon them, neither shall they grieve" (2, 112).

Ibn Arabi, then, is but elaborating upon the principle of universality clearly implied in this verse; and his counsel should also be seen in relation to a saying of the Prophet regarding the vision of God on the day of Resurrection. This is a saying, found in the collection of Muslim, according to which God will appear to the believers on the day of Resurrection and proclaim Himself as their Lord. The believers deny Him, and though He "transmutes" Himself (*yatahawwal*) into different forms, they persist in denial until He manifests Himself to them according to a sign by which they will recognize Him; in other words, according to the forms of their religious beliefs on earth (Path, 38).

Implicit reference to the principle of this divine self-transformation and limited beliefs is clear in the passage which precedes his advice to believers not to remain bound up by the forms of their beliefs:

> Generally speaking, each man necessarily sticks to a particular creed (*'aqida*) concerning his Lord. He always goes back to his Lord through his particular creed and seeks God therein. Such a man positively recognizes God only when He manifests Himself to him in the form recognized by his creed. But when He manifests Himself in other forms he denies Him and seeks refuge from Him. In so doing he behaves in an improper way towards Him in fact, even while believing that he is acting politely towards Him. Thus a believer who sticks to his particular creed believes only in a god that he has subjectively

posited in his own mind. God in all particular creeds is dependent upon the subjective act of positing on the part of the believers (Sufism, 254).

The degree to which the universality of religious belief and knowledge is realized is then established as an important criterion of spiritual preeminence, both in this world and the next: those who know God best now are the ones who will most clearly see Him on the day of Resurrection.

Behold how the degrees of men concerning their knowledge of God correspond exactly to their degrees concerning the seeing of God on the day of Resurrection (Sufism, 254).

Thus, Ibn Arabi urges the believer to make himself receptive to all forms of religious belief, both for the sake of objective veracity—that is, "the true knowledge of the reality" that God is immanent within all forms of His Self-revelation—and in the interests of one's posthumous condition—the "great benefit" that accrues to the soul in the Hereafter in proportion to the universality of knowledge of God attained on earth.

It now remains to be seen how the *'arif* apprehends the Divine residing in the conceptions and forms attributed to it in the different faiths. Ibn Arabi's answer to this question is oriented more towards intellectual or principial considerations rather than going into the concrete modalities of spiritual assimilation or intuition of the divine contents of the different religions. It has already been seen how Ibn Arabi recommends that one investigate all doctrines concerning God, the sources of these doctrines, and their relationship to the needs and orientations of those possessing them, in order to judge of their veracity and efficacy. In addition to this, there is a more objective criterion that stems from the very fact of the universal ontological poverty: everything depends on God, being poor in relation to Him, and thus can but worship Him, objectively speaking, even if the subjective intention and focus of this worship be on something that is—in appearance only—"other than God," as is the case with polytheistic worship. This point is made with reference to the following Quranic verse: "Thy Lord has decreed that you shall not worship any but Him" (17, 23). Ibn Arabi interprets this as a descriptive statement rather than as a normative injunction, God being "identical with everything toward which there is poverty and which is worshipped" (Illuminations (Chittick), 319).

In other words, the idol-worshipper cannot, objectively, worship anything other than God, since only God can be the real recipient of worship; his "sin" resides, on the one hand in detaching the object of worship from its divine source, and on the other hand, in himself instituting this worship instead of submitting to a divine dispensation ordaining it as legitimate. But this cannot detract from the truth that "in every object of worship it is God who is worshipped" (Bezels, 78).

This brings one back to the decisive criterion of provenance: if objects "other than God" are established by God Himself, as objects of worship, in the context of His Self-revelation, then these objects are spiritually invested with the properties of Divinity and are legitimated as authentic religious forms. This is the import of God's words addressed to Ibn Arabi in a visionary experience during which he entered a spring of milk (signifying spiritual knowledge): "He who prostrates himself to other than God seeking nearness to God and obeying God will be felicitous and attain deliverance, but he who prostrates himself to other than God without God's command seeking nearness will be wretched" (Path, 365).

It is in this light that the *'arif* is able to discern that, whatever names be given to the "gods" as objects of worship, these are but the theophanies of the one Divinity:

> The perfect gnostic is one who regards every object of worship as a manifestation of God in which He is worshipped. They call it a god, though its proper name might be stone, wood, (etc.) . . . Although that might be its particular name, Divinity presents a level that causes the worshipper to imagine that it is his object of worship. In reality, this level is the Self- manifestation of God to the consciousness of the worshipper . . . in this particular mode of manifestation (Bezels, 247).

The concrete mode of spiritual assimilation of the divine substance in religious forms must be regarded as forming the basis of these principial considerations. This mode, involving as it does the deepest levels of spiritual intuition, can be alluded to symbolically rather than communicated definitively; implicit in Ibn Arabi's approach is that this mode of assimilation flows as a consequence of the essential intuition of the Divine in its supra-formal reality: having concrete knowledge of this transcendent Essence, its immanent presence within forms is unveiled. One again returns to this fundamental metaphysical principle.

Since this mode intrinsically involves the imponderables of spiritual intuition, only certain of its extrinsic aspects are susceptible of communication; in this domain, Ibn Arabi does not write in detail about the different religions and their specific conceptions of the Divine; what he does communicate, however, in symbolic terms, is the resolution of the apparent paradox that the same unique, objective Divinity can be represented by a variety of conceptual and formal expressions, often mutually exclusive and contradictory. Ibn Arabi addresses this question by means of the saying of Junayd, mentioned earlier, to the effect that water takes on the color of the cup. Applying this principle to the diversity of beliefs and degrees of knowledge of God, he writes:

> He who sees the water only in the cup judges it by the property of the cup. But he who sees it simple and noncompound knows that the shapes and colors in which it becomes manifest are the effect of the containers. Water remains in its own definition and reality, whether in the cup or outside it. Hence it never loses the name "water" (Path, 341-342).

In this image, the cup symbolizes the form of the "preparedness" of a particular belief, water symbolizing the divine revelation; water in itself is undifferentiated and unique, whilst undergoing apparent change of form and color by virtue of the accidental forms of the receptacles in which it is poured. The one who knows "water" as it is in itself, that is, the substance of revelation as such, will recognize it in receptacles other than his own, and will be able to judge all such receptacles according to their content, rather than be misled into judging the content according to the accidental properties of the container.

To accept God fully, therefore, means to accept His presence and reality in all forms of His Self-expression, while to limit Him to one's own particular form of belief is tantamount to denying Him:

> He who delimits Him denies Him in other than his own delimitation. . . . But he who frees Him from every delimitation never denies Him. On the contrary, he acknowledges Him in every form within which He undergoes self-transmutation (Path, 339-340).

Nonetheless, the ordinary believer who may thus "deny" God by adhering exclusively to his own belief is not punished because of this implicit denial: as seen above, since God is Himself the "root of every diversity in beliefs . . . everyone will end up with mercy," and also, in terms of the water/cup image: the water in the cup, however delimited it may be by the container, remains water nonetheless, hence the ordinary believer benefits from his possession of the truth. Even if this truth be limited by the particularities of his own conception, it adequately conveys the nature of its intrinsic reality; thus, one returns to the notion that all "religions" are true by virtue of the absoluteness of their content, while each is relative due to the particular nature of its form.

The only "punishment" conceivable for the implicit denial constituted by exclusively identifying God with one's own belief is the deprivation of that plenitude of bliss that flows from the unrestricted beatific vision which is the fruit of full recognition of God in all His forms. Thus, the inner reality of the affirmation of God is bliss—whether this be conceived in celestial/eschatological mode or in terms of spiritual experience, *hic et nunc*, which prefigures that mode: to the extent that one recognizes and affirms the Divine, to that very extent one will be assimilated to the bliss proper to the divine nature. Thus, one rejoins the fundamental principle established earlier: true Being is "the finding of the Real in ecstasy." Applying this principle to the universality of religious belief, one can say that in proportion to one's capacity to "find" God in the forms of His Self-revelation—the various religions—one will experience the spiritual bliss which is the inner content of all the diverse modes in which the Essence communicates itself as form and in which forms return to the Essence, this very movement of return constituting what Ibn Arabi calls the "religion of Love" or religion as such, which both transcends and comprises all its particular facets.

# CHAPTER 3

# MEISTER ECKHART: The *Geburt*

The Birth of the Word in the soul: this sums up the essence of Eckhart's spiritual teachings. This Birth is at once the transcendent summit of realization and the criterion of all other spiritual practices and attitudes. To understand the meaning, nature, and consequences of this Birth is then essential for a proper appreciation of Eckhart's teachings on transcendent realization.

These teachings, as found in his sermons, are distinguished from his more scholastic Latin treatises by their direct relevance to the spiritual life in its immediate and concrete aspects. In these sermons, Eckhart all but dispenses with elementary religious teachings, which are employed as so many bases for advancing towards their higher and more profound spiritual dimensions; what is externally "given" by the formal religion is thus transmuted into an internally experienced reality for the supra-formal spirit. It is because Eckhart is so explicit on the modalities of this ascent from the formal to the essential that his sermons are a particularly valuable source for exploring themes of transcendence.

If it was necessary in the previous chapter on Ibn Arabi to sift the purely vertical and transcendent material from the horizontal "spread" of his doctrine, in the case of Eckhart one is faced with an almost opposite problem: virtually all of his sermons are of a "transcendental" nature, being so many imperious and authoritative summons to realize transcendence *hic et nunc*.

This emphasis on the concrete experience of transcendence—rigorously and relentlessly pressed home—helps to explain the audacious formulations for which Eckhart was attacked by the religious authorities of his day. One of the secondary aims of this chapter will be to elucidate the important relationship in Eckhart's perspective between the highest realization and the antinomian, elliptical, and paradoxical expressions thereof, expressions which flow out of the gulf that separates all non-transcendent realities from the One; and it is union with the One which is considered not just as the highest beatitude, but as the only beatitude that there is, properly—or "absolutely"—speaking.

In relation to this "highest" which alone "is," all lesser forms of happiness, along with the acts leading thereto and the contexts presupposed by these acts, are described in strikingly negative terms: all that is not this highest good is by that very token a kind of evil in relation to it. When Eckhart goes so far as to say that ordinary prayer for "this" or "that" is a prayer for evil, it is easy to see why conservative guardians of Catholic orthodoxy had difficulty in distinguishing between dialectical ellipsis and heretical extravagance.

This chapter is divided into three parts; the first will concentrate on the metaphysical doctrine of transcendence, with much of the discussion taken up by Eckhart's distinction between the level of the Godhead and that of the Trinitarian Divinity; the second, dealing with the spiritual aspects of the path to the realization of transcendence, comprises two sections: the first examines the mode of transcending virtue as conventionally conceived and practised, and the second focusses on the experience of the *Geburt*, the "Birth" of the Word in the soul, and the *Durchbruch*, the "Breakthrough" or union with the Absolute; and the final part will be concerned with the "existential return," the manner of being proper to the one in whom the "Birth" and "Breakthrough" have taken place.

The principal source for this chapter is the most recent complete translation of Eckhart's sermons, that by Maurice O'Connell Walshe;[1] all references to this work will be made simply by the volume number followed by the page number. One other English translation of the sermons, that by C. De B. Evans,[2] will be referred to in those places where Eckhart's meaning is rendered more intelligible by it.

## Part I: Doctrine of the Transcendent Absolute

### 1. Beyond the Notion of God

The first point that should be made in connection with Eckhart's view on the status of doctrine is that he firmly rejects the notion that God can be circumscribed by any concepts or descriptions. He repeatedly emphasizes the necessarily apophatic nature of all "less inadequate" statements about God; whatever is positively attributed to Him is unavoidably and immeasurably short of the mark: "Whatever we say God is, He is not; what we do not say of Him, He is more truly than what we say He is" (I:237).

Nevertheless there are important aspects of this apophatic doctrine that are susceptible of communication, even if their main function is to clear the ground for, and enhance receptivity to, the higher and necessarily incommunicable nature of the Divine. Thus: "Whatever can be truly put into words must come from within, moved by its inner form: it must not come in from without, but out from within. It truly lives in the inmost part of the soul" (I:283).

If received opinion, "coming in from without," is not going to be "truly put into words," this is because its inner form is not alive in the soul: it is not realized there. Hence any verbal formulations, however technically accurate they may be, will not "truly" convey the reality in question; inner realization must come first, and then verbal expression deriving therefrom will effectively convey, if not the thing itself, then at least that aspect of the realization which is communicable.

But if verbal expression is thus predicated on realization, comprehension by the hearer is also dependent upon a degree of realization; for example, in discussing the deepest meaning of poverty—to be dealt with more fully in the final section of this chapter—Eckhart pleads with his listeners:

---

[1] *Meister Eckhart: Sermons & Treatises* (Vols. I-III), translated and edited by Maurice O'Connell Walshe, Element Books, Dorset, 1979.

[2] *Meister Eckhart* (Vols. I-II), C. De B. Evans, Watkins, London, 1947.

I beg you to be like this in order that you may understand this sermon: for by the eternal truth I tell you that unless you are like this truth we are about to speak of, it is not possible for you to follow me (II:269).

In other words, a particular mode of being is the prerequisite for understanding. Something "like" the poverty of which he is to speak is thus a kind of opening through which the meaning of profound poverty may enter the soul, and help bring to fruition that partial mode of poverty that is already existent and which prefigures, by its very intention, the complete or integral poverty in question here.

Effective communication, then, depends on the realization both of the speaker and the hearer—albeit in lesser degree for the latter. Also relevant here is the following statement: "He who has abandoned all his will savours my teaching and hears my words" (II:144).

This point will be elaborated further in Part III. Turning now to address directly the question of whether any particular conception or doctrine about the Absolute is either useful or necessary, Eckhart says categorically that all such conceptions, being incommensurable with the reality of the Absolute, must be excluded from consciousness if the highest realization—the Birth—is to be attained:

[T]he question arises, whether a man can find this birth in any things which, though divine, are yet brought in from without through the senses, such as any ideas about God being good, wise, compassionate, or anything the intellect can conceive in itself that is divine. . . . In fact, he cannot (I:39-40).

He adds that it is God who knows Himself in this Birth; and this principle implies that there is a necessary hiatus between all things creaturely—even though they be conceptions of the Divine—and the reality of the uncreated Absolute; to the extent that creaturely knowledge subsists in the soul, in that very measure God is excluded. The distinction between the extrinsic functions or "powers" of the created intellect and the intrinsic mode of the uncreated intellect within man will be dealt with in the next section; at this point, the relative aspect of all conceptions, *qua* human categories of thought, is being emphasized, in order to show the unbridgeable gap between created and uncreated knowledge.

Human conceptions of the essence of the Divine constitute so many veils over it; to think of it as good, just, wise, etc., is to project something of one's own understanding of these attributes onto That which transcends all such limitative attributions; even to attribute some kind of "nature" to the essence is to do it an injustice, since:

It is its nature to be without nature. To think of goodness or wisdom or power dissembles the essence and dims it in thought. The mere thought obscures essence (II:32).

That the essence comprises the intrinsic realities noetically intended by such conceptions is not being denied here; it is the mental understanding of, for example, goodness that veils the essence of this and all other positive realities; the essence, then, is not incompatible with goodness as such: rather, it is incompatible with the human thought which delimits and thus distorts the true nature of this goodness. If this may be said to constitute the subjective aspect of incommensurability between concept and reality, the objective counterpart, within the divine order itself, is found in the fact that any particular and thus distinctive attribute that is held to pertain to God is a specification which is transcended by the essence. Thus:

> For goodness and wisdom and whatever may be attributed to God are all admixtures to God's naked essence: for all admixture causes alienation from essence (II:39).

In regard to the relationship between doctrine and realization, then, it would appear that, far from positing as necessary any particular conception of the divine reality, Eckhart on the contrary emphasizes that the essential precondition for the highest realization is precisely the absence of any limiting conceptions, for the sake of a state of pure receptivity to the divine influx.

It would be misleading, however, to leave the matter there; for it appears that Eckhart is extolling, as the ideal starting-point for the highest realization, a complete ignorance—or absence—of all conceptions of God, while this is not exactly the case. This is an ignorance that is to be methodically precipitated, on the basis both of a clear understanding of the reasons for this spiritual necessity, and of a certain necessary knowledge of fundamental doctrine concerning religion. It would be more accurate to say that this ignorance is advocated exclusively to those already in possession of a preexisting set of ideas about God and also a way of life corresponding thereto; in other words, he takes it for granted that this knowledge—albeit relative and provisional—is present as a basis to be transcended by "ignorance."

This is clear from the following extract which comes after a declaration that "real union" can only take place when all images are absent from the soul; his words are meant, he says, only for the "good and perfected people" in whom dwell "the worthy life and lofty teachings of our Lord Jesus Christ. *They* must know that the very best and noblest attainment in this life is to be silent and let God work and speak within" (I:6, emphasis added).

Only those who have assimilated the "lofty teachings" of Christ should be taught of this necessity of ignorance; prior to the realization of union, then, aspirants thereto must have assimilated a certain degree of doctrine and, moreover, they must be "perfected" in their life of virtue deriving from this doctrine. So if Eckhart, at a higher stage in the spiritual life, and having transcendence in view, belittles and excludes all narrowly human conceptions as hindrances, this is only on the assumption that these same conceptions have been comprehended, at the level appropriate to them; the level in question being the human individual in the face of the teachings revealed by "our Lord Jesus Christ." Therefore, it is fair to conclude that, for Eckhart, the integral assimilation of the basic data of revelation constitutes the indispensable qualification for starting the journey along the path towards union, even if the next stage of this path calls for an unknowing and a "forgetting," in order to transcend, not revelation as such, but one's own inescapably limited grasp thereof; for the transcendent aim is to be one with the essential content and source of revelation itself, the Word. Union with the source of revelation thus presupposes an emptiness of all conceptions, even those derived from the data of revelation itself.

These points will be dealt with in more experiential and methodic terms in Part II. At this juncture the central conceptual distinction between God and the Godhead needs to be addressed.

## 2. From God to Godhead

A useful starting point is Eckhart's statement about the limits to which the natural intellect can go; this is illustrated by means of Aristotle's conception of the angels gazing on the "naked being of God":

> This pure naked being is called by Aristotle a "something." That is the highest that Aristotle ever declared concerning natural science, and no master can say greater things unless prompted by the Holy Ghost. I say, however, that the noble man is not satisfied with the being that the angels cognize without form and depend on without means—he is satisfied with nothing less than the solitary One (II:52-53).

In other words, Aristotle, here personifying all purely natural science, goes only so far as the level of Being; Eckhart, evidently fulfilling the condition—inspiration by the Holy Ghost—for saying a "greater" thing, affirms the transcendence of this level by the "solitary One," which thus implicitly stands for what is "beyond" Being. Elsewhere, he says that "Being is the first Name" (II:244); and this can be readily understood in relation to the "first effusion" or self-manifestation, by which God is rendered "Father": "The first outburst and the first effusion God runs out in is His fusion into his Son, a process which in turn reduces him to Father" (Evans, I:93).

God *qua* Godhead is thus neither Father nor Son, taking these in their aspect of personal affirmation; but in His first outpouring, God becomes intelligible as the Principle of all subsequent manifestation—divine and creaturely; here, the Godhead can be referred to as "Beyond-Being," Father as the Principle is the level of Being, and Son as the immediate source of universal manifestation, is the Logos "by which was made all that was made."

This interpretation is supported by the following:

> God is a word, an unspoken word. . . . Where God is, He utters this Word—where He is not, He does not speak. God is spoken and unspoken. The Father is a speaking work and the Son is the speech at work (I:177).

At the plane of Being—"where God is"—the Word is spoken, whilst on the plane of Beyond-Being—"where He is not"—there is silence, no-thing. That this does not mean "nothing" in the sense of the negation of Being, but rather nothing as That which surpasses and comprises all "things" as well as Being itself, is clear from the fact that Eckhart says: "God is spoken *and* unspoken." The "unspoken" therefore is not equated with nothingness pure and simple, but rather with that dimension of God which transcends the realm of Being and existents: the Father being the "work" of God that speaks, the Son being the speech of God that works; the first pertaining to the articulation of the principle of supra-manifest potentiality at the level of Being, the second relating to the principle whereby particular possibilities are transcribed from that level into the domain of universal manifestation.

The idea of a principle or a reality that transcends the Trinity, conceived as a hypostatic determination of that reality, would certainly have been problematic to many of Eckhart's listeners; but he clearly establishes the unity of essence by which the three Persons are but one God, even while asserting the transcendence of the Essence in relation to the distinctive affirmation of the Persons as such. On the first point:

> For anyone who could grasp distinctions without number and quantity, a hundred would be as one. Even if there were a hundred Persons in the Godhead, a man who could distinguish without number and quantity would perceive them only as one God. . . . [He] knows that three Persons are one God (I:217).

Eckhart seems to be expressing here the possibility of making distinction without the concomitant of separation: the three Persons are distinct on the outward plane, without this implying mutual exclusion on the inward plane; each is identified with the other two by virtue of its inward identity with the Essence, while being distinct from the others by virtue of its mode or function which deploys the Essence, without this implying any numerical or material differentiation from it. There is here the application of a principle which plays a role of the utmost importance in Eckhart's perspective, and to which discussion will return repeatedly: everything pertaining to the spiritual realm is inclusive and unitive by nature, whilst matter is by its nature exclusive and implies separative particularity; the more spiritual a thing is, the more inclusive and thus universal it is, and the more material a thing is, the more it excludes other things by the very rigidity of its specific contours.

As for the second point, the transcendence of the Essence, Eckhart speaks clearly on the basis of his own spiritual experience when he says, in the course of describing the "citadel" of the soul:

> [S]o truly one and simple is this citadel, so mode and power transcending is this solitary One, that neither power nor mode can gaze into it, nor even God Himself! . . . God never looks in there for one instant, in so far as He exists in modes and in the properties of His Persons. . . . [T]his One alone lacks all mode and property. . . . [F]or God to see inside it would cost Him all His divine names and personal properties: all these He must leave outside. . . . But only in so far as He is one and indivisible (can He do this): in this sense He is neither Father, Son, nor Holy Ghost and yet is a something which is neither this nor that (I:76).

It should be noticed that the "citadel" in the soul is described in terms identical to those relating to what was beyond the "bare being" attained by means of "natural" science: the "solitary One" is the Absolute that is both transcendent and immanent, residing in the innermost essence—the "citadel"—of the soul as well as surpassing the level of Being, the plane presupposed by the modes, properties, and names of God.

That the citadel is here described as a "place" which cannot be entered or even "peeped into" by any but the pure Godhead leads one to the conclusion that Eckhart's conceptual distinction between God *qua* Trinity and God *qua* Godhead could only have been the fruit of a concrete realization of this Godhead; and it is exclusively in the light of that transcendent level that the relativity of the Trinitarian hypostasis is discernible. Elsewhere, one finds another daring formulation which is fully explicable only in terms of the above distinction: "Intellect forces its way in, dissatisfied with goodness or wisdom or God Himself. . . . [I]t is as little satisfied with God as with a stone or a tree" (I:298).

One should understand that the "God" with which the intellect is not satisfied is the aspect of Divinity that is intelligible as the immediate principle of creation, at the level of Being, as opposed to the Godhead with which alone the intellect is "satisfied" because it is its own essence. In an extremely important passage this distinction is clearly enunciated:

> While I yet stood in my first cause, I had no God and was my own cause. . . . I wanted nothing and desired nothing, for I was bare being and the knower of myself in the enjoyment of truth. . . . I was free of God and all things. But when I left my free will behind and received my created being, then I had a God. For before there were creatures, God was not "God": He was That which He was. But when creatures came into existence and received their created being, then God was not "God" in Himself—He was "God" in creatures (II:271).

The "I" in question in the first paragraph can clearly be identified with the Self as Essence or Godhead and not to Eckhart's personal self, or his "created being."[3] The term "bare being" is here to be identified with unconditioned Being or "Beyond Being," in keeping with the above points.[4] Eckhart as Self "had no God" because there was no creaturely "I" over whom an uncreated God held sway: in the Godhead there are no such distinctions. But at the stage of acquiring created being, the existentiated individual is subject to the transcendent Divinity as the absolute principle of his relative existence: thus God is distinctly definable as such only in relation to the existence of creatures. In Himself, God is neither transcendent nor immanent, acquiring these extrinsic aspects only in regard to creatures: to say He becomes "God in creatures" means not just that He is immanent within them, but also transcendent in regard to them, thus God "in relation to" creatures as well as "in creatures."

Eckhart continues:

> God, inasmuch as He is "God," is not the supreme goal of creatures. . . . [I]f a fly had reason and could intellectually plumb the eternal abysm of God's being out of which it

---

[3] The striking correspondence to the Vedantin *Sat-Chit-Ananda* and Ibn Arabi's *Wujud wijdan al-haqq fi'l-wajd* should be noted in the phrase "I was bare being and the knower of myself in the enjoyment of truth": this will be commented upon further in Chapter 4.

[4] Evans' translation has the more appropriate term "conditionless being" (I:218).

came, we would have to say that God, with all that makes Him "God" would be unable to fulfill and satisfy that fly! (II:271).

Here, one can also understand the "eternal abysm of God's being" as implicitly referring to Beyond-Being: hence, if the intellect is capable of conceiving of this transcendent Essence, it must be because it is not other than it, and therefore it cannot be satisfied or fulfilled by anything other than, or below it; and "God," defined as such in relation to creatures, is below this Essence of Godhead, hence the dissatisfaction of the intellect. This can be seen as a metaphysical version of the classical ontological proof of God: whereas for St. Anselm, the reality of God is proven by the human capacity for conceiving Him, for Eckhart, the relativity of God *qua* Creator is proven by the intellectual capacity for conceiving the Essence, which surpasses the level of being proper to that aspect of God; and this intellectual capacity, in turn, proves or expresses the spiritual capacity for realizing identity with that Essence. This aspect of realization anticipates the discussion in Part II; here, it is important to further substantiate this manner of interpreting Eckhart's key distinction between God and Godhead in terms of the ontological distinction between Being and Beyond-Being. In focussing and commenting upon relevant extracts pertaining to this question, further aspects of the meaning of the concept "Beyond-Being" will be brought to light.

There are many sentences dealing with the supra-ontological aspect of the Divine; what follows is an attempt to select and comment upon the most important ones. First, one may cite this:

> God and Godhead are as different as heaven and earth. . . . God becomes and unbecomes.
> . . . God works, the Godhead does no work: there is nothing for it to do, there is no activity in it. It never peeped at any work (II:80).

Insofar as there is activity or manifestation on the part of God, in that measure there is change, and change implies a "becoming," which in turn implies an "unbecoming"; only the non-acting, thus non-changing, Godhead transcends all process of becoming and unbecoming, remaining eternally what it is, and is thus as different from God as heaven is from earth: just as the earth manifests impermanence and change in contrast to the permanence and immutability of heaven, so the acting God manifests, and by this very manifestation is distinguished from the non-acting, unmanifest Godhead which nonetheless comprises within itself the principle of all being and manifestation. Here again, one observes that the spiritual principle of inclusive unicity is not contradicted by the affirmation of manifest diversity. Rather, there emerges a hierarchical vision of the planes of reality, intrinsically one, but extrinsically ordered according to the degree of manifestation: for even though heaven be "permanent" in relation to earth, it is in its turn subordinated to its principle, God, thus representing a degree of relative impermanence in relation to the principle of Being; and this principle in turn can be viewed in its aspect of relativity from the perspective of its Essence, Beyond-Being, or the non-acting Godhead.

Several key points on this question are found in Sermon No. 67. Firstly: "God is something that necessarily transcends being. . . . God is in all creatures insofar as they have being, and yet He is above them. By being in all creatures, He is above them: what is one in many things must needs be above those things" (II:149).

All things that *are*, by that very token, "have" being, but are not equatable purely and simply and in every respect with Being; this distinguishes them from Being and from each other. Being is thus common to all existents, and is itself endowed with a degree of relativity in relation to its principle, Beyond-Being, even while representing the Absolute in relation to relative existents; in regard to the Godhead, Being is thus the first relativity, precisely on account of its positive determination, which allows one to say of it that it "is": of the Godhead one cannot predicate any such determination, for determination is limitation. This line of interpretation coheres with the following statement: "God works beyond being . . . and He works in non-being: before there was being, God was working: He wrought being where no being was" (II:150).

In other words, God's first "act" was to establish being, this corresponding to the Father as the "working speech," noted above, and also to the notion that "Being is the first name of God." Since this first act necessarily derives from something of God that "is," the question may be asked: how can God's act establish the being that is presupposed by that act? The answer to this question helps to clarify the necessity of understanding the rigorously metaphysical concept of "Beyond-Being." For it is clear that the God that acts to determine Being must in some sense also "be," but this in a "mode above modes," in a mode, that is to say, which has no common measure with that being that is the common factor in all entities which "are"; thus, when Eckhart says that "God works beyond being" this would appear to mean that the "work" of Beyond-Being is to establish Being, and this, in a place "where no being was"—thus, He works also "in non-being." Speaking in accordance with Eckhart's temporal and spatial imagery, one could say that Being crystallizes in an intelligible, not existential, "space" formerly occupied by nothingness, and it is by the very fact of the conceivable opposition between Being and the non-being that it replaces or displaces, that the relativity of Being is manifest; conversely, the impossibility of opposing non-being to Beyond-Being proves the absoluteness of Beyond-Being.

Therefore, Being is not only relativized by virtue of serving as the common substratum underlying and unifying all relative beings, it is also relativized by the fact that it is susceptible of negation—albeit in a purely intelligible manner—by non-being or nothingness. This may be understood as a metaphysical interpretation of the *creatio ex nihilo*: taking note of the earlier principle of God "becoming" and therefore "unbecoming," one could say that God becomes Being, where previously there was nothing, in order to unbecome; this unbecoming flows not into the emptiness of non-being but rather rejoins the plenitude of Beyond-Being. One is also reminded here of a dictum to be met with later in this chapter: God became man that man might become God.[5] Continuing with this sermon, Eckhart says:

[5] A patristic formula often paraphrased and employed by Eckhart for the purposes of expounding his doctrine of union; see for example I:138.

> Masters of little subtlety say God is pure being. He is as high above being as the highest angel is above a midge. . . . [W]hen I have said God is not a being and is above being, I have not thereby denied Him being: rather I have exalted it in Him. If I get copper in gold, it is there . . . in a nobler mode than it is in itself (II:150-151).

The angel and midge exist and thus both participate in, and are qualified by, Being; but the great qualitative distinction between them must be transposed to the distinction between Being and Beyond-Being. From the simile used by Eckhart one understands that Beyond-Being comprises Being, and thereby all that it contains, while transcending the delimitation attendant upon the determination of Being: Being is in Beyond-Being as traces of copper may be in gold, without this meaning that gold in itself loses any of its value in regard to the value of copper; insofar as copper—or Being—stands apart from gold—or Beyond-Being—it is in that very measure devalued—or relativized.

Being is thus exalted in Beyond-Being, finding therein an unconditioned plenitude not attainable on the determined plane of its own affirmation as such, conditioned as this plane is by its immediate relationship with those existents which it transcends in one respect, but with which it shares a common attribute in another respect, that of Being itself.

These considerations highlight the necessity for the apophatic dialectic when dealing with the Godhead: having nothing in common with anything at all, no positive attribute can be predicated of it, not even that most fundamental and seemingly indeterminate attribute which is Being; for even though it be the most indeterminate of all attributes, it remains nonetheless an attribute, which as such, inescapably constitutes a determination, hence a limitation, which the Godhead infinitely transcends.

A further nuance to the relationship between work, act, and being is found in the following extract; here, Eckhart speaks of the soul being borne up in the Persons, according to the power of the Father, the wisdom of the Son, and the goodness of the Holy Ghost—these three being the modes of "work" proper to the Persons; following this come two further stages, transcending this plane of activity:

> Above this is being that does not work, but here alone is being and work. Truly where the soul is in God, just as the Persons are suspended in being, there work and being are one, in that place where the soul grasps the Persons in the very indwelling of being from which they never emerged. . . . Now mark my words! It is only above all this that the soul grasps the pure absoluteness of free being, which has no location, which neither receives nor gives: it is bare "beingness," which is deprived of all being and beingness. There she grasps God as in the ground, where He is above all being (II:174-175).

Three levels are thus to be discerned within the divine Nature: the first level of the Divinity is here represented by the Persons as agents whose activity derives from the plane of Being; the second level is where Being is itself "work," prior to any particular modalities of activity: the "act" is Being itself, which means, in passive terms, that it is the "en-actment" of its principle, Beyond-Being, and, in positive terms, its activity is constituted by the potentialities which it comprises and which flow therefrom. The Persons are "suspended" at this level of Divinity, meaning that they do not manifest their particular properties.

At the final level, "above all this," is to be found the "pure absoluteness of free being"—understanding by "free," the notion of unconditioned and non-delimited Beyond-Being. "Deprived of all being and beingness": it is deprived, dialectically speaking, only insofar as Being itself constitutes a limitation in relation to this highest degree, so that to be deprived of this limitation is tantamount to being deprived of all possible deprivation, and thus to "be" infinite plenitude.

It should now be easier to comprehend Eckhart's paradoxical statements about the "nothingness" both of the creature and of God. In regard to the former, he declared, in a thesis condemned in the Bull of 1329:

> All creatures are pure nothing. I do not say that they are a little something, or anything at all, but that they are pure nothing (I: Note C, No. 26).

The creature is nothing because in itself it is an implicit negation of all that which is excluded by its own limitations: to negate that which is unconditionally Real is to be negated by it, hence to be reduced to nothingness. On the other hand:

> One is the negation of the negation and a denial of the denial. All creatures have a negation in themselves: one negates by not being the other . . . but God negates the negation: He is one and negates all else, for outside of God nothing is (II:339).

Only the negation of all negation is the supreme, unconditioned affirmation—all other affirmations are but affirmations of negation inasmuch as their very specification implies limitation and hence negation: not being all other things nor the One transcending all things, the particular creature, in its own right and standing apart from God, is but the expression of the principle of negation, hence, in Eckhart's elliptical dialectic, "a pure nothing." Moreover, since "outside of God nothing is," the creature is strictly nothing only in the measure that he is envisaged apart from or "outside of" God; and this gives a clue as to the converse truth, relating to God's immanence in creatures: if God's transcendent and exclusive unicity negates all that is other than it, His indivisible and inclusive totality encompasses and thus affirms all that there is, so that the creature is nothing apart from God and only a "something" in God.

Finally, if the creature is nothing in one respect, so too is God—though in a very different respect—a nothing which is a non-being, in the sense which has by now been sufficiently established as Beyond-Being; the Godhead surpasses—and thus in one sense negates—Being from above, while the creature's separative affirmation limits—and hence negates—Being from below:

> God is nothing: not in the sense of having no being. He is neither this nor that that one can speak of: He is being above all being. He is beingless being (II:115).

To conclude: Judging by his pronouncements, Eckhart's doctrine on the transcendent Absolute appears to emerge as the fruit, rather than the precondition, of transcendent realization; the key theological distinction between the "acting"

God and the "non-acting" Godhead is expounded parallel with the metaphysical distinction between Being and Beyond-Being; both of these distinctions being presented on the basis of Eckhart's spiritual experience and not simply from discursive ratiocination. Part II explores the nature of this spiritual experience.

## Part II: The Spiritual Ascent

This part consists of two sections. The first deals with the spiritual ascent in terms of the transcendence of virtue as conventionally conceived, with special attention given to the key spiritual values inherent in detachment; the second will directly address the experience of the Birth, focussing on the most transcendent aspects and implications of this spiritual state, and critically evaluating the nature and function of the intellect in regard to the modalities of the Birth and "Breakthrough."

### 1. Virtue and Transcendence

Just as it was seen in Part I that the transcendence of limitative conceptions of the Divine presupposed their existence as a basis for such transcendence, so too in relation to virtue, transcendence thereof implies its perfect attainment. For Eckhart, the eternal Word is only spoken in the perfect soul:

> For what I say here is to be understood of the good and perfected man who has walked and is still walking in the ways of God; not of the natural, undisciplined man, for he is entirely remote from and totally ignorant of this birth (I:1).

And, describing the state of the "perfected" man, as already noted in Part I above, Eckhart emphasizes that the essence of all the virtues has been assimilated to such an extent that they all emanate from him naturally, or, taking account of the undisciplined aspect of the "natural" man in the above quotation, they may be said to flow from him in a "supernaturally" natural manner.

It is only from the vantage point of the transcendent realization that a dimension of relativity attaching to human virtue becomes discernible, a realization, it must be stressed, that is inaccessible except on the basis of a prior attainment of the essence of the virtues.

Strictly speaking, virtue, along with all aspects of the individual's relationship with the "other"—including in this category God insofar as He is Creator and Lord—is transcended fully only in the pure experience of union, which will be the central theme of the next section.

At this stage, the degree of transcendence envisaged pertains to the most profound concomitants of a key virtue, that of detachment; in Eckhart's perspective detachment from self is the essential ontological—and not merely ethical—condition for receptivity to the Birth. This is clear from the range of values that are associated with detachment in this perspective: renunciation, objectivity, inwardness, love of God, assimilation to the universal—these are key modes by which the outward acts of piety and virtue are transcended, and by which the soul is oriented towards its highest beatitude.

It should be noted that transcendence of the virtues not only presupposes their realization but also raises them to an even higher degree of perfection; one might almost say that, if natural and existential virtue be the prerequisite for union, then supernatural and ontological virtue is its fruit. Transcendence of the virtues, far from entailing their cessation, results in a flow of even greater plenitude, this flow, indeed, constituting one of the signs by which the realized man is to recognized:

> [A]ll virtues should be enclosed in you and flow out of you in their true being. You should traverse and transcend all the virtues, drawing virtue solely from its source in that ground where it is one with the divine nature (I:128).

If drinking directly at the source of virtue corresponds in one respect to assimilating a mode of the divine nature which transcends the flow of virtue, in another respect it strengthens the current of the flow.

Turning now to pious practices, Eckhart stresses that their intention is to turn the man inwards, detaching him from outward objects, so that the "inner man" will be ready for God's salvific action, and God will not have to "draw him back from things alien and gross." Such practices, then, diminish the pain that results from being separated from outward objects, and are thus themselves constitutive of the beginning of Grace:

> For the greater the delight in outward things the harder it is to leave them, the stronger the love, the sharper the pain (I:34).

If pious actions are performed with self-interest, then they, too, become objects of attachment and hence hindrances; in a sermon based on the story of Christ's expulsion of the merchants from the Temple, Eckhart symbolically identifies as merchants those who, while abstaining from sin and seeking to be virtuous, "do works to the glory of God, such as fasts, vigils, prayers and the rest . . . but they do them in order that our Lord may give them something in return" (I:56).

God cannot be treated as the means to some individualistically conceived end; this would be to love God as one would a cow, "for her milk and her cheese and your own profit" (I:127); God Himself must be the intention of all actions and orientations, inward and outward, not just because true love of God excludes all selfish motivation, but also for the metaphysical reason that everything other than God is, as noted above, nothing:

> Remember, if you seek anything of your own, you will never find God, for you are not seeking God alone. You are looking for something with God, treating God like a candle with which to look for something; and when you have found what you are looking for, you throw the candle away. . . . [W]hatever you look for with God is nothing (I:284).

Whatever being the creature has is entirely derivative and hence, on its own account, is equatable with non-being, depending for its being on the presence of God; therefore this presence of God—His Being—not only encompasses all possible beings but also infinitely surpasses them. To have something without God is to have nothing, while to have God alone means having an absolute and infinite plenitude to which no thing can be added. Eckhart is here urging his listeners to establish God alone as the focus of their aspirations, and not His reward, paradisal though this be. The reward is nothing in the measure that, on the one hand, it is appended to the individual, and on the other, it is sought after apart from God Himself, thus using God as the means for the sake of a lesser end. This is the "sin" for which the "merchants" must be expelled from the Temple of true worship.

It should be noted that the "doves" also must leave the Temple; the error of these believers is more subtly defined, since they do indeed work solely for the sake of God, seeking no reward for themselves, and yet they too must leave the Temple:

> He did not drive these people out or rebuke them harshly, but said quite mildly "take this away," as though to say it is not wrong, but it is a hindrance to the pure truth. These are all good people, they work purely for God's sake, not for themselves, but they work with attachment, according to time and tide, before and after. These activities hinder them from attaining the highest truth, from being absolutely free and unhindered as our Lord Jesus Christ is absolutely free and unhindered (I:57-58).

The important point to grasp here is that it is the attachment to the notion of individual ownership of works that acts as a hindrance to the highest truth; for this attachment constitutes an entrenchment of particularity, both subjectively and objectively: subjectively, it intensifies awareness of an individual self working for, but nonetheless apart from, the Divine; and objectively, the work itself is conceived of in separative mode, tied down to a particular time, and assumed to give rise in the future to a determinately conceived commensurate reward. Even if one is not acting for the sake of the reward, one's action may still be qualified as "attached" in the measure that it is performed in accordance with a fixed awareness of this chain of temporal causality, and in the framework of an act-reward relationship; such an awareness is a hindrance to the highest truth which does away with such temporal distinctions, being situated in eternity; and which excludes alterity—the distinction between the actor and God—because it is absolutely One.

Further light is shed on this important notion of attachment to works in time by comparing Eckhart's position on the value of austerities with that of more conventional "masters." Taking the scriptural injunction: "Deny yourself and offer up your cross," Eckhart comments: "The masters say this is suffering: fasting and other pains. I say it is putting away suffering, for nothing but joy follows this practice" (II:182). While the masters see austerities as modes of suffering with a view to earning merit, Eckhart says that self-denial itself constitutes the reward: the negation of the suffering inescapably attendant upon attachment to the ego and its pretensions. On the one hand, with Eckhart, there is a disinterested and ontological approach, and on the other, with the masters, an interested and individualistic approach: the objective ontological *cause of* suffering is tacitly emphasized by Eckhart, and identified with the subsistence of the egocentric individuality, while with the traditional masters, the religious and subjectively interested *motive for* suffering is stressed, with the accent on penitence and individual effort, along with its concomitant, individual reward—all of which assumes and thereby reinforces the subsistence of the self-willed individuality.

To work with any kind of fixed awareness of temporal causality is to entrench oneself in the vicissitudes of the created order; and within this order any particular good is but an impermanent veil over the immutable nature of universal good:

> How has he abandoned all things for God's sake, who still considers and regards this or that good? . . . [T]his and that good adds nothing to goodness, rather, it hides and covers up the goodness in us (III:73).

This detachment from self and from all particular, hence limiting, good—with which this self is wont to identify—contains within it not just a mode of objectivity in relation to oneself, but also a mode of receptivity to the substance of universal good; the "good" man who says: "my work is not my work, my life is not my life" is also able to claim that "all of the works that all of the saints and all the angels and Mary, God's Mother, too, ever did, from this I hope to reap eternal joy as if I had done it all myself" (I:94).

The key to the explanation of what one might call this "transferral of merit" wrought by detachment lies in a later statement near the end of this sermon: "When you have God, you have all things with God." In other words, when Eckhart does not claim his works as "his," but refers everything, works and will, to God, then he is one, not just with God, but with all the saints and angels whose works and will likewise are not claimed by themselves, but are given over utterly to God: thus Eckhart reaps "their" reward, since what is "his" and what is "theirs" are equally God's, and "when you have God, you have all things with God." Likewise, from another sermon: "He who seeks God alone, in truth finds God but he does not find God alone—for all that God can give, that he finds with God" (I:94).

These considerations elucidate a key meaning of spiritual objectivity—the seeking of God alone and for His own sake; it is as if Eckhart were saying: be determined and motivated by the supreme and transcendent *object* of divine truth and not by the desire to append this truth to the inescapably defective subject. This subject, then, has its nature transmuted in the very measure of its objectivity. This principle emerges clearly from another sermon, in which Eckhart tells his listeners that if their love of God were purified of attachment to self, they would possess the deeds of virtuous men—even those of the Pope himself—more purely than these men possess them themselves:

> For the Pope has often tribulations enough for being Pope. But you have his virtues more purely and with greater detachment and peace, and they are more yours than his, if your love is so pure and bare in itself that you desire and love nothing but goodness and God (I:104).

In the very measure that one loves God "purely," one is assimilated upwards, out of the limitations of individual subjectivity, into the universal nature of objective reality—or universal subjectivity—which God is, the Object upon whom that love is fixed. This universal Object then subsumes the particular subject so that the subject that subsequently "possesses" all virtuous deeds can no longer be "himself," but is now the subject universalized by virtue of (and to the extent of) his effective identification with the Universal. This universal subjectivity more completely enjoys virtue—being one with its supra-manifest source—than does the particular subject—the Pope, for example, insofar as he remains affected by circumstances of outward manifestation, or "tribulation."

Eckhart is underlining here the disproportion between the unlimited receiving that comes through detachment from self, on the one hand, and the limited merit that comes through attachment to self and the works that flow from the self; it is in this light that the following principle of bliss through passivity may be understood: "But our bliss lies not in our activity, but in being passive to God. For just as God is more excellent than creatures, by so much is God's work better than mine" (I:22).

God's work for the individual, given as a gift, takes place in eternity and is conditional on the detachment of the individual both from himself and from the ties of the temporal condition; this is a key aspect of pure love of God, which is thus conceived as a transcendence in relation to the normal dualistic notion of love, and is more akin to a mode of union with Him: "In the love that a man gives, there is no duality, but one and unity, and in love I am God more than I am in myself" (I:110).

This totally detached love transforms the lover into the Beloved: the particular is universalized by its love of—and union with—the Universal. To thus live in God means that it is God that lives in the man. Further discussion of this theme is reserved for Part III of this chapter, on the "existential return," since the possibility of fully living in this manner presupposes the prior realization of union, the theme of the next section.

Continuing for the present with the theme of works and detachment, Eckhart, in a sermon remarkable for its boldness, contradicts the masters of his day on the question of whether good works wrought by a man in a state of mortal sin are lost eternally or whether they bear fruit once the man enters into a state of grace. Eckhart took the latter position in contrast to the former, upheld by the masters, but does so from an entirely different viewpoint: *all* works without exception, along with the time in which they occurred, are "totally lost, works as works, time as time. . . . [N]o work was ever good or holy or blessed." A work only gives rise to goodness or blessedness to the extent that its transient nature is fully acknowledged and its "image" or trace in the mind is immediately shed:

> If a good work is done by a man, he rids himself of this work, and by this ridding he is more like and closer to his origin than he was previously. . . . That is why the work is called holy and blessed (I:131).

It may be *called* holy and blessed, but this is "not really true, for the work has no being . . . since it perishes in itself." In reality, it is the man who performs the work that is blessed, since it is within his soul that the work bears fruit, not as work nor as the time in which it was performed, but as a "good disposition which is eternal with the spirit as the spirit is eternal in itself, and it is the spirit itself" (I:131).

Insofar as the soul is freed from the work and its time, such work and time are "blessed" in that they contribute to the blessedness of the soul above works and time. By contrast, if the works cling to the soul, then they act as blockages, preventing the light of the unhindered spirit from penetrating the soul. The performance of these good works, then, is a positive spiritual factor when it is for the sake of a "working out" of images that would otherwise inhibit receptivity to union. Good works will thus be useful to a man insofar as they create the "readiness for union and likeness, work and time being of use only to enable man to work himself out" (I:132-133).

It is because God is Himself untouched by work that man, to be "like" Him, must rise above works as works: "And the more a man frees himself and works himself out, the more he approaches God, who is free in Himself; and inasmuch as a man frees himself, to that extent he loses neither works nor time" (I:133).

The process of detaching oneself from works even while performing good works means, in concrete terms, being rid of, or freed from, the images of these works, and thus approximating the state of freedom enjoyed by God, who acts, but without in any way being bound by His activity. Hence, the richness of the inner fruit of works depends upon their being performed with detachment and objectivity, knowing that they derive from, and thus properly pertain to, the spirit, which is universal, and not from the individual. Only then can one say that neither works nor time can be lost: in contributing to the actualization of the consciousness of God, their true value is consummated in the union to which this consciousness ultimately leads—that union in which is to be found all blessedness, above time. The *raison d'être* of good works is thus union; they are valuable in the measure that they are performed and shed immediately.

Finally, on this question of works, one should note that, although the work as such perishes, nonetheless, insofar as it "corresponds to the spirit in its essence, it never perishes" (I:134). This means that a good work is the outward reflection in time and space of that intrinsic goodness, the essence of the spirit of God, a goodness which constantly flows into creation and into itself: the essential content of the work—radiating goodness—is thus imperishable, being at one with the Spirit which is imperishable, while the contingent container of the work, or the form vehicling this essence, is what perishes. To the extent that one acts for the sake of the fruits of the work on its own level, and in its own terms on the plane of contingency, to that extent there is attachment to the perishable, and this in turn diminishes the soul's capacity for attaining likeness to—and still less, union with—God. By contrast, when performed with perfect detachment, the essential and imperishable content of the work is activated and generates a corresponding disposition of soul which attracts grace and union.

Eckhart calls this kind of work "rational"; it is distinguished also by its interiorizing efficacy: rather than being dispersed by outward works, one must be drawn ever more inward, toward the ground of one's own being: "It is thus with all rational creatures that the more they go out of themselves with their work, the more they go into themselves. This is not the case with physical things: the more they work, the more they go out of themselves" (I:177-178).

To be qualified as fully "rational," the individual must distance himself from that "physical" element of his own nature which, in acting, degenerates by "going out of itself"; to work with attachment is here shown to imply that the soul flows in the direction of the work to which it is attached, along with its time, both of which are transient. The "rational" element of one's relationship with works, on the contrary, leads to a comprehension that work and its time are destined for nothingness, and hence one cannot but work with detachment from the work, thereby actualizing a movement of inwardness on the very basis of an outward act: outward acts are performed only in order to take one deeper within oneself. In this way, detached activity becomes not just a force of interiorization but also a luminous exteriorization:

> They are unhindered who organize all their works guided by the eternal light. . . . [H]e who works in the light rises straight up to God free of all means: his light is his activity and his activity is his light (I:82).

One who is thus detached from all outwardness, knowing that works as such do not lead to God, is able to rise up to God im-mediately or "free of all means," free, that is to say, of the notion that attainment of God can be the result of some outwardly performed acts; such a man's acts are thus performed in the light of discrimination, so that each act is an act of light, a projection outwardly of an inward luminosity.

This manner of working with discrimination and detachment joins man to God more effectively than anything else "except the vision of God in His naked nature" (I:85). This exception is extremely important: for this mode of detached activity is a mode of unification with God which is realized within the necessarily restrictive framework of outward existence, a framework which is transcended inwardly by the correct attitude, but not abolished outwardly. This mode relates to the way of being at one with God in the world, of the manner by which exteriority is to be interiorized, and therefore remains at a relative level when considered in relation to the experience of unconditional union. This should be borne in mind when reading the following: "[I]f a man thinks he will get more of God by meditation, by devotion, by ecstasies . . . than by the fireside or in the stable—that is nothing but taking God, wrapping a cloak round His head and shoving Him under the bench" (I:117).

What Eckhart appears to saying here is that one must relate to God according to His measures and not according to creaturely efforts; one should not set up a formal or deterministic relationship between one's own effort—as cause—and His reality—as effect—for if God is posited as the "achievement" of a particular "way," initiated by the creature, then He, as effect, depends on the creature, as cause, whereas in reality it is the opposite that is true. It is as if Eckhart is saying: you impose on Him your own measures, bringing Him down to your level—"shoving His head under the bench"—and this, after having veiled His true nature—"wrapping a cloak round His head"—by smothering Him with your particular "ways," which thus arrogate to themselves the status properly belonging to the ostensible object of devotion. Thus, to "shove" God beneath the bench can be understood as the human reduction of the Divine to the level of a horizontally determined chain of conventional causality: to give God His due, by implication, is to be perpetually—and "vertically"—aware    of Him as the omnipresent and inalienable Reality towards which man must ever gravitate.[6] The following quotation is more intelligible in the light of these considerations:

> [L]ove constrains me to love God, but detachment compels God to love me. Now it is a far nobler thing my constraining God to me than for me to constrain myself to God . . . because God is more readily able to adapt Himself to me and can more easily unite with me than I could unite with Him (III:117).

There are further, metaphysical aspects of detachment which can more easily be understood on the basis of the transcendent realization to be addressed below, and these aspects will be further examined in the final part of the chapter. For now, the more volitive aspects will be addressed.

Closely related to detachment is the volitive notion of renunciation, and on this question Eckhart is characteristically uncompromising: "Now our Lord says, 'Whoever abandons anything for me and for my name's sake, I will return it to him a hundredfold, with eternal life . . .'" (Matt. 19, 29). But if you give it up for the sake of that hundredfold and for eternal life, you have given up nothing. . . . You must give up yourself, altogether give up self, and then you have really given up" (I:142).

In another sermon Eckhart rhetorically puts to himself the question: how can one strive for nothing but God—how can one renounce all desire for reward? He answers by emphasizing that the reward is inevitable, but that purity of devotion must take precedence over the individualistic implications of one's knowledge that this reward is inevitable: "Be assured, God will not fail to give us everything. . . . It is far more necessary for Him to give than for us to receive, but we should not seek it—for the less we seek or desire it, the more God gives. In this way God intends only that we may be the richer and receive the more" (II:6).

The renunciation of self thus includes renouncing all desire of relative reward for oneself, and this total renunciation enhances receptivity to the absolute reward; there must be a pure intention for God alone, untainted by any yearning for individual reward: only when the soul and all its desires are offered up as sacrifice for the sake of the transcendent reality of God, does God pour out His infinite riches as reward for the soul.

It is as if Eckhart were saying: know that you will be rewarded, but do not allow this reward to insinuate itself as the motivation for the gift of self: the sole motivation of the gift of self to God must be the glorification of the absolute Object, not the adornment of the relative subject.

Returning to the idea that the soul will receive all that has been renounced, multiplied a hundredfold and with eternal life, this is clearly founded on the principle already referred to, that of spiritual—as opposed to numerical or material—unity, comprising within itself the universal reality of multiplicity.

---

[6] One is reminded here of Shankara's principle that the lower may be treated as if it were the higher, but the higher must never be treated as if it were the lower.

In the context of the above extracts, this principle can be seen to apply thus: sacrifice phenomenal multiplicity at the altar of the all-exclusive One, and then regain principial multiplicity in the bosom of the all-inclusive One. In the phenomenal order multiplicity divides unity, but in the principial order unity unites multiplicity. Thus, one sees Eckhart, in another sermon, saying: "Unity unites all multiplicity but multiplicity does not unite unity" (II:168).

This notion of the inclusivity of unity leads to the final part of this discussion: the correct way to pray. One should bear in mind that in Eckhart's order, the Dominican, the utmost stress was placed on contemplative prayer, several hours of such prayer each day being customary; what is in question at present is more in the nature of "interested" prayer, the making of personal requests, rather than disinterested contemplation which, as will be seen in the next section, is of the greatest value.

The important principle to grasp as a basis for understanding Eckhart's highly unconventional attitude to prayer is, again, that while material multiplicity veils spiritual unity, spiritual unity contains the essence of all possible material things in eternal, perfect, and infinite mode: to say "spiritual" is to say "universal"; the more spiritual a thing is the more inclusive and thus universal it becomes: "[A]ll spiritual things are raised above material: the higher they are raised, the more they expand and embrace material things" (II:10).

Likewise: "[I]n the heavenly realm all is in all and all is one and all ours. . . . [W]hat one has there, another has, not as from the other or in the other, but in himself, so that the grace that is in one is entirely in the other as his own grace. Thus it is that spirit is in spirit" (I:65).

Not only is the spiritual more universal than the material, but as seen in the first section, it is infinitely more real, the material or created order as such being reducible to "nothing." With these points in mind, one is better equipped to appreciate the following statements which appear to equate prayer with idolatry and unrighteousness:

> When I pray for aught, my prayer goes for naught; when I pray for naught, I pray as I ought. When I am united with That wherein all things are existent, whether past, present, or future, they are all equally near and equally one; they are all in God and all in me. Then there is no need to think of Henry or Conrad. If one prays for aught but God alone, that can be called idolatry or unrighteousness. . . . If I pray for someone I pray at my weakest. When I pray for nobody and for nothing, then I am praying most truly, for in God is neither Henry nor Conrad (I:52).

Since all things are in God, when one prays only for His sake, it is impossible to exclude any particular thing from that prayer; but in praying for some particular thing, all others are perforce excluded from that prayer; the best way to pray for all things is therefore to consciously integrate them into their universal and unique source, wherein all existents "past, present, or future" are equally each other and equally one. On the other hand, to pray for this or that is to affirm material particularity over and above spiritual universality; it is thus to uphold limitation at the expense of the infinite, choosing exclusivity and imperfection instead of inclusivity and perfection; all of these reductions are then hyperbolically assimilated to the status of idolatry and unrighteousness. But, as stated above, this is only an apparent equation, for it can be argued that Eckhart did not intend this to be unconditionally applied.

The points made earlier regarding the relativity of particular conceptions and pious acts may be used as a basis for construing the above statement in the following way: for those who are striving towards transcendence, on the path of absolute commitment to the Divine in its uncreated unicity, it is necessary to know that any prayer other than that for all in the One is tantamount to praying for a privation in respect of the totality of the One, and to say privation is to say "evil"; even if it be a relative good in itself, it is nonetheless an evil when considered in relation to the absolute Good. In this sense the following thesis— condemned as "erroneous or tainted with heresy" in the Bull of 1329—can be more profoundly appreciated:

> Whoever prays for this or that, prays for something evil and in evil wise, for he prays for the denial of good and the denial of God, and he prays for God to deny Himself to him (I:xlvii).

The methodic implications of this principle will be clearer in the discussion of the next section, where it will be seen that any kind of image is regarded as hindering that emptiness and stillness required for the Birth. In relation to that emptiness, personal prayer is relative and thus a kind of "evil": emptiness is to union what prayer is to duality; that is to say, in itself prayer may not only be good, but even necessary on its proper plane, but this ontological plane itself pertains to separativity, and it is separativity which is "evil" in comparison with that infinite Good which is One, transcending the plane on which the distinction between good and evil has any meaning. What, then, is the prayer made by the detached heart?

> My answer is that detachment and purity cannot pray, for whoever prays wants God to grant him something, or else wants God to take something from him. But a detached heart desires nothing at all, nor has it anything to get rid of. Therefore it is free of all prayer or its prayer consists of nothing but being uniform with God (III:126).

It is clear that Eckhart is here describing the state of the heart of one who has attained to complete detachment: such a person cannot pray with that central point of his consciousness which is aware of the nothingness of the created order and the unique reality of God. One may argue here that Eckhart is not saying that one must not pray in order to be detached; rather, he is stressing that a fruit of the realization of spiritual detachment is absolute contentment, which does preclude all need on the most inward plane of consciousness, that of the "heart," precisely.

If the heart is detached and thus empty of all desire, the arising of a desire in the heart would signify that the heart is not in fact empty, so that it becomes a contradiction in terms to say: the detached heart desires this or that. If there is to be any kind of petition it should be for union with God and resignation to His will:

A man should never pray for any transitory thing: but if he would pray for anything, he should pray for God's will alone and nothing else, and then he gets everything (II:76).

This section has emphasized the transcendent aspect of the key virtue of detachment in the preliminary stages of the "ontological ascent"; hitherto, discussion has assumed the framework of diversified being, but the tendency of the dialectic employed by Eckhart has consistently been directed upwards and beyond this framework, having in view the supra-ontological level to which consciousness must rise. Thus, the principal value of detachment and its concomitant virtues is derived from the extent to which it enhances receptivity to the Birth of the Word in the soul, or union with the Godhead which this Birth implies. The next section deals directly with this attainment.

## 2. Unitive Concentration, *Raptus*, and the Birth
The first important principle to establish in the description of the Birth is the absolute necessity of divine grace, without which the soul can achieve nothing in its quest to transcend itself. Following on from the previous discussion on detachment, it could be said that the pure emptiness which spiritual detachment effects is the inner receptivity to the influx of grace; God is continuously seeking the creature, who, for his part, is unreceptive to God by reason of his preoccupation with—hence "fullness" of—himself and the world:

God is always at great pains to be always with a man and to lead him inwards, if only he is ready to follow. . . . God is always ready, but we are unready. God is near to us, but we are far from Him. God is in, we are out. God is at home, we are abroad (II:169).

A decisive opening towards grace is effected by the creature's recognition of his inherent incapacity, and this opening is also identified with the awakening of the higher reaches of the intellect; thus, the created aspect of the intellect must become aware of its inescapable limitations, and then fervently seek the grace of God; for it is only by virtue of this grace that the "highest" or the "uncreated" aspect of the intellect can be actualized. So whatever is "achieved" by means of this intellect pertains more to the work of the grace of God than to the efforts of the creature: "When a man is dead in imperfection, the highest intellect arises in the understanding and cries to God for grace. Then God gives it a divine light so that it becomes self-knowing. Therein it knows God" (I:267).

This awareness of the necessity of grace does not imply a fatalistic or quietist attitude with regard to one's actual state of imperfection; on the contrary, recognition of this imperfection is tied strongly to resolute action: it goes hand in hand with an unremitting struggle against one's failings, a "hatred of one's own soul" in the measure that the soul remains imperfect: "[W]hoever loves his soul in the purity which is the soul's simple nature, hates her and is her foe in this dress; he hates her and is distressed that she is so far from the pure light that she is in herself" (I:171).

One must make the continuous effort of transcending oneself—overcoming one's faults—into a way not just of prefiguring and anticipating the effective victory over oneself actualized by grace, but also of opening oneself up to that grace; thus, in speaking of the "functions" of the angel in respect of preparing the soul for the Birth, Eckhart adds that one must strive to become ever more like the angel in the performance of its triple functions: the purification, illumination, and perfection of the soul (I:212). Elsewhere this process is assimilated to the growth of likeness to God: "[J]ust so far as all (the soul's) failings drop away from her, just so far does God make her like Himself" (I:219).

One must now address the question of what exactly is meant by "failing" and what is the corresponding "success." To answer this, one needs to appreciate the most significant aspect of the nexus of relationships subsisting between the Father and the Son, the Son and humanity, and humanity and the individual human being. Taking first the relationship of Divine paternity, Eckhart quotes the scriptural principle: No man knows the Father but the Son (Matt. 11, 27) and adds: "if you would know God, you must not merely be like the Son, you must be the Son yourself" (I:127). To thus "be" the Son means to be at one with the Word eternally spoken by the Father, as opposed to being the man Jesus who was born in a particular time and place. To distinguish between the eternal Birth and the temporal birth makes clear the necessity of realizing within oneself the reality of this ceaseless Birth, of which the temporal birth is but a consequence. Herein lies the crux of Eckhart's teachings, which he expresses by quoting St. Augustine: "What does it avail me that this birth is always happening, if it does not happen in me? That it should happen in me is what matters" (I:1).

The assumption by the Word of human nature is the key to the individual human being's realization of the Birth: "God took on human nature and united it with His own Person. Then human nature became God, for He put on bare human nature and not any man. Therefore, if you want to be the same Christ and God, go out of all that which the eternal Word did not assume . . . then you will be the same to the eternal Word as human nature is to Him. For between your human nature and His there is no difference: it is one, for it is in Christ what it is in you" (II:313-314)

In other words, when the accidents of individuality are once eliminated, universal human nature is revealed: not such and such a human being, but humanity as such. This "such-ness," having constituted the existential container of Divinity, is absorbed by its divine content: becoming one with humanity is thus a stage on the path of ascending to become one with Divinity, describing thereby the inverse of the movement whereby the Divinity descended to become humanity: "Why did God become man? That I might be born God Himself" (I:138).

Therefore, the true or transcendent meaning of humanity is Divinity, which amounts to saying that man is only true to his deepest nature to the extent that he transcends himself, which he does, in the first instance, by purifying himself from "all of that which the eternal Word did *not* assume." It is clear that Eckhart is here stressing the necessity of the divinization of the human and not the humanization of the Divine: the lower must extinguish itself in the face of the higher and only then be reabsorbed by it; it is not a question of bringing down the higher to its own level and assimilating it crudely to one's personal actuality.

These considerations are reinforced by an alchemical analogy employed by Eckhart: "By being poured into the body, the soul is darkened. . . . [T]he soul cannot be pure unless she is reduced to her original purity, as God made her, just as gold cannot be made from copper by two or three roastings: it must be reduced to its primary nature. . . . Iron can be compared to silver, and copper to gold: but the more we equate it without subtraction, the more false it is. It is the same with the soul" (I:202-203).

The essence of the soul is darkened and enshrouded by the body: the alchemical "reduction" or "dissolution" required is evidently not aimed at the body *qua* material, but rather at the soul insofar as it has taken on itself the darkness of its covering: the psychic traces of matter and corporeality, passion for the perishable, attachment to the transient material that is "created after nothing" (I:203). The more the natural, fallen, and actual state of the soul—the unrefined copper—is taken for the essence of its being and consciousness, the more false it becomes, the more susceptible to pride, which here means deifying the creature as such, taking darkness for light. One should recall here the idea of copper being more exalted in gold than it is in itself: earlier this image was used in regard to the distinction between Being and Beyond-Being, but it applies with equal relevance to the soul and God: the soul realizes a plenitude in God that is strictly excluded on the plane of its separative affirmation as soul.

If this reduction to pure humanity constitutes the aim and limit of the human being's capacity—the modalities of which will shortly be addressed—and renders him at one with the Word, the question now arises: what is it that the Son "knows" of the Father, and that now the individual, reduced to "bare humanity" and thus the Word, also knows? In what does this knowledge consist? "What does the Son hear from his Father? The Father can only give birth, the Son can only be born. All that the Father has and is, the profundity of the divine being and the divine nature, He brings forth all at once in His only-begotten Son" (I:138).

The content of this knowledge is inseparable from the Being of the Absolute; the ontological distinction between the Son as Person and the Godhead *qua* Essence is not operative in this supra-ontological dimension of essential identity—that identity which allows Eckhart to assert that the Persons are but one Godhead despite their outward personal distinctions. Thus: "The hearer is the same as the heard in the eternal Word" (II:83).

Just as the Son *is* the Father in this unitive dimension, so, if the individual man has become born as the Son by virtue of his effective reduction to pure humanity, it follows that he, too, cannot be other than the One. To say "Birth" is to say "Union": "God the Father gives birth to the Son in the ground and essence of the soul, and thus unites Himself with her . . . and in that real union lies the soul's whole beatitude" (I:5).

Regarding the nature of the Being that is thus communicated and consummated in union, Eckhart's description closely corresponds, again, to the Vedantin ternary *Sat-Chit-Ananda*; for there are said to be three aspects of the Word as spoken in the soul: "immeasurable power," "infinite wisdom," and "infinite sweetness" (I:60-61).

Eckhart emphasizes that in this integral nature, he possesses everything that was given to Christ; this was another thesis for which he was condemned in the Bull of 1329: "All that God the Father gave His only-begotten Son in human nature He has given me: I except nothing, neither union nor holiness" (I:xlviii).

In one of his sermons he proposes and answers the key question implicit in the condemnation of such an idea: if we have everything that Christ was given "why then do we praise and magnify Christ as our Lord and our God?" He answers: "That is because he was a messenger from God to us and has brought our blessedness to us. The blessedness he brought us was our own" (I:116).

In other words, Jesus—the man—"re-minded" mankind of the blessedness within them, a blessedness derived from God, in the first instance, inasmuch as each human soul is made in the image of God—that is, in essence, each soul is born as the Son, and thus with all the blessedness of the Son; a blesssedness which is clouded, only, and not abolished by the Fall. This blessedness is only "our own" in the essentialized human nature, where all creaturely aspects are transcended. It is as though Eckhart were saying: the Principle which transcends me transmits to me a message that reminds me that it is immanent within me; that it is more truly "myself" than this empirical psycho-physical shell that enshrouds me.

Turning now to the means by which this transcendent immanence is to be realized, Eckhart describes the uncreated aspect of the soul as something more unknown than known, "a strange and desert place"; hence self-effacement is the *sine qua non* of its realization: "If you could naught yourself for an instant, indeed I say less than an instant, you would possess all that this is in itself. But as long as you mind anything at all, you know no more of God than my mouth knows of color or my eye of taste" (I:144).

One must now focus on the meaning of this self-naughting and the ontological principle whence its spiritual necessity derives. One should recall here the idea that any specific thing—albeit something good in itself—is a veil over the universal Good and is thus a kind of negation thereof. Anything which "is" in itself is "not" in regard to God: "insofar as *not* adheres to you, to that extent you are imperfect. Therefore if you want to be perfect, you must be rid of *not*" (I:117).

Ontological perfection is thus the transcendent negation of negation. Any trace of alterity excludes this perfection, for otherness is the affirmation of negation. Union means total oneness with that which is, while separativity entails an inevitable relationship with nothingness. This is a relationship which detracts from the Real in the measure that it moves one in the direction of a nothingness which can be postulated as a negative tendency, its existential status deriving not from its own nature, which by definition is non-existent, but from its capacity to negate the Real.

It is important to distinguish two types of "nothingness" which pertain to the soul: the first is when the soul is affirmed as such apart from God, and which may be called its negative nothingness, inasmuch as it negates the unique reality of God; and the second is a methodically precipitated nothingness which is, on the contrary, eminently positive, inasmuch as it is a deliberate negation of the soul's own apparent "somewhat," and is thus a nothingness which is receptive to the Divine "somewhat." To attain to the "somewhat" of God, His Reality, that is as it were on the thither side of the Void, the soul must first fall into her own nothingness, here implying the concrete and "upward" or "inward" negation of her own apparent "something-ness"; then God "with His uncreatedness upholds her Nothingness and preserves her in His Something" (I:59).

If in terms of Being, the soul must become void to itself, the same applies, *mutatis mutandis* in terms of cognitive consciousness: the soul can only come to know by an unknowing, a complete stripping away of all contents of thought: "There must be a stillness and a silence for this Word to make itself heard. We cannot serve this Word better than in stillness and silence: there we can hear it and there too we will understand it aright—in the unknowing. To him who knows nothing, it appears and reveals itself" (I:20).[7]

What is being stressed is that what is ignorance from the human perspective is but the underside of an absolute mode of knowledge from the divine perspective; just as the ear has no knowledge of taste, so human modalities of knowledge have no means of assimilating the divine verities, there being an unbridgeable incommensurability as between the finite processes of cognition and the infinite content of divine reality. To "unknow," from the human point of view is the precondition for knowledge of the divine order: "Then we shall become knowing with divine knowing and our unknowing will be ennobled and adorned with supernatural knowing" (I:21).

To thus "unknow" means in concrete terms to ingather all the powers of the soul, interiorizing them for the sake of unitive concentration; concentration, not on this or that image, but on the Truth itself in the inmost depths of silent stillness: "[We must] concentrate all our powers on perceiving and knowing the one, infinite, uncreated, eternal truth. To this end, assemble all your powers, ally your senses, your entire mind and memory; direct them into the ground where your treasure lies buried" (I:19).

The "unknowing" thus pertains to all modes of the individual powers of the soul: pure concentration is an ignorance, so far as the individual is concerned, subsuming within itself in undifferentiated mode all aspects of the soul's functioning, resulting in a "modeless mode" of ignorance, which is a void, receptive only to the influx of the divine Being, Truth, and Blessedness. This is the "treasure" that lies buried deep beneath the superficial layers of cognition which are so many veils over the Truth.

All images, insofar as they are received from without, must be firmly excluded. Even the image of Christ is held to be a hindrance to the highest realization. Quoting John, 16, 7, "It is expedient for you that I should go away from you, for if I do not go away, the Holy Spirit cannot come to you," Eckhart comments: "This is just as if he had said: 'You rejoice too much in my present form, and

---

[7] Cf. the dictum of Shankara: the Self is known only by him who knows it not at all.

therefore the joy of the Holy Ghost cannot be yours.' So leave all images and unite with the formless essence" (III:128).[8]

Eckhart's position becomes more intelligible when the notion of "image" is understood, along with the corresponding state of freedom from all images; in the Birth, all things in their objective reality within God are attained, in contrast to their outward forms as images refracted through the limited and hence distorting prisms of creaturely consciousness. If any image—whether noble or base—is present in the mind, God must necessarily be absent:

> The least creaturely image that takes place in you is as big as God. How is that? It deprives you of the whole of God. As soon as the image comes in, God has to leave with all His Godhead. . . . Go right out of yourself for God's sake, and God will go right out of Himself for your sake! When these two have gone out what is left is one and simple. In this One the Father bears His Son in the inmost source (I:118).

One observes here a cognitive reflection, in the domain of spiritual method, of an ontological process, in the realm of metaphysical reality: the abstention from all images is the negative aspect of unitive concentration, and this reflects and prefigures that self-effacement which is the negative aspect of unitive realization: no sooner is the self effaced—gone right out of itself—than the immanent Godhead is realized, in a union which precludes all exclusive affirmation of either the self or God: the Godhead alone abides in this union.

It is in this sense of the abandonment of all sense-impressions and mental constructs that Eckhart interprets the scriptural passage about the child Jesus being lost by his parents, and only being found by them upon returning to the point from which they had started: one must leave behind the "crowd"—of powers, functions, works, and images of the soul—and return to the source (I:39).

In another sermon he puts to himself the question: is it always necessary to be so "barren and estranged from everything, outward and inward"—can one not pray, listen to sermons, and so on, to help oneself? He answers: "No, be sure of this. Absolute stillness for as long as possible is best of all for you. You cannot exchange this state for any other without harm" (I:43).

One again observes a clear parallel between the operative elements of spiritual method and the structure of metaphysical reality: just as the Godhead was distinguished from the Trinity by "non-working," so the non-acting essence of the soul must be stripped of its outward modes of functioning: "The soul works through her powers, not with her essence" (I:3).

---

[8] This recalls the final mental act performed by Ramakrishna before attaining *nirvikalpa samadhi*: unable to go beyond the vision of the Mother Kali in his attempt at concentrating on the Self, he says: "With a firm determination I sat for meditation again and, as soon as the holy form of the divine Mother appeared now before my mind as previously, I looked upon knowledge as a sword and cut it mentally in two with that sword of knowledge. There remained then no function in the mind, which transcended quickly the realm of names and forms, making me merge in *Samadhi*" (*Sri Ramakrishna: The Great Master*, Swami Saradananda, trans. Swami Jagadananda, Sri Ramakrishna Math, Madras, 1952, p. 484).

In the previous part of this section, it was seen how the virtues were to be first assimilated and then transcended; that aspect of the spiritual ascent may be said to relate primarily to the lower powers of the soul: the lower intellect, anger, desire, and the senses. At this higher stage of the ascent, represented by the degree of pure concentration or "stillness," it is the modalities of the higher powers of the soul that must be transcended, these higher powers being: the higher intellect, memory, and will. All cognitive contents deriving from the function of the intellect, on the basis of the images stored in the memory, and with the operation of the self-seeking will—all of this must be transcended if the ground and essence of the soul is to be attained, the imageless "silent middle," which is by nature receptive to nothing save "the divine essence without mediation. There God enters with His all, not merely with a part" (I:3).

Eckhart does not give many descriptions of the unitive experience, the highest *raptus*, *gezucket*, or "ecstasy" as it is conventionally termed, but which would be more appropriately called "enstasis," given the fact that the beatitude experienced derives, as Eckhart so insistently maintains, from the deepest ontological dimension *within* and not without oneself. This recalcitrance doubtless derives, in large part at least, from the ineffability of the experience and thus its intrinsic incommunicability. But in one important sermon, he does give an extrinsic description, in speaking of St. Paul's *raptus*, to which Eckhart clearly attributes the highest status in regard to the experience of union. In the context of exhorting his listeners again to abandon all powers, images, and works so that the Word be spoken in them, he says:

> If only you could suddenly be unaware of all things, then you could pass into an oblivion of your own body as St. Paul did, when he said: "Whether in the body I cannot tell or out of the body I cannot tell: God knows it" (2 Cor. 12, 2). In this case the spirit had so entirely absorbed the powers that it had forgotten the body: memory no longer functioned, nor understanding, nor the senses, nor the powers that should govern and grace the body, vital warmth and body-heat were suspended, so that the body did not waste during the three days when he neither ate nor drank (I:7).

He commends the listener likewise to "flee his senses, turn his powers inward, and sink into an oblivion of all things and himself."

In another sermon he points to the necessarily limited duration of this state:

> Were [the soul] always conscious of the good which is God, immediately and without interruption, she would never be able to leave it to influence the body.... [B]ecause this is not conducive to this life and alien to it, God in His mercy veils it when He will and reveals it when He will (I:27).

The amount of time spent in this state, then, is determined by God and not the individual, who is entirely passive in this respect. Another question that presents itself is the following: in the unitive state, does the soul lose its identity completely—in which case there could be nothing to which consciousness could return "after" union—or is there something of the soul's identity which remains—in which case union could not have been total? In regard to this question, Eckhart insists on the attainment of pure one-ness as opposed to united-ness:

> Where two are to become one, one of them must lose its being. So it is: and if God and your soul are to become one, your soul must lose her being and her life. As far as anything remained, they would indeed be united, but for them to become one, the one must lose its identity and the other must keep its identity (I:52).

How then does the soul not perish in this union, entailing as it does the loss of its entire "being and life"? The answer to this, in Eckhartian terms, can be extrapolated from the answer he gives to a similar question, how the soul can "endure" union:

> Since He gives to her within Himself, she is able to receive and endure in His own and not in her own, for what is His is hers. As He has brought her out of her own, therefore His must be hers, and hers is truly His. In this way she is able to endure union with God (I:184).

In the state of union the soul is completely possessed by God in such a way that the soul's endurance of this state is conferred by God's being, replacing that of the soul; just as the soul is incapable of attaining to what transcends its own created nature, so it is incapable of enduring union on the basis of its created capacity. God is the active agent in both respects, bestowing His capacity upon the soul which has faithfully extinguished its own capacity. If this transferral of capacity did not take place then, logically, one would have to conclude that all creaturely other-ness would be extinguished, not just in the unitive state— which is the eternally real state—but even in the temporal domain of ontological multiplicity, to which the soul does indeed return.

Therefore, one can say that the soul's created nature is suspended or negated for the duration of the state, while its uncreated essence is revealed in its true identity, one with God, not just united to God. It is important to stress here that this union is posited as a state of limited duration only from the viewpoint of the created nature that is excluded from the union, while from the viewpoint of the Absolute, this "state" is the eternal reality, intrinsically immutable, while being extrinsically susceptible to apparent exclusion—or veiling—only by the "nothingness" represented by the created order, for this union is in truth the "eternal birth which God the Father bore and bears unceasingly in eternity" (I:1). Everything else in the temporal, created order is strictly "nothing."

This same idea is suggested in another sermon where Eckhart speaks of the soul being united; one should bear in mind the distinction between "one" and "united": "God created the soul that she might become united with Him" (II:263). To "become united" is quite distinct from "being one": there can be no question of "becoming" in the pure state of oneness; whatever is in the realm of becoming is subject to a process—in this case the process of unification, a "becoming united," whilst pure being is the immutable reality of oneness. Therefore, starting from its created nature, the soul must become united with God; that which is shed in the process of unification is everything which the

Word did not assume when it assumed human nature. That is, all that separates man from his perfect prototype, the image of God in which he was created. This process of "unification" is the essential condition for that "union" with which it, however, has no common measure. Unification means eliminating otherness by degrees; union is the abrupt transcending of all otherness, the revelation of the nothingness of otherness and the sole reality of the One.

The created aspect of the soul is thus susceptible to a transformation both in the spiritual ascent—the process of unification—as well as after the attainment of union, a transformation by means of which it becomes perfectly conformed to the image of God in which it was created; but this conformity of the outer soul to God is to be distinguished from the total identity between the essence of the soul and the Godhead. Conformity relates to the soul insofar as it is made in the "image" of God, whereas identity pertains strictly to that of which the soul is an image, the divine reality itself.

### 3. Intellect and Grace

In assessing the nature of the important relationship between the intellect and grace in the context of the Birth, it is essential to grasp the following two-fold distinctions: within the intellect, one must distinguish between individual, creaturely understanding, and the supra-individual, uncreated substance of the intellect; and within grace, one must grasp the distinction between, on the one hand, its relative aspect, which delimits it as a specific function of the Divine, thus stopping short at the source of its effusion, and, on the other hand, its aspect of absolute necessity in regard to the conscious effort to transcend creaturely limitations. Without a clear understanding of these distinctions, it would be easy to see in Eckhart's many and scattered pronouncements an apparent contradiction, whereby intellect is sometimes placed above grace and at other times beneath it.

As seen earlier, man cannot turn the created light of his understanding into a comprehension of the uncreated; he must be illuminated by the light of Grace:

> [T]he light that flows from intellect is understanding, and is just like an outflow . . . a stream compared to that which intellect is in its own being. . . . [T]here is another light . . . that of grace: compared to this the natural light is as small as what a needle-point can pick up of the earth compared with the whole earth (II:194).

The first statement clearly distinguishes the "flow" of the intellect from its source, and the second emphasizes the negligible light of this flow compared to the light bestowed by grace. However, the function of the lower intellect is the necessary starting-point for grace:

> [H]ere and now that power in us by which we are aware and know that we see is nobler and higher than the power by which we see; for nature begins her work at the weakest point, but God begins His work with the most perfect (III:113).

The "weakest point" of nature is the contact between the senses and a material object, while the witness of this contact is the intellect, the "most perfect" element with which God's work begins; while nature works with sensible/empirical consciousness, God begins with that element of objectivity in the intellect which is conscious of this consciousness, and thus superior to it.

The preliminary function of the intellect is to establish the distinction between itself—consciousness—and that of which it is conscious—things outward or inward—and to be dissatisfied with all such objects in the very measure that they are not pure Being, or in the measure that they are susceptible to distinction therefrom. As seen above, this involves the unremitting rejection of all images, those traces in the mind of external existents which all imply and entrench the nothingness of alterity. By this process—strongly reminiscent of the Vedantin *neti, neti*—the flow of light from the intellect is drawn in towards its source, but it cannot shed light on this source, for the "flow" is created, while the source, the "spark" of the intellect is uncreated:

> There is a power in the soul. . . . If the whole soul were like it, she would be uncreated and uncreatable, but this is not so. In its other part it has a regard for and a dependence on time, and there it touches on creation and is created (I:190).

While that aspect of the intellect which "touches on" creation is by that very token created, the aspect that touches on the uncreated must itself be uncreated, and that is why, continuing the above quotation, "To this power, the intellect, nothing is distant or external. . . . [It] seizes God naked in His essential being. It is one in unity, not in likeness." The intellect, then, while being one in itself, is nonetheless extrinsically differentiated in accordance with the ontological plane of its operation: when focussing on the created order it is itself endowed with a created aspect and is moreover individualized in proportion to its contact with that order; but when reposing within itself, having been reabsorbed back into its source, it is wholly uncreated, and it is universalized to the extent that its oneness with the "naked being" is realized. However, to make contact with this uncreated substance of the intellect, grace is indispensable:

> A master who has spoken best of all about the soul says that no human wit can ever come to know what the soul is in her ground. . . . What we can know of it must be supernatural: it must be by grace (I:190).

The natural resources of the personal intellect are insufficient to grasp the source of the intellect, the "spark" of the soul which transcends the soul itself even while mysteriously residing within it. This coincidence of presence and transcendence can only be understood if the dimension of depth comes to denote height: the spark in the depths of the soul is that transcendent source whence flow the powers of the intellect. That which flows cannot turn back and grasp the source of its own flow—therefore the natural functions of the intellect must be stilled as the condition for that miraculous reflux or "inflowing," that is, the return to the source; and this can only be a supernatural operation, an act of divine grace, the result of which is that the point of actual consciousness is transported into the immanent depth that the ground of the soul is.

Henceforth, whatever is claimed in regard to the operation or tendency of this uncreated aspect of the intellect is at the same time necessarily an affirmation of the operation of grace, inasmuch as the former depends for its actualization on the latter; the "fruits" of the intellect, then, far from being assimilable to the individual as such, are inescapably the fruits also—and preeminently—of grace, even when, as will be seen shortly, the intellect is described as transcending the limits proper to grace.

The operation of this principle is clear in the process of purification whereby the soul is rendered more "like" God and less like "nothing": "When God works in the soul, whatever is unlike in the soul is purified and cast out by the burning heat. . . . [T]here is one power in the soul that splits off the coarser part and becomes united with God: that is the spark in the soul" (I:237).

God's work in the soul—the purification of what is "unlike" Him—is here identified with the power of the intellect—that which eliminates coarseness; thus, the operation of the intellect is identified as the work, not of the individual, but of God: the discriminating activity of the intellect is the initial principal means by which God acts in the soul. When this discrimination is allied to the tendency to move away from the base and towards the good, it is given the name "synteresis"; this is a tendency or an inclination which is "always striving against whatever is ungodly . . . and is always inclined to the good"; it is "a binding and a turning away from": one of its functions is to "bite against that which is impure," the other, "it ever attracts to the good" (I:238).

This synteresis is the function of the spark, and not a power of the soul; it is, as Evans' translation has it, a "permanent tendency to good" (Evans: I:88). While the powers relate to individuality and are bound up by it, this tendency, though profoundly affecting the individual, pertains to a higher order and is ever moving towards its true nature; that which tends by its nature to be reunited with its own source is the uncreated intellect, the spark; and to the extent that it is frustrated in this tendency, it gives rise to remorse for imperfection, "hating" the soul in its actual corruption because it loves the soul in its pure essence. This "striving against whatever is ungodly" thus has its root in that objective element in the soul which is in essence completely independent of it, failing which there would not be the possibility of conceiving of, or acting against, its "ungodliness." In other words, objectivity in relation to the soul is only possible through the transcendent faculty of the intellect, this objectivity being itself an aspect or expression of transcendence, and thus gives rise in turn to the possibility not just of striving against oneself but also of transcending oneself: if objectivity is the function of the created intellect, transcendence is the function of the uncreated intellect, always remembering that both functions are inseparable from grace.

The nature and function of the intellect is further clarified by viewing it in relation to the will: whereas the highest mode of the intellect seizes upon God "naked" in the very source of His being, the highest mode of the will—which is love—only goes so far as the primary effusion of His being, which is goodness; commenting on the scriptural injunction: "Stand in the gate of God's house and proclaim the word," Eckhart identifies God's house with "the unity of His being" and the gate as the first "melting out" as goodness:

Love infatuates and entangles us in goodness, and in love I remain caught up in the gate. . . . If I am caught up in goodness, in the first effusion, taking Him where He is good, then I seize the gate, but I shall not seize God. Therefore knowledge is better, for it leads love. . . . [L]ove seeks desire, intention. Knowledge does not add a single thought, but rather detaches and strips off and runs ahead, touches God naked and grasps Him in His essence (I:258).

Just as love can only go so far as the "gate," so too the interiorizing power of grace can only take the soul as far as this first effusion; having emphasized the necessity of the work of grace, by which the soul is continuously drawn closer to God, Eckhart then adds:

[T]he soul is not satisfied with the work of grace, because even grace is a creature: she must come to a place where God works in His own nature . . . (where) He who is poured out and that which receives the outflowing are all one (II:114).

This indicates the point at which the uncreated intellect predominates over the non-transcendent elements of the created soul; it is the intellect that is not "satisfied" with the work of grace, since this work can be seen to imply three elements: the source of grace; an outflow from that source, which is then distinguished from the source; and an agent receptive to the grace, again distinct both from the source and the flow of grace.

To say here that grace is a "creature" is to affirm hyperbolically the relativity of all that can in any way be distinguished from the unconditional oneness of the Godhead. Since, elsewhere, Eckhart identifies grace with the work of the Holy Ghost, it can hardly be referred to in creaturely terms; rather, one should understand this ellipsis in the light of the concept of a "lesser absolute," or *apara Brahman*; in other words, anything that is not in every respect identified with the pure Absolute, the Godhead, even though it be divine, must be endowed with a degree of relativity, a relativity and therefore an alterity at which the uncreated intellect cannot stop, its quest being for absolute union: the commitment to the Absolute must itself likewise be absolute.

This interpretation of Eckhart's dialectical intention is given support by a statement in another sermon on the aspect of the soul that is subject to the experience and benefit of grace: "God shines in a darkness where the soul outgrows all light; true, in her powers she receives light and sweetness and grace, but in her ground she receives nothing but God barely" (II:328). The individual powers are receptive to the relatively transcendent outflows that constitute the graces of God, while the supra-individual ground of the soul is receptive only to the absolutely transcendent Godhead, with which it is completely one; it is therefore in one's created nature that grace is felt, while with one's uncreated nature that identity with the source of grace is realized.

With these points in the background it will be easier to understand the next—at first sight paradoxical—stage of the ascent. For though earlier it was established that the Birth was equivalent to union, wherein the "whole beatitude" of the soul lay, it now appears that there is a stage higher than the Birth, at which occurs a "breakthrough" to the Godhead, a begetting of the begetter.

In one sermon there is an indication that the Birth of the Word is to be distinguished from the life that proceeds from that Birth; asking himself the question whether the highest beatitude lies in love or in the vision of God, Eckhart answers that it is in neither: "Once born, he neither sees nor pays heed to God: but at the moment of birth *then* he has a vision of God. . . . The spirit is in bliss then because it has been born, and not at being born, for then it lives as the Father lives, that is in the simple and naked essence" (II:100).

In other words, the eternal beatitude that has previously been identified with the Birth *qua* union is here shown to be more in the nature of an implicit seed within the experience of the Birth: at the actual moment of the Birth there is what might be called a specifically human beatitude, an experience of the Divine which, on the one hand, is conditioned by the previous absence of this beatitude—this contrast deriving from the very confrontation between the human and the Divine—and, on the other hand, prefigures or anticipates an eternal beatitude, proper to the One alone in its infinite essence. This is the mode of living as the "Father lives . . . in the essence."

To "live" according to the life of the essence can be understood in two ways: firstly, in terms of spiritual experience or "state": there is an allusion to a higher state than the Birth, one which is implicit in it, namely, the "Breakthrough" (*Durchbruch*). This aspect will be addressed below. Secondly, it can be taken to refer to what has been termed here the "existential return": the fundamental orientation and way of life that flows from the consummation of union. This aspect will be examined in Part III of the chapter; the focus at present will remain on the experiential dimension of the ascent of consciousness to the summit of spiritual realization.

The human experience of beatitude—"at the moment of birth"—is limited, but only in relation to the eternal, essential beatitude which has never not been; the human beatitude experienced at the Birth pertains to the nature of a change of state, hence a "becoming," and it thereby involves the relatively transcendent bliss of "being born," as opposed to the absolutely transcendent bliss of the essence. The spirit enjoys a foretaste of this eternal beatitude "because it has been born"; that is, because it lives in the life that flows forth or unfolds from the Birth.

This final ascent into oneness with the Father must be understood as union with the supra-personal essence or Godhead, and not with the Father *qua* Person, for this pertains to the level of the Trinitarian "acting" God. As will be seen shortly, Eckhart offers another schema for the Trinity, whereby Father denotes the essence, Son, union with the essence, and Holy Ghost, the goodness flowing from this union. In attaining to union with the Father *qua* essence, the "I" of Eckhart is extinguished, so for him to say "I beget my begetter" means simply that whatever flows from the essence by way of hypostatic determination—on the plane of the Principle, or Being—and by way of further specific manifestations—on the plane of existentiated souls, Eckhart's own included—all of this becomes Eckhart's "act" by virtue of his effective identification with the essence. In this light, the following statement is more clearly understood: "He has been ever begetting me, his only-begotten son, in the very image of His eternal Fatherhood, that I may be a father and beget Him of whom I am begotten" (II:64).

In the same sermon in which Eckhart so rigorously distinguished between the working God and the non-working Godhead, he says: "When I return to God, if I do not remain there, my breakthrough will be far nobler than my outflowing. . . . [W]hen I enter the ground, the bottom, the river and fount of the Godhead, none will ask me whence I came or where I have been. No one missed me, for there God unbecomes" (II:82).

Not to remain at "God" means not being restricted by the plane of personal affirmation on the ontological degree of Being, but "breaking through" to the supra-ontological essence, where, if there is no possibility of the distinctive affirmation of the threefold personality of God, there is *a fortiori*, no question of Eckhart's personality as such being affirmed either in this transcendent attainment. If "no one missed me" this is because there was or is no "other" that could either miss or be missed: the essence can but be one, even while comprising within itself all-possibility, in absolutely undifferentiated mode, Beyond-Being.

One observes that the process of return to the Godhead describes the inverse of the movement by which the Godhead "melts outwards" into the Trinity: "Essence is the Father, unity is the Son with the Father, goodness is the Holy Ghost. Now the Holy Ghost takes the soul in her purest and highest and bears her into her source which is the Son, and the Son bears her further into his source which is the Father, into the ground, into the beginning, where the Son has his being" (I:265).

Goodness, or the Holy Ghost, in this schema, is the first effusion, and it also corresponds to that grace which is necessary for the soul to be drawn into its own ground, this contact resulting in the Birth of the Son; that which flows out of the essence, communicating its goodness to creatures is thus that which attracts the creatures back towards the essence: the grace of pure goodness is a flow and an ebb. The Son, having been born in the soul, then transports the soul's uncreated element by a total reabsorption back into its own ground which is identical to the ground of the Son, that is, the Father *qua* essence. So this final "breakthrough" denotes the absolutely transcendent mode of union between the soul and the Godhead.

Although in one respect this attainment is called the soul's breakthrough, it must in another, more fundamental respect, be called God's breakthrough: "This spirit must transcend number and break through multiplicity, and God will break through him: and just as He breaks through into me, so I break through in turn into Him" (I:136).

God's breakthrough into Eckhart depends upon Eckhart's transcendence of outward diversity, which diversifies and thus dissipates consciousness; and Eckhart's breakthrough into God is strictly conditional upon God's breakthrough into him: the act of pure transcendence by which the uncreated intellect realizes the essence is thus only conceivable as the counterpart of the divine breakthrough into the soul's essence, so that it would be more accurate to say that it is the Absolute as transcendent object that breaks through and assimilates to itself the divine element present within the depths of the relative subject, rather than to assert baldly that the uncreated intellect "attains" or breaks through into the essence.

This point emerges with clarity from the following principle, which is enunciated immediately after stating that the spark seeks only the source of being, "the silent desert into which no distinction ever peeped of Father, Son, or Holy Ghost": "In the inmost part, where none is at home, there that light finds satisfaction, and there it is more one than it is itself" (II:105).

In other words, the last trace of any individuality is effaced from the intellect in this highest realization; it is not so much an affirmation of the intellect within this "inmost part," as its complete identification with that "part" with which it is "more one than it is itself." It is important to elaborate on this principle for it shows clearly that Eckhart cannot in good logic be accused of intellectual hubris, the reduction of the essence of God to the level of human intellect. Rather, it is the converse that is true: "If you were to cast a drop into the ocean, the drop would become the ocean, and not the ocean the drop. Thus it is with the soul: when she imbibes God, she is turned into God, so that the soul becomes divine, but God does not become the soul" (II:323).

The return of the drop to the ocean is a useful image for establishing the consubstantiality of the soul and God, while simultaneously affirming the transcendence of the Divine over the human; but to indicate more directly the nature of the immanence of the Divine within the soul, this image needs to be complemented by the following notion: transcendent height is identical with interiorization in depth. Eckhart establishes this perspective by saying: "The deeper the well, the higher it is; height and depth are one" (III:53); and again, more elaborately:

> God is brought down, not absolutely but inwardly, that we may be raised up. What was above has become inward. You must be internalized, from yourself and within yourself, so that He is in you. It is not that we should take anything from what is above us, but we should take it into ourselves, and take it from ourselves, and take it from ourselves into ourselves (II:46).

The "highest" is revealed as the "inmost" when consciousness is most fully interiorized; it is thus that the highest is taken "into ourselves"; taking it "from ourselves" means understanding that our inner substance is itself the "highest" inasmuch as this is immanent in all that exists; and finally taking it "from ourselves into ourselves" means sublimating the outer personal consciousness— an exteriority which implies alterity—within the inner unitive dimension, wherein no differentiation subsists. The notion of not taking "anything from what is above us" can mean, in this perspective, not attempting to appropriate to one's outer being any properties relating to the transcendent aspect of God: again one observes the crucial principle, noted in the previous chapters, that the transcendent is realizable only by way of immanence, an interiorization to a point in consciousness which transcends by way of depth the empirical consciousness of the outer ego.

In another description of the state of union between the soul and the uncreate, Eckhart says: "When the soul has got so far it loses its name and is drawn into

God, so that in itself it becomes nothing, just as the sun draws the dawn into itself and annihilates it" (III:126). The dawn experiences a loss of identity as dawn, but this loss is the price paid for the brilliance of unobstructed sunlight, before which no "dawn" can subsist; the dim light of dawn must be annulled, but only by a light infinitely more refulgent, and so it is with the soul: the limited light of its intellect must give way to the infinite light of the Absolute.

In another sermon Eckhart says that the light by which the intellect sees must be the light of the Absolute if it is to see the Absolute as it is in itself: "Supposing my eye were a light, and strong enough to absorb the full force of the sun's light and unite with it, then it would see not only by its own power, but it would see with the light of the sun in all its strength. So it is with the intellect. The intellect is a light, and if I turn it away from all things and in the direction of God, then, since God is continually overflowing with grace, my intellect becomes illumined and united with love, and therein knows and loves God as He is in Himself" (II:281).

This extract also helps to underline the methodic necessity of unitive concentration: the intellect, stripped bare of all contingent content, must concentrate on the exclusive reality of God so that, by virtue of its own uncreated substance, it may be sublimated within the uncreated light of God; one observes here a useful clarification of the point made earlier about the implication of the intellect's capacity to conceive the supra-ontological esssence: the eye of the intellect can only gaze on the light of God because of the affinity—and, in the final analysis, identity—between its own uncreated substance and the uncreated reality of God.

This methodic capacity to concentrate on the Absolute is closely related to the intellectual capacity to conceive of the Absolute; as seen earlier, the Absolute can only be referred to, in discursive terms, by an apophatic dialectic, so the question arises, what is it that the intellect can conceive of, that then serves as the object upon which attention is concentrated? One plausible answer that may be extrapolated from Eckhart's perspective is that, since the intellect is satisfied only by the Absolute, this means that the realization of union in supra-ontological mode alone represents the apotheosis of the intellect; but in its quest for that union, the intellect's powers of conception function in such a manner as to exclude all that can form the basis for determinate—hence limited—conception; therefore, one may say that, in its conceptual mode, the intellect is only "satisfied" by that which surpasses its own power of conception—the properly limitless, infinite, transcendent One. To say that the intellect "conceives" of the Absolute—upon which it then concentrates—means that it can conceive of a "somewhat" which is intelligible only by way of negation: a "somewhat" which surpasses the limits of determinate conception; thus it is a conception of the intrinsically inconceivable, but remains nonetheless a conception since it is present to the mind. In other words, it is possible to conceive *that* it is, but impossible to conceive *what* it is, except in antinomian terms, as seen in Part I.

One may observe here the inverse of the process by which the Father "speaks" the Son: "The object of the Father's thought is the eternal Word" (II:300). If the Son as Word is the determinate object of the intellection of the Father, then the supra-personal essence is the indeterminable object of the intellection of the soul. While the first is a downward movement intending manifestation, determination, and hence limitation, the second is an upward movement intending the non-manifest, indeterminate, and limitless. It must be stressed that the *raison d'être* of such a conception is, not its extrinsic formulation *qua* conception, but its inner content which remains inexpressible in discursive terms, and ineffable in terms of spiritual realization.

Returning now to the question of the essential identity between the intellect and its object, Eckhart gives an extremely important analogy, about which he says: "If you can understand it, you will be able to grasp my meaning and get to the bottom of all that I have ever preached about (II:104)." The analogy is based on the relationship between the act of seeing, the eye that sees, and a piece of wood that is seen:

> When my eye is open it is an eye: when it is shut it is the same eye; and the wood is neither more nor less by reason of my seeing it. . . . Suppose my eye, being one and single in itself, falls on the wood with vision, then though each thing stays as it is, yet in the very act of seeing they are so much at one that we can really say "eye-wood," and the wood is my eye. Now, if the wood were free from matter and wholly immaterial like my eyesight is, then we could truly say that, in the act of seeing, the wood and my eye were of one essence. If this is true for material things, it is all the more true of spiritual (II:104).

One should note first of all that the eye remains quite distinct from the wood when considered apart from the vision wherein the two are united; and the wood does not change by virtue of being seen by the eye. This can mean, by appropriate transposition, that the Absolute, as object of the intellective vision, is not affected in its transcendent essence either by being "realized" or not realized, the change in question relating to the eye which so completely enters the wood in the act of vision that it becomes one with it; while a complete identity of essence on the level of matter is precluded due to the principle of separativity inherent in matter, such is not the case in the spiritual domain, where the lower is assimilable by the higher.

This analogy is useful in elucidating the nature of pure, unitive concentration which may be envisaged as the methodic counterpart to this transcendent intellectual vision: what, *a priori*, is a focussing of attention on the supreme object that transcends the personal intellect, becomes through methodic concentration a realization of identity with that object, but not as object, rather as immanent subject, the very word "con-centration" suggesting this process of assimilation within one's own center, a "taking from oneself into oneself."

This is also implicit in Eckhart's insistence that "whatever a man draws into himself or receives from without is wrong"; one must not consider God as outside oneself, "but as one's own and as what is within oneself" (II:136). In other words, it is one's deepest oneself that in reality furnishes the transcendent object of that intellection that initially pertains to a relatively more outward mode of one's own being: that upon which one concentrates is one's own deepest self, even if the subjective starting point of concentration is necessarily located on the relative plane of one's being whence the innermost subjectivity must at first be envisaged as the transcendent object.

This concentration is thus an essential condition for the process whereby the object of concentration "digests" the concentrating subject; whereas in material terms, food consumed is assimilated to the individual, in spiritual terms, this is reversed: that which the individual takes into himself changes him into it: "The bodily food we take is changed into us, but the spiritual food we receive changes us into itself" (I:50).

This idea is well expressed, with a nuance that opens up the principle of identity, in terms of another analogy using wood; this time, wood symbolizes the relative soul, in relation to the "fire" of the Absolute: "Fire changes into itself what is added to it, which becomes its own nature. The wood does not change the fire into itself, but the fire changes the wood into itself. Thus we are changed into God that we may know Him as He is" (II:137).

The wood can only be changed into fire to the extent that it has within its nature a profound affinity with fire; and this, despite the outwardly tangible differences between their respective natures that render them incommensurable in the very measure that they are physically kept apart from each other. One can see the relevance of this image to the relationship between the soul and God: to the extent that the soul subsists in its created awareness, it is remote from God, and there is a strict incommensurability between the soul as such and God as such; but on contact between the wood and fire—the awakening of the soul to the divine reality—an unsuspected affinity is revealed, and, eventually, a total union is consummated. Going back to what Eckhart said above about union, the one agent is reduced to nothing, while the other remains what it is.

This useful analogy sheds light on what is meant by the following statement expressing the spiritual inversion of natural processes, and the gift that *is* the Giver preceding the gifts *of* the Giver:

> Nature makes a man out of a child and a hen out of an egg, but God makes the man before the child, and the hen before the egg. Nature first makes wood warm and hot, and thereafter creates the essence of fire; but God first gives all creatures their being and after that, in time yet timelessly, He gives individually all that belongs to it. And God gives the Holy Ghost before He gives the gifts of the Holy Ghost (III:113-114).

That to which man's consciousness attains is attainable only because it is inherent in his very being: attainment or union is then considered not so much as an effect of a preceding cause, rather, it is seen as the cause which is only apparently produced by its own effect; apparently, because in truth it is the eternally preexistent element, hence the paradox that, having given creatures their being, God then gives all that properly pertains to that being "in time yet timelessly"; that is, given in time, with regard to the extrinsic chain of temporal causality in which the gift or the effect—the realization of union being of all gifts the most precious—comes after the cause—God's unifying grace; while the intrinsic truth of the union is that it is a timeless reality, more "real" therefore than the whole dimension of relativity presupposed by temporal causality.

Prior to realizing pure being, man is already, by virtue of his very actuality, endowed with that being; the process of perfection is God's "giving individually" all that which already inheres in being, and this involves the reabsorption of the individual consciousness back into the immanent universality whence that consciousness sprang. The gift that *is* the Holy Ghost is thus inherent in the very gift of life, and is the inner condition which produces receptivity to the gifts *of* the Holy Ghost: one can receive these gifts because one already has the Giver, in turn a gift from the One who alone is real, so that the giving and the receiving are experienced by the same subject, exteriorized only for the sake of the glory of the inward return, inwards after the outward radiation: "my breakthrough will be far nobler than my outflowing" (II:82).

These considerations lead us to pose the question: if there is but one subject, what dimension of that subject is the locus for the experience of union? An answer to this emerges from the following extracts. In the first, Eckhart describes a debate between "understanding" and "love," each claiming preeminence over the other. Then the "highest intellect" intervenes:

> He to whom you (two) have led me, and whom I have hitherto known, He knows Himself now in me, and He whom I have loved, He loves Himself in me. Thus I realize that I need no one any more. All created things must remain behind (I:267-268).

Understanding and love initiate the movement towards God, but are surpassed by the uncreated aspect of the intellect at the summit of that process. It is important to stress that by the word "understanding," Eckhart here implies distinctive knowledge in which the subject and object remain separate, and "love" is likewise a mode which is mediated by the terms of a polarity defined by the lover and the beloved. But the highest intellect, while comprising both aspects, nonetheless abolishes their limitative specificity, and realizes their union in a dimension which surpasses the ontological degree proper to their distinctive affirmation; both knowledge and love, and the duality subject-object implied by their individualized operation, are resolved within an undifferentiated oneness, so that the "hitherto known and loved"—that is, the transcendent object intended by both knowledge and love—becomes the absolute subject, having as object nothing outside itself: thus it is God who is the agent of knowledge "in me."

The created soul, on its own account, is a "pure nothing"; and yet, since the Divine can only know and love itself in itself, to say that this supreme Self-knowledge and Self-love is realized in the soul, means that the soul, in another respect, is not just a "something," but that it is identical with the One in its uncreated substance and ground. It is as though Eckhart were saying: it is only in me-as-God, and not in me-as-creature, that God can love and know Himself in me. By means of these affirmations, attention has been focussed on the divine subjectivity within man that experiences union; the following extract sharpens further this focus:

> The soul must dwell above herself if she is to lay hold of God: for however much she might achieve with that power whereby she grasps created things . . . yet she cannot

grasp God. The infinite God who is in the soul, He grasps the God who is infinite. Then God grasps God, God makes God in the soul and shapes her after Himself (II:259).

If it is only the Infinite that can grasp the Infinite, then that which is described as the "inmost man" must be identified with the immanent presence of God, it must be a center which unfolds in infinitude: "The inner man and the outer man are as different as heaven and earth. . . . [A]ll creatures are savored by my outer man as creatures, . . . but my inner man savors things not as creatures but as God's gift. But my inmost man savors them not as God's gift, but as eternity" (II:80-81).

Three subjectivities are delineated here: the first clearly pertains to formal manifestation and has in view the senses and the reason or lower intellect; the second to supra-formal manifestation, having the higher intellect for its mode of cognition, a mode which is itself supra-formal, but individualized in the measure that there can still be a distinction between the "savoring" subject and the object "savored"—in this case the creature as divine gift; the third degree of subjectivity pertains to the eternal, transcending all manifestation, wherein the uncreated and uncreatable substance of the intellect is fully identified with the universal and hence the eternal, within which all things are encompassed. Hence the inmost man savors no particularity in regard to creatures, but rather has a taste only for that eternity with which "it is more one than it is itself," to recall the phrase used by Eckhart in relation to the highest mode of being for the intellect. These three degrees of subjectivity can be seen to correspond to the following ontological ternary: the creature—standing in synecdochic fashion for the level of formal existence; the Creator, standing for the level of supra-formal Being; and the Godhead, standing for the level of Beyond-Being. Thus the passage from the inner man to the inmost man is an inverse reflection—in depth and subjectively—of the passage from God to the Godhead—in height and objectively; this reveals once again the identity between transcendent height and immanent depth.

This still leaves the question: if it is God Himself that is the proper locus for the subjective experience of union, what can Eckhart the created soul know about this degree of knowledge and being? An answer is forthcoming in the sermon called "The Nobleman." Its basis is the verse: "A certain nobleman went away to a distant country to gain a kingdom for himself, and returned" (Luke, 19, 12). In this sermon, Eckhart recapitulates many of the essential points elaborated above, and, towards its end, interprets the meaning of the journey and the "return"; the "going away" means that man must "be one in himself . . . to see God alone" while "returning" means "being aware and knowing that one knows God and is aware of it" (III:114).

"To see God alone" clearly means to exclude all but the One from consciousness, to interiorize oneself by means of the methodic unitive concentration described above; and then the nobleman can find God—the "kingdom" that is "within you," Eckhart might well have added—only when he is in a "distant land," that is to say: only when, in the innermost depths of his own being, there is a radical rupture with individual consciousness, so that it can no longer be said to be the individual that is the agent or subject of the experience; on his "return" to himself, he is aware that it could not have been him *qua* individual who knew God in that state, but that nonetheless this knowledge was attained or realized within him. As an individual, then, he knows both that transcendent knowledge is "known" in him and that, as an individual, he can *only* know that this transcendent consciousness was realized, and is eternally being realized within him; while he cannot as an individual know the Transcendent in itself: he knows that That which can be known only by itself does so within his own soul at a level which, precisely, excludes his own limitative, personal affirmation, that is: his "nothingness." Hence this knowledge is realized in a "distant land": a supra-ontological degree that is incommensurable with his own existential actuality.

Finally, it should be emphasized that this distant land is in reality the immutable and eternal unity of the divine nature, being "distant" only in relation to the extrinsic plane of outwardly diverse phenomena; it is precisely because of its supra-phenomenal degree that, comprising all phenomena within itself in undifferentiated unity, it must be regarded as infinitely transcending—hence "distant" from—the plane of phenomena. It is with this unconditional divine oneness that the individual's consciousness is indistinguishably identified in the highest realization: Commenting on Hosea, 2, 14: "I will lead the noble soul into a wilderness, and there I will speak into her heart," Eckhart adds: "one with One, one from One, one in One, and a single One eternally" (III:114-115).

To conclude this discussion: properly transcendent consciousness is attained in the experience of the Birth and Breakthrough, the union of the soul with the Godhead; and this union is possible only on the basis of that element of absoluteness already present in the uncreated essence of the intellect. The process by which this uncreated intellect comes to realize its identity as the Absolute is based in the first instance on the operation of grace, which draws this element up through the degrees of being until it is finally reabsorbed back into the source whence it derived, a source that transcends the plane presupposed by the operation of grace. The individual in whom this realization takes effect knows that he, as such, cannot be the agent of the transcendent knowledge revealed in the state of union, and he also knows that his knowledge as an individual is as limited, in relation to that transcendent knowledge, as the very limitation constituted by his empirical individuality in relation to the infinitude of transcendent being. The manner in which he lives henceforth, oriented towards that higher reality, whilst necessarily subject to the framework of the lesser reality of this world, is the subject of Part III.

## Part III: Existential "Return"

Eckhart's position on the return to phenomenal awareness can be assessed in relation to four broad and interrelated categories: the *modus operandi* of the perfect saint, the man in whom the Birth has been—and is being—consummated;

his manner of "seeing God in all things"; the question of whether the saint is susceptible to ordinary suffering in the world; and finally the nature of the "poverty" that characterizes the saint in his relationship with God.

## 1. Thought and Action in the World

The first question to ask about the realized man is the following: how does he act, think, and move "outside" of his state of supra-phenomenal union, in the world, and with the awareness of diverse outward phenomena and images?

Eckhart's answer would include the following important principle: it is God Himself who acts through such a man, in the measure that he has realized his oneness with the Godhead. What then flows from such a man is the Holy Ghost, just as the first effusion of the transcendent deity is the goodness that the Holy Ghost is: "It (the Holy Ghost) flows forth from all who are God's sons, according as they are in greater or lesser degree born purely of God alone" (III:85).

That this flow, in ontological mode, directly stems from union in supra-ontological mode, is shown in one of his descriptions of the Birth; he begins with the key Augustinian proposition: "it is in the nature of the good to diffuse itself," and then proceeds to say that the Birth is always accompanied by light: "In this birth God streams into the soul in such abundance of light, so flooding the essence and ground of the soul that it runs over and floods into the powers and into the outward man" (I:16).

Having concentrated all outer powers of the soul upon the silent and non-working center of the soul, none can be said to subsist as powers, rather, each is merged into the undifferentiated concentration required for the Birth; but, outside of this concentration, and in the light flowing from the Birth, the powers of the outward man are illuminated in the field of their respective activities: the "sleep" of his powers corresponds to the "unknowing" of the outward man in relation to the unitive state, which is pure "wake" and supernatural knowing for the inner man; while the powers in their turn are fully awake only in the light that floods into the outward man by virtue of the consummation of the Birth.

The next question that logically presents itself is: given this mode of grace, to what extent does the intellect still function in a conventional manner when dealing in the world with particular phenomena? Eckhart's answer to this can be extrapolated from his response to a similar, rhetorical question posed by himself. First, he distinguishes between the active and the passive intellect; the former abstracts from phenomena their appropriate images and implants them into the passive intellect. Under normal functioning, the intellect thus works with one image at a time, but if a man's active intellect be stilled for and by God, then God perforce takes over its role and impregnates the passive intellect, not with one image, but with "many images together in one point," those images, that is to say, that are necessary for the proper accomplishment of the particular work in question.

> For if God prompts you to a good deed, at once all your powers proffer themselves for all good things: your whole mind at once tends to good in general. Whatever good you can do takes place and presents itself to you together in a flash, concentrated in a single point (I:30).

The man who thus attains to union with the non-acting Godhead, Beyond-Being, recapitulates his experience within being by what may be termed a "unitive activity," and this to the extent that his own active intellect is inactive, so that the divine intellect operates within him, not with multiple images but with what one might call a "polysynthetic" image containing all those images required by the lower powers and bodily members for the accomplishment of the good work.

However, this does not mean that such a man is rendered infallible; it is clear that this *modus operandi* is not applicable in each and every circumstance of life, but seems rather to refer to the essential work undertaken by the individual; this is because Eckhart concedes that it is possible that even great saints may "slip" or "err in speech": "[S]hould it happen that such a man slipped or erred in speech, or that something wrong crept in, since God began the work He must bear the damage. . . . In this life we can never be quite free from such incidents" (III:28).

Despite this possibility of negligible error, the man in whom the Birth is consummated is no longer liable to gross error and, still less, to sin: "I am sure that the man who is established in this (Birth) cannot in any way ever be separated from God. I say he can in no way lapse into mortal sin" (I:11-12).

It should be noted that it is the outer man who is prevented from sinning by the realized consciousness of the inner man; in another sermon, Eckhart says that, after union with the Word, "the outer man will be obedient to his inner man until death, and will at all times be at peace in the service of God for ever" (I:61). While the inner man is conscious of identity with the One, the outer man acts in the framework of multiplicity, but in a manner that conforms to this consciousness; and this conformity or "obedience" translates into serene devotion to God in all things, in contrast to that disobedience constituted by sin.

It would appear that Eckhart has in mind this "outer" man when he speaks of the possibility of "slips," since the inner man is "impeccable," in the strict sense of "incapable of sin." This interpretation finds support from the following statement: "The soul has two eyes, one inward and one outward. The soul's inner eye is that which sees into being, and derives its being without any mediation from God. The soul's outer eye is that which is turned towards all creatures, observing them as images and through the powers" (II:141).

If, then, there is the possibility of error for the saint, this can only pertain to his outer man—or his "outward eye"—not his inner man, and it can only relate to phenomenal existence, not principial realities, and it can involve only minor details, not important actions; thus this type of error possesses a significance as relative as the plane of phenomena to which it is restricted. In other words, the closer to the plane of principial realities, to Being and the divine order, the less possibility there is of error, which is thus limited—intellectually, ontologically, and morally—to the peripheric or epiphenomenal planes of existence. The saint is thus in a quasi-permanent state of inspiration, the fallibility of his specific human nature being manifest only in proportion to the distance from the realm of pure Being, this fallibility therefore partaking of an insignificance commensurate with peripheral levels of existence.

## 2. Seeing God Everywhere

Perpetual consciousness of God within oneself is the basis for the perception of God in the world. Earlier, it was seen how Eckhart criticized the notion that God was more present or attainable by some particular "way" than another, saying that one must be as close to God by the fireside as at prayer. This attainment appears to be more in the nature of a description of the saint than a normative prescription for the ordinary man—without this distinction implying any mutual exclusion. The aim is to be united to God in all circumstances, an aim which is realized by the saint and intended by the ordinary man, who, prior to the realization of this degree of awareness, should be aware of it as the aim, even while applying himself to those practices which are most conducive to that interiorization which is the *sine qua non* of this realization. This interpretation derives in part from the following extract from Eckhart's "Talks of Instruction":

> [W]hen we speak of "equality," this does not mean that one should regard all works as equal, or all places or people. That would be quite wrong, for praying is a better task than spinning, and the church is a nobler place than the street. But in your acts you should have an equal mind and equal faith and equal love for your God (III:17).

It is the inner man that sanctifies outer works and circumstances, thus making God equally present, so far as his own consciousness is concerned, this being the subjective counterpart of the objective reality of God's inalienable presence within all things: "Do not think to place holiness in doing; we should place holiness in being, for it is not the works that sanctify us but we who should sanctify the works. . . . [I]n so far as we are and have being, just so far do we hallow all that we do. . . . Those in whom being is slight, whatever deeds they do amount to nothing" (III:15).

Although Being can but be one, the notion of degrees of Being, enunciated in Part II above, permits one to distinguish between individuals having only a "slight" degree of being and others who "are" pure being; the latter type corresponding, in terms of an earlier image, to the drop of individuality which is submerged by the ocean of which it is an infinitesimal part, and the former corresponding to those who, while still being—that is to say, whose drops cannot be other than water—nonetheless are as if separated from their source because of the opacity of their personal substance. This is in contrast to the sanctified man whose substance is transparent and thus allows the full glory of Being to shine through him; and it is through this very radiance that he may be said to "sanctify" all that he does.

The man distracted from God by phenomena is prevented from participating in the vision of God in phenomena only by his own heedlessness; it is thus "in *him* (that) God has not become all things" (III:17) (emphasis added). This shows that the accent is not on the "things" in themselves, which, as such, are unequal and subject therefore to gradation, but rather, all the stress is on the man, and more particularly, his consciousness: it must be in his awareness that the Divine is revealed within all things. Then all things are rendered equal by means of the spiritual transmutation effected upon them inwardly by the sanctified man, who, being at one with the undifferentiated nature of pure Being, is alone capable of reducing the multiple phenomena of outward existence to their inherent, unitive principle which is the very same, pure Being.

Another way of putting this idea is to say that things are rendered transparent to the light of Being pervading them immanently, by virtue of the spiritual quality of this man, since his own phenomenal existence—his "outer" man—has likewise become a transparent veil over the Being of God: having seen through himself—the subjective illusion attendant upon the empirical ego—he likewise sees through its objective correlate, the existential opacity of outward phenomena.

The following question arises: does this manner of seeing God in all things require, or on the contrary preclude, the active faculty of discernment? Given what was said above about God assuming the role of the active intellect, the answer to this question may be assumed to be in favor of the idea of preclusion; and Eckhart does say that while discriminatory effort is required in the early stages of the spiritual life, it is no longer necessary for the man who is totally pervaded by the divine presence. To begin with, the man must strive to take or grasp all things as divine, that is to say, "as greater than they are in themselves" (III:18). This perception does not imply a suspension of discernment such that one should see God even in evil things; rather, it requires a higher, ontological mode of discernment: one must distinguish between the particular qualities of a thing and its pure being. On this basis, if the thing be bad, its privative quality is rejected, while if good, its positive quality is referred back to its divine source. Awareness of God's presence within the positive being of all things is thus enhanced; such a discernment, it may be assumed, is what, among other things, Eckhart implies when he says, in regard to the above exhortation to take things as divine:

> [T]his requires zeal and love and a clear perception of the interior life and a watchful, true, wise, and real knowledge of what the mind is occupied with among things and people (III:18-19).

This process is compared to the art of writing: at first requiring much practice, careful attention to each letter, memorizing of its image, etc., this effort bears fruit in the ability to write fluently, effortlessly, and spontaneously: "Thus a man should be pervaded with God's presence, transformed with the form of his beloved God, and made essential by Him, so that God's presence shines for him without any effort" (III:19).

At this stage the personal, active intellect may be said to have given way to the divine intellect, so that the passive intellect intuitively and spontaneously receives the appropriate divine images from things; put differently, once the uncreated essence of the intellect is actualized, the divine element in outward things is grasped by means of the divine element within the intellect. One observes here a reflection, in manifest mode, of the supra-manifest realization of union: just as it is the infinite God within the soul that, alone, can know and be one with the infinite God above the soul, so it can only be the fully awakened uncreated substance of the intellect that can see through created accidents and grasp the uncreated substance of the Divine within all things.

In terms of the concept of "possession," Eckhart states that "all things" thus "belong" only to the man who, in turn, belongs to all things, but not as they are in themselves, rather, as they are in God, to whom this man belongs exclusively: "He is altogether our own, and all things are our own in Him. . . . [W]e must take Him equally in all things, in one not more than in another, for He is alike in all things" (I:111-112).

In regard to "things" as persons, Eckhart elucidates the nature of this supra-empirical perception of God within them by means of a comparison with the theological principle given earlier, that of the undifferentiated Godhead transcending, even while comprising, the distinctiveness of the Persons:

> Whoever would exist in the nakedness of this nature, free from all mediation, must have left behind all distinction of person, so that he is as well disposed to a man who is across the sea, whom he has never set eyes on, as to the man who is with him and is his close friend. As long as you favor your own person more than that man you have never seen, you are assuredly not right and you have never for a single instant looked into this simple ground (I:116).

This shows the total objectivity that characterizes the consciousness of the realized man: he regards his own creaturely personality—his empirical ego—as no more worthy of affection or attachment than that of any other person. In regard to the "simple ground," the differentiated affirmations or personal specificities constituted by creatures are equally far removed; and yet, since the ground is absolutely simple and unique, each of these personalities can but be one with this ground, but only at an ontological degree which precludes both their creatureliness and their specificity. In other words, for the man who has attained to the Birth, by virtue of his effective identification with humanity as such, and by virtue of his transcendence of the created nature attendant upon being such and such a human being, for such a person, all particular beings can be grasped in their deepest essence: they are viewed as so many recapitulations of integral human nature, or as so many modes of the One, he does not stop short at their limitative particularities. Only for one who has realized his own inmost nature is it possible to view others in a corresponding depth, grasping thereby the Divinity that constitutes their essence, and also knowing that this Divinity can but be one and the same within them and oneself, so that there can be no question of making rigid distinctions between oneself and others.

Another way of putting this mode of permanent awareness of the Divine within all things is given by Eckhart in terms of a vision of the sun; explaining that one of the key criteria for establishing the authenticity of the Birth is that all things must remind one of God, he goes on to say: "All things become simply God to you, for in all things you notice only God, just as a man who stares long at the sun sees the sun in whatever he afterwards looks at" (I:44).

In accordance with the threefold nature of the Word as Power-Wisdom-Sweetness, the invariable concomitant of this consciousness of the Divine is the experience of beatitude; one of the proofs of having effectively realized union is that henceforth, even in the world, the presence of God is inalienable, and awareness of this presence is blessedness:

God is closer to me than I am to myself. . . . So He is also in a stone or a log of wood, only they do not know it. . . . And so man is more blessed than a stone or piece of wood because he is aware of God and knows how close God is to him. And I am the more blessed, the more I realize this. . . . I am not blessed because God is in me . . . but because I am aware of how close He is to me and that I know God (II:165-166).

In other words it is not the objective and inalienable presence of God that produces blessedness, but the degree to which awareness is attuned to this presence or proportioned to this Being.

## 3. The Saint and Suffering

These points form an appropriate bridge to the next question: whether the man sanctified by the Birth is subject to suffering. For if awareness of God is perpetual, and if this awareness produces blessedness, how is it possible for such a man to undergo suffering? Eckhart's various statements on this question may lead some to conclude that he contradicts himself, sometimes denying and at other times affirming that suffering takes place; but the key to understanding his position lies in correctly grasping, within the very consciousness of the saint, the locus or agent that experiences suffering, and the ontological degree occupied by this agent.

One may usefully begin the discussion with the following unequivocal statement: "When you have reached the point where nothing is grievous or hard to you, and where pain is not pain to you, when everything is perfect joy to you, then your child has really been born" (I:68). He gives, by way of illustrating concretely the nature of this impassibility, the example of witnessing the slaughter of his loved ones: "[I]f the child is born in me, the sight of my father and all my friends slain before my eyes would leave my heart untouched. For if my heart were moved thereby, the child would not have been born in me, though its birth might be near" (I:68).

On the other hand he says, "never was there a saint so great but he could be moved"; all saints then, however great, are still subject to being "moved." This appears to be a contradiction, until one notes carefully the nature of this "movement": "Yet . . . I hold that it is possible for a saint even in this life to be so that nothing can move him to turn from God" (I:86).

The saint can be moved, then, but not in such wise as to be removed from the consciousness of the divine presence; he is moved—emotionally or otherwise— to some extent, but at the same time he remains inwardly impassible in the permanent awareness of God. This simultaneous movement and impassibility is expressed by Eckhart in terms of an image of a well-anchored boat: the wind may blow, and the boat may "move," but it cannot be carried away (II:124-125).

In other words, even if pain be experienced, and one is to a certain extent "moved" by it, it is the mark of the saint to relativize this pain, accepting it as the will of God, and remaining inwardly one with the reality of God that transcends all such contingencies. Thus he is not "carried away" either from his awareness of God or from the joy that this awareness entails for the inner man, once this inner man be realized, once "the child is born." It can only be the inner man that has the capacity to objectify, and thus distance himself from, the pain experienced by the outer man, an experience willed by God, and for that very reason being rendered susceptible of spiritual transmutation into joy:

> You have neither sickness nor anything else unless God wills it. And so, knowing it is God's will, you should so rejoice in it and be content, that pain would be no pain to you: even in the extremity of pain, to feel any pain or affliction would be altogether wrong, for you should accept it from God as the best of all, for it is bound to be best for you. For God's being depends on His willing the best. Let me then will it too, and nothing should please me better (I:281).

Pain, therefore, must be understood on two distinct levels: the psycho-physical, on the one hand, and the spiritual, on the other; in the absence of this distinction, the above statement is incomprehensible, or else the notion of pain loses its meaning. What Eckhart appears to be saying is the following: it is possible to experience painful states of being—physical, psychic, and emotional—without the pain penetrating into the spiritual core of the individual; in this core there subsists the awareness of the reality of God's nature and will, an awareness which takes precedence over all transient states, and can thus result in a serenity which may coexist with the experience of pain on the more superficial levels of being. He seems to be asserting the possibility—and hence the necessity—of the spiritual man attaining to a state of spiritual objectivity in relation to his own subjective states such as can eliminate, not necessarily the surface experience of pain, but the ramifications in depth of painful conditions, whether emotional or physical. It is a question of maintaining consciousness impassibly within the highest intellect:

> There is one power in the soul to which all things are alike sweet: the very worst and the very best are all the same to this power, which takes things above "here" and "now": now meaning time, and here the place where I am standing (II:237).

To return to the earlier example of witnessing the slaughter of loved ones: to the extent that consciousness resides in this power which grasps universal realities beyond time and space—realities that are inherently beatific—it will not experience distress; but inasmuch as one's outer consciousness is not penetrated by this awareness in the moment of being alive to phenomenal modalities, that same level of outer consciousness will be subject to a degree of pain; but this by no means contradicts the fact that the witnessing of such a scene "would leave my heart untouched."

In other words, one may be "moved" by such a sight, but never "carried away"; in terms of the boat image employed earlier, this inmost awareness acts as an anchor for the boat of individual consciousness in the ocean of phenomenal experiences.

If suffering has no access to this plane of the intellect, neither has joy, in the measure that the joy can be qualified as "creaturely," for the one goes inexorably with the other. If one is susceptible to profane pleasure, so that God is forgotten or eclipsed in that pleasure, then there will be an inverse opening towards its opposite, misery, which will appear to pervade the core of one's being; "appear" because, objectively speaking, that core is receptive only to the joy of God, the joy, that is, of "being born." What then suffers is the individual insofar as he is "not": the illusory nature of creaturely subsistence "apart from God" makes itself felt in the form of suffering. To be rid of "not" or of illusion is to be rooted in the immutably real; Eckhart refers to one key aspect of this impassibility as "mental satisfaction" which results "when the summit of the soul is not brought so low by any joys as to be drowned in pleasure, but rather rises resolutely above them. Man enjoys mental satisfaction only when creaturely joys and sorrows are powerless to drag down the topmost summit of the soul. 'Creature' I call whatever a man experiences under God" (I:80).

That is, joy as well as sorrow may be experienced, but the summit of the soul remains unaffected, the heart "untouched"; only non-creaturely joy is divine joy: and it is exclusively in this joy that the summit of the soul can fully participate, being raised up into the highest beatitude rather than lowered and drowned in passing creaturely joys. The negation of creaturely joy is expressed with particular clarity in the following:

> [A]s long as you are or can be comforted by creatures, you will never find true comfort. But when nothing can comfort you but God, then God will comfort you. . . . While what is not God comforts you, you will have no comfort here or hereafter, but when creatures give you no comfort, and you have no taste for them, then you will find comfort both here and hereafter (III:76).

Eckhart is here emphasizing the aspect of God's transcendence above creatures at the apparent expense of His immanence in creatures; "apparent" because if comfort is derived from creatures insofar as they manifest Divinity, then in reality this comfort comes not from creatures as such, but from the divinity that is present and real within them; the question then becomes: how to ascertain whether it is truly the divine immanence within the creature that is the source of comfort, as opposed to the creature "apart from God"; is it an orientation towards God or towards the creature that is in question? The answer emerges when deprivation of the object is experienced: if deprivation is accompanied by sorrow, then the object whence one derived comfort was creaturely, but if deprivation is accompanied by equanimity, then the true source of comfort was indeed the divine essence within the creature, an essence which eternally subsists while its creaturely vehicle perishes. On the one hand: "[A]ll sorrow comes from love of that whereof I am deprived by loss. If I mind the loss of outward things, it is a sure sign that I am fond of outward things and really love sorrow and discomfort" (Evans, II:49). And on the other hand: "[H]e who loves only God in creatures, and creatures in God only, that man finds real and true and equal comfort everywhere" (Evans, II:49).

The same point emerges from the consideration of what Eckhart refers to as the two faces of the soul, the inner face being that which is turned towards God and the outer face being the one turned towards the world: "The one is turned towards this world and the body; in this she [the soul] works virtue, knowledge, and holy living. The other face is turned directly to God. There the divine light is without interruption, working within, even though she does not know it, because she is not at home" (I:231).

Against this background, one can more clearly discern Eckhart's position both on the general question of the suffering endured by the spiritual man and on the particular question of how to interpret Christ's words: "my soul is grieved unto death":

> He did not mean his noble soul according as this is intellectually contemplating the highest good, with which he is united in person, and which he is according to union and person: that, even in his greatest suffering, he was continually regarding in his highest power, just as closely and entirely the same as he does now: no sorrow or pain or death could penetrate there (II:291).

Even as his body was dying in agony on the cross, Christ's "noble soul" was maintained in the presence of this beatific contemplation; it was only in the "part whereby his noble spirit was rationally united to the senses and life of his blessed body" that grief was necessarily experienced, for "the body had to perish." In other words, the suffering endured by Christ as a person could not affect the exalted state of his inner consciousness, his true being; this suffering was endured only at the point of contact between his outer consciousness and the sensible elements, and thus, though the suffering was real enough at its own level, it is this very level that is "unreal" or "is not" when considered from the point of view of the inner man or the inner face, and in the measure that this inner man has awakened to his own true identity as the immutably Real, the One-and-only.

In another place, where Eckhart addresses himself to the suffering of the Virgin and Christ, he gives the useful simile of a door that swings on its hinge: that which suffers, the outer man, is likened to the wood of the door, while that which remains impassible, the inner man is likened to the hinge. Therefore, the lamentations uttered by Christ and his mother are to be understood as expressions of their "outer man, but the inner man remained in unmoved detachment" (III:124).

Another way in which suffering is divested of its painful character opens up as a result of resignation in depth to the will of God. Whatever grief is endured in the world, in the very measure that it is taken as the necessary expression of God's will, the result for the individual will always be joy: the joy of accepting the will of God, since whatever God wills can only be for the good, in the final analysis, "for God's being depends on His willing the best." Even if the immediate manifestations of the consequences of God's will be privative, this will not necessarily involve suffering: if the inner consciousness of the individual is rivetted to the unimpeachable goodness of God, then His will can but be an expression of that goodness:

> Now observe what an amazing and blissful life this man must lead "in earth as in heaven"—in God Himself! Discomfort serves him as comfort, grief as well as joy—for if I have the grace and goodness of which I have spoken, then I am at all times and in all

ways equally comforted and happy; and if I lack it then I shall do without it for God's sake and by God's will (III:71).

In this way the deprivation of grace and goodness can equally well serve as the bestowal of this same grace and goodness, to the extent that, on the one hand, the deprivation is assimilated by the individual as the expression of God's will, and on the other hand, this will is understood in its inalienably beatific context: "If God wills to give me what I want then I have it and have the pleasure of it; if God does not will to give it to me, then I get it by doing without, in God's same will, and thus I take by doing without and not taking" (III:71).

To thus "get by doing without" means that one can never be "without": without the beatific consequences that flow from the permanent awareness of God and of His absolute goodness, exalted far above the privations of the relative world. Therefore, it follows that, for the man whose will is completely identified with the will of God, all suffering loses "its bitterness through God and God's sweetness, becoming pure sweetness before ever it can touch the man's heart" (III:94).

Here again, one observes the key distinction between the outward or empirically determined consciousness and the "inner man," the "heart" which experiences only the sweetness of God, whatever the external state of soul may be. Elsewhere, this condition is referred to by Eckhart as "justice": only he is just who accepts all things equally from God, and grieves at nothing: "[N]othing made or created can grieve the just, for everything created is as far beneath him as it is beneath God" (III:64).

## 4. Poverty

This is a suitable place to enter into discussion of Eckhart's conception of poverty; for this critically involves, even while surpassing, the relationship between the individual and the divine will.

In one sermon, he says that there are three ways of "running" with—or aligning oneself to— God's will: to run in front of God, beside Him, or behind Him (III:183). In the first category are those who follow only their own will, which is "altogether bad"; in the second are placed those who claim to will only what God wills, but when afflicted, will that it be God's will that they are relieved: "that may pass," Eckhart says, but it is not the best. As for the "perfect ones," they accept absolutely everything that God wills, and this is identified, *de facto*, with everything that takes place in life, since nothing happens but by the will of God.

These points serve as a useful introduction to the analysis of a powerful and important sermon on the true nature of poverty, a sermon which summarizes many of Eckhart's most striking teachings, extracts from which have already been examined in earlier sections. The dialectical approach employed in this sermon seems calculated to distinguish, with the utmost rigor, between a relative and an absolute mode of poverty; this may be seen as a mirror-image, on the plane of the individual soul, of his doctrine of the Godhead as the absolutely transcendent "modeless mode" of the Divinity, on the plane of supra-personal Beyond-Being.

The sermon is based on the text from Matthew (5, 3): "Blessed are the poor in spirit for theirs is the Kingdom of Heaven," and begins with an exhortation, already mentioned in Part I of this chapter; he appeals to his listeners to be "like" the "poor" in question, "for unless you are like this truth we are about to speak of, it is not possible for you to follow me" (II:269). The listener has to identify with the transcendent conception of poverty which Eckhart has in view, this being a prerequisite for grasping or realizing its true nature, while discarding all other preconceptions as to the conventional meanings of poverty. It is as if Eckhart were saying: let your conscious intention to identify with this poverty act as an opening through which its deepest reality may enter the soul, bringing to fruition that partial mode of poverty constituted by the very intention to be poor.

He proceeds to cite Albertus Magnus on the "poor" man: he is one who "finds no satisfaction in all things God ever created"; which is "well said," according to Eckhart. It is not, however, completely adequate. "But we shall speak better, taking poverty in a higher sense: a poor man is one who wants nothing, knows nothing, and has nothing" (II:269-270).

He then goes on to explain this threefold aspect of poverty: willing, knowing, and possessing nothing. As for the first, Eckhart again uses a conventional or non-transcendent view of willing nothing in order to situate its relativity and surpass its limitations, doing this by means of a daring—if not abusive—dialectical contrast. He criticizes those people, attached to "penances and outward practices," who claim that the poor man who wills nothing is one who "never does his own will in anything, but should strive to do the dearest will of God." Eckhart then evaluates this position thus:

> It is well with these people because their intention is right, and we commend them for it. May God in His Mercy grant them the Kingdom of Heaven! But by God's wisdom I declare that these folk are not poor men or similar to poor men. . . . I say they are asses with no understanding of God's truth. Perhaps they will gain heaven for their good intentions, but of the poverty we shall now speak of they have no idea (II:270).

It is significant that Eckhart posits the gaining of heaven as the reward to which the intention of the "asses" is proportioned, in implicit contrast to the ultimate realization of the Birth; this shows that it is exclusively from the perspective of the absolutely transcendent level that even heavenly intentions are revealed in their aspect of relativity: by using the provocative word "asses," one feels that Eckhart, in the manner of a Zen master, is delivering a salutary shock to his listeners for the sake of heightening their sensitivity—and thus receptivity—to the absolute mode of poverty which he is about to describe; this he does, after explaining the key limitation inherent in the relative mode of poverty:

> As long as a man is so disposed that it is his will with which he would do the most beloved will of God, that man has not the poverty we are speaking about: for that man has a will to serve God's will—and that is not true poverty! For a man to possess true poverty he must be as free of his created will as he was when he was not (II:270-271).

Eckhart is here describing the condition of one who truly "wills nothing" because he is liberated from his own creaturely will, so that he identifies completely with the will of God; this liberation is strictly a function of knowing the nothingness of one's own willing and being, in contrast to the unconditional reality of God's will and being, to which the creature can add nothing; and this knowledge, in turn, is a function of union: in that state the man "is not" and God alone "is."

The key condition for this absolute mode of poverty is that "a man be as free of his created will as he was when he was not"; there is here what one feels to be a deliberate ambivalence, for on the surface the statement means that the man must be as free from this will as he was prior to his existence, but a deeper meaning, centering on the fact that Eckhart says "as he *was* when he was not" relates to the subtle reality revealed in the unitive state: that the man's subjectivity is absorbed within that of the Divinity, in such wise that he as a man cannot be said to exist, and yet his essence "is" and is one with the Absolute. This highest mode of willing nothing, in the framework of outward existence in the world, can be fully realized, then, only by the consciousness of one who has effectively realized the supra-ontological plenitude that contains within it all that is. This realization gives rise to a permanent awareness of the immutable plenitude of the Godhead—where man "is not"—and the consequently immutable nothingness of all that is other than this reality, which also implies the futility of the creature's engagement with his own created will: his will is not distinguishable from the will of the Absolute, inasmuch as the lower will of man identifies with the higher will of the Divine, which expresses itself *de facto* in each and every happening in his life, as well as *de jure* in everything that takes place in the cosmos.

The next part of the sermon has already been dealt with earlier in this chapter, in the context of defining the distinction between the Godhead and the personal God: Eckhart "had no God" while he stood in his "first cause": "I was bare being and the knower of myself in the enjoyment of truth." Only when he received his "created being" did he become subject to "God": "For before there were creatures, God was not 'God': he was That which He was."

It is necessary to bear in mind this crucial defining characteristic of the personal God in order to properly understand the "prayer" that follows the enunciation of these points, and in order to situate the intended condition in the context of the absolute mode of poverty:

> Therefore let us pray to God that we may be free of God, that we may gain the truth and enjoy it eternally, there where the highest angel, the fly, and the soul are equal, there where I stood, and wanted what I was and was what I wanted (II:271).

Just as the Divine, in one dimension, is circumscribed by the fact of being "God" in relation to creatures, so the individual is likewise limited by being the inverse, a creature in relation to God; and this is the relationship within which the first, lower or non-transcendent mode of poverty is situated: where one wills to do the will of God, assuming and thereby strengthening the ontological delimitations of the duality constituted by the two agents involved; therefore, to be "free of God" means living in conformity with the knowledge of the undifferentiated nature of infinitude within the essence or Godhead, wherein all things are equally present, equally each other, and equally the selfsame Godhead. Absolute non-differentiation thus implies absolute non-manifestation of exclusive specificity; and it is the absolute mode of poverty that alone transcribes, within the created order, this highest reality, by reason of the absolute non-manifestation of the will of the created being, the total extinction of individual self-will.

It should also be noted that when Eckhart speaks of receiving his "created being," this reception goes hand in hand with the loss of his "free will": "when I left my free will behind and received my created being, then I had a God" (II:271). To be "free of God" thus means to be free of that relationship which entailed the loss of absolute freedom in the uncreate: just as this integral freedom was lost upon the assumption of created being, entailing subordination to God *qua* Creator, so the extinction of creaturely self-will—partaking of a conditional and relative freedom—in the very framework of existing creaturehood in the world, describes the inverse movement: the shedding of all limitation and determination—even while subsisting in the realm of limitation. Thus, true freedom is attained only in the context of the absolute poverty which wills nothing other than what is; that which is, in turn, being the necessary expression of the integrally free will of the Absolute, so that there is no distinction between the will of the creature and the will of the Creator, no engagement in the terms of cosmic dualism, but simply a reflection or recapitulation, within the created order, of the non-differentiation of the uncreated and metacosmic Godhead; considered in this manner one can better appreciate Eckhart's intention when he says "if a man is to be poor of will, he must will and desire as little as he willed and desired when he was not."

Turning now to the second aspect of this poverty, knowing nothing, Eckhart again sets up a distinction between what might be called a relative and an absolute mode; he begins by mentioning that he himself has "sometimes said that a man should live as if he did not live either for himself or for truth or for God." He does not elaborate any further on this, so it is necessary to venture an interpretation, based on principles enunciated elsewhere by him, in order to situate the higher position to come. What he appears to mean is that, even though one be living in a holy manner, if this is accompanied by the idea that it is in accordance either with one's own self-interest, or by the idea that it is in conformity with the dictates of truth, or by the idea that it is in obedience to the will of God, then the mode of living will be relativized inasmuch as these concepts necessarily pertain to a non-absolute ontological degree, wherein the distinctive notions of "self," "truth," and "God"—defined as the "other"—veil the true nature of the One Self, the Godhead, beyond all determinative attributions, and *a fortiori*, beyond all limitative conceptions. One must live, then, not for oneself, nor for the truth, nor for God. But even this position is inadequate in the present context:

> But now . . . we go further: for a man to possess this poverty, he must live so that he is unaware that he does not live for himself or for truth or for God. He must be so lacking in all knowledge, that he neither knows nor recognizes nor feels that God lives in him: more still, he must be free of all the understanding that lives in him (II:272).

Eckhart now seems to be saying that whereas in the first case, a man must so live that he is completely at one with the Absolute in terms of his being (life) and his knowledge—that is, by not attributing to his mode of being any conceptually circumscribed "position" defined in terms of a relationship with some distinctively affirmed, and thus non-transcendent, entity—in the present case, one must be completely *unaware of the fact* that one is living in accordance with this condition. By this may be understood a degree of unself-consciousness, an absence of the specific knowledge that one is living in accordance with the true nature of the unconditional One; in other words, there should be such a degree of absorption in this holy way of life that there is no room for any superadded content of knowledge over and above this mode of being, which would thus be relativized by virtue of being conditioned by, or subordinated to, the human aspect of this knowledge. In other words, being must not become compromised by thought. This interpretation accords with what follows:

> For when that man stood in the eternal being of God, nothing else lived in him: what lived there was himself. Therefore we declare that a man should be as free from his own knowledge as he was when he was not. That man should let God work as he will, and himself stand idle (II:272).

In the Godhead—here described as "the eternal being of God"—knowledge is not a distinctive element added to being: the two are inextricably one; so, in his "poor" state, the individual must reflect this non-differentiation, and must not see his knowledge of things as a distinct possession attaching or superadded to his individual substance, for any such possession not only contradicts poverty, but also constitutes an object to which the individual may become abusively attached: thus there is, objectively, an entrenchment of ontological separativity—as inescapable concomitant—and subjectively, pride and attachment—as ever-present possibility—in the measure that the man is not "free of all the understanding that lives in him."

There must be no individualistic awareness of one's "own" knowledge as a distinct element, for this not only belies the reality that all knowledge and truth "belong" exclusively to the One, the only true agent of knowledge, but it also contradicts the integral holy life in which one's knowledge is effectively and totally identified with one's being; negatively, this absence of hypocrisy—the contrast between what one knows and what one is—may be viewed as the moral reflection of the state of union; and positively, the impersonal identity between knowledge and being reflects both the particular state of union—again, "as he *was* when he was not"—and the universal, eternal, and immutable condition of the Godhead: "God is not a being and not intellectual and does not know this or that. Thus God is free of all things and so He is all things" (II:272).

In other words, the formless essence of God cannot be reduced to the status of a particular entity, knowing other particular entities; it is precisely because He is all things—constituting their very essence and true being—that He is free of all things—defined in terms of their existential limitations. He does not know distinctive particulars—this and that—as we would know them in conventional cognitive terms, because this would imply a separation between Him as a knowing being and others as objects known: the reality is that His being is one with His knowing, and since His being encompasses—even while transcending—all things, so He knows all things because "He is all things," this very being constituting in itself the absolute mode of knowledge of all things. Therefore man, to be absolutely poor in spirit, "must be poor of all his own knowledge: not knowing anything, not God, nor creature, nor himself. For this it is needful that a man should desire to know and understand nothing of the works of God. In this way a man can be poor of his own knowledge" (II:273).

Only the man who has realized the true source of his own being and knowledge can thus be ontologically "poor" of his own creaturely knowledge; this is because he is utterly pervaded by the awareness that universal truth is inseparable from the absolute being of the Godhead; and that, consequently, all possible creaturely knowledge is a pure nothing in comparison. It should also be noticed here that it is such a person, alone, who can be legitimately unconcerned with the "works of God," since he has realized the non-working Godhead, and it is exclusively in the light of this realization that all works—even those of God—are revealed as inescapably marked by relativity.

It is important to note that Eckhart says that this poverty of knowledge is a "poverty in spirit"; one may understand this as meaning, not that such poverty necessarily precludes all creaturely contents of knowledge on the outer spheres of consciousness, but that none of these contents can be distinctively affirmed in the innermost sphere of consciousness, that, precisely, of the "spirit." For, if a certain conceptual and thus provisional knowledge of God can coexist with knowledge of particular relativities on the outer spheres of awareness—those with which one necessarily operates in the world—this coexistence is strictly excluded as a possibility within the innermost "spirit," for therein any creaturely knowledge of particulars can only be an impediment to the uncreated universal Truth. The way in which the outer man lives in conformity with this absolute mode of poverty of knowledge, realized by the inner man in the spirit, is by remaining detached from the contents of his outward consciousness, seeing through them, as it were, and perceiving this knowledge to be more in the nature of an ignorance in relation to that supreme Knowledge which, from the viewpoint of the created world, itself appears as a "darkness" or an "unknowing"—as seen in the earlier sections.

The intention behind Eckhart's enunciation of this principle of "poverty" of knowledge can be understood primarily as descriptive and secondarily as normative: in the first instance he is implicitly describing the condition of one who has so fully realized the absolute plenitude of this uncreated knowledge, that he cannot but be absolutely poor of his own created knowledge. Normatively, this principle can serve as a point of reference from which the listener's own particular knowledge assumes a proper degree of relativity; and by thus correctly situating his relative knowledge in the light of absolute values, he is assisted in his effort to be detached from his own knowledge, rather than abusively endowing it with an undue significance. For the individual to attribute any significance to his particular, finite stock of knowledge renders him "full" rather than empty of himself, bearing in mind that for Eckhart, emptiness of self is the essential condition for transcending oneself.

These points lead on to the third aspect of poverty, possessing nothing, which Eckhart again introduces by a relatively transcendent perspective which he himself had adopted:

> I have often said . . . that a man should be so free of all things and all works, both inward and outward, that he may be a proper abode for God where God can work. Now we shall say something else. If it is the case that a man is free of all creatures, of God, and of self, and if it is still the case that God finds a place in him to work, then we shall declare that as long as it is *in* that man, he is not poor with the strictest poverty . . . for poverty of spirit means being so free of God and all His works that God, if He wishes to work in the soul, is Himself the place where He works (II:273-274).

The meaning of this passage becomes clearer if it is considered in relation to selections from Eckhart's treatise "On Detachment." The importance of the spiritual virtue of detachment has already been seen earlier, and it was noted that further aspects of this key principle would be addressed in the context of the existential return, aspects which are more clearly discernible in the light of the attainment of the Birth.

One can understand what Eckhart intends in the above passage about God being Himself the "place" wherein He works by examining the deepest meaning of detachment. In this treatise, Eckhart asserts that of all virtues, detachment is the highest because it takes man closest to "his image when he was in God, wherein there was no difference between him and God"; this is because all other virtues "have some regard to creatures, but detachment is free of all creatures" (III:117). Even when compared with the love of God, detachment is held as superior, since this love constrains the individual to love God, whereas detachment compels God to love the individual:

> That detachment forces God to me, I can prove thus: everything wants to be in its natural place. Now God's natural place is unity and purity, and that comes from detachment. Therefore God is bound to give Himself to a detached heart (III:117-118).

So, for God to be Himself "the place where He works," means that the soul in which God's activity most completely bears fruit must subsist in absolute detachment. To clarify further the nature of this detachment, Eckhart compares it with humility. While humility can exist without detachment, "perfect detachment cannot exist without perfect humility"; in this comparison, humility is seen to relate to a certain mode of willing on the part of the individual, since it "means abasing oneself beneath all creatures," and is consummated in "the destruction of self"; whilst detachment is seen in a supra-volitive light, as a condition which presupposes this destruction, so that "detachment comes so close to nothing that between perfect detachment and nothing no thing can exist" (III:118).

In other words, detachment is the plenary realization of the state intended by humility, implying a complete awareness that one is truly "nothing," as opposed to humility which implies the active will to be as nothing, this very will belying the intended state. The difference between the two virtues is again brought out in an answer to the question why the Virgin gloried "in her humility and not in her detachment," that is, in the words: "He regarded the humility of His handmaiden" (Luke, 1, 48). The roots of both virtues are found in the divine nature, according to Eckhart, but whereas humility relates to the descent of the Divine into human form, detachment pertains to the "immovable" aspect of God, that is to say, His aspect of transcendence. Now the Virgin could express her humility but not her detachment:

> For if she had thought once about her detachment and said "he regarded my detachment," that detachment would have been sullied and would not have been whole and perfect, since a going forth would have occurred. But nothing, however little, may proceed from detachment without staining it (III:119).

In other words, whereas one may be conscious of possessing the virtue of humility, in personal mode, without this consciousness detracting from the virtue, in the case of the spiritual degree of detachment, the moment one establishes any personal awareness thereof, the degree in question is unavoidably undermined. Total detachment means complete disengagement from the personal self: this abandoned self cannot then become aware of the very quality which extinguishes it.

While it would seem that this highest aspect of detachment can only relate to the state of union attained in the Birth, and cannot therefore strictly speaking be called a personal virtue for the individual living in the world, there is a mode of personal being which may be said to prolong or reflect this highest aspect of detachment, which must be viewed in relation to the divine archetype of detachment. In this way, detachment may be understood not just as a conceivable mode of being in the world, but also, as the necessary manifestation, in the context of the existential "return," of the highest realization. This becomes clear in the section of the treatise where Eckhart writes that "immovable detachment brings a man into the greatest likeness to God"; it should be noted that "likeness" implies the duality of the soul and God, and thus relates to the manner in which the soul may participate in the nature of this divine quality. He continues:

> For the reason why God is God is because of His immovable detachment, and from this detachment He has His purity, His simplicity, and His immutability. Therefore, if a man is to be like God, as far as a creature can have likeness with God, this must come from detachment. This draws a man into purity, and from purity into simplicity, and from simplicity into immutability (III:121).

God's most transcendent aspect, His absoluteness, which is in no wise affected by His creation, is here referred to as "detachment"; and the most appropriate way in which man can reflect this aspect of God is by means of his own detachment from creation, to the extent that this is possible for man: what is detachment for man corresponds, *mutatis mutandis*, to absolute transcendence for God.

It could also be said that only the man who has concretely realized his inner identity with and as God—and hence the nothingness of all that is other than this identity—only such a man is in a position to reflect, in appropriate fashion, that detachment which properly speaking belongs solely to the transcendent Godhead. In other words, while a degree of detachment is the prerequisite for the attainment of the Birth, its complete realization is a fruit of the Birth: only one who has realized the immanence of the Divine within the soul can properly reflect within the world, the transcendence of the Divine with regard to creation.

To conclude this discussion of the existential return, it is necessary to underline the importance of the practice of what may be called the "conventional" virtues for the realized man, lest one be left with the impression that this poverty and detachment render him aloof from non-transcendent modes of devotion. As seen in Part II, the realization of the essence of the virtues is a prerequisite for the Birth, and the spontaneous flow of the virtues is a mark of the authentic consummation of the Birth. Here, one may make mention of Eckhart's stress on the necessity of the "fruitfulness" of the Birth; the fruits of the Birth are constituted by gratitude and praise; then one is not just a "virgin," but a fruitful "wife":

> "Wife" is the noblest title one can bestow on the soul—far nobler than "virgin." For a man to receive God within him is good . . . but for God to be fruitful in him is better, for only the fruitfulness of the gift is the thanks received for that gift, and herein the spirit is a wife, whose gratitude is fecundity (I:72).

Without this "wifely fruitfulness . . . and praise and thanks" the gifts received in virginity perish, "and all comes to naught." One may understand this kind of praise that emanates from the realized man as more akin to what may be called "ontological worship," comprising, even while surpassing, the more conventional forms of devotional praise, in the sense that every aspect of such a man's being constitutes a mode of praise. This understanding accords with what Eckhart says elsewhere on the true nature of praise: that which properly praises God is "likeness":

> Our teachers ask, "What praises God?" Likeness does. Thus everything in the soul that is like God praises God . . . just as a picture praises the artist who has lavished on it all the art that he has in his heart, making it entirely like himself. The likeness of the picture praises the artist without words. That which one can praise with words is a paltry thing, and so is prayer with the lips (I:259).

Thus, only the man who has been made fully "like" God is capable of reflecting the "work" of the divine Artist, and he does this not only by means of verbal or active praise but more in terms of what he actually *is*; more, that is to say, by his inner quality of being and not just by his outer manner of doing. Only the man who has realized identity of essence with the Absolute is fully capable of possessing this "likeness" which constitutes pure praise, for he alone, knowing the true nothingness of his own outer man, will be unimpeded by any traces of egotism in his praise, egotism being of all things most "unlike" the divine nature.

Furthermore, such a man, by virtue of his realization, possesses not just a conceptual understanding but a veritably ontological certitude that nothing less than the One can be the legitimate object of praise; whilst all those who fall short of this realization are, in the very measure of this shortcoming, "unlike" God, and their praise consequently partakes of a more superficial or less ontological nature; their continuing attachment to the idea of specific selfhood, or their persisting and limiting self-consciousness, acting as a kind of prism of alterity through which their praise necessarily passes, assuming thereby an individualistic coloring.

It may be observed that, far from belittling the value of the relative, personal virtues on the plane of diversified Being and being unconcerned with the relatively transcendent level of God as Lord of creatures, Eckhart's transcendent realization implies, on the contrary, that these virtues are revealed and practised in their plenary nature, on the level to which they correspond, by the fully realized man. Humility, charity, praise, devotion, gratitude—all are given their deepest significance and highest value by the man who has concretely realized the essence which transcends not only the plane on which all human virtues are situated, and the degree of being they presuppose, but also the level of the personal Divinity to which these virtues relate, and of which they are so many reflections on the human plane.

If to "know" the essence of God is to "be" Beyond-Being, in the "distant land" which excludes one's personal being, the fruit of this realization, in terms of the existential return to the world and oneself, is to be humbly and gratefully devoted to the One who is simultaneously Lord of all creatures, and the absolute Godhead both transcendent and immanent.

# CHAPTER 4

# THE REALIZATION OF TRANSCENDENCE:
## Essential Elements of Commonality

As the reader will no doubt have seen, the similarities between the three sages studied here are remarkable. There are so many areas where their doctrines and experiences overlap that it would be vain to try and offer an exhaustive appraisal of the commonalities in this final chapter. Instead, we will focus on what appears to us as the most *essential* elements of commonality. In the course of evaluating these common elements the question posed at the outset—whether the different religions have different summits, or whether the summit is in fact one and the same—is answered emphatically in the positive. In respect of conceiving and realizing transcendence the evidence presented here leaves no doubt that the sages are indeed speaking of the selfsame reality. Coming from such prominent mystical authorities within their faiths, this evidence of spiritual unanimity on the ultimate values and goal of religion is of particular importance in demonstrating the oneness of religions, not on the formal, but on the transcendent plane, precisely.[1]

Important differences between the perspectives will not be ignored; rather, we shall try to evaluate their significance in the light of the metaphysical principles that have been expounded by the sages themselves. The structure of this chapter will reflect that of the preceding ones, with the first part addressing doctrinal aspects of transcendence, the second and third dealing with concrete aspects of the highest spiritual realization.

## Part I: Doctrines of Transcendence

### 1. Dogma and Beyond

The most significant aspect of the doctrinal approaches to the Transcendent put forward by the three mystics lies in their tendency towards a supra-dogmatic or "unramified" mode of expression. The key distinction made by all three on this level of discourse—which goes beyond the conventional confines of religious thought proper to the theistic contexts of Ibn Arabi and Eckhart—is that between the absolute transcendence of the "One" and the relative transcendence of the Personal God—that plane to which relate, in the first instance, all possible determinate designations, personal distinctions, particular names, and thus dogmatic definitions and concepts.

---

[1] For the most important exposition of this principle, see Frithjof Schuon's *The Transcendent Unity of Religions*, trans. Peter Townsend, Faber & Faber, London, 1953.

All three insist on an apophatic dialectic in regard to the transcendent Absolute: Shankara subjects all nominal, formal, and conceptual designations of the Absolute to the double negation of *neti, neti*, the Absolute in itself being without "name and form"; Ibn Arabi likewise writes that the Essence has no definition "since it has no attribute"; and Eckhart says that God is much closer to what is not said than to what is said. This apophatic approach must be seen as the necessary conceptual expression of the ontological incommensurability between all determinate and relative forms—and hence conceptions, since these partake of the formal order—and the essence of the Absolute; this great gulf that separates the Absolute from all relative conceptions means that all three mystics are compelled to assert the final inadequacy, as well as the initial necessity, of the designations of the Absolute found within their respective traditions.

Taking Shankara first: while the scriptural definition of *Brahman* as "Reality-Knowledge-Infinity" is deemed necessary to point to a divine reality, it must in its turn be negated by the *neti, neti* in order to indicate the incomparability of this reality in itself, which transcends all relative "name and form."

For Ibn Arabi, the Essence is posited as that which surpasses, even while constituting the true substance of, the Name *Allah*, and all other Names of God, which are the ontological foundations of the cosmos, while themselves possessing no ontological substance other than that of the Essence, the modes of whose relationship with the relative world they embody. The Names pertain, then, to the "Level" of Divinity, and only the Name "the One" can be said to be a Name of the Essence inasmuch as it includes all that is, even while excluding all that can be distinctively conceived as other than it. Thus the Essence is alone real, all the Names being reduced, in the very measure of their distinctive properties, to the nature of "imagination."

Eckhart likewise refers to a transcendent Godhead which is as far above the God of the three Persons as heaven is above earth.

This transcendent degree, then, can only be indirectly alluded to, and this, always in terms that are metaphysical rather than dogmatic or theological: for Ibn Arabi to call the Essence "the One" corresponds with Shankara's abstract designation *advaita*, "non-dual," as does Eckhart's reference to the Godhead as the "solitary One." This unity refers to reality such as it is in itself, a transcendent reality which perforce comprises within itself all things, but in a manner which excludes their separative manifestation; in the very measure that reference is made to the principle of the manifestation of these "things"—that is, to the principle of Being—all three mystics unite in asserting that this very principle is itself not only the first relativity, but also the first degree at which formal designations become metaphysically intelligible: in Shankara, the "Lord" as *Isvara* is identified with the Absolute insofar as it is endowed with qualities, *Brahma saguna*, and the latter is identified with *Sat* or Being; for Eckhart, the Persons are "suspended in Being" at the level where "God works"; and in Ibn Arabi's doctrine, the existentiating command "Be!" (*kun*) devolves upon the level of the Divinity, at which level are affirmed the distinctive properties of the Names "Creator," "Judge," etc.; while the Essence has absolutely no relation with the created cosmos.

There is, therefore, an intimate link between ontology and conception, or being and theology: determinate concepts can be applied to the determinate level of Being, while only indeterminate or apophatic concepts are applicable to that which transcends Being as the primary causal principle of universal manifestation. Both Shankara and Eckhart explicitly refer to the Absolute as "Beyond-Being": *Brahma nirguna* is dissociated from the causal attribute *Sat*, Being, according to Shankara; and in the "ground," God is "above all being," according to Eckhart.

This notion of Beyond-Being, however, is not found explicitly in Ibn Arabi's perspective; it may be objected, indeed, that it is antithetical to his perspective which stresses, above all, the metaphysical principle of the unity of Being as counterpart to the theological principle of the unity of God (*tawhid*). To answer this objection, it is necessary to show two things: first, that the unity of Being is not contradicted by the notion of degrees within it; and second, that what is positively designated as "Being" by Ibn Arabi is, at its summit, not other than what is apophatically referred to as "Beyond-Being" by the other two mystics.

First, it must be stressed that it is the Absolute and nothing else that assumes the relativity of Being; or, to put it another way, that it is the supra-personal Essence that assumes the personal attributes of Lordship at the level of Being. According to Shankara, the Absolute takes on the appearance of relativity in order to rule over it as Lord so that "That which we designate as the Creator *is* the Absolute." Similarly with Eckhart: Being is the first "name" of the Absolute: it is the Absolute and nothing else that "overflows" into, and as, the Persons: "The first outburst and the first effusion God runs out in is His fusion with the Son, a process which in turn reduces him to Father."

This corresponds closely to Shankara's formulation: the Father or "Creator" is only rendered such in relation to the relativity of which He is the Principle—the "Son" here standing for the image in, from, and by which manifestation proceeds.

In Ibn Arabi, one finds a similar picture: although from the point of view of *tanzih* or incomparability, the "Real" has nothing at all do with creation, which latter proceeds from, and is ruled by, the Lord as Divinity, nonetheless, the Real and creation do "come together" from the point of view of *tashbih* or similarity and this "in respect of the fact that the Essence is described by Divinity." The Essence is thus transcribed within relativity by the Divinity: to revert to Shankara: the Creator *is* the Absolute. This is also implicit in the fact that the Names of God have no distinct ontological entities: each Name is the Named in respect of its inner substance and is only distinct therefrom in the measure of its specific properties, which presuppose the forms of the cosmos. To say, then, that the Name is the Named is to say also the converse: the Essence is the Divinity; the Essence not as it is in itself, but in the already relative aspect it must perforce assume in order to enter into relationship with the relative world.

It is this very relativity within Being, which remains nonetheless one, that furnishes the basis for a convergence between Ibn Arabi and the other two mystics on the question of "Beyond-Being." This term, though it does not appear in Ibn Arabi, is implicit in his doctrine; for the oneness of Being, actually presupposes a hierarchical distinction of degree, rather than being contradicted by it: it presupposes the distinction between the following planes, degrees, or dimensions: the lowest plane of cosmic existence, the intermediate plane of divine existentiation, and the highest plane which transcends the relativity entailed by causal relationship with the relative existence of the world. Without these distinctions, the oneness of Being would imply the abolition of the difference between the relative and the Absolute; that is, transcendence would be negated. On the other hand, without the doctrine of oneness, these distinctions would imply the attribution to the world of a separate and autonomous existence: the immanence of the Real throughout existence would then be negated. The distinction between the Essence and the Divinity/Level can therefore be seen as corresponding, functionally, to the distinction between Beyond-Being and Being, given the way in which these two aspects of the self-same Reality are conceived.

Furthermore, it could be argued that Ibn Arabi's view of the ultimately illusory nature of everything apart from the Essence—the Names being "imaginary" in the measure of their distinction from the Essence—brings him even closer to Shankara's most rigorous metaphysical denial of the reality of all but *Brahma nirguna*: the Absolute is alone fully real and this is because, to use Shankara's phrase, it is *prapañcha-upasama*—without any trace of the development of manifestation.

Being, then, constitutes the first "trace"—albeit principial—of the development of manifestation; and if Being is itself the first self-determination of Beyond-Being, and the Divinity is the first self-determination of the Essence, then one can legitimately posit Ibn Arabi's distinction between the Divinity and the Essence as analogous to the distinction between Being and Beyond-Being; Universal Manifestation has its immediate principle in Being or, in Ibn Arabi's terms, the Divinity, and not in Beyond-Being, or the Essence.

## 2. One Absolute or Three?

The next basic question that arises is the extent to which there is convergence as regards the conceptions of the Absolute proposed by the three mystics. As seen above, it is only to the "lesser Absolute" that determinate conceptions apply, so the question needs to be formulated: at the level of conception itself, to what extent can the outwardly differing names and designations of the lesser Absolute be regarded as converging upon a unique higher Absolute? The answer to this question can be pitched at two levels: the one negative and deriving from mode of expression, and the other positive, deriving from metaphysical intelligibility.

Turning first to the negative level: it is the very apophatic character of all references to the transcendent Reality evinced by the three mystics that opens up the possibility of convergence. They all assert that there is an epistemological disjuncture between the word/name/concept and the Reality so named; this very fact brings closer together their respective provisional designations of the Absolute. If there were no assertion of the transcendence of the Absolute over all conceptions thereof, then these conceptions would be endowed with an absolute status, and, consequently, with a rigorously exclusive character: each conception would then perforce exclude the validity of other conceptions found in different perspectives. On the other hand, in the measure that the designations of the Absolute be regarded as transcended by the Absolute, it is legitimate to posit, albeit in negative terms, a convergence of conception of the Absolute.

A more positive affirmation of convergence arises out of reflection upon the metaphysical principles and symbols given by the mystics. To begin with, Eckhart's principle of spiritual inclusivity may be cited: while all material things limit and exclude each other, all things of a spiritual or divine nature include each other; material exclusivity entails separative particularity, whilst spiritual inclusivity is equated with unitive universality. Applying this principle to the question of differing conceptions of the lesser Absolute, one may say: in the measure that these conceptions intend an indefinable spiritual reality, one which transcends the formal and possibly dogmatic character of the conceptions themselves, they can be regarded as inwardly united by the very content of that intended reality, which is identified as absolute infinitude: this infinitude, being of a supereminently spiritual nature, is by that same token unitive and thus all-inclusive. Outwardly differing formal conceptions thus converge insofar as their supra-conceptual referent consists in a spiritual reality that is infinite and unitive, outside or apart from which nothing exists; it is only by virtue of their formal and thus separative character that each conception diverges from the others.

This may be seen as an articulation of one level of meaning in Ibn Arabi's image of the water and the cup: the cup may be taken to be the limited receptacle that the faculty of conception is, the water as "structured" by the cup standing for the conception of the Absolute, and water in its own nature representing the Absolute as it is in itself. This image at one and the same time expresses the two fundamental points made earlier in regard to identity and distinction: on the one hand, the personal God/Being that is susceptible of determinate conception is not other than the Essence/Ground/Beyond-Being—the water in the cup is in essence not other than water; and on the other hand there is a strict incomparability between the ontological degree proper to the personal God/Being and that pertaining to the transcendent Essence which is beyond Being—the accidental properties of shape, form, color etc. imparted to the water by the cup can in no wise be attributed to the true nature of water. In Shankara's terms, the cup is the *upadhi*, the relative adjunct which imparts to the object it limits the appearance of its own qualities; when divested of this *upadhi* the object stands forth in its own right. Each conception of the lesser Absolute is then essentially identifiable with other such conceptions by virtue of its content or what it intends, even while being separate therefrom by virtue of its form.

Finally, drawing on Ibn Arabi's explicit universalism, one can conclude with the following metaphysical principle: the very infinitude of the Real implies the impossibility of enclosing it within one conception to the exclusion of all others. Therefore each conception of the Absolute is assimilable to the other in the measure that it opens out onto and intends the infinite and transcendent Reality. In the case of the three mystics studied here, the fact that their determinate conceptions of the "lesser" Absolute are emphatically subordinated to the apophatically defined "higher" Absolute which transcends all limited conceptions and definitions—this fact constitutes in itself a persuasive argument in favor of the thesis that these conceptions diverge as regards their formal nature but converge in respect of their intended content. This intended content is the Absolute itself, that which cannot be defined or named, but which can be provisionally referred to, on condition that such references are understood to be incommensurable with the reality of the Absolute, which is absolutely one. Indeed, in this crucial notion of the oneness of the Absolute there lies another argument: insofar as the absolute Reality is one, and insofar as each mystic conceives of this Absolute, the essential content of their respective conceptions must likewise be one, even if the formal structure or outward delineation of the conceptions as such necessarily differ.

# Part II: The Spiritual Ascent

## 1. Virtue

It has been observed that a key prerequisite for setting out on the path of transcendence is the attainment of integral virtue. The highest teaching about the Birth, Eckhart tells his listeners, is intended only for those who fully live up to Christian precepts; transcending virtue as conceived in its human aspect, then, presupposes its perfect realization on the plane corresponding to it. Shankara stresses likewise that his doctrine of the Self is to be expounded only to those who possess all the fundamental virtues; these are assimilated as so many aspects and means of knowledge, while egoism and pride are on the contrary seen as so many intellectual dysfunctions, in addition to being moral vices. Ibn Arabi also accords to virtue a status that goes beyond its moral ramifications, inasmuch as virtue is seen as an ontological participation in the very nature of God: the adoption of virtuous qualities is tantamount to "assuming the character traits of God," and constitutes the "accidental perfection" without which the "essential," that is, transcendent perfection cannot be attained. Virtue is also considered as a methodic precondition for entering the spiritual retreat.

While there is fundamental agreement on the necessity of virtue, there is nonetheless a difference to be noted in respect of the ritual framework within which virtuous action is to take place.

## 2. Ritual and Action

For Ibn Arabi and Eckhart, the performance of the orthodox rites is taken for granted as one of the foundations of the path of transcendence, and is not abandoned at any point of that path, whereas for Shankara such an abandonment is, practically if not dogmatically, part of the discipline for the aspirant to Liberation. This is an important difference and may be seen as deriving from the following contextual factor: the adoption of the path of the *sannyasin* is structurally integrated into the framework of the Hindu tradition, rather than being a deviation from it, whereas the place of the rites in the historically founded religions of Islam and Christianity is far more central, being definitive of religious identity and essential to sacramental participation within those faiths. To renounce or abandon the rites for the sake of the Absolute is then tantamount to a heretical innovation.

On the other hand, if one looks carefully both at the motivation and the proviso relating to Shankara's formal abandonment of the rites, the difference between the two positions is substantially modified, albeit not totally overcome. The motive for ceasing to perform the ordinary rites is grounded, on the one hand, in the general principle that action does not lead to Liberation, and on the other, in the subjective principle that the aspirant to Liberation must cultivate a "disgust" for all the rewards—terrestrial and heavenly—proportioned to ritual action. Seen in this light, Shankara's position is not so far removed in substance from those of Eckhart and, though to a lesser extent, Ibn Arabi. Eckhart's views regarding action, and his antinomian reference to the limitations of heaven, can in fact be more clearly appreciated in the light of Shankara's explicit pronouncements on the relativity of all but the transcendent aspiration: heaven is dialectically posited as the reward given to "asses" who may have noble intentions and commit the most pious actions, but whose knowledge is defective as regards the intrinsic reality of the Absolute. Shankara succinctly states a principle which greatly clarifies Eckhart's antinomian hyperbole: "When the Self has once been known, everything else is seen as evil."

For Shankara, even *Dharma* is a sin for the one seeking knowledge of the Self, In Eckhart, it is the "Birth" or "union" that would be stressed rather than the "Self," since it is in this union that is found "the soul's whole beatitude"; and it is in this light, alone, that all lesser attainments are seen as "evil." Moreover, inasmuch as Eckhart insists that one not take God from anywhere but within oneself, his perspective comes even closer to that of Shankara, despite not sharing with the latter the continuing explicit stress on the absolute Self.

Shankara's principle helps elucidate Eckhart's intention in saying that "to pray for this and for that" is to pray for evil, as well as numerous other, at first sight, scandalous pronouncements. Also to be noted is the way in which Shankara's view of the limitations of action clarifies the motive behind Eckhart's dismissal even of the "doves" as well as the "merchants" from the Temple; while it is clear why those who perform good acts out of attachment to the reward ("merchants") are to be excluded, it is less clear why those who perform good acts selflessly, only for the sake of God ("doves"), are also sent away. In his elliptical explanation Eckhart merely says: "they work with attachment, according to time and tide, before and after"; they are said to be "hindered" by these activities without the nature of the hindrance being spelt out. It is not clear, at first sight, what the object of this attachment is, given that the "doves" are "detached" and work only for the sake of God.

The attachment in question is clearly seen when one turns to Shankara, who makes an explicit distinction which applies perfectly to Eckhart's teaching. Shankara distinguishes between the lower type of renunciate who has renounced selfish action and acts only for the sake of the Lord, and the higher type who renounces action because he sees "inaction in action," that is, he has a disinterested view of action because of his knowledge that the Self is independent of action and is thus to be realized only through knowledge and not through even "ten million acts." This accords well with Eckhart's view of detachment and works: these are only valuable insofar as they are shed immediately. For both Shankara and Eckhart it is attachment to the ontological status of action that constitutes the "hindrance"; even if works be accomplished in a spirit of selflessness, and in exclusive devotion to God, this subtle attachment entails a twofold entrenchment of relativity: the relativity of the empirical agent of the act on the one hand, and the relativity of the acting personal God, *qua* "other," as the object of devotion, on the other hand.

Turning now to the second point, Shankara's proviso: ritual action may continue to be performed not only by the one seeking Liberation but also by the one who has realized it, if it be for the sake of setting an example. Thus, given the fact that the formal dimension of Islam and Christianity—that is the exoteric dogmas and prescriptions—derives in large part from the needs of the community, Shankara's proviso permits one to see the compatibility between his own position on the rites and that of the other two; though this latter position be structurally defined in respect of outward action, it is nonetheless intellectually and spiritually governed by the highest aspiration.

This argument does not imply that Ibn Arabi, for example, only counsels, and himself abides by, the external prescriptions of the Law for the sake of setting a good example; for his esoteric interpretations of these prescriptions show that, in more positive terms, he enacts them as symbols relating to the principial realities they embody and intend. In this respect, moreover, he rejoins Shankara's view that the performance of rites has a purificatory function with a view to knowledge—describing the rites as "remote auxiliaries to knowledge," in that they are "instrumental in extinguishing that demerit, arising from past sins, which obstructs knowledge of the Absolute." Shankara's abandonment of the rites, it should be remembered, involves the adoption of the quintessential rites of the *sannyasin*; but the important point here is that this formal renunciation of the external rites is not laid down as an absolute prerequisite for the adoption of the "Direct Path," especially given the fact that the Vedas speak of householders also attaining enlightenment. Therefore, there is no essential or necessary contradiction between the path of transcendence which excludes all external rites of the religious form, and the path of transcendence followed by Ibn Arabi and Eckhart wherein these rites continue to be performed, with a view to realizing their deepest significance.

## 3. Methods of Ascent

One point of similarity between the three mystics, which at first sight may appear as a difference, lies in their respective attitudes to the mystical vision of God, seen as "other." All three are at one in regarding this as a relative attainment and one that must be transcended by realization of the Absolute as one's own innermost identity. But an apparent difference may be construed as between the way in which Ibn Arabi endows this vision with a relatively transcendent and, ultimately, a wholly divine nature, and Shankara's more rigorous exclusion of all attainments short of Self-realization.

For Shankara, any attribution of objective alterity to the Absolute—and therefore, implicitly, any mystical vision thereof—entails the imprisonment of consciousness within the confines of the dualistically defined ego, and, therefore, within the domain of illusion.

Ibn Arabi's position, in one respect, is not dissimilar: the vision of God is defined in terms of the contact between the self-manifestation of God and the receptivity of the immutable entity, the *'ayn* of the individual, and is thus in one sense reducible to the level of the individual. So far, this is close to Shankara: there is in both cases a reduction to the individual conceived as subjective correlate of the Divine *qua* object. But Ibn Arabi's position is nuanced by the fact that this very preparedness of the entity is itself fashioned by the first "most holy effusion" of the Divine: this preparedness is thus itself reducible to the Divine, which in turn is reducible to the Essence. There appears, then, a difference: Shankara's view of the ego's imprisonment within alterity seems to be undermined by the principial assimilations made by Ibn Arabi. However, the difference is only apparent inasmuch as for Shankara, also, the "Creator is the Absolute": the individual ego as "creation" of the Absolute, in seeing the Lord/Creator, sees in fact nothing but the Absolute appearing, on contact with *Maya*, as *Isvara* in one of its manifestations. While this position may be affirmed for both Ibn Arabi and Shankara, it is in any case superseded for both by the methodic principle that the Absolute alone is the object of the highest aspiration; all lower attainments are to be firmly resisted.

Ibn Arabi stresses that in the spiritual retreat all visions—celestial and divine—are strictly relativized; the aspirant at every stage of illumination is told not to "stop" with what is offered but to persevere with the invocation of the Name and the corresponding intention firmly focused on the Named, for if "you stay with what is offered He will escape you, but if you attain Him nothing will escape you." One must resist all bestowals of God for the sake of realizing God Himself. This corresponds closely with Eckhart's insistence that all images must be excluded for the sake of that receptivity to the Word which consists in the absolute stilling of all intellectual powers and functions; even Christ, insofar as he is present to the mind in his corporeal form, is to be excluded, and one is told to unite with the "formless essence."

This firm rejection of all but the Transcendent relates to the key methodic principle common to the three mystics: a concentrated withdrawal from the outer dimension of awareness and existence towards the innermost center of consciousness and being. This interiorization, whatever be the different modes it may take, constitutes the essential methodic principle in the path of transcendence: that which is most inward is that which is most exalted: depth equals height, according to Eckhart.

Shankara's *adhyatma-yoga*, the superior type of meditation, hinges on abstention; the result of abstaining from all outward modes of sense, feeling, and thought is a progressive dissolution of the outward faculties whose respective essences are successively reintegrated into their anterior and interior principles.

Ibn Arabi also uses the concept of dissolution in describing the path of interiorization, which is simultaneously the path of ascent to the Absolute; in the course of the ascent, the composite dimensions of the individual are dissolved within their respective principles until all contingency is finally transcended. Eckhart, too, stresses the same withdrawal, but in terms this time of "stilling" all the powers of the intellect; this entails the exclusion of all empirical content inasmuch as the "silent middle" is receptive to nothing but the Word; hence it is "unknowing" and "silence" that most conduce to the Birth of the Word.

The methodic efficacy of this interiorization is grounded in a metaphysical principle of the utmost importance, a principle affirmed by all three mystics: the inmost essence of the individual is not other than the transcendent Essence of the Absolute. It is because of this preexisting identity at the inmost degree of being that interiorization is put forward as the principal means of realizing the Transcendent.

In Shankara's case, the scriptural maxim "That thou art" establishes this identity in the clearest possible manner, but he explains its foundation in relation to the concept of *tadatmya*, which expresses the paradoxical relationship between the ego and *Brahman*: the ego is non-different from *Brahman*, while *Brahman* is not non-different from the ego. The ego thus has two dimensions: in respect of the external dimension, there is no possible relation between the ego and *Brahman*, but in the inner dimension, that of pure consciousness and being, the ego is non-different from *Brahman*. In Ibn Arabi, one finds the corresponding principle of non-reciprocal identity is expressed, albeit inversely, as follows: "the transcendent Reality is the relative creature, even though the creature is distinct from the Creator."

In Eckhart the same principle is found: the fact that the essence of the intellect is "uncreated" means that it can only be divine, hence the identity between the inmost "citadel" of the soul and the most transcendent "solitary One" above the soul; at this point of identity, only, the soul is "divine" but "God does not become the soul: the drop cast into the ocean is the ocean, while the ocean is not the drop."

This is the reason why Eckhart urges concentration upon God not as something other, but as He is "in oneself." To concentrate on this inmost dimension of oneself is, to apply Shankara's principle, to become that upon which one concentrates. This same idea is expressed by Eckhart in an image to which he says the utmost attention should be paid, since, if this be understood, one will "get to the bottom of all that I have ever preached about": in the point of contact between the eye and wood in vision, there is a single reality, "eye-wood": "the wood is my eye." In other words, such is the totality of concentration upon the object that it subsumes within itself that subject which had been the agent of the concentration: spiritual food assimilates to itself the one who "eats" it, in such a manner that the spiritual substance itself is revealed as one's true identity. This recalls the fact that "the gazelle" which Ibn Arabi loved is ultimately revealed as being his own self.

In addition to these two fundamentally identical factors in all three mystics— the non-reciprocal identity between the essence of the soul and that of the Absolute; and the method of interiorizing concentration employed for realizing that transcendent identity—there is a further important correspondence between one methodic support advocated by Shankara and the principal such support for Ibn Arabi: concentration on the Name of the Absolute. Even though, from the strictly metaphysical and objective viewpoint, the Name was distinguished from the Named, from the methodic and subjective viewpoint, the complementary relationship of identity is stressed; as Shankara says, the Name is the Named. The Named is immanent in the Name even while simultaneously transcending it. Returning to the image of the cup and water: the water in the cup is water, even though water as such cannot be reduced to that quantity in the cup. Thus, Shankara emphasizes the efficacy of invoking *Om* and Ibn Arabi, that of *Allah*. Shankara explains that realization of the Absolute is brought about as a result of the actualization of the grace inherent in the Name which sacramentally represents the Absolute. On the basis of this realization, the relativity of the very relationship Name-Named is itself transcended, inasmuch as the contingency or alterity presupposed by the formal affirmation of the Name is surpassed; hence "the purpose of knowing the identity of the name and the named is to enable oneself to dismiss name and named altogether and realize the Absolute which is quite different from either."

It should be noted that in Shankara's perspective the realization of the Absolute is not restricted to any one method: it can be crystallized even on the basis of one hearing of the text *tat tvam asi*; it can result from "hearing, cogitating over, and sustained meditation upon" the sacred texts; it can come about through the concentration on the inmost source of consciousness effected through the technique of abstention; and it can be the effect of the grace attracted to the invoker as a result of the invocation of the sacred syllable *Om*. In Ibn Arabi, on the other hand, invocation is given as the central if not exclusive methodic practice which relates to the ultimate realization; and in Eckhart, it is only the technique of concentration through abstention that is explicitly mentioned. The fact that both of these are included in Shankara's methodic perspective shows that there is nothing incompatible between them, so that this difference between Eckhart and Ibn Arabi on the central methodic practice leading to the final realization is a relative one, and is rendered less significant in the measure that, on the one hand, the function of these methods is identical, viz. interiorization of consciousness, and, on the other, the goal of these practices is one and the same. The next sections deal with the essential aspects of the final stages of this realization.

## 4. Bliss and Transcendence

As the consciousness of the aspirant approaches the summit of realization, an exalted state of bliss is experienced; but this is to be surpassed, according to all three mystics. Ibn Arabi writes that, prior to extinction, the aspirant is not to "stop" at the degree of blissful experience. Eckhart speaks of the lesser attainment of love over that of knowledge: stopping with love involves being "entangled" and "infatuated" in goodness and love; this means remaining "caught up in the gate" which is the first effusion of God. Knowledge, on the other hand, "runs ahead" and "grasps God in His essence." Shankara also writes in similar vein: as one approaches the state of *samadhi*, bliss is experienced, but the *mumuksu* must not "pause to savor it."

However, all three mystics also affirm that, to the extent that one can speak of the final realization, it entails the following three elements: Being, Consciousness, and Bliss. The essence of this formula, associated with Shankara, is found in Ibn Arabi: "Being is the finding of the Real in ecstasy"; and in Eckhart: the content of the Word that is spoken in the soul is "immeasurable power, infinite wisdom, and infinite sweetness." One could also cite here his saying: "I was bare being and the knower of myself in the enjoyment of truth."

The question that imposes itself is the following: how is one to distinguish between the relative bliss that must be surpassed through concentrating on the Absolute, and that absolute Bliss that is entailed by realization of the Absolute? In answering this question attention is brought to bear on the crux of the problem of "experience" in relation to transcendence.

It is again to Shankara that one turns for the key to understanding this question, as it is he who spells out in more explicit terms the difference between relative and absolute bliss. Firstly, the lower, non-transcendent bliss is noted as something which can be seen to "increase by stages": this means that there is some common measure between the joy experienced in everyday life and the degree of bliss here in question; the latter may be more intense, but it occurs within the same basic ontological framework. The nature of this framework is clarified by Shankara's statement that the transcendent Bliss is "totally different from all objects . . . unborn because it is not produced like anything resulting from empirical perceptions."

In other words, the non-transcendent degree of bliss *is* something like an "object," that is, it resembles that which results from empirical perception; it is thus conditioned by the relationship between a subjective agent and an object distinct therefrom, an object which, albeit internal to the subject, is constitutive of a particular experience *of* the relative subject. It is only when this ontological dualism, as ground of all subjective experience, is transcended that one can speak of the realization of that bliss which is proper to the Self, being absolutely indistinguishable therefrom in any respect. This is the bliss inherent to the "one without a second," which, precisely because it surpasses the context of ontologically differentiated experience, is "indescribable": description, along with all individual modes of cognition, presupposes this context and is proportioned to events occurring within it, while being strictly inadequate with regard to whatever goes beyond it. To give a description of this highest reality or the realization that assimilates it, is to confuse levels of being: transcendent Being cannot be reduced to modes of contingent thought and language. As Eckhart put it: so long as one tries to encompass this reality in language and thought, one knows no more about it than the eye knows of taste.

Hence, to say that in transcendent realization the mystic has an "experience" of the transcendent Real is misleading; it is only when there has been a conscious transcendence of the conditions in which experience is grounded that it becomes possible to refer to transcendent realization. It is for this reason that Shankara compares the realization of the Self to the state of deep sleep: in deep sleep there takes place a negation of all differentiation between consciousness and being, and this eliminates the basis of subjective experience. Nevertheless, the deep sleep state only prefigures the realization of the Self, and this in inverse fashion: even though only the consciousness of the Self abides in the deep sleep state, the "seeds of ignorance" have not been burnt up, so the individual, upon awakening, is as ignorant of the Self as he was before falling asleep: he remains unaware of his identity as that Self whose consciousness alone persisted in deep sleep. When, on the contrary, realization of the Self is attained, individuality is consciously transcended: consciousness, in other words is liberated from the bonds of the individual condition, or more precisely, of the ontological dualism of which individuality constitutes the subjective pole.

Thus, it is not a state of bliss that defines realization; it is the conscious transcendence of duality, with the concomitant realization of supra-personal identity, that necessarily entails the "unutterable joy," the "whole beatitude," and the "ecstasy" mentioned, respectively, by Shankara, Eckhart, and Ibn Arabi. The next section examines more closely this transcendence of duality.

## 5. Transcendent Union

To say "transcendence" is to say "union"; a union in which consciousness persists, but in a mode which nullifies the individual condition. If consciousness itself were nullified, then the mystics would not be able to assert that duality was in fact transcended; and if the individual condition is not nullified, the claim to have attained the degree of absolute transcendence is undermined.

According to Eckhart: if there is to be a true union, one of the two agents so unified must lose its "whole identity and being"—failing which there will be "united-ness" but not union; this crucial point must be seen in connection with the claim he makes regarding "his" being, such as it was in the "first cause": therein he "had no god" and was "bare being and the knower of myself in the enjoyment of truth." It is to this condition that he "breaks through" in his "return" to the Essence, for it is there—and there only—that "God unbecomes"; so that it is there and only there that Eckhart can be said to have "no god." But to say "Eckhart" here is elliptical; for, taking together the above points, one must conclude that in union, the "whole identity and being" of Eckhart *qua* individual is lost, and what is found is transcendent identity and being in and as the Godhead: the identity attained is so completely one that Eckhart is able to claim, again most elliptically, that he "begets his begetter." Everything, in other words, that proceeds from the Godhead by way of hypostatic determination becomes his own act, by virtue of this transcendent identity, which is attained only on the basis of the "naughting" of his specific, personal identity.

The same fundamental points are to be observed in the writings of Ibn Arabi. On the one hand, he writes that God removed from him his contingent dimension, resulting in the realization that he was himself the essence of the one "Named" by all the divine Names; and on the other hand, the transcendent degree of this identity is affirmed by the claim to have transcended not only all the *a'yan*, or immutable entities, but also the very plane on which the Lordship of the Divine is defined as such, that is, in relation to the cosmos over which this first of all relativities reigns as Lord: the "King" becomes a "prince" to him. This corresponds closely with Eckhart's assertion that in his first cause and final return he "has no god"; in both cases there is the claim to have not only realized a transcendent identity that is ontologically premised on the negation of contingent existence and individual identity, but also to have realized in this identity a degree that surpasses the level of the personal God. The one, indeed, may be said to be inconceivable without the other: it is only possible to realize the transcendent Absolute as one's own identity insofar as the duality presupposed by the degree proper to the personal God has been transcended; to thus go "beyond God" can, metaphysically, only be the prerogative of the Self that is the Essence of God, the Essence that is realized as his own true identity by the consciousness of the mystic, but only upon the effacement of his own contingent and specific identity.

In Shankara, also, these two essential aspects of the highest realization are found. Firstly, as regards the transcendence of the ontological dualism inherent in the persistence of the individual as such, the individual ego is likened to an "arm which has been cut off and thrown away"; only upon the full elimination of the ego-notion through the *neti, neti* can the remaining, pure subjectivity in the "I" be legitimately identified with *Brahman* in the sentence "I am *Brahman*." The "immediate experience" (*anubhava*) that ensues at the point of the effective, and not merely theoretical, negation of the ego is "the Supreme Self."

Here, the comparison with an arm makes it clear that the ego is something which by its very nature is an extrinsic object, dependent for its life and being on a superior conscious agent, just as the arm needs a mind to direct it; to say "ego," then, is to say fundamental and irreducible duality: the ego has no self-subsistence, but presupposes another for its very existence. The transcendence of the ego is the transcendence of ontological dualism; the realization of the Self is the realization of *advaita*, the "one without a second."

Secondly, as regards the transcendence of the personal God: it will be recalled that the realization of identity with the Lord was the attainment proper only to the "indirect path," identity with the Self being attained by the "direct path." It is important to note that the identity attained with the Lord in the "indirect path" is of a transient and partial nature: there remains always and inescapably an ontological distinction between the Lord and the individual soul; and even in the case of one whose identification with the Lord results in the acquisition of superhuman powers, there still persists an unbridgeable chasm separating this soul and the Lord, inasmuch as the Lord alone has the prerogative of "governing the universe." There cannot be complete identity, then, between the Lord and the soul, the very affirmation of one presupposing the existence of the other. On the other hand, the Self brooks no alterity, so that realizing one's identity as the Self necessarily entails the transcendence of the dualism inherent in the affirmation of the plane of the Lord. It is thus said by Shankara that even the god *Brahmà*, one of the *Trimurti* of the Lord, becomes an "object of pity" for the one who has realized the Self.

It is clear, then, that Shankara, Eckhart, and Ibn Arabi are in perfect accord on the essential nature of transcendent realization. For Shankara to posit a degree of realization that surpasses the level of the Lord, *Brahma saguna*, entails less "scandal" inasmuch as this is implicitly found as the highest truth in the Hindu scriptures; for this reason, he is able consistently to adopt this viewpoint and all its ramifications, whereas in the case of Ibn Arabi and Eckhart, this transcendent identity is more often alluded to in veiled and elliptical terms, and but rarely stated in as explicit a manner as one finds in Shankara.

## 6. Agency in Transcendent Realization

Another very important principle shared in common by all three mystics is that, as Shankara has it, "only the Self knows the Self"; just as earlier it was noted that they were united in the view that the relative soul was both outwardly distinct from, and essentially identical with, the Absolute, so too now they are at one in asserting that it is only that element of absoluteness immanent in the soul that can be the agent in the realization of the Absolute which infinitely transcends the soul. Preexisting metaphysical identity of substance, in other words, is the basis on which transcendent spiritual realization takes place.

As already noted above, Ibn Arabi writes that the creature is distinct from the Creator, even though the Real is identical with the creature. The creature as such does not realize or become the Absolute; it cannot even truly "see" the Absolute: in transcendent realization, the seer is identical to the one who sees—remembering that "seeing" here is to be identified with "extinction in contemplation" and, thus, union; He "to whom nothing is similar" is seen only by him "to whom nothing is similar." The consciousness of the individual must be rendered incomparable to all things, and this implies, as seen above, the transcendence of the individuality. This is possible only because the consciousness *in* the individual is, in its essence, not *of* it; it is on this metaphysical premise that Ibn Arabi distinguishes between two types of gnosis: knowing God through knowing yourself—the lower type, entailing knowing one's Lord; and knowing God "through you as Him, not as yourself"—the higher type relating to the Absolute. Knowledge of the Absolute in itself is attainable exclusively through *being* the Absolute, which is possible only insofar as one already *is* the Absolute, on the one hand, and insofar as one's specific contingency is negated, on the other.

Similarly with Eckhart: "The hearer is the same as the heard in the eternal Word"; and more explicitly: "The infinite God who is in the soul, He grasps the God who is infinite."

The only manner in which this can take place is through the reduction of the soul to its bare humanity, which is what was assumed by the Word; this Son, only, knows the Father; therefore "to know the Father one must be the Son." In order to know the ultimate Truth—the "Father"—one must be that which knows—the Son; recalling here another interpretation by Eckhart of the Trinity whereby the Father stands for the Essence, and the Son, union with the Essence. The knowledge, in other words, that the Son has of the Father is actually constitutive of the self-knowledge of the Father, recalling that God knows Himself in the Birth.

It is clear that, while the essential nature of transcendent realization is being expressed in terms of the Trinity, this realization should not be regarded as reducible to the dogmatic elements of the Trinity, nor should it be deemed to be exhaustively and exclusively expressed in terms of the Trinity; Eckhart goes far beyond the conventional theological meaning of the relationship between the Persons, and expresses a supra-dogmatic reality, albeit by means of elements proper to the dogma.

The possibility of establishing concordance with the other two perspectives arises from the following important fact: that which is symbolized by the Father and the Son—the supra-personal Essence and union with this Essence—along with the concomitant assertion that the Son's knowledge of the Father is identical with the knowledge the Father has of Himself, can be expressed equally well by other conceptual schemas. In particular, one may note its correspondence with Shankara's view that "the essence of the Self . . . verily knows Itself by means of unborn Knowledge"; just as the heat of the fire is non-different from the fire, so knowledge of the Self is non-different from the Self. The "heat" in this image is the functional equivalent of the Son in Eckhart's schema: they both refer to that knowledge which is inseparable from the Essence, that knowledge by means of which alone the Essence can be known, with which the consciousness of the individual is fully identified, and the price of union with which is the negation of the individual.

Turning back to the question of agency, the above points show that the true agent or subject in transcendent realization is nothing but the Transcendent itself; the individual as such ceases to be the cognitive subject in this realization. Hence, knowledge of the Absolute implies an "unknowing" from the point of view of the contingent subject. Eckhart's stress on the poverty of knowledge corresponds to Shankara's affirmation that in enlightenment there is no "particularized consciousness" nor are there any "empirical means of knowledge"; and it corresponds also to Ibn Arabi's reference to the distinction between ignorance and inexpressibility: while certain knowers of the Absolute say that this knowledge implies ignorance, he says it implies not ignorance but the inexpressible. In other words, "ignorance" is only as the shadow cast upon the contingent subject by the light of pure consciousness, which is "inexpressible" in terms that are intelligible to that subject. Shankara refers to this also in saying that enlightenment can neither be called cognition nor non-cognition: it is a flash of intuitive awareness in which there is a supra-cognitive comprehension of "that which transcends all empirical knowledge." Just as it was seen in the last section that there can be no particular experience of the Transcendent, so it is observed now that there can be no particular empirical knowledge thereof: the complete identity between the essence of the soul and that of the Transcendent is realized at a degree which strictly precludes the duality that is the basis, existentially, for particular experience, and, cognitively, for particular contents of knowledge.

A further fundamental, if paradoxical, point is to be observed in the case of all three mystics: the very process of realization is reduced to the status of illusion in the light of that which is revealed as fully real. For Shankara, both bondage and Liberation are "conjured up by *Maya*" and do not exist in reality; when Eckhart "returns" to "the ground, the bottom, the river and fount of Godhead, none will ask me whence I came or where I have been. No one missed me . . ." This is because he had never left that Godhead, in reality, inasmuch as nothing can be added to, nor taken away from, that Godhead on pain of reducing it to a relativity. For Ibn Arabi also "there is no arriving and no being afar": in extinctive union, that which is extinguished "never was," while that which remains "never was not."

It would seem that this mystery must be entered under the category of "inexpressible." It is certainly why the gnostic in Ibn Arabi's perspective is called *al-'arif bi-Llah*—knower *through* God, as opposed to knower *of* God. Without pretending to diminish the aspect of mystery, one can nevertheless point to Shankara's concept of *abhasa* as the most fitting means of expressing the simultaneous affirmation of two apparently irreconcilable propositions: on the one hand, the content of realization reveals that no "other" can be said to exist; on the other, the very process of realization presupposes something "other" as yet unrealized. Shankara's reflection theory points to the existence of something in the soul that is at once both one with the Self, and distinct therefrom, and this is the reflection of the consciousness of the Self in the ego. It is the return of this "ray" to the source of its projection that, on the one hand, accounts for the experienced change of consciousness entailed by the process of realization, and, on the other, does not contradict the affirmation that only the Self knows the Self.

This point of view is implicit in Ibn Arabi's chapter on Adam in the *Fusus* where God is said to have created man because he wished to come to know Himself from the starting point of another, as it were in a mirror; and it is explicit when Ibn Arabi refers to the vision of Light only being possible through the Light itself: "it is as if it (the light) returns to the root from which it became manifest."

As the discussion on Shankara's *abhasa* concept showed, this reflection is the only thing that can conceivably be the agent in the act of realization: the ego is ever bound by nature and the Self is ever free by nature; thus, insofar as there can be any agent in realization, it can only be this ambiguously defined entity, whose nature is the Self by virtue of its essential identity and source, but whose existence *qua* reflection presupposes a plane of alterity—the ego. It is important to stress that this reflection is posited as the agent only *insofar* as there be any agent; for, in the actual moment of realization, when the reflection is absolutely indistinguishable from its source, there is no longer any reflection, but only the Self, which was never not-realized, since it is eternally realized (*nitya-siddha*): hence one returns to the mystery that the process of Liberation is revealed as illusory for want of any subject that could conceivably undergo it.

The reflection theory, then, graphically suggests, without pretending to explain exhaustively, the nature of enlightenment or transcendent realization, which remains incommunicable in its essence, the Self being *anirukta*—inexplicable—from the viewpoint of the non-Self. The mystery remains, in the measure that the content of realization transcends all "empirical knowledge."

Nonetheless, the theory is valuable in giving at least an extrinsic symbolic expression which points to that which remains inexpressible. It is also useful in providing an answer to the logical problem that could be put to the self-realized individual: how can you as an individual know what was revealed when your individual nature/identity was extinguished?

From Shankara's *abhasa* concept can be extrapolated the following answer: by means of the reflection of the consciousness of the Absolute subsisting in the individual, he knows that identity with the Absolute was attained, and he knows that this One is unconditional Reality, infinite Consciousness, and absolute Bliss; this he knows by virtue of the positive aspect of the reflection. But he is unable fully to encompass, in discursive and cognitive terms, the plenary nature of the Absolute; this limitation deriving from the fact that the reflection is not in every respect identical with the object it reflects: a ray of sunlight is both something of the sun and at the same time reducible to an infinitesimal quantity before the source of its projection.

The positive knowledge of what was revealed in the moment of realization remains permanently with the *jivan-mukta*; but it is not a mode of knowledge limited to the mind; rather, it is one that pertains to the "heart": nothing can cause him to deviate from the "conviction in his own heart that he has direct knowledge of the Absolute and is also supporting a physical body at the same time." The reference to the "heart" brings the discussion back to the question of who or what is the subject that undergoes realization: that element of absoluteness that is found at the inmost center—the "heart"—is alone capable of realizing the Absolute. All three mystics have stressed interiorization as the path of transcendence, and, applying here the reflection principle, it could be said that the attainment of the center of the soul is the attainment of that point of contact between the "ray" of light of the Absolute and the "mirror" of the being of the individual: from that point of contact the reflected image "returns to the root from which it became manifest," in Ibn Arabi's phrase. In Eckhart's terms, at that point of contact the "eye" of the soul sees the "wood" of the Absolute, so that the two are absolutely one; and according to another of his images, the soul is absorbed into God, thus losing its "name" in just the same way as "the sun draws the dawn into itself and annihilates it." While in Shankara's terms, the Self that had been present in the soul "in the form of a reflection of consciousness . . . returns to its own nature, abandoning its form as the soul."

Finally, it is to be remembered that this "return" takes place inwardly: the mirror of the ego reflects the Absolute that transcends it, certainly, but this transcendence is by way of immanent depth, an inner infinitude which unfolds at the center of the being. It is for this reason that Ibn Arabi claims that "my voyage was only in myself and pointed to myself"; and that Eckhart says: "What was above must become inward. You must be internalized, from yourself and within yourself, so that He is in you. It is not that we should take anything from what is above us, but we should take it into ourselves, and take it from ourselves, and take it from ourselves into ourselves."

The same principle pervades the whole of Shankara's perspective: the Self is not "other" than the individual, and in this respect can be said to be immanent "within" the individual; but in reality, it is the individual as "other" that is illusory, inasmuch as "nothing different from Me can exist so as to belong to me."

## 7. Grace

Before turning to discussion of questions pertaining to the existential return, the following factor will be briefly addressed: the necessity of grace for transcendent realization.

Shankara not only writes of the realizatory power of grace that issues from the sacred syllable *Om*, but also assimilates all conscious efforts of the individual to a mode of preexisting grace, inasmuch as the Self is the source of the individual's intelligence; therefore, even when it appears that Shankara attributes to the intellect of the individual the capacity to realize its true nature as the Self, this capacity is itself a grace: "liberation of the soul can only come through knowledge proceeding from His grace."

Eckhart also speaks of the intelligence requiring illumination by supernatural grace, and of the fact that the gifts *of* the Holy Ghost can only be assimilated on the basis of having already received the gift that the Holy Ghost *is*: the very fact of having been created in the image of God constitutes the preexisting grace that allows of union, which comes about through the subsequent modalities of grace, on the one hand, but which surpasses the relative degree proper to grace as an effusion from the Godhead, on the other. Nonetheless, it is only that already uncreated element—thus that bestowal of grace that the Holy Ghost is—within the intelligence that can surpass this relative degree within the divine nature: it is thus grace, rather than the individual, that penetrates beyond the "work" of grace in order to realize union with the Godhead that as far transcends all work as heaven transcends earth. Furthermore, Eckhart's "breakthrough" to the Godhead only takes place as a result of the divine "breakthrough" into him.

Ibn Arabi, writing of the summit of his spiritual ascent, claims not that he realized the transcendence of his contingent dimension, but that God took from him this dimension: thus it is grace that is again stressed, implicitly, as being instrumental in consummating the final transcendence.

What this common emphasis on grace shows is that, despite the fact that transcendent realization entails the attainment of a degree which surpasses the personal God, the very capacity to realize this degree is dependent on the grace that proceeds, by definition, from the personal God, since nothing can proceed from the Essence without relativizing it. This point reinforces the stress placed on the necessity of faith and devotion—both of which relate *a priori* to God as the "other"—as prerequisites for setting out on the path that transcends the personal God; it also helps, as will be seen below, to explain the persistence and deepening of these same elements even after that transcendence has been realized.

## Part III: Existential "Return"

### 1. Poverty

Ibn Arabi expounds at great length on the "poverty" of the saint, as does Eckhart; not only is the same term applied in both cases, but it seems clear that the self-same ontological quality is intended by both: the one in whom realization of the plenitude of the Absolute is attained cannot fail to be aware of the nothingness of his own personal dimension; this is the nothingness of an apparent "something"—the creature in its own right—and must for this very reason be all the more stressed. Both Eckhart and Ibn Arabi go to great lengths, dialectically, in order to distinguish between a volitive "poverty" which relates more to the moral and affective aspects of detachment, and an ontological "poverty," the ground of which is the effacement of the ego.

Eckhart refers to the "asses" who believe that poverty of the will involves willing only what God wills; this is done in order to reveal the individualism implicit in this non-transcendent position: the individual ego, along with an independent will, is assumed as the active agent in this mode of poverty, "for that man has a will to serve God's will—and that is not true poverty!" No trace of individual will is to be found in "true poverty" for therein the creature must be "as free of his created will as he was when he was not." This position corresponds closely to Ibn Arabi's conception of poverty: the distinction between "slavehood" (*'ubudiyyah*) and "servitude" (*'ubudah*) is made in order to show that the perfect man is subsumed within the latter quality rather than possessed of the former, such possession implying personal affirmation prior to subordination to the Absolute.

That this absolute degree of poverty is the existential reflection of the realization of the Absolute is clear in both Ibn Arabi and Eckhart: it was seen in the case of Eckhart that man "is not," and is realized as such, only in the plenitude of the Godhead wherein all things "are not" in respect of their exclusive specificity, but "are," in respect of the undifferentiated ground of their Being. In this manner one can understand what is meant by his saying that man must be as free of his created will "as he was when he was not." Similarly with Ibn Arabi: servitude is the transcription within relative existence of that condition of total effacement realized in the unitive state, wherein God removes from the individual his "contingent dimension": through this, Ibn Arabi says, "I came to know that I was a pure 'servant' without a trace of lordship in me at all."

It may appear at first sight that this exaltation of poverty and "enslavement" runs directly counter to Shankara's consistent and repeated affirmation of freedom and "Deliverance." Indeed, there is to be found here a fundamental difference in respect of style or tone of spiritual discourse, as well as content: that so much of Shankara's output expounds the *paramarthika*, or absolute, viewpoint almost to the point of marginalizing the *vyavaharika*, or relative, viewpoint clearly distinguishes his perspective from those of Eckhart and Ibn Arabi. This contrast is revealed as a difference in emphasis resulting from a different vantage point: from the point of view of the realized man as an individual, the stress is on poverty, servitude, and nothingness, but when focus is directed to the essential content of the realization in question, the stress will, on the contrary, be on plenitude, deliverance, and Reality. There is complementarity and not mutual exclusion as regards these two views.

For Ibn Arabi, so long as the individual subsists as such, his poverty/servitude is his immutable station, while freedom is a transitory "state"—union with God, which strictly negates the individual condition. If this were as far as Ibn Arabi went, there would be a serious contradiction with the perspective of Shankara, for whom the very subsistence of the individual is itself reduced to illusion—and is thus a transitory "state" in relation to the immutable reality of the Self, which is eternally free: and the "delivered one" is free precisely because he is identified with that eternal freedom.

But the two perspectives are in fact reconcilable as soon as it becomes clear that Ibn Arabi sees the freedom of the Essence as pertaining to the one and indivisible Reality: whatever, then, is not one with this Reality *is not*. That is, it cannot be regarded as ultimately real: "the final end of the gnostics is that the real is identical with them while they do not exist." Insofar as the individual is qualified by existence, he is, and is described as, a "slave" before the One; there can be no freedom for the individual except insofar as he is aware of his own nothingness: "no thought of existence occurs to him, poverty disappears, and he remains free in the state of possessing nonexistence like the freedom of the Essence in Its Being."

One should stress the word "like" in the above quotation: the freedom attained is not totally identified with the absolute freedom of the Essence but may be likened to a reflection, within the consciousness of the individual, of that immutable freedom which infinitely transcends the individual. This closely corresponds to Shankara's position: the individual participates in the Self—and therefore its eternal freedom—by means of the reflection of the consciousness of the Self in the intellect. This reflected consciousness is not only an effect of the realization of the Self—source of the reflection—but also a prefiguration of the "final peace" which comes at the moment of the physical death of the individual; the fact that the *jivan-mukta* remains alive and subject to the unfolding of his *prarabdha karma* entails an inescapable engagement with contingent existence, even though, by virtue of his realized consciousness, there is also transcendence of all contingent existence. This, it seems, is precisely the meaning behind Ibn Arabi's assertion that to cling to one's existence entails poverty, while clinging to the immutable non-existence of one's own entity results in freedom.

While for Shankara the emphasis is on the metaphysical consciousness, "I am the Real"—with the existential corollary "I, as a particular individual, am illusory" being largely implicit—it is the converse that holds for both Ibn Arabi and Eckhart: the emphasis in the first instance is on the non-existence of the individual, with the metaphysical corollary—consciousness of being the Real—being left largely implicit.

Shankara maintains a dialectical position which is consistently derived from the perspective of the Self, even within the context of the subsisting individuality. He is able to do this since the reflection of consciousness is of an essentially ambivalent nature: in respect of the element "consciousness" it is the Self, while in respect of the element "reflection" it presupposes a plane of alterity—the individual ego—and thus illusion, given the fact that all but the Self is illusory in the very measure of its distinction therefrom.

It is the reflection of the consciousness of the Self in the individual that makes possible the paradoxical capacity to use the mind as the vehicle for the expression of truths which render illusory the mind; here, the aspect "consciousness"—hence the Self—predominates over the aspect "reflection"; whereas in the perspective of Ibn Arabi, there is a greater degree of emphasis—implicitly—on the aspect of "reflection," hence "otherness"—whence the stress on the poverty and slavehood of the individual. It is thus a question of viewing the same fundamentally ambiguous relationship between the relative and the Absolute—or, what amounts to the same thing: between the individual and the content of realized consciousness—from two different perspectives, which, far from being mutually exclusive, in fact presuppose each other: Shankara's elliptical statements, such as "I am the Absolute," would be unintelligible without the crucial corollary that, on the one hand, his own personal nature *qua* ego is as insignificant as "an arm that is cut off and thrown away"; and on the other, that liberation does not pertain to the ego.

Likewise, in the case of Ibn Arabi: to affirm the non-existence of the individual entity presupposes some consciousness to take cognizance of this non-existence; and this can only be the consciousness of the Absolute, in the last analysis, that very consciousness whence was derived the capacity to affirm, after being "lifted" out of the contingency of the individual condition, "the King is a prince to me." The same applies to Meister Eckhart: the full ontological, rather than simply mental, assimilation of the fact that the creature is a "pure nothing" presupposes the realization of pure Being: "I was bare being, knower of myself in the enjoyment of truth." That the "I" in question has absolutely nothing to do with Eckhart's personal subjectivity is clear from his description of what takes place in "union" as opposed to "unitedness": it is only in the former that the creature loses its entire "being and identity."

It can also be argued that this principial complementarity between the two modes of dialectical emphasis is further underlined when one considers the question of objectivity in regard to the ego: as a result of the transcendent realization, both Ibn Arabi and Eckhart maintain a view of the empirical self as being quite distinct from the realized locus of awareness. It is not only in Shankara that the consciousness of the Self persists as a reflection within the self by means of which the self is grasped—even outside the moment of enlightenment—as the "other" and thus as illusory: Ibn Arabi also regards the ego as the "first stranger" that the gnostic comes across; and Eckhart likewise is no more concerned with his own self than with the individual "across the sea."

## 2. Existence and Suffering

Although Shankara asserts that the *jivan-mukta* is, despite his deliverance, still outwardly bound to the contingencies of relative existence because of the unspent portion of his *karma*, the relationship he has with the fruit of this *karma* is determined by the consciousness of the Self and not by the empirical phenomena constituted by this fruit of past action: he maintains an attitude of supreme indifference to the outward world and to the empirical ego as subjective agent in the world, since he identifies in a permanent fashion with the Self; he thus sees in the empirical ego nothing but a transient aspect of the non-Self. The mutability of empirical experience is viewed from the perspective of the immutability of the Self. This is analogous with Ibn Arabi's position: the saint sits in the "house of his immutability, not his existence," gazing on the manner in which God "turns him this way and that." Similarly, Eckhart in his sermons repeatedly comes back to the detachment of the saint regarding his destiny in the outer world, accepting absolutely everything that happens to him as the expression of the will of God.

While it is clear that all three mystics share the same fundamental spiritual attitude towards the exigencies of outer existence, there is a difference between the more theistic conception of Ibn Arabi and Eckhart—it being the personal will of God that determines phenomena—and the impersonal causality expressed in Shankara's position, in which the experience of phenomena is assimilated to the fructification of past action. Again, there is here an important difference of emphasis, but by no means an irreducible opposition: for Shankara does affirm that it is *Isvara* who macrocosmically distributes the fruits of past action and establishes a pattern of interlocking destinies such that the law of *karma* is upheld throughout time and space with an impeccable justice that could only derive from an "Inner Controller."

It will readily be admitted that Shankara affirms this theistic aspect more in the context of his exegetical writings than in his independent doctrinal treatises, and therefore as one who is duty-bound to defend the scriptural tenets; to this extent it may be said that his theistic position on existence does not characterize his fundamental perspective on the world as *Maya*, that is, on the creation as unreal (*ajati*). This may be acknowledged, without necessarily inferring that his theistic conception is but a formality, still less a pretence, on his part: it would be a pretence only if the *paramarthika* perspective precluded, rather than included, the *vyavaharika* one. On the contrary, though, there is no contradiction between them: from the point of view of the Absolute, there is no creation, while from the point of view of the relative, creation has its own rhythms, structures, provenance, and divine causality.

The three mystics share, then, a fundamental attitude of detachment with regard to the exigencies of the external world, an attitude which derives from their realization of that which infinitely transcends the world. It might be argued that there is, however, a contradiction between Eckhart and Ibn Arabi in respect of the nature of the response to a particular modality of empirical experience, namely, suffering. It will have been seen that for Eckhart, suffering is likened to the swinging of the door on its hinge: the inner man—the hinge—remains impassive, while the outer man—the door—will be "moved" by the experience of suffering. The point that would be emphasized in this argument is that Eckhart does not say that personal prayer is to be resorted to: rather, his general opposition to "prayer for this or that" would be presumed to apply in this instance, remembering that for Eckhart such prayer is described as a "prayer for evil." Ibn Arabi, on the other hand, commends as exemplary the supplication made by the prophet Job when afflicted; there is here, it will be argued, a direct contradiction.

One will readily concede that there is here an important difference, resulting from a divergence as regards the consequences of the methodic imperative to concentrate on the Absolute: with Eckhart, personal prayer is a relativity and thus an evil with respect to the absolute good it eclipses, while for Ibn Arabi, such prayer—despite being "accident" relating to "accident," the soul addressing the Divinity—is an important aspect of the individual's immutable relationship with God. For the soul to pray for relief from suffering is an obligation, for subjective and objective reasons: subjectively, the making of personal prayer enhances awareness of the permanent state of need that characterizes the empirical self, and objectively, such prayer is an acknowledgment of the incommensurability between the creature's limited resources and the infinite power of God. The obligation to pray is, furthermore, willed by the Lord for the express purpose of manifesting mercy, through the granting of relief from suffering.

This significant difference of perspective on personal petition is, however, mitigated by two factors, the one ontological and the other contextual. Ontologically, this difference can only be attributed with a significance that is proportionate to the level of being on which it is manifest: as both Ibn Arabi and Eckhart affirm the nothingness of the creature in the world in contrast to the reality of the Essence, the question of how the creature responds to a relativity cannot be regarded as having any absolute or final status. It is clear that Ibn Arabi is substantially at one with Eckhart in respect of the ontological degree to be accorded to the experience of suffering: from the perspective of "unveiled consciousness" there is but the One Reality, and only from the viewpoint of veiled consciousness arises the injunction, "worship Him and trust in Him"; and it is solely in the context of the latter relationship that praying to God for help in overcoming affliction is commended.

Sitting in the "house of immutability" does not then exclude the possibility that one of the ways in which the hand of God moves the saint "this way and that" is to make him pray for help (one also notes the fact that Eckhart often appends a personal prayer to the end of his sermons): this duo-dimensionality constituted by inward immutability and outward "movement" corresponds closely in fact to Eckhart's image of the moving door swinging on its immobile hinge, as well as to Shankara's distinction between the *paramarthika* and *vyavaharika* perspectives.

Turning to the consideration of the contextual factor, the two perspectives can be rendered even more harmonious if it be accepted that Eckhart's intention in equating prayer for particular things with evil is more dialectical than practical: it could be argued that he is attempting—by use of striking, if not scandalous, hyperbole—to heighten the receptivity of his listeners to the transcendent mode of prayer, that "absolute stillness" in which, alone, the Word can be heard. It might be argued that this dialectical intention arises in response to a particular contextual need: such may have been the predominance of personal over contemplative prayer in Eckhart's social context that the greatest fruit of the spiritual life was lost in the maze of indefinite lesser goods that were constantly being sought.[2] This is plausible in the light of other instances of this dialectical

---

[2] There is strong evidence to suggest this: many of the nuns to whom Eckhart preached, and for whom he had pastoral responsibility, typically engaged in severe ascetic practices, and had a prayer life that was "dominated by the practice of petitionary prayer." See Oliver Davies, *Meister Eckhart: Mystical Theologian*, SPCK, London, 1991, p. 73.

intention to focus attention sharply on the rigorous requirements of that union in which is to be found the "soul's whole beatitude": all lesser works and attainments being akin to the "doves" that must be expelled from the temple, that is: things good in themselves but wrought to the accompaniment of attachment to the self.

Ibn Arabi, on the other hand, seems to have been faced with a different context: he refers to the lower class of Sufis who believed that the virtues of resignation and patience precluded the resort to personal prayer in moments of trial. Against this view—and the concomitant possibility of spiritual pretension: the presumption, on the part of the shallow aspirant, that he does not need God's help, aspiring only to His Essence—Ibn Arabi stresses that the individual's unveiled consciousness never blinds him from his existential dependence on God. Just as God's infinitude is not relativized by virtue of the assumption of finitude, so the gnostic's consciousness of his outward need of God's qualities does not relativize his inward identity with God's Essence.

The understanding of this principle of two poles of consciousness is important in assessing the next point: the status of personal devotion to the Absolute as "other."

### 3. Devotion and Praise

It might have been thought that, realization of the One having been attained, any distinctive relationship grounded in the duality of worshipping subject and worshipped object would be strictly excluded. But all three mystics affirm—with varying degrees of emphasis—both the ontological validity and the existential duty to render homage, devotion, or praise to all that which surpasses them as individuals.

One of the keys to understanding this can be found in Ibn Arabi's formulation that one should praise God "accident for accident." As the One cannot be made the object of devotion, this object can only be its necessarily relative self-determination, that is, the Divinity; this Divinity is "accident" when considered in relation to its own transcendent Essence, just as that exterior dimension of man which praises the "other" is "accident" when considered in relation to his immanent substance, which is "the Reality." This accords with Shankara's explanation of how it is possible for him to salute, bow, and prostrate not only to *Brahman* but even to the knowledge of *Brahman*. Though neither *Brahma nirguna* nor this knowledge can be "subjected to any relative treatment, yet we view it from the relative standpoint and adore it to the best of our ability."

Likewise, Meister Eckhart stresses that to be a "wife" is superior to being a "virgin": to be virgin is to receive the gift of God while to be a "fruitful wife" is to offer praise and gratitude for that gift; such is the importance of this dimension that Eckhart says that without this "wifely fruitfulness" the gifts received in virginity perish. One feels that in making this point so strongly, Eckhart, in common with both Ibn Arabi and Shankara, wishes to underline the fact that humble adoration of the Divine, far from being precluded by the realization of transcendent union—in which the relativity of the distinctively conceivable and thus worshipable Divinity is surpassed—is in fact strengthened as a result of the highest spiritual attainment. Having known and realized one's true ontological identity in and as the Absolute, the realized man necessarily knows and realizes his outward existential identity in and as a relative being: each dimension has its rights and duties, without there being any confusion or contradiction between them. Just as the accidental or "outer man" cannot aspire to union with the Essence, so the substantial or "inner man" aspires exclusively to this union and has nothing to do with anything less: it is this that explains both Eckhart's and Ibn Arabi's antinomian statements and Shankara's near-exclusive concern with expounding on the nature of "his" true identity as the Absolute.

There is, moreover, another reason why transcendent realization should entail, by way of consequence, a deepened devotion to the personal God: the mystic knows that this realization was only attained through the grace of God, as seen earlier; the aid of the relative Divinity is absolutely necessary for the relative individual; the metaphysically conceivable limitation of the Lord does not blind the individual to his spiritual and existential dependence upon Him, a dependence which subsists for as long as does the individual.

## 4. Vision of God in the World

The three mystics affirm that, once the transcendent Absolute is realized, that same Absolute will be grasped as immanent in the world. A useful image for conveying the relationship between the two modes of realization—and which explains both Shankara's vision of "all is *Brahman*" and Ibn Arabi's vision of the entire cosmos as the deployment of the divine Name "the Outward"—is given by Eckhart: just as the man who stares at the sun for a long time sees the sun in whatever he looks at afterward, so the man who has realized the Absolute transcending the world cannot fail to see it also in the world.

However, the manner in which this vision is described by Shankara and Ibn Arabi differs in one important respect: for Ibn Arabi, the cosmos is itself the manifestation of the divine quality "the Outward," and its very substance is thus assimilated to the divine Nature; creation, then, is taken seriously as an ontological quality in its own right. This is to be contrasted with Shankara's categorical denial of the metaphysical reality of creation, his theory of *ajati*. The world is illusion and can be grasped as the Real only when it is "seen through"; to say that it is *Atman* means that the substratum of the world is perceived through the world which is an illusory superimposition thereon: the snake is the rope only when the conception, name, and form of "snake" disappears. The substance of the snake is not assimilated to the substance of the rope except on pain of the snake ceasing to exist as such.

Such a view of the world as *Atman* contrasts markedly with Ibn Arabi who emphasizes the Divine intention regarding creation, an intention which renders it sacred; thus one finds him quoting such verses of the Qur'an as follows: "What, do you think that We created you only for sport?" (23, 115).

It is clear that, in terms of spiritual style, dialectical emphasis, and psychological ramifications, this divergence on the question of the existence of creation constitutes a significant difference between the two approaches. This having been admitted, it is nonetheless important to see that the gap between these two views of the world is narrowed considerably as soon as the apparently opposite—but in fact complementary—view is shown to be present in both cases; this shows that the difference is of a contextual and not principial order, since it does not impinge on the metaphysical principles held in common by the two mystics.

Taking Shankara first: we can consider two other similes which he employs in order to convey the nature of the relationship between *Brahman* and the world, the clay-pots image and the image of water. In terms of these images, the very stuff of the pots is clay, and the very substance of the waves, foam, and spray is water: the world is, in its very manifestation, a transmutation of *Brahman*, even if this be *Brahma saguna* and not *nirguna*, which latter remains always *prapapañcha upasama*—without any trace of the development of manifestation. This accords perfectly with Ibn Arabi's position: in every existential degree or "presence" the *'arif* sees that "the Real has transmuted Himself in keeping with the property of the presence."

Furthermore, when one looks at the texts in which Shankara is defending the theistic conception against atheism—when, that is, he speaks as commentator and theological defender of scripture against unorthodox interpretations—it becomes evident that the doctrine of *satkarya-vada* implies this same view of the ontological continuity between *Brahman* and the world: if all effects subsist within Being prior to their outward manifestation, and if Being is thus both efficient and material cause of the world, then the very substance of the world is itself constitutive of what Ibn Arabi would call the Divine Self-manifestation. It is again true that in his independent treatises and at his most characteristically metaphysical, Shankara inclines more to the view of the illusory nature of the world; the snake-rope image is more characteristic of Shankara's approach, even while the complementary view conveyed by the clay-pots image is present though not so much emphasized.

Similarly, but in an inverse manner, for Ibn Arabi: creation as theophany is doubtless more characteristic of his approach to the world, but the complementary view of the illusory nature of the world, stemming from his most rigorous metaphysical conceptions, is strongly present also: the two dimensions of *tanzih*—incomparability and transcendence—and *tashbih*—similarity and immanence—must both be affirmed if a complete picture of the relationship between the relative and the Absolute is to emerge.

Despite the fact that the Real transmutes itself into the forms of the world, the Real in itself undergoes no change. The Real is said to be "perpetually in a state of union with engendered existence" only in respect of its descent as Divinity: it is through this descent that the Real "is a god." That is, only the already relative aspect of the Divine—not its transcendent aspect, the Essence—is subject to this transmutation: this accords with Shankara's distinction between *Sat* or *Brahma saguna* as the material cause of the world and *Brahma nirguna* as being without any trace of the development of manifestation.

Furthermore, if, in Ibn Arabi's perspective, the divine Names are of an "imagined" nature, in respect of their distinctiveness, then the world must itself also be so, *a fortiori*, since these Names are the ontological roots of the world. In both Ibn Arabi and Shankara, then, the world is both real and illusory, depending on the point of view adopted: real when seen as the expression of the Absolute in its relative dimension; and illusory when the emphasis is on the exclusive reality of the Absolute, in which light all else is illusory or "imagined"—including even the relative aspect of the Absolute, *Brahma saguna* or the Names of God.

As between the respective dialectical positions of Shankara and Ibn Arabi, then, it is again a question rather of emphasis and point of view than of mutually exclusive alternatives: the difference of emphasis is real enough on its own level, but it is a difference which is overcome inasmuch as the complementary perspective is simultaneously affirmed within each perspective.

In Eckhart, one finds the same compatibility between denial and affirmation of creation. On the one hand, the creature is described as a "pure nothing" and on the other, there is no time when creation is not occurring as the "overflow" of the divine Nature. As to its being an overflow, the very notion and reality of "god" requires the created world as object over which to be Lord, but for which there would but be the Godhead. As to its nothingness, the created world "is not," from the point of view of this Godhead, firstly because each created thing excludes everything else and is thus itself negated by this very opposition with the Universal, for true reality cannot be subject to any opposition; secondly, because there is no created element in the Godhead—all things being contained therein, uncreate, in the absolute non-differentiation of the "Solitary One."

On the one hand, then, there is the affirmation of creation, and on the other, a denial of its final ontological reality: the creature is both image of God—and by that very fact reducible in its essence to that of which it is an image—and at the same time a "pure nothing." In Shankara's terms: the snake is the rope when grasped as the rope, but an illusion when considered in itself. And with Ibn Arabi: man is "the transient, the eternal"—a creature in respect of his "corporeal formation," but the Real in respect of his "spiritual formation."

## EPILOGUE

# RELIGION AND TRANSCENDENCE

It has been said earlier that the attainment of the transcendent essence of religion entails surpassing, but not bypassing, the boundaries of formal religion. Realizing that which transcends religion can only be achieved by means of religion itself, through identifying with what religion spiritually and metaphysically "intends," rather than remaining at the level of what it formally establishes and dogmatically propounds. To transcend religion is very different from subverting it. This same process—surpassing but not bypassing—applies, *mutatis mutandis*, to the other two fundamental "objects" that are transcended by the summit of spiritual realization: the individuality as such, and the personal God.

Individuality cannot be surpassed except by means of Divine grace; therefore, except on condition that the individual be fully in conformity with the requirements of grace, or to put this "theological" condition in more metaphysical terms: in conformity with the existential and ontological imperatives of the individual's situation in the hierarchy of being. Existentially, the individual human soul must be characterized by faith and virtue; ontologically, the soul must be extinguished in the ultimate object of faith and in the divine roots of human virtue. One cannot bypass or ignore the individual dimension of the spiritual path in the quest for an ostensibly supra-individual attainment; for without giving the individual nature its due, without feeding it with the faith and virtue that are its very life-blood, the channel of grace is ruptured, and no transcendence whatsoever is conceivable, let alone attainable: such a quest for a "supra-individual" realization does nothing but eliminate the possibility of that objective "leaven" of grace from entering the soul, and thus results only in a further entrenchment of the individual within his own subjective limits. Far from being receptive to the objective power of grace, which alone can lift consciousness above the confines of the empirical ego and lead it towards its Infinite source, there is, for the soul which lacks faith and virtue at the outset of the path, nothing but an intensification of egotism: instead of the infinitude of pure consciousness there are but the vagaries of indefinite pretension.

Indeed, there is nothing more pretentious than for the individual to believe that, because he conceives of something which transcends the personal Divinity, he can bypass God in his quest for transcendence. The three mystics studied here are at one in stressing that the grace of God is the indispensable means of attaining transcendence. Even if, on the discursive plane, there seems to be a contradiction here—grace emanating from the personal God giving rise to the realization of the Essence that transcends the personal God—the appearance of contradiction disappears as soon as one understands the following essential principle: the personal God is nothing other than the Divine Essence affirming or determining itself at the level of Being; it is the one-and-only Reality expressing itself as personal Divinity, whatever be the dialectical means of indicating the relativity of this level of Being in the face of the supra-ontological Absolute. Thus, in this connection, the "grace of God" is nothing but that ontological attraction exerted by the transcendent Essence upon the innermost consciousness of the individual; the means by which the God within is summoned to realize the God above; the process by which immanence rejoins transcendence.

Each of the three fundamental "objects" transcended, then—religion, individuality, the personal God—must be given its due, at the appropriate level, prior to being surpassed: when religion is observed, when the soul is governed by spiritual virtue, and when there is complete faith in and submission to God, conceived as the infinitely "Other." Only then, and in accordance with the specific means and conditions laid down by tradition, does one embark in earnest on the path of transcendence.

But there is also a fourth element that must be transcended: transcendence itself. That is, the unitive state—wherein the individual as such is effaced and there remains nothing but Reality unqualified—this state is also to be surpassed, not insofar as its essential content is concerned, but insofar as it is a *state*. The particular experience of enlightenment, however exalted, gives way to a permanent manner of being: the content of the supra-individual state, "beyond-being," is transcribed by the realized sage within the framework of diversified existence. Indeed, realization—"making real"—goes far beyond the realm of particular experiences; it is not such and such an experience that defines realization; rather, it is realization that determines the manner in which experience as such is assimilated, conferring on life itself a continuously intuited, quasi-miraculous quality. The thirst for experiences and the aspiration for transcendence are in fact poles apart; in concrete, human terms, the aspiration for transcendence implies, above all else, an effort to open oneself up to the infinite power of grace; and this, in turn, demands an awareness that the individual as such is an "illusion" (Shankara), a "pure nothing" (Eckhart), and that his only property is "poverty" (Ibn Arabi). The desire for experiences to be appended to the individual, or even the individualistically conceived desire to transcend individuality, on the other hand, is nothing but a desire for the enrichment of the individual, not its effacement, a reassertion of the ego's congenital claim to existential autonomy, and thus a violation of the indispensable prerequisite for the operation of grace. Schematically speaking: without self-effacement there is no grace, and without grace there can be no transcendence.

Therefore it can be asserted that an individual whose life accords with the basic requirements of grace—faith in God, fidelity to a revealed religion, the pursuit of a life of virtue—is, *ipso facto*, following a path that leads to transcendence, even if the conception thereof be simple, and even if the governing aspiration of such an individual be limited to salvation in the Hereafter. In the measure that such a person sincerely follows a religious, even an exoteric, path, there is receptivity to grace, and thus a degree of transcendence is realized; or at least: the process of transcendence has effectively begun, one has set out on the path to the Transcendent. On the other hand, a cavalier attitude towards religion, a pseudo-metaphysical marginalization of the personal God, a disdain for the relativity of human virtue, together with a hunger for tangible experiences—all of this stands at the very antipodes of authentic aspiration for the Transcendent, such as this principle has been expounded here.

In other words, there is both continuity and discontinuity as regards the relationship between the two paths of transcendence: the exoteric path of transcendence, leading to salvation in the Hereafter, and the esoteric path, aimed at realization here and now. There is a certain solidarity between the two paths insofar as they are both based entirely on the necessity of grace, both are oriented towards the Divine Principle—at whatever level this be conceived—and both are governed by aspiration towards the ultimate purpose, and the ultimate happiness, of the human soul; so much so that it might almost be said that realization is salvation herebelow, just as salvation is realization in the Hereafter. We say "almost" because of the necessity of taking into account different levels of realization and of salvation: just as there are different degrees of mystic and esoteric realization, so there are different degrees of Paradise.

This having been said, the element of discontinuity between the two paths must also be stressed. We have seen in this study various ways in which the path of mystical realization involves the radical exclusion of ideas and practices of conventional religion; Eckhart's reference to the "asses" who will nonetheless earn a heavenly reward most strikingly expresses the disjuncture between the two paths. But the element of discontinuity is not just to be found as between the one path and the other: the root of this discontinuity is to be found even within the path of transcendence itself. It is expressed as the incommensurability between the path leading to transcendence and the summit itself. This is another way of saying that as between the finite and the infinite, or between form and essence, there is no common measure: the summit of transcendence, one with the Absolute itself, is infinitely beyond anything that is encountered along the path leading to that summit. This principle is expressed by Shankara as follows: "the two active causes of the fruit of liberation—the preliminary mental activity and the ensuing cognition in its empirical aspect—are not of the nature of the fruit." The realization of transcendence has nothing in common with its apparent causes, its "seeds," or the path leading up to it; there is a radical disjuncture at the threshold of this summit, the point at which the relative is at once obliterated and assimilated by the Absolute. This is the point when, in Ibn Arabi's words, "God removed from me my contingent dimension"; that ineffable moment when, to use Eckhart's evocative and eloquent image, "the sun draws the dawn into itself and annihilates it."

The difference between the religious or exoteric path and the metaphysical or esoteric path critically involves the distinction between the relative and the Absolute. This distinction is, moreover, applied within each dimension: there is an element of relativity within the Absolute: the personal Divinity; it is this which is ultimately surpassed. And there is an element of absoluteness within the relative: the immanent Self; it is this that must be realized. To surpass the personal Divinity entails the surpassing of the individuality. Whereas in the path of exoterism the relationship between the individual and the personal God is absolute and exhaustive, this same relationship takes on a more nuanced quality in the esoteric path: it is absolute, but only within the realm of relativity, and therefore for as long as the individual as such subsists; but this realm of relativity is itself grasped as an illusion in the light of the Absolute. The two viewpoints, *paramarthika* and *vyavaharika*, do not so much exclude each other as imply each other. The individual may have an "experience" of God, but can never "realize" Him: in the realm of relativity the individual remains always the individual, God remains always God. On the other hand, the individual cannot "experience" the Transcendent, but it is nevertheless "realized" within him; in the realm of transcendence there is neither experience nor individuality.

From a strictly metaphysical point of view, there can be no "experience" of the Transcendent: from the perspective established by that which is realized, the essential condition for "experience" is revealed as illusory, namely, a subject which is distinguishable from that which is experienced. The concept and reality of experience presuppose an essentially dualistic ontological framework, for experience is the result of an encounter between an experiencing subject and an object experienced, even if this object be of an inward order. To experience "something" is to be contrasted with "being" that thing. To say experience, then, is to say irreducible alterity; at the transcendent level, alterity—and thus experience—is illusory; transcendent realization entails complete identity with the Absolute, and this Absolute does not experience anything "other," for nothing "other" truly exists. Since the Absolute does not have any "experience" which can be distinguished from that which it immutably is, it follows that identity with the Absolute cannot, in good spiritual logic, be described in terms of an experience.

It is precisely because of the effacement of the individual in the highest realization that there can be no experience of this realization: for experience presupposes the individual as its subjective ground. Once it is established that, in the realm of transcendence, the notion "individual experience" has no currency, then the "problem" of ineffability is easily resolved. In its essence this realization is necessarily incommunicable because communicability is predicated upon human language, which in turn is a function of the individual, and the individual is effaced in the realization of transcendence. Language cannot adequately express that which nullifies the foundation of its own operation.

It may be objected here that Shankara does precisely this when says to his own mind: "thou art illusory." Here he uses language, mediated by his mind, to express a truth that renders illusory his own mind. The response to this objection is that he is not, in this instance, expressing the nature of plenary realization, but enunciating a key concomitant of this realization, one which relates to the non-existence of that which appears to exist, the non-self, the individual human mind. This he does by adopting the viewpoint of the Self, which is possible inasmuch as the realized intellect functions as a positive reflection of the consciousness of the Self, taking on its point of view in a provisional, but nonetheless effective, manner.

A second objection can be envisaged: if realization be ineffable, what does it mean to say that it consists in Being-Consciousness-Bliss? To say that the content of this realization can be designated as Being-Consciousness-Bliss does not mean that these three elements are distinctively encountered, but that their undifferentiable common essence is realized in infinite mode; this last qualification is crucial: the finite modes of being, awareness, and joy commonly experienced in the framework of existential diversity are incommensurable with their infinite archetypes, of which they constitute so many distant reflections. To offer this triple designation affords to the imagination some idea of the transcendent realization, starting from one's experience in the world, but this approximate notion is then to be dialectically negated by the *neti, neti*: the realization of the Self, and therefore of the undifferentiated essence of absolute Being, Consciousness, and Bliss, infinitely transcends the experience which the limited self has of outward existence, conditioned awareness, and finite joy.

Just as the attribution of qualities, such as Being, to the Absolute is provisional and requires, dialectically, a negation in order to indicate less inadequately the undesignatable Absolute, so the notion "experience of the Absolute" is provisional, having some meaning exclusively from the vantage point of the individual; the notion is also valuable discursively insofar as "experience" can be complementarily contrasted with "concept" or "doctrine"; but it, also, requires a spiritual negation, which emerges as the shadow of the realization in question: that is, the "one liberated" knows that the experience of Liberation is illusory *qua* experience, given, on the one hand, the immutability of the Self, and on the other, the unreality of the empirical agent or non-self which undergoes change and thus "experience."

At a higher level, the liberated individual also knows that, since the Absolute is infinite, and since there is no conceivable limit to the infinite, there can likewise be no conceivable "point" at which transcendence is exhaustively and finally attained: the "path" leading to transcendence in one sense never comes to an end: having reached the summit, that summit becomes the center of a totality that ceaselessly pulsates with infinite life. The path can thus be said to have a beginning, but no end, this being the inverse of the nature of *Maya*, which has no beginning but does have an end.

The individual cannot have any experience of the Absolute; but this does not prevent the consciousness in the individual from realizing its transcendent identity as the Absolute. There is no common measure between the individual as such and the Self, so when the mystics affirm that they are not other than the Self this cannot refer to their individuality, on pain of reducing the Absolute to the "illusory superimposition" (Shankara), the "nothingness" (Eckhart), or "poverty" (Ibn Arabi), of the relative creature as such. To know that one "is" the Self is the corollary of knowing the Self: once the Self is "known," no other reality can be distinguished from it, except in illusory mode; that consciousness in the individual which "knows" the Self can therefore only "be" that which is "known"; this transcendent identity is "realized"—made "real," that is: fully effective as opposed to conceptual, actual as opposed to virtual, concrete as opposed to abstract—this realization taking place in the first instance in the moment of Liberation at a supra-individual degree; and this realized knowledge is thereafter permanent, becoming appropriately transcribed within relativity by the consciousness of the individual now liberated from the illusion of separativity.

This cognitive transcription and "return" to diversified existence, what we have called above "transcending transcendence," or what the Sufis call subsistence after annihilation (*baqa'* after *fana'*) outwardly modifies, but does not essentially alter, the consciousness attained in the unitive state; again, one returns to the principle of essential identity giving rise to continuity, and formal difference giving rise to discontinuity. Consciousness of the Absolute subsists, even in the framework of those relative modes of awareness with which it has no common measure. Herein lies one of the great paradoxes of mystical realization: how the knowledge of the Absolute, or absolute Knowledge, persists even in the context of the individuality. One possible answer to this problem has been extrapolated in this study from Shankara's *abhasa* concept: it is the existence of a reflection of the consciousness of the Self, in the intellect of the finite self, that can maintain the viewpoint of its source, and thus permits a vision of all things from the *paramarthika* or absolute perspective, that perspective which Eckhart attributes to the "uncreated intellect" and "the inmost man," and which is indicated by Ibn Arabi in terms of "unveiled consciousness."

But to speak of this knowledge persisting in the context of the individuality also entails the reemergence of the perspective of *vyavaharika*/ "the outer man"/ "veiled consciousness." Despite the fact that the absolute perspective takes precedence within the consciousness of the realized sage, the coexistence of the two perspectives—a coexistence which is inescapable for as long as the individual self subsists—entails the paradox that the Self is "known" whilst simultaneously being "unknowable": the individual as such cannot cognitively encompass the very principle—pure Consciousness—of cognition itself.

The individual, as we have stressed repeatedly, can never "become" the Self or the Absolute: only the Self, immanent in the individual, can come to realize its transcendent identity. This crucial point—along with the necessary qualification: the Absolute that transcends the personal God can only be realized as a result of the grace of the personal God—cannot be too strongly emphasized. It is because of the incommensurability between the relative individual and the Absolute Self that, outside of the unitive state wherein being and consciousness are absolutely undifferentiated, the individual cannot know—because he cannot "be"—the Absolute Self.

What the individual does possess, however, on the very basis of his realization, is an accurate reflection of the consciousness of the Self, and this transmits to him an awareness of the transcendent bliss and unconditional reality of the Absolute, as well as the conviction that in his essence he is no other than this One Reality, the only ultimate reality. This knowledge stems from the positive aspect comprised in the reflection of consciousness, while the negative aspect— that of the inversion proper to reflection—results in the fact that the awareness in question is not total identity. Total identity implies absolutely "unobstructed metaphysical knowledge" and this is realized only at the "fall of the body," as Shankara says. For the individual to adopt the absolute vantage point is, then, a prefiguration of the final identity, a taste, one might say, and not its final consummation; but this identity is nonetheless known, despite the apparent subsistence of the self and the world as distinct from the Absolute, to be the only true reality. The realized sage is no longer deluded by the appearance of otherness: the Absolute is grasped not only through the objective veil of the world, but also through the subjective veil of the ego.

Finally, this vision of the realized sage, far from diminishing the devotional instinct, in fact deepens it: to know the Absolute is to devote oneself to it absolutely. Devotion to all that which surpasses one in the hierarchy of Being, rather than being subverted by the realization of the Absolute, is on the contrary an inescapable corollary of the highest realization. Indeed, the devotion of these sages may be said to be more "real" than that of ordinary worshippers insofar as their devotion is impregnated with "realization," not just of the Absolute, but of their own nothingness in the face of the Absolute; hence they have an ontological and not just notional awareness of their own utter dependence on the Absolute for their very being.

> The final end and ultimate return of the gnostics . . . is that the Real is identical with them, while they do not exist.

# APPENDIX

# AGAINST THE REDUCTION OF TRANSCENDENCE:
## A Critical Appraisal of Recent Academic Approaches
## to Mystical Experience

In the light of the assessment of the principal dimensions of transcendent realization common to all three mystics studied in this work, the shortcomings of certain influential academic analyses of mysticism can be clearly seen. What these analyses have in common is a tendency to reduce the nature of mysticism to categories that cannot do justice to the higher, transcendent aspects of mystical realization. This appendix comprises four parts: the first deals with the reductionist epistemology of Steven Katz's "contextualism"; the second, with the reductionist theoretical concomitants of Robert Forman's "Pure Consciousness Event"; the third addresses the reductionist typologies of mystical experience proposed by W.T. Stace, R.C. Zaehner, and Ninian Smart; and the fourth offers a critique of the surface universalism espoused by Fritz Staal and Aldous Huxley.

## Part I: Against Reductionist Epistemology: Katz and "Contextualism"

The central element in the approach propounded by Steven Katz, labeled "constructivism" by his critics, and "contextualism" by himself, essentially consists in a denial of the possibility of transcendence, that is, of any mystical experience or consciousness which transcends the context—cultural, doctrinal, linguistic—in which the mystic perforce operates. The crux of his argument is that, *a priori*, there can be no "pure (i.e. unmediated) experiences":

> All experience is processed through, organized by, and makes itself available to us in extremely complex epistemological ways. . . . This epistemological fact seems to me to be true because of the sorts of being that we are, even with regard to the experiences of those ultimate objects of concern with which mystics have intercourse, e.g. God, Being, nirvana, etc.[1]

All possible "intercourse" with the "ultimate objects of concern" is therefore constructed out of elements proper to the context in which the complex epistemological processes make experience available to the individual: the transcendence of this context is ruled out *a priori* by Katz. While none would doubt the need to respect the context in which mystical experience occurs, there seems to be no reason to accept the axiom that the context will necessarily determine the content of all possible mystical experience and consciousness. Nor

---

[1] "Language, Epistemology, and Mysticism," p. 26, in *Mysticism and Philosophical Analysis*, ed. S.T. Katz, Sheldon Press, London, 1978.

is there any reason for accepting the inductive reasoning, based on conventional experience or the "sorts of beings that we are," which generalizes in such wise as to subsume within its own non-transcendent and even non-mystical nature, all possible mystical experience. This is precisely what Katz does, in asserting that the "synthetic operations of the mind" which process all epistemological activity are the "fundamental conditions under which, and under which alone, mystical experience, as all experience, takes place."[2]

The simple reason for refusing to adopt this starting point is that mystics themselves do claim to have attained a spiritual degree which transcends all context. It is this which Katz cannot take seriously because of the limitations inherent in his own epistemological context:

> The metaphysical naiveté that seeks for or worse, asserts, the truth of some meta-ontological schema in which either the mystic or the student of mysticism is said to have reached some phenomenological "pure land" in which he grasps transcendent reality in its pristine pre-predicative state is to be avoided.[3]

This categorical exclusion of transcendent realization is made despite his own insistence that due weight be accorded to the actual reports of their experiences offered by the mystics themselves; indeed he claims that his sole concern is "to try and see, recognizing the contextuality of our own understanding, what the mystical evidence will allow in the way of legitimate philosophical reflection."[4]

Katz appears to uphold the phenomenological principle of "intentionality": evaluating that which the religious believer or mystic himself says or "intends," rather than reducing the data to the categories of the external analyst. However, the simple retort to his contextualist denial that transcendence is a possibility is that, were one to take seriously the mystical evidence, the analyst may—and indeed does—find that mystics claim to have attained to just such a "transcendent reality": philosophical reflection will then either entail a Katzian reduction at the expense of mystical or metaphysical intentionality, or else one remains faithful to this intentionality to the necessary detriment of the Katzian notion of constructivism.

Certain objections to the conclusions of this study will obviously be forthcoming from a Katzian perspective, and, it is hoped, in the course of responding to these objections, the import of these conclusions in respect of transcendent aspects of mysticism will be thrown into sharper relief.

The first objection that could be made is the following: the claim that transcendent mystical realization is identical in the three mystics studied is itself founded upon, and thus reducible to, an *a priori* assumption of the ontological validity of the ostensibly "transcendent" degree of realization attained; it is thus the expression of a preexisting belief rather than an inference based on examined evidence.

---

[2] Ibid., pp. 62-63.

[3] "The Conservative Character of Mystical Experience," p. 41, in *Mysticism and Religious Traditions*, ed. S.T. Katz, Oxford University Press, 1983.

[4] "Language, Epistemology, and Mysticism," pp. 65-66.

To reply: it will readily be admitted that all forms of analysis inescapably involve some form of "reduction"; in this study the reduction in question has been explicitly in favor of the ontological status of mystical and religious claims: to elucidate meaning within religion, it is better to opt for that form of reduction which in principle coheres with that which is held to constitute religion in the minds of the subjects to be studied, that is, religious believers. This reduction is, moreover, justified by the principle of intentionality; and this principle compels the analyst to focus on the evidence forthcoming from the reports of the mystics in order to generate therefrom appropriate analyses: in the measure that this occurs, the structure of analysis is grounded in this evidence, and is by this very fact independent of the question of the validity or otherwise of the claims implicit in that evidence. The charge of a priorism would then be untenable since the deductions and conclusions would be rooted in the evidence itself: it is this evidence which, rather than being the subject of dispute or denial, is accepted in an *a priori* way, as being the very data—the "given"—on which comparative religion as a discipline is based. ·

Now Katz, on the contrary, conceals his own *a priori* judgment behind the veil of academic objectivity. For, in rejecting the possibility of transcendence of context, in denying that the fundamental conditions of everyday experience can be surpassed in mystical realization, he is in fact advancing, not a value-free epistemological principle, but a set of claims that are ontological in their turn: namely, that everyday experience is absolute; that the individual, on the one hand, and his terrestrial context, on the other, are the unsurpassable poles of universal existence; that the empirical context of all conventional experience cannot in any way be transcended. From the perspective of the mystics studied here, these claims would quite clearly be seen as "absolutizing" the relative, and by the same token, relativizing the Absolute; if it be contended that the Absolute cannot be realized starting from the context of relativity, then this entails an implicit limitation on the Absolute itself, since, as seen clearly in this study, it is in reality the Absolute that realizes itself through the individual: to thus limit the Absolute is to relativize it.

To apply here the approach of Ibn Arabi: to deny the Absolute the capacity to know itself through an apparent "other," as it were in a mirror, is to delimit it to but one mode of Self-knowledge—"seeing Himself in Himself"—that is, the immutable Self-consciousness of the Essence. But the Absolute cannot be excluded from the possibility of Self-knowledge starting from relativity inasmuch as this very relativity itself is a necessary aspect of the "completeness" of the Absolute: without relativity and thus delimitation, the non-delimited Absolute would be delimited by the very absence of delimitation. If the Absolute must have an extrinsic dimension of relativity, without this impairing its transcendence, the converse is also true: the relative, even while remaining distinct from the Absolute in respect of ontological degree, must be reducible in its essence to the Absolute, but for which it would lack existence. It is this subtle metaphysical point that appears to elude Katz's analysis; for Katz, the relative must remain in every way relative, with no possibility of transcendence included within it, because relativity is implicitly conceived as absolutely distinct and separate from the Absolute; from this point of view, there is no room for the notion of divine immanence, the mysterious penetration of the relative by the Absolute. Only when the fundamental metaphysical assumption of immanence be accepted can there be any question of positing the possibility of transcendence for the consciousness of the individual.

To argue against Katz's reification of conventional experience one need not assert that the individual can realize, and still less experience, the Absolute, but that, in Eckhart's terms, the infinite God within man realizes the infinite God above man; or: none knows Him to whom nothing is similar but Him to whom nothing is similar (Ibn Arabi); only the Self knows the Self (Shankara).

Only when the transcendent Absolute is regarded as already immanent in the world, and more particularly in the soul, can the conception arise of the possibility that transcendence can be realized, and this at a degree which perforce surpasses the boundaries of contingency, the "context," both microcosmic and macrocosmic.

It is because the consciousness in man is not exclusively "created" or relative that this possibility of transcendent realization arises; Eckhart's affirmation of the uncreated aspect of the intellect here corresponds with Shankara's identification of *Atman* with *Brahman* and Ibn Arabi's identification of Adam's essence with *al-Haqq*, the Real: it is this already absolute dimension hidden in man that becomes realized as such. If Katz is unable to conceive of the possibility of transcendence in terms of spiritual realization, it can only be because this essential metaphysical principle of immanence—so clearly expressed by the mystics studied here—has not been given sufficient attention.

Proper consideration of this principle also gives rise to a clearer perception of the metaphysical inadequacy of the notion of "experience" in respect of transcendent realization. The very incommensurability between the Essence and the Divinity, *Brahma nirguna* and *Brahma saguna*, the Godhead and God, that is posited in respect of the objective transcendence of the pure Absolute above all relativities—this incommensurability must be transposed onto the planes relating respectively to the empirical self and the immanent Self. All the rigor of that metaphysical distinction between the non-acting Absolute and the acting Divinity must be brought to bear upon the ontological distinction between all possible experiences of the individual self, and the transcendent realization of the Absolute: to say "experience" is to affirm duality and hence the non-transcendent, while to say "transcendent realization" is to exclude dualistic experience. Just as "mere thought obscures the essence" (Eckhart) in respect of the transcendence of the Essence of the Divine above all conceptions thereof, so, in respect of spiritual realization of that Essence, all thought "obscures" the essence of this realization. This is because thought—and therefore language, which operates only as the expression of thought—is inescapably tied to the individual, and the individual is extinguished in the unitive state of realization, like the dawn which is annihilated by and absorbed into the sunlight (Eckhart). Hence ineffability is a central aspect of this transcendent realization: the only means to express this realization are already compromised by their unavoidable entanglement with the very order that is transcended. If the analyst accepts the claim of the mystics that the individuality is transcended in the highest realization, then he must also accept the logical corollary: all contextual factors are likewise transcended since they cannot operate in the absence of the individuality, neither *a fortiori* can they "determine" or "construct" an outcome that undermines the very foundation of their own influence—the individual agent.[5]

This does not mean denying the importance of cognitive processes preceding enlightenment; they are simply given an appropriately relative status. In Shankara, for example, they are even called "active causes," but he adds that these causes do not participate fully in the "effect" to which they apparently give rise. In other words there is a radical disjuncture between individual cognition and realization of the Self. According to Shankara, the "active causes" of enlightenment consist of two elements: the "previous mental activity" and the "liberating cognition in its empirical aspect"; but they nonetheless are not "of the nature of the fruit"; this means that what, in Katz's view, would determine the nature of the mystical experience is here explicitly separated from the realization whose fruit—Liberation—has nothing in common with the cognitive processes that apparently produced it.

This fundamental point can be approached from a different angle, that of the affirmation, consequent to enlightenment, "I am *Brahman*"; according to Katz, this would be seen as an expression of the way in which experience is shaped by the preexisting concept of "*Brahman*," so that there is an ontological and epistemological continuity between this concept and its experiential referent. According to Shankara, however, the affirmation is not only the expression of the highest truth, it is also an "object," distinct from the reality it expresses and therefore illusory, in the final analysis. The verbal affirmation is, on the one hand, an expression of a truth whose intrinsic reality has nothing in common with any linguistic or conceptual processes, since these pertain to the individual, the non-Self; and on the other hand, the affirmation is predicated on cognition, which is "an act that can be referred to by a verb and characterized by change."

This radical disjuncture between linguistic/conceptual affirmation and the spiritual realization it either prefigures or expresses *post facto*, indicates that the realization in question transcends the contexts—conceptual, linguistic, doctrinal, cultural etc.—from which it springs. If Shankara had insisted that there was a

---

[5] In his latest contribution, "Mystical Speech and Mystical Meaning" (in *Mysticism and Language*, ed. S.T. Katz, Oxford University Press, 1992), Katz argues that "ineffability" should be taken to mean: communicable, but only by means of extraordinary language. Again, one is asked to choose between, on the one hand, accepting the explicit claims—based on extraordinary experience—made by the mystics to have attained to a spiritual degree that surpasses the plane on which language operates, and on the other, accepting the claim—based on generalization from ordinary experience—made by Katz that nothing is incommunicable. He is forced by the logic of his contextualist thesis to contradict the mystical evidence: he cannot take at face value the claim of the mystics to have transcended the epistemological plane of language as this would necessarily undermine the foundation of the postulate that all experience is epistemologically constructed. This is a clear case of the distortion of intentionality by a preconceived theoretical assumption.

relationship of interdependence between the linguistic/conceptual affirmation of identity and the realization of identity, then the claim could, in good logic, be advanced that the realization in question is essentially determined by its cognitive context. But Shankara maintains, on the contrary, that this affirmation is but a remote reflection of the identity it expresses, one which, far from determining this identity, is itself absolutely dependent on, and therefore determined by, it; and this dependence is by no means reciprocal: identity with *Brahman* is the immutable reality that can either be contradicted by the cognitions of the mind or else affirmed by them, without this having any bearing on the identity itself. In this respect, denial and affirmation are equally far from realization: they both have in common the extrinsic plane of individual cognition, which is an "object" in relation to the supra-individual Self. In another respect, affirmation of identity is closer to the truth inasmuch as it is expressive of a reflection of the truth on the limited plane of the mind; but the important point here is that the very capacity of the mind to affirm this identity is itself derived from the already extant identity and thus predetermined by it, rather than being the determinative factor in regard to the content of the realization of identity.

One is faced here with rival ontological claims: either one accepts the explicit claim made by Shankara regarding the subordination of the concept to the reality of realization, or one accepts the implicit claim to the contrary made by Katz: that privileged ontological status be accorded to the mental and linguistic context which predetermines the nature of all possible mystical attainments. A decisive factor which should incline one to accept Shankara's claim is that while he unambiguously and authoritatively asserts that Liberation transcends all conceivable contextual factors—hence its very designation—Katz is compelled by the logic of his argument to admit that his own perspective is constructed by context. Katz, of course, does not claim to arrive at his position through mystical experience, but through epistemological principles of his own construction, based on everyday experience; now Shankara, Eckhart, and Ibn Arabi claim, on the contrary, that it is precisely this ordinary experience, along with all epistemological principles proportioned to, and thus limited by, that experience, that is transcended in the highest realization. Seen in this light it is Katzian constructivism that is the position predetermined by, and imprisoned within, contextual conditions. Furthermore, a critique of all perspectives that are limited by context presupposes a vantage point that is itself liberated from its own context: this is precisely what Katz admits to *not* having, and precisely what the three mystics confidently assert at having realized.[6]

---

[6] "The axiom of relativism is that 'one can never escape from human subjectivity'; if such be the case, then this statement itself possesses no objective value, it falls under its own verdict" (Schuon, *Logic and Transcendence*, trans. P. Townsend, Perennial Books, Bedfont, 1975, p. 7). Schuon's compelling critique in this chapter, "The Contradiction of Relativism," can be usefully employed as a refutation of the premises of Katz's analysis. The Kantian relativism which implicitly provides the foundation for Katz's perspective is noticed and properly criticized by Perovich in his chapter, "Does the Philosophy of Mysticism Rest on a Mistake?" in *The Problem of Pure Consciousness*, ed. R.K.C. Forman, Oxford University Press, 1990.

Another argument against Katz can be derived from the importance attributed by the three mystics to the role of grace: they all assert that the summit of spiritual realization is attained not as the result of their own unaided efforts but as a "grace"; this means that not only is the content of the realization of a supra-individual nature, but also the means whereby it is attained is derived from a supra-individual source; one returns to the fundamental point that refutes the Katzian thesis: if the individual as such is transcended both in respect of the means and the content of realization, then all contextual factors that presuppose the individual as the ground of their mediating influence are *ipso facto* transcended.

Two further points may be considered before concluding this discussion: the role of scripture and the role of the invocation of a Name of the Divine in the process of spiritual realization. What is to be stressed here is the manner in which the mediating context of specific revelation is surpassed in the realization of that from which the revelation derives its value.

According to Shankara, the Veda is said to "disappear" on enlightenment; their purpose realized, they play no further role and do not enter into, and still less determine, this realization: for the Veda does not produce liberating knowledge, it does not "reveal what is unknown." On the contrary, its capacity to assist the individual in the quest for Liberation derives from the fact that the Self is already attained and never non-attained, being the "eternally realized fact"—*nitya-siddha*. Far from scripture determining the nature of realization, it is the preexisting and immutable Self that determines scripture: to the extent that the attainment of the Self has a preceding cause, this cause can only be the already extant state of being the Self, and cannot be attributed to scripture, which is itself an effect.

This view of revelation is mirrored in its essentials by Eckhart's description of the function, not so much of scripture, but of Christ: he was sent as a messenger to bring the blessedness "that was our own." It is thus this blessedness, which, being the content of the message, takes precedence over the form of the messenger and indeed constitutes an essential condition for the efficacy of the messenger's function. This ontological and spiritual priority of the essence of realization—blessedness—over the form that vehicles it—Christ as outward messenger—is further underlined by Eckhart's injunction: unite with the formless essence, even if this be at the expense of the elimination of the formal image of Christ, to which one must not become attached. Moreover, the supreme realization of this blessedness is found in union with the Godhead which surpasses the plane of the Persons, and thus Christ, envisaged in his distinctive form; therefore Christ is successful in actualizing for Eckhart the blessedness he already has, a blessedness whose consummation surpasses the plane on which Christ's deifying function can be manifested.

The whole discussion of the station of "proximity" in the chapter on Ibn Arabi shows how closely his position corresponds to the ones outlined above. The essential point here is that, in principial terms, prophecy, and the formal, specific revelation that defines it as such, is subordinated to sanctity and the essential and universal quality that constitutes its defining characteristic; this priority is moreover to be observed even within the soul of the prophet. Sanctity, then, in static terms, refers to that qualitative and universal essence which is intended by formal revelation, and in dynamic terms, consists in that realization which transcends the context within which formal revelation perforce operates. Far from the context determining the content of realization, and thereby relativizing it through making of it an element within that context, it is the realization which confers a vantage point whence the relativity of the context is apparent. The understanding of the relativity of the context of specific and formal revelation is a key element of the "station of proximity"; and it is also implicit in Ibn Arabi's assertion that the Qur'an, along with the other formal scriptures, "point only to the Divine Names and are incapable of solving a question that concerns the Divine Essence."

This is not to deny the fundamental importance of the Qur'an for Ibn Arabi's metaphysics; for it is readily apparent that his whole perspective is rooted in Quranic symbols and terms, the deepest meanings of which he brings out in accordance with his spiritual insight and "unveiling." But to bring implicit and profound meaning to light is not to be equated with transcendent realization: hermeneutical profundity may arise as a consequence of spiritual realization, but the two occupy different ontological planes. It may be admitted that Ibn Arabi's "context"—the Qur'an, principally—is an inalienable part of his metaphysical exposition of meaning, while at the same time affirming that this context is transcended by the ultimate degree of spiritual realization, the realization, that is, of the Essence; for it is the Essence, in the last analysis, that constitutes the *raison d'être* of the context: the forms that make up the context exist only for the sake of the Essence which they embody and to which they lead.

Finally, the question of the role of invocation in determining realization must be assessed. One will readily agree with Katz that more attention should be given to this question.[7] But whereas Katz tries to show that the generative power of the invocation with regard to mystical experience proves the determinative power of language *per se*, the conclusion here is that this generative power is derived from the sacramental presence that inheres in the revealed Name of the Absolute. The chapters on Shankara and Ibn Arabi show that there is a crucial distinction to be observed between the efficacy of the Name as it is employed methodically in the quest for transcendence, and the inadequacy of all Names, considered doctrinally, in any attempt to define the transcendent. If the invocation of the Name leads to realization of the Named, this means, not that the epistemological structure inherent in language somehow constitutes, or determines, or even enters into, the Absolute, but rather the converse: that something of the Absolute enters into language. The Named assumes a Name in order to be realized, not as the linguistic essence of the relatively defined Name, but as an Essence that strictly transcends the domain of relativity presupposed by all linguistic and epistemological structures.

Thus, far from supporting the thesis that transcendent realization is determined by the linguistic basis of the invocation that precedes realization,

---

[7] See Katz, "Mystical Speech and Mystical Meaning," pp. 5-15.

the spiritual efficacy of the invocation proves, rather, that it is only through the sacramental presence of the Named in the Name—the "grace" that inheres in *Om,* according to Shankara—that the invocation of the Name can lead to the realization of that which transcends all Names: the purpose of knowing the identity of the Name and the Named, as Shankara said, is to realize the Absolute which is different from both. The Self to be realized, then, cannot be regarded as the correlate of any finite form, or *nama-rupa,* being beyond even that trace of relativity pertaining to the Unmanifest, Being, as source of all manifestation and existence; the Self is *prapañcha-upasama,* beyond any trace of the development of manifestation, and it thereby infinitely transcends both the Name—which is formal, linguistic manifestation—and the Named, not insofar as this is identified with the Self, but insofar as it is distinguished as the supra-formal counterpart to the Name: the Self is beyond all relationship with relative form; and if the realization of the Self can be said to have any "content," this can only be the infinitude of the Self, and not any "experience" derived from the reconstituted elements of prior conceptual and linguistic processes.

To conclude: once the notion of individual experience ceases to define the parameters of one's epistemological viewpoint, it can readily be grasped how all contextual factors which both construct and presuppose individual experience are transcended by the highest spiritual realization. From the perspective of the outside observer it requires an imaginative leap, a "paradigm-shift," to affirm an epistemology that is not limited by the parameters of one's own ontological premises—of one's own experience; but this is exactly what is urged by the mystics themselves: in order to understand the "poverty" of which Eckhart, for example, speaks, it is necessary to "be like it," to some degree at least. Appropriately transcribed into academic terms, this means that if the outside observer is to have any proper understanding of the essence of mysticism, he must be prepared to accept the possibility in principle that his own experiential categories and premises are proportioned to, and operative within, a plane of being that is transcended by certain degrees of spiritual realization. In this way, the analyst can then be said to be, relatively speaking, "poor"—that is, empty of, or detached from—the limiting confines of his initial starting-point.

## Part II: Against Reductionist Experience: Forman's "Pure Consciousness Event"

Although there are several aspects of Forman's critique of Katzian constructivism with which one will readily agree, his own alternative is, in its turn, clearly reductionist. In place of constructivism, he proposes, on the basis of mystical intentionality, the notion of "forgetting": he asserts that the mystical evidence, far from supporting the idea of contextual predetermination, on the contrary supports the notion of "pure consciousness events," which, being contentless, are therefore unconstructed. His position is intimately bound up with his own apparent experience of just such a "pure consciousness event." He claims to have undergone a certain content-free state of consciousness during a retreat involving some unnamed technique of Hindu meditation. During one session, there was a knock on the door:

> I knew that . . . before hearing the knock, for some indeterminable length of time prior to the knocking I had been awake but with no content for my consciousness. . . . The experience was so unremarkable, as it was utterly without content, that I simply would have begun at some point to recommence thinking and probably would never have taken note of my conscious persistence devoid of mental content.[8]

The non-transcendent nature of this experience is immediately apparent from the observations made in this study. In particular, the clear exposition by Shankara of different degrees of spiritual experience allows one to situate Forman's state with some measure of precision.

First of all there is no mention of the bliss that one would expect from the realization of pure consciousness; on the contrary, it is described as "unremarkable." Secondly, the realization of transcendent consciousness cannot be equated with the mere cessation of cognition; as Shankara says, this consciousness is neither cognition nor the simple cessation of cognition, but a supra-cognitive or spiritual intuition of the Self grasped once and for all as one's own true identity. Forman's "Pure Consciousness Event" is clearly free of cognitive content, but this absence, alone, does not qualify it as "pure" in the sense understood by Shankara: the absence of distinctive content is but the reverse side of a positive realization of the plenitude of the Self which contains everything within itself in undifferentiated mode; it is because of this very non-differentiation that there can be no question of distinctive content, while the converse does not hold: the absence of distinctive content does not necessarily entail realization of the undifferentiated plenitude of the consciousness of the Self. This point will be amplified below in relation to Forman's interpretation of Eckhart's *raptus*.

Staying for the moment with his own experience, what Forman seems to be describing is a state that is analogous in one respect to *sambija samadhi*, that is, to a state of enstasis in which the "seeds" of ignorance remain intact, so that distinctions born of ignorance reemerge as soon as the state ceases; it is dissimilar from this state in another key respect, however, since in this *samadhi*, blissful experience is an essential element, while Forman's experience is devoid of blissful, joyous, or any other, content. With reference to the absence of distinctive content proper to this lower *samadhi*, Shankara makes a comparison with the deep sleep state: there is the attainment of a certain mode of undifferentiated consciousness, but this is unaccompanied by the realization of the Self. It is only the knowledge of identity as the Self that burns up all seeds of ignorance, and this occurs only in the higher state of *nirbija samadhi*.

In Forman's "Pure Consciousness Event" a break in the flow of the stream of relative consciousness does seem to have taken place, but since it is unaccompanied by liberating and blissful knowledge of true Selfhood, it is to be located within the

---

[8] "Mysticism, Constructivism, and Forgetting," in *The Problem of Pure Consciousness*, p. 28.

realm of relative consciousness: for the simple negation of finite consciousness shares with this finite consciousness a common ground—that which is affirmed, sharing with that which is negated, a common referent—even if this negation appears, from the viewpoint of relativity, to share a key attribute with absolute consciousness, namely, the absence of specific content. The state of deep sleep likewise appears to share this attribute, and it is for this reason that Shankara employs it to such good effect as an inverted image of pure consciousness: any specific content of consciousness is distinct from consciousness itself and thereby proves, by its very presence, that pure consciousness has not been attained. It is in order to express graphically this point that the comparison with the state of deep sleep is made; but then Shankara asserts that it is only beyond this non-differentiation, which is but the negation of differentiation, that pure consciousness, or *Turiya*, the "Fourth," is to be found. It is beyond all states that are susceptible of cancellation, and the deep sleep state is, after all, but the cancellation of the two preceding states of wake and dream; hence it is, as said above, only an *inverted* image of the nature of pure consciousness: what is seen as the absence of cognitive content from "below" is in reality absolute and infinite plenitude from "above." Forman's description affords a phenomenological report of the "underside" of this realization but is silent on that which would qualify the "experience" as being of the transcendent order, namely the positive affirmation of identity with pure being, pure consciousness, and pure bliss.

Forman does admit that the "Pure Consciousness Event" is not necessarily "ultimate or salvific";[9] but problems of interpretation arise when, on the basis of his own experience, he applies this category to the *raptus (gezucken)* described by Eckhart:

> I characterize the pattern of mental functioning denoted by Eckhart's term *"gezucket"* as a pure consciousness event, a mind which is simultaneously wakeful and devoid of content for consciousness.[10]

This means, according to Forman, that the silencing of the "cognitive mechanism and the senses is none other than the encounter with God." Eckhart is then quoted in support of this assertion: "where the creature stops, God begins to be."[11]

One should like to emphasize in this citation the word "begins": this means that human silence does not of itself constitute the consummation of the divine Word, that is, it is a necessary but not sufficient condition for its "utterance" or Birth; silence is, in other words, the prerequisite for hearing God's Word, and must not be identified with this Word itself.

This line of reasoning is clearly in accordance with Eckhart's perspective on the Birth; in the sermon describing St. Paul's *raptus* he says:

---

[9] Ibid., p. 9.

[10] "Eckhart, *Gezucken*, and the Ground of the Soul," in *The Problem of Pure Consciousness*, p. 106.

[11] Ibid., p. 109.

> When the powers have been completely withdrawn from all their works and images,
> then the Word is spoken. . . . [T]he further you can get from creatures and their images,
> the nearer you are to this, and the readier to receive it (I:7).

In other words, silent stillness is a mode of enhanced receptivity to the Word,
but by no means constitutive of it, or with the "encounter with God"; the Birth
is clearly distinguished from the silence that must precede it: "if God is to speak
His Word in the soul, she must be at rest and at peace, and *then* He will speak
His Word" (I:7, emphasis added).

The ramifications of this basic error in interpretation are clearly to be seen in
Forman's book on Eckhart, *Meister Eckhart: The Mystic as Theologian*.[12] Given
the limitations of space a detailed critique of this work cannot be undertaken
here; it will suffice for the purposes of this analysis to draw attention to one
important example of the error in question. Forman writes:

> [W]hen Eckhart asserts that one is "locked in the embrace of the Godhead" in *gezucket*,
> he is offering a term, the Godhead, for the "something" encountered in this "nothing"
> experience. He may be understood to be providing an *analytical*, theological "content"
> for a phenomenological contentlessness.[13]

On the contrary, Eckhart expresses by the word "Godhead" a symbol for the
absolute plenitude that is the positive counterpart to the phenomenological
emptiness; as Eckhart says elsewhere, "our unknowing will be ennobled and
adorned with supernatural knowing" (I:21).

There appears to be at work here a basic misinterpretation arising out of an
erroneous extension of Forman's own experience to cover other, higher degrees
of spiritual realization which may happen to share a similar extrinsic character
when viewed from the vantage point of conventional consciousness; what is
similar in phenomenological terms may be quite different in spiritual or supra-
phenomenal terms; phenomenal emptiness is distinct from supra-phenomenal
plenitude, despite the fact that this plenitude will appear, from the specifically
human point of view, as nothing but "contentlessness."

Despite concurring with Forman's critique of Katz, and accepting some of his
conclusions—in particular, the notion that contextual factors are "forgotten" in
the highest spiritual attainments rather than determinative in regard to them—
his "Pure Consciousness Event" cannot be accepted as "pure" in the sense given
this term explicitly by Shankara and implicitly by Eckhart and Ibn Arabi: pure
consciousness is nothing short of the consciousness of the Absolute, which is
devoid of particular content by virtue of its very infinitude.

[12] R.K.C. Forman, *Meister Eckhart: The Mystic as Theologian*, Element Books, Dorset, 1991.
[13] "Eckhart, *Gezucken*, and the Ground of the Soul," pp. 111-112.

## Part III: Against Reductive Typologies: Stace, Zaehner, and Smart

### 1. Stace and the "Universal Core"

The first major problem with the ostensible "universal core" of mysticism proposed by Stace is that the distinction between "introvertive" and "extrovertive" mystical experience ensures that certain essential elements of mystical realization are excluded from his list of core characteristics only because they are not shared in common by both of his theoretically defined "types." Thus, the following two characteristics belonging to the introvertive type are excluded from the common core: (i) unitary consciousness; the One; the Void; pure Consciousness; (ii) non-spatial/non-temporal experience. While the following two extrovertive characteristics are excluded: (i) unifying vision—all things are One; (ii) the One is the subjectivity/life in all things.[14]

From the perspectives addressed here, it is clear that what are called "extrovertive" characteristics do but constitute the transfigured vision of the world enjoyed by the mystic who has realized the "introvertive" elements in the unitive state. The key link between the two dimensions of realization lies in the nature of the One—the "voidness" of which is not properly understood by Stace.

The One, having been realized *above* all things is then realized *in* all things. This is because the One is not simply Void: it is a void in respect of its exclusion of distinctive phenomena, the apparent plenitude of the world; but in itself it principially contains all things in absolute non-differentiation. Thus, "all things" can be grasped as differentiated aspects of their unique and transcendent source, by the mystic who has realized this source: the One is therefore their true "life."[15]

This failure to recognize the organic connection between the two "types" of mysticism is closely related to the second principal problem with his analysis, namely, his misunderstanding of the role and status of the individual in the realization of unitary consciousness, the "nuclear characteristic" of the introvertive mystic. This is clearly discernible in his comment on Tennyson's report of "extinction" in which "individuality itself seemed to dissolve and fade away into boundless being"; Stace, wishing to bring out the paradoxical nature of this extinction, says that "it was Tennyson who experienced the disappearance of Tennyson."[16] Stace does not see that there must be something beyond the individuality that takes cognizance of the extinction of individuality, and this

---

[14] W.T. Stace, *Mysticism and Philosophy*, MacMillan, London, 1961, pp. 131-133.

[15] That Stace has not understood the meaning of the Void in respect of the One is clear from his statement that the Godhead in Eckhart and the higher *Brahman* in Shankara "carry the negative side of the paradox, the vacuum," while God/lower *Brahman* "carry the positive side, the *plenum*" (*Mysticism and Philosophy*, p. 172). As argued in the critique of Forman, the Godhead/higher *Brahman* is only void from the relative viewpoint; in its intrinsic reality it is the source of all being and therefore infinitely more "positive" than its first self-determination *qua* God/lower *Brahman*.

[16] *Mysticism and Philosophy*, p. 119.

something is the "spark" (Eckhart), the "secret" (Ibn Arabi), or the "reflection" (Shankara); that which is mysteriously within—but not of—the soul, that which is divine, and which takes cognizance of the "disappearance" of the soul, is necessarily distinct from that which disappears. It is the supra-individual source of individuality that is realized in the unitive state which, as necessary concomitant, entails the dissolution of the individual.

Finally, attention should be drawn to the problems inherent in the terminology employed by Stace. "Dualism" is defined as the view that the relation between God and the world, including therein the individual soul, is one of "pure otherness or difference with no identity"; "monism" is the view that this relation is "pure identity with no difference"; and "pantheism" is the view that the relation is "identity in difference."[17]

The inadequacy of these definitions is clear once one has grasped the distinction between the *paramarthika* and *vyavaharika* perspectives: there is at once identity—from the absolute viewpoint—*and* difference—from the relative viewpoint, without there being any contradiction since the two perspectives pertain to incommensurable degrees of reality.

On the basis of these rigid definitions, Eckhart is regarded by Stace as having experiences that tend towards monism and pantheism, but "in his defense he repudiated these 'heresies' thus accepting dualism at the behest of the papal authorities."[18] To this one must object: there is no contradiction between Eckhart's "dualistic" affirmation of the distinction between the creature and the Creator, on the one hand, and his "monistic" view of identity with the One: his realization of transcendent identity, "above all being" evidently did not prevent him, *qua* creature, from expressing "devotion and praise" to the Lord—which he insisted upon as the "wifely fruits" of union. The duality presupposed by devotion and praise is transcended in supra-ontological realization, but not abolished on the outward plane of being, where it retains its validity; there is, then, not so much a "pantheism" defined as "identity in difference," but a more subtle relationship, taking into account both transcendence and immanence, which may be defined as "identity *and* difference": the immanence of the Absolute in the soul means that there is identity, but an identity which can be realized only at a supra-personal degree, given the fact that the Absolute is simultaneously transcendent in relation to the soul: and from this transcendence derives the relative reality of difference; relative, because final reality pertains to the Absolute, identity with which is realized "above all being." It is to be stressed again that ontological "dualism" is reduced to the status of illusion exclusively when it is regarded from the perspective of the pure Absolute (*Brahma nirguna* or the Godhead/Essence); outside of this perspective, which properly pertains to the essence of transcendent realization, the dualistically conceived Lord (*Isvara* or God/Creator) retains all its rights as object of devotion and praise.

[17] Ibid., p. 219.

[18] Ibid., p. 226.

## 2. Zaehner: "Monism" vs. "Theism"

The reductive aspect of theoretically defined categories is even more pronounced in the writings of R.C. Zaehner. His analysis is flawed by a singular misunderstanding of the position of Shankara, whom he takes as the representative *par excellence* of "monism." All the neat juxtapositions between the "monist" and the "theist" collapse once Shankara's actual position on the nature and status of God conceived as "the other" is fully grasped. In his *Mysticism: Sacred and Profane*,[19] he asserts that for Shankara "God" is pure illusion, which Zaehner interprets as meaning "absolute nothingness."[20] Illusion does not mean absolute nothingness for Shankara; it is, rather, a relative reality, with its own internal structure, rhythms, and modalities—and disappears only in the measure that it is reduced to the substratum on which it is superimposed and from which it derives its very capacity for appearance as a relative reality; Shankara calls this relative reality "illusion" in order, dialectically, to highlight its aspect of appearance. For the unenlightened need no proof or argument that the world is "real"; on the contrary, it is the ultimately illusory character of the relative reality of the world that needs to be understood, hence the references to dream and illusion.

It is true that Shankara says that this world is a dream: but it is a dream dreamt and ordered by the *Antaryamin*, the "Inner Controller," and possessed therefore of a degree of reality that surpasses the dream-world of the individual soul; furthermore, if the world were but absolute nothingness, there would be no reason for Shankara to address himself so sedulously to the task of refuting the doctrines of the atheists, and advancing the theistic argument from design regarding the creation of the world. The significance of the relative reality of the world is further implicitly underlined by Shankara by the lengths to which he goes in proving that the Lord is the only being capable of distributing the fruits of *karma* in the world, refuting the view of the *Purva Mimamsakas* that *karma* contains the principle of its own distribution within itself. The fact that in the face of the absolutely Real the world is reduced to the status of illusion by no means implies, then, that this world lacks a reality, provenance, and structure proportioned to its level of being.

Zaehner also asserts that Shankara cannot accept the idea of the "grace of God";[21] on the contrary, as seen in Chapter 1, according to Shankara there is no possibility of realization apart from the grace of the Lord. It is also claimed by Zaehner that the monist is forced to see himself as identical to the Creator;[22] on the contrary, Shankara writes that not even on the "indirect path"—leading to the lesser Absolute—is there ever a question of complete identity between the soul and the Creator: each presupposes the other, so that any identity can only

---

[19] R.C. Zaehner, *Mysticism: Sacred and Profane*, Oxford University Press, 1961.

[20] Ibid., p. 156.

[21] Ibid., p. 170.

[22] Ibid., p. 204.

be partial and transient, the distinction between the two being insuperable in the measure that one or the other be present as such. Total identity relates only to the essence of the soul and the higher *Brahman*, that is, the transcendent essence of the Creator and not the Creator as such. Apart from this identity, and insofar as the soul subsists in the world, the framework entailed by the *vyavaharika* perspective retains all its rights; hence devotion, homage to the Lord, to the *guru*, even to the knowledge that liberates—all of which is conceived as "other"—is incumbent on Shankara the man, and duly expressed by him, as seen in Chapter 1.

According to Zaehner, theists and monists can never agree;[23] now while it is true that the theist—such as Ramanuja—cannot accept the ultimate metaphysical conclusions of the non-dualist, the converse is not true: the non- dualist can accept the validity—within its own terms of reference—of the dualist, since the non-dualist contains within his perspective the principles proper to the dualist, giving them their due, but locating them in a framework which surpasses their ontological limitations. This is expressed by Shankara in the following terms: "the non-dualist does not conflict with the dualist"; this is because "non-duality is the ultimate reality, therefore duality or multiplicity is only its effect." Whereas the dualist perceives a duality comprised of the Absolute and the relative, the non-dualist perceives duality only in respect of the relative, and from its vantage point, knowing it to be unreal from the viewpoint of the Absolute. To illustrate this Shankara uses the following image:

> It is like the case of a man on a spirited elephant, who knows that none can oppose him, but who yet does not drive his beast upon a lunatic who, though standing on the ground, shouts at the former, "I am also on an elephant, drive your beast on me" (Karika, 165).

The non-dualist, from a higher vantage point, sees everything that the man on the ground can see, while also enjoying a perspective to which the other has no access; thus there will be contradiction and incompatibility between the two perspectives from the standpoint of the lower of the two, but no incompatibility as far as the higher one is concerned.

When Zaehner asserts that the monist sees in the raptures of the theists nothing but homage to "a deity which one has oneself imagined,"[24] the extent of the error is clear in the light of the above discussion. One could also add that, according to Shankara, it is first the Lord who "imagines" the soul and only after this does the soul proceed with its own constructions: this shows clearly the ontological priority of the Lord over the soul; and the fact that the Lord *qua saguna* is ultimately an illusion before its own essence, *Brahma nirguna*, by no means invalidates its ontological precedence within the framework of the relative reality "imagined" by itself.

[23] Ibid., p. 206.
[24] Ibid., p. 206.

In making these criticisms, one is not pretending that the distinction between the non-dualist/monist and the dualist/theist is meaningless; it obviously does correspond to a genuine division in the ranks of the world's mystics; but in order to be more useful in analytical terms it needs to be considerably nuanced: one has to be clearer about the subtlety and complexity of the non-dualist perspective, and thus correspondingly more flexible in drawing the line that separates the two viewpoints.

### 3. Smart: The "Numinous" vs. the "Mystical"; "Union" vs. "Identity"

Turning now to Ninian Smart's approach, his distinction between "numinous" (in which category are placed the mystics of Christianity, Islam, and Judaism) and "mystical" (comprising those of Hinduism, Buddhism, and Taoism) may be regarded as a useful but provisional starting point of analysis.[25] It is when rigidity enters into the picture that problems arise: when it is claimed, for example, that neither type is reducible to the other. As seen in this thesis, the Muslim mystic Ibn Arabi, while wholly dependent upon the "grace of the other" (the key characteristic of the "numinous" category) nonetheless attains to a unitive state of consciousness, after practicing a particular, intentional, mystical method (the key characteristic of the "mystical" category). Conversely, Shankara is not excluded from positing realization as a grace, despite his emphasis on individual effort, concentration, and knowledge—all of which are in turn reducible to effects of grace. There is, however, a marked difference of emphasis in regard to the place and importance of the "other" as between the two mystics, and this justifies to some extent the employment of these categories; but this difference of emphasis does not give grounds for setting up an irreducible duality.

Rather more important is Smart's distinction between "union" and "identity," the latter being the "organizing concept" when mysticism is combined with the principle of "Ground/Being," the former serving this function when mysticism is combined with "theism."[26] This means that for the mystic whose organizing concept is union, the realization of union with God is seen as an event which occurs and then ceases, leaving intact the distinction between the soul and God, this distinction having been temporarily overcome only for the duration of the particular state of union. For the "identity" mystic, on the other hand, that which is revealed in the unitive state is assimilated as the expression of a preexisting and immutable identity which subsists as such whether the soul be plunged in the unitive state or not.

This reminds one of a criticism made by Shankara against those who feel at one with the Self only in the state of *samadhi*, only to feel bereft of this union once the state has passed; these are contrasted with the *jivan-mukta* who knows that identity with the Self is the reality that is subverted only in appearance by outward modes of existence.

[25] N. Smart, *Reasons and Faith: An Investigation of Religious Discourse, Christian and non-Christian*, Routledge and Kegan Paul, 1958.

[26] "The Purification of Consciousness and the Negative Path," in *Mysticism and Religious Traditions*, p. 125.

Smart's distinction, then, tallies with Shankara's. But again it is important to see that "identity," when considered from the *vyavaharika* viewpoint, necessarily comprises the dualism inherent in the category "union." To illustrate this, the following image may be useful; it was proffered by Ramakrishna in response to a question regarding what is revealed in the state of *samadhi*:

> Once a salt doll went to measure the depth of the ocean. No sooner was it in the water than it melted. Now who was there to tell the depth? . . . [T]he "I" which may be likened to the salt doll melts in the ocean of Existence-Knowledge-Bliss Absolute and becomes one with it.[27]

The mystery, however, is not so much this dissolution, but the fact that the "salt doll" returns from the ocean; this means that, from the point of view of the "reconstituted doll," final, complete, and unalterable identity has not in fact been realized. In other words the "identity" achieved in the unitive state takes on the characteristic of "union," that is, it is grasped as a temporary state. It is only when the *paramarthika* viewpoint is adopted that the mystic will say, with Shankara, that his true identity is the Self/ocean; but this does not make contradictory the affirmation from the viewpoint of the subsistent individual, that a temporary unitive state had been attained, after which the distinction between the soul and the Self retains a certain relative reality. Shankara also admits, as has been noted, that totally "unobstructed metaphysical knowledge only comes after the fall of the body," that is, at physical death. This means that there must in fact be some distinction between Shankara and the Self, for as long as Shankara is still alive—which again returns one to the organizing concept of "union."

To reiterate what has been noted above: Shankara does not mean that, while still living, he has realized complete consummation of identity as the Self; his statements affirming this identity are to be understood rather as anticipations or reflections of that final "unobstructed" knowledge of the Self which is absolutely one with the Reality of the Self: total identity implies a complete union between absolute knowledge and absolute being, and this in turn requires that the knowledge in question be "unobstructed," which in turn is possible only after death. Thus, to say that in *de facto* terms, union with the Self was attained by Shankara—a union which does not permanently abolish the distinction between the two—does not contradict either Shankara's own *de jure* affirmation of identity as the Self, nor his knowledge that this identity is the only true and unconditional Reality, duality being but an appearance which is "seen through." As seen in the chapter on Shankara, he is able to adopt the absolute viewpoint by virtue of the reflection of the consciousness of the Self in the intellect; and it suffices to note that "reflection" both participates in its source and is also distinct therefrom, in order to see the point being made here.

The following description of the state of identity by the Shaykh al-'Alawi is of great value in the present context; after the "veil of the senses" are drawn aside

---

[27] Cited in Mahendranath Gupta ("M"), *The Gospel of Sri Ramakrishna*, trans. Swami Nikhilananda, Ramakrishna-Vivekananda Center, New York, 1969, p. 148.

there remains of man "a faint gleam which appears to him as the lucidity of his consciousness":

> There is a perfect continuity between this gleam and the Great Light of the Infinite World, and once this continuity has been grasped, our consciousness can flow forth and spread out as it were into the Infinite and become One with It, so that man comes to realize that the Infinite alone is, and that he, the humanly conscious, exists only as a veil. Once this state has been realized, all the Lights of Infinite Life may penetrate the soul of the Sufi, and make him participate in the Divine Life, so that he has a right to exclaim "I am Allah."[28]

What is important to note here is that "man comes to realize that the Infinite alone is"; this is what ultimately distinguishes the theistic/union type from the non-dualist/identity type: the realization that the Absolute is the sole reality means invariably that the true identity of the soul—whether in or out of the unitive state—can only be as that Absolute, in that it is concretely realized that nothing else truly exists: the Islamic testimony, "There is no god except it be God" thus acquires the esoteric meaning that there is "no self except it be the Self." The theist/dualist, on the other hand, may well realize a state of union, without this being accompanied by the realization "that the Infinite alone is"; this means, in Shankara's terms, that all the seeds of ignorance cannot have been burnt up, hence the state is qualified as *sambija* and the degree of being with which union has been attained goes no further than *Brahma saguna*, the goal of the "indirect path," involving, as seen earlier, partial and temporary states of identity with the Lord: full and permanent identity is the exclusive preserve of the "direct path" leading to the realization of *Brahma nirguna*, anticipation or reflection of which allows the individual soul to participate in this reality even in this life, hence his designation *jivan-mukta*.

The difference between the two types can also be seen by examining Shankara's statement that after union, the lower *yogin* "sees distinctions as before"; in contrast to this, the *jivan-mukta* is not described simply as one who no longer sees distinctions—because he does, since he continues to operate in the world— but as one who no longer sees them "*as before*," that is, he no longer takes "his perceptions as real": he sees, but does not see, acts, but does not act. The dualistic mystic, on the other hand, sees himself in existential subordination to the Lord in all but the unitive state; the ontological distinction between the two entities thus remains insuperable. Shankara also sees his soul as subordinate to the Lord, but his liberated consciousness at the same time has access to the truth that the distinction between the two, albeit insuperable on the plane of existence proper to it, is conditioned by the relativity of this plane itself, a relativity which is grasped as illusion from the viewpoint of the Absolute and non-dual Self.

---

[28] Cited in M. Lings, *A Sufi Saint of the Twentieth Century*, George Allen and Unwin, London, 1971, p. 136.

## Part IV: Against Reductive Universalism: Staal and Huxley

The question of what constitutes the essence or summit of mysticism lies at the root of the discussion about whether the different religions are outward expressions of a single, universal Truth, or on the contrary derive from fundamentally incompatible conceptions of the Truth. The key conclusion from this study is that the three sages studied here certainly appear to be at one when it is a question of the summit of realization—the transcendence of all finite conditioning attendant upon individuality, and the attainment of identity with the unique Absolute, which is at once pure Being, pure Consciousness, and pure Bliss; while in respect of the return to the finite world, there are substantial similarities as well as important differences of style and emphasis; these differences, far from being essential or irreducible *de jure* are of secondary importance, precisely because they pertain to the relative dimension, that of the relationship with the world, and not to the absolute dimension, the essence of transcendent realization which surpasses all relativities. Thus the overall conclusion supports the universalist position on religions. However, it is important to distinguish carefully between the type of universalism which emerges as the fruit of reflection on the metaphysical principles proper to the highest mystical realization, and a less convincing, but very prevalent, version of universalism which reduces religion to a putatively independent mystical essence which, shorn of religious trappings, is then held up as the universal reality obscured by religious forms.

The first point to make is that both in respect of theory and practice, mysticism is inconceivable in the absence of the religious context that furnishes its formal foundation.[29] Mysticism, such as we have explored it in this study, cannot be isolated from its traditional religious context and then analyzed or practiced employing whatever is available in the way of an abstracted mystical "technique" or through the use of drugs. The clearest and most forthright exposition of a universalist view of religion based on this kind of abstraction comes from Fritz Staal.[30] His basic premises are as follows: mysticism essentially consists of intense phenomenal experience; this experience is uniformly attained by religious and non-religious mystics alike; the means by which it is attained involve various techniques of meditation; and these techniques have nothing to do with religious "superstructure"—the corpus of traditional dogma, doctrine, and ritual that constitute the specific form of the religion in question. From these premises are derived the conclusion that the student of mysticism should eschew any involvement with the superstructure of religion, and actively pursue a meditative path under the guidance of a "guru" who has mastered an appropriate mystical "technique."

There are too many problems inherent in such a position to allow of a comprehensive critique here, but a few major points of criticism need to be

[29] See S. Katz, "The Conservative Character of Mysticism."

[30] F. Staal, *Exploring Mysticism*, Penguin, Harmondsworth, 1975.

stressed. First of all, one wonders what kind of "guru" would find Staal's notion of "guidance" acceptable; for the essence of the master-disciple relationship is defined by the master and not by the disciple: it is the master and not the disciple who lays down the conditions for the engagement.

Staal, on the other hand, says: "But despite the initial need for the uncritical acceptance of certain methods of training, it is equally important that the student of mysticism does not turn into a follower of the guru."[31] What this means in practical terms is that the "student" should distinguish between instruction on meditation—which he must accept uncritically—and instruction on doctrine, relating to religious and philosophical "superstructure"—which is to be ignored because it is something "which is added and which is often worthless if not sheer nonsense."[32] Among such "nonsense" is the belief in God, which Staal sees as being a "special outcome of mystical experiences."[33] To juxtapose the above with Shankara's notion of the guru and the conditions of guidance: The guru is defined as such by his assimilation of *agama*, traditional teaching, on the one hand, and his position in the chain of gurus handing down that teaching, on the other: reverence not just for his own guru but for the whole line of gurus (*parampara*) is a *sine qua non* of his own authority. Staal, however, who shrinks from the idea of reverence for the guru and his teaching, would find nonsensical the notion that the guru is the living embodiment of the ideal to be realized, and would reject out of hand any attempt to include virtue as part of what he calls "methods of training," quite ignoring the fact that training of character is the foundation—as seen in all three mystics studied here—for any higher teaching and instruction. Shankara, quite definitely, would find Staal's notion of "obedience" at best futile—in respect of the true aim of deliverance—and at worst dangerous—given the preoccupation with "experiences" as the goal of the mystical life: futile, because *samsara* is not so easily overcome, and dangerous, because illusion is capable of inflicting painful deceptions on those whose aim is not to transcend, but to seek experiences within, its domain.

Sound metaphysical doctrine, in other words, is an inalienable part of integral "instruction": meditation is, according to Shankara, a mode of action, and action cannot bear fruit as knowledge, hence the necessity of teaching; but this aspect Staal rejects as "superstructural."

Regarding Staal's rejection of faith in God: one need only recall that for Shankara—not to mention the other two sages—faith in the Lord is a prerequisite for the disciple: without faith, no further instruction is to be imparted; however inadequate be the initial conception of the Lord in the first instance, the Absolute must at least be acknowledged and believed in, albeit as a mental construct, prior to the rectification of this conception in the light of realized knowledge of the Self; this being an instance of the principle of *adhyaropana-apavada*, false attribution and subsequent denial.

---

[31] Ibid., p. 142.

[32] Ibid., p. 143.

[33] Ibid., p. 179.

Apart from these basic problems, Staal's idea of the essence of mysticism as being reducible to a set of phenomenal experiences is the most serious flaw in his approach: in the light of this study, the essence of mysticism is, on the contrary, that which transcends all possible experiences which have the individual as their subjective ground.

The fact that the greatest mystics transcend the formal limitations of their respective traditional contexts does not justify the assertion that these contexts can then be ignored, marginalized, or subverted: the mystics both transcend *and* "conserve" the religious form. The ritual forms of the traditions are not to be discarded because they are relative, but, once they are perfected on the plane of being proper to them, they are to be surpassed as relativities before the Absolute can be realized; and the realization of the Absolute demands a commitment that is absolute—hence the rigor with which the relative forms are "rejected" for the sake of the higher discipline. Thus Eckhart insists that his sermons are only intended for those who live according to the basic precepts of the Faith, in perfect virtue; they are not for the "natural, undisciplined man." When, therefore, he appears to marginalize these precepts, it must be understood that it is only on the basis of their perfect realization: Staal and Huxley mistake dialectical hyperbole for practical instruction when they take literally the antinomian pronouncements of one such as Eckhart, so often cited as the epitome of the "subversive" mystic.[34]

Although Aldous Huxley differs from Staal in respect of the importance of virtue,[35] he nonetheless shares with Staal the idea that the rites of religion are dispensable in practical terms: the "perennial philosophy" is something that is expounded and practiced by the mystics without any necessary connection to the ritual aspect of their traditions. Rituals, he argues, either function as channels for a flow of collective psychic energies, or else they do assist in the process of deliverance, but not because of any special sacramental efficacy, but because of

---

[34] The conservative character of Eckhart is further underlined by the very fact that, rather than confront the ecclesiastical authorities of his day, he strenuously endeavored to have his case submitted to the Pope; also, he emphasized in his defense that he could not be a heretic as this involved willful intention, and he had no intention of introducing heretical innovations, his only aim being to expound the deeper meanings of orthodox doctrine. (See his defense in *Meister Eckhart: The Essential Sermons, Commentaries, Treatises, and Defence*, trans. E. Colledge, B. McGinn, SPCK, London 1981.) As argued above, this is perfectly intelligible if it be understood that mysticism involves transcendence of forms from within, and not a rupture of forms on the plane proper to them: the mystic transcends the boundaries of his religious tradition by plumbing its infinite essence and not breaking its outward forms. See O. Davies, *Meister Eckhart: Mystical Theologian*, pp. 65-68, for a discussion of the contrast between Eckhart's response to accusations of heresy with that of Margaret Porete, who openly subverted the forms of the Faith in the name of a higher truth and was burnt as a heretic in 1310.

[35] "Transformation of character" is deemed the prerequisite for a "spiritually fruitful transformation of consciousness." A. Huxley, *The Perennial Philosophy*, Chatto and Windus, London, 1946, p. 31.

the fact that "every thing, event, or thought is a point of intersection between creature and Creator."[36]

While both Eckhart and Ibn Arabi stress the need for perfecting the practice of the ritual dimension of religion, even while interpreting all rites according to their most transcendent symbolic associations, Shankara also upholds, albeit in a more qualified manner, the efficacy of the rites which are *arad-upakaraka*, remote auxiliaries to knowledge; rites, correctly performed, are "instrumental in extinguishing that demerit, arising from past sins, which obstructs knowledge of the Absolute." Only at a certain point, where ignorance is sufficiently overcome in the soul, are the external rites to be substituted by the supreme rite of the invocation of the sacred syllable, in which there is, contrary to the idea of Huxley, a special unitive grace.

There is, then, no support from this study for the type of "universalism" which posits an identity of the religious traditions on the grounds of the rejection of their respective ritual and dogmatic "superstructures." The conclusion here, on the contrary, is that the forms of the traditions may be seen as so many paths leading to a transcendent essence, realized as one by the mystics only at the summit of spiritual realization; short of this summit the differences between the traditions are to be seen as relative but nonetheless real on their own level. The forms of the traditions, at one in respect of their single and transcendent essence, are expressions of this essence, and, for this very reason, should be taken seriously as paths leading back to the essence, rather than rejected on the basis of their unavoidable relativity in the face of the Absolute. This conclusion is in accordance with the principles made explicit by Ibn Arabi in this study, and also with the universalist perspective associated chiefly with the name of Frithjof Schuon; his position on the relationship between the esoteric, universal essence and the exoteric, particular forms of religion is summed up thus:

> [E]soterism on the one hand prolongs exoterism—by harmoniously plumbing its depth—because the form expresses the essence and because in this respect the two enjoy solidarity, while on the other hand esoterism opposes exoterism—by transcending it abruptly—because the essence by virtue of its unlimitedness is of necessity not reducible to form.[37]

This esoteric essence is none other than the Absolute; and it is in the realization of the Absolute—which is One—that the mystics of the different

---

[36] Ibid., pp. 309-310.

[37] *Esoterism as Principle and as Way*, trans. W. Stoddart, Perennial Books, Bedfont, 1981, p. 26. This position is more fully elaborated in the chapter, "Transcendence and Universality of Esotericism," in Frithjof Schuon, *The Transcendent Unity of Religions*, pp. 48-79. For the importance given by Schuon to the role of the virtues in spiritual realization, see Part II of *Esoterism as Principle and as Way*, entitled: "Moral and Spiritual Life"; and for his understanding of the role of invocation as the principal—and universally practiced—means of realization, see *Stations of Wisdom*, trans. G.E.H. Palmer, John Murray, London, 1961, pp. 128-145.

religions can be seen to be at one; apart from or below this realization there may be similarities and differences but they are to be regarded as incidental in the measure that one's interest lies in the quintessence of the religious forms and in the realization of this quintessence. Judging by the pronouncements of the three great sages from different religious traditions who have been studied here, the summit of spiritual realization is conceived of in fundamentally similar terms: the transcendence of all finite conditioning—including, crucially, the individuality as such—entails the realization of the one and only Absolute; to the extent that this attainment—which cannot in the last analysis be identified as an "experience"—can be expressed analytically, it is said to consist in the realization of the Self as the undifferentiated Essence of pure Being, pure Consciousness, and pure Bliss.

# BIBLIOGRAPHY

1. SHANKARA:

Alston, A.J (trans.). *Samkara on the Creation*, Vol. II, Shanti Sadan, London, 1983.

——. *Samkara on the Soul*, Vol. III, Shanti Sadan, London, 1985.

——. *Samkara on the Absolute*, Vol. I, Shanti Sadan, London, 1987.

——. *Samkara on Discipleship*, Vol. V, Shanti Sadan, London, 1989.

——. *Samkara on Enlightenment*, Vol. VI, Shanti Sadan, London, 1989.

——. *The Thousand Teachings* (*Upadesa Sahasri*), Shanti Sadan, London, 1990.

Jagadananda, Swami (trans.). *A Thousand Teachings: Upadesa Sahasri*, Sri Ramakrishna Math, Madras, 1979.

Madhavananda, Swami (trans.). *Vivekachudamani*, Advaita Ashrama, Calcutta, 1957.

Nikhilananda, Swami (trans.). *The Mandukyopanisad with Gaudapada's Karika and Sankara's Commentary*, Sri Ramakrishna Ashrama, Mysore, 1974.

—— (trans.). *Self-Knowledge* (*Atma-Bodha*), Sri Ramakrishna Math, Madras, 1975.

"Raphael" (trans.). *Atma-Bodha*, Asram Vidya, Rome, 1986.

Sastry, A.M. (trans.). *The Bhagavad Gita with the Commentary of Sri Shankaracharya*, Samata Books, Madras, 1988.

Shastry, H.P. *Direct Experience of Reality* (*Verses from Aparokshanubhuti*), Shanti Sadan, London, 1985.

Tapasyananda, Swami (trans.). *The Sankara-dig-vijaya of Madhava-Vidyaranya*, Ramakrishna Mission, Madras, 1983.


2. IBN ARABI:

Addas, C. *Quest for the Red Sulphur: The Life of Ibn Arabi*, Islamic Texts Society, Cambridge, UK, 1993.

Austin, R (trans.). *The Bezels of Wisdom*, Paulist Press, New York, 1980.

Burckhardt, T (trans.). *La Sagesse des Prophètes*, Editions Albin Michel, Paris, 1955.

Chittick, W. *The Sufi Path of Knowledge*, SUNY, Albany, New York, 1989.

——. *Imaginal Worlds: Ibn al-'Arabi and the Problem of Religious Diversity*, SUNY, Albany, New York, 1994.

——. *The Self-Disclosure of God: Principles of Ibn al-'Arabi's Cosmology*, SUNY, Albany, New York, 1998.

—— (trans.). "Towards Sainthood: States and Stations," in Chodkiewicz, M. (ed.), *Les Illuminations de La Mecque*, Sindbad, Paris, 1988.

Chodkiewicz, M. *Seal of the Saints: Prophethood and Sainthood in the Doctrines of Ibn 'Arabi*, trans. Liadain Sherrard, Islamic Texts Society, Cambridge, 1993.

—— (ed.). *Les Illuminations de La Mecque*, Sindbad, Paris, 1988.

Corbin, H. *Creative Imagination in the Sufism of Ibn Arabi*, trans. R. Manheim, Princeton University Press, 1969.

Gril, D. (trans.). "Le terme du voyage," in Chodkiewicz, M. (ed.), *Les Illuminations de La Mecque*, Sindbad, Paris, 1988.

Harris, R.T (trans.). *Journey to the Lord of Power*, Inner Traditions, New York, 1981.

Hirtenstein, S. and Tiernan, M (eds.). *Muhyiddin Ibn Arabi: A Commemorative Volume*, Element Books, Dorset, 1993.

Izutsu, T. *Sufism and Taoism*, University of California Press, Berkeley, 1983.

Morris, J.W (trans.). "The Spiritual Ascension: Ibn Arabi and the *Mi'raj*," *Journal of the American Oriental Society*, Vol. 108, 1988.

———. "Ibn Arabi's Spiritual Ascension," in Chodkiewicz, M. (ed.), *Les Illuminations de La Mecque*, Sindbad, Paris, 1988.

Nicholson, R.A (trans.). *The Tarjuman Al-Ashwaq*, Royal Asiatic Society, 1978.

Valsan, M. *Le Livre de l'Extinction dans la Contemplation*, Les Editions de l'Oeuvre, Paris, 1984.

———. "Le Livre du Nom de Majesté," *Études Traditionnelles*, Jan-Feb, 1948, No. 265, July-Aug, 1948, No. 268, Dec, 1948, No. 272.

———. "Sur la notion de *Hal*," *Études Traditionnelles*, July-October, 1962, No. 372-373.

———. "La notion de *Chari'ah*," *Études Traditionnelles*, July-Oct, 1966, Nos. 396-397.

———. "Sur la notion de *Khalwah*," *Études Traditionnelles*, March-June, 1969, Nos. 412-413.


3. MEISTER ECKHART:

Colledge, E. and McGinn, B (trans.). *Meister Eckhart: The Essential Sermons, Commentaries, Treatises, and Defense*, SPCK, London, 1981.

Davies, O. *Meister Eckhart: Mystical Theologian*, SPCK, London, 1991.

Evans, C. De B (trans.). *Meister Eckhart* (vols. I-II), Watkins, London, 1947.

Forman, R.K.C. *Meister Eckhart: The Mystic as Theologian*, Element Books, Dorset, 1991.

Walshe. M.O'C (trans.). *Meister Eckhart: Sermons & Treatises* (vols. I-III), Element Books, Dorset, 1979.


4. GENERAL:

Allen, D. *Structure and Creativity in Religion*, Mouton, The Hague, 1978.

Barbosa da Silva, A. *The Phenomenology of Religion as a Philosophical Problem*, W.K. Gleerup, Uppsala, 1982.

Bianchi, V., Bleeker, C.J. and Bausani, A (eds.). *Problems and Methods of the History of Religion*, E.J. Brill, Leiden, 1972.

Chavchavadze, M. *Man's Concern with Holiness*, Hodder and Stoughton, 1972.

Eliade, M. *The Sacred and the Profane*, Brace and Co., Harcourt, U.S.A., 1959.

———. *Shamanism: Archaic Techniques of Ecstasy*, trans. W.R. Trask, Bollingen Series 76, New York, 1964.

———. *Yoga: Immortality and Freedom*, trans. W.R. Trask, Routledge, Kegan Paul, London 1969.

Eliade, M. and Kitagawa, J.M (eds.). *History of Religion*, University of Chicago Press, 1967.

Farber, M. *The Foundations of Phenomenology*, SUNY, Albany, New York, 1943.

Forman, R.K.C (ed.). *The Problem of Pure Consciousness*, Oxford University Press, 1990.

Gupta, M. *The Gospel of Sri Ramakrishna*, trans. Swami Nikhilananda, Ramakrishna-Vivekananda Center, New York, 1969.

Hawley, J.S. *Saints and Virtues*, University of California Press, 1987.

Husserl, E. *Cartesian Meditations*, Martinus Nijhoff, The Hague, 1960.

Huxley, A. *The Perennial Philosophy*, Chatto and Windus, London, 1946.

Katz, S.T (ed.). *Mysticism and Philosophical Analysis*, Sheldon Press, London, 1978.

—— (ed.). *Mysticism and Religious Traditions*, Oxford University Press, 1983.

—— (ed.). *Mysticism and Language*, Oxford University Press, 1992.

King, W. *Introduction to Religion: A Phenomenological Approach*, Harper and Row, New York, 1968.

Kockelmans, J.J (ed.). *Phenomenology*, Anchor Books, New York, 1967.

Kristensen, W.B. *The Meaning of Religion*, trans. J.B. Carman, Martinus Nijhoff, The Hague, 1971.

Lings, M. *A Sufi Saint of the Twentieth Century*, George Allen & Unwin, London, 1971.

——. *Muhammad*, Islamic Texts Society, Cambridge, UK/George Allen & Unwin, London, 1983.

Otto, R. *Mysticism: East and West*, Macmillan, New York, 1960.

Saradananda, S. *Sri Ramakrishna: The Great Master*, trans. Swami Jagadananda, Sri Ramakrishna Math, Madras, 1952.

Sells, Michael. *Mystical Languages of Unsaying*, University of Chicago Press, 1994.

Schuon, F. *The Transcendent Unity of Religions*, trans. P. Townsend, Faber and Faber, London, 1953.

——. *Stations of Wisdom*, trans. G.E.H. Palmer, World Wisdom Books, Bloomington, IN, 1995, pp. 121-145.

——. *Logic and Transcendence*, trans. P. Townsend, Perennial Books, Bedfont, 1975.

——. *Esoterism as Principle and as Way*, trans. W. Stoddart, Perennial Books, Bedfont, 1981.

Sharpe, E.J. *Comparative Religion*, Duckworth, London, 1975.

Sherry, P. *Spirit, Saints and Immortality*, Macmillan, London, 1984.

Smart, N. *Reasons and Faith: An Investigation of Religious Discourse, Christian and Non-Christian*, Routledge and Kegan Paul, London, 1958.

Smith, J.E. *Experience and God*, Oxford University Press, 1968.

Smith, Q. "An Analysis of Holiness," *Religious Studies*, Vol. 24, No. 4, 1988.

Staal, F. *Exploring Mysticism*, Penguin, Harmondsworth, 1975.

Stace, W.T. *Mysticism and Philosophy*, MacMillan, London, 1961.

Suzuki, D.T. *Mysticism: Christian and Buddhist*, George Allen & Unwin, London, 1979.

Van Baaren, Th.P. and Drijvers, H.J.M (eds.). *Religion, Culture, and Methodology*, Mouton, The Hague, 1973.

Waardenberg, J. *Reflections on the Study of Religion*, Mouton, The Hague, 1978.

Zaehner, R.C. *Mysticism: Sacred and Profane*, Oxford University Press, 1961.

# BIOGRAPHICAL NOTE

**REZA SHAH-KAZEMI** is a Research Associate at the Institute of Ismaili Studies, London. His areas of research are Comparative Religion, Islamic Studies, Shi'i Studies, and Sufism. He has edited, translated, and written numerous books and articles, including *Doctrines of Shi'i Islam* (London, 2001), *Avicenna, Prince of Physicians* (London, 1997), *Algeria: Revolution Revisited* (London, 1997), *Turkey: The Pendulum Swings Back* (London, 1996), *Bosnia: Destruction of a Nation, Inversion of a Principle* (London, 1996), and *Crisis in Chechnia* (London, 1995). Currently in preparation for publication are: *The Other in the Light of the One: Unity, Universality, and Dialogue in the Qur'an* (London, 2006) and *Justice and Remembrance: An Introduction to the Spirituality of Imam Ali* (London, 2006). At present he is engaged on a new, annotated English translation of Imam Ali's *Nahj al-balagha*.

# INDEX

For a glossary of all key foreign words used in books published by World Wisdom,
including metaphysical terms in English, consult:
www.DictionaryofSpiritualTerms.org.
This on-line Dictionary of Spiritual Terms provides extensive definitions, examples and
related terms in other languages.

# Other Titles on Christianity
# by World Wisdom

*Christian Spirit,*
edited by Judith Fitzgerald and Michael Oren Fitzgerald, 2004

*The Destruction of the Christian Tradition: Updated and Revised,*
by Rama P. Coomaraswamy, 2006

*For God's Greater Glory: Gems of Jesuit Spirituality,*
edited by Jean-Pierre Lafouge, 2006

*The Foundations of Christian Art: Illustrated,*
by Titus Burckhardt, edited by Michael Oren Fitzgerald, 2006

*The Fullness of God: Frithjof Schuon on Christianity,*
selected and edited by James S. Cutsinger, 2004

*In the Heart of the Desert: The Spirituality of the Desert Fathers and Mothers,*
by John Chryssavgis, 2003

*Not of This World: A Treasury of Christian Mysticism,*
compiled and edited by James S. Cutsinger, 2003

*Paths to the Heart: Sufism and the Christian East,*
edited by James S. Cutsinger, 2002

*Paths to Transcendence: According to*
*Shankara, Ibn Arabi and Meister Eckhart,*
by Reza Shah-Kazemi, 2006

*The Sermon of All Creation: Christians on Nature,*
edited by Judith Fitzgerald and Michael Oren Fitzgerald, 2005

*Ye Shall Know the Truth: Christianity and the Perennial Philosophy,*
edited by Mateus Soares de Azevedo, 2005

# Other Titles on Hinduism
# by World Wisdom

*The Essential Sri Anandamayi Ma,*
by Alexander Lipsky and Sri Anandamayi Ma, 2007

*The Essential Swami Ramdas: Commemorative Edition,*
compiled by Susunaga Weeraperuma, 2005

*The Essential Vedanta: A New Source Book of Advaita Vedanta,*
edited by Eliot Deutsch and Rohit Dalvi, 2004

*A Guide to Hindu Spirituality,*
by Arvind Sharma, 2006

*Hinduism and Buddhism,*
by Ananda K. Coomaraswamy, 2007

*Introduction to Hindu Dharma: The 68th Jagadguru of Kanchipuram,*
edited by Michael Oren Fitzgerald, 2007

*Lamp of Non-Dual Knowledge & Cream of Liberation:*
*Two Jewels of Indian Wisdom,*
translated by Swami Sri Ramanananda Saraswathi, 2003

*Paths to Transcendence: According to*
*Shankara, Ibn Arabi, and Meister Eckhart,*
by Reza Shah-Kazemi, 2006

*Timeless in Time: Sri Ramana Maharshi,*
by A.R. Natarajan, 2006

*Tripura Rahasya: The Secret of the Supreme Goddess,*
translated by Swami Sri Ramanananda Saraswathi, 2002

*Unveiling the Garden of Love: Mystical Symbolism in*
*Layla Majnun & Gitagovinda,*
by Lalita Sinha, 2007

## Other Titles on Islam
## by World Wisdom

*Islam, Fundamentalism, and the Betrayal of Tradition:*
*Essays by Western Muslim Scholars,*
edited by Joseph E. B. Lumbard, 2004

*The Mystics of Islam,*
by Reynold A. Nicholson, 2002

*The Path of Muhammad: A Book on Islamic Morals*
*and Ethics by Imam Birgivi,*
interpreted by Shaykh Tosun Bayrak, 2005

*Paths to the Heart: Sufism and the Christian East,*
edited by James S. Cutsinger, 2003

*Paths to Transcendence: According to*
*Shankara, Ibn Arabi and Meister Eckhart,*
by Reza Shah-Kazemi, 2006

*The Sufi Doctrine of Rumi: Illustrated Edition,*
by William C. Chittick, 2005

*Sufism: Love and Wisdom,*
edited by Jean-Louis Michon and Roger Gaetani, 2006

*Sufism: Veil and Quintessence*
*A New Translation with Selected Letters,*
by Frithjof Schuon, 2007

*Tierno Bokar: The Sufi Sage from Mali,*
by Amadou Hampaté Ba, translated by Fatima Jane Casewit, 2007

*Understanding Islam,*
by Frithjof Schuon, 1994

*The Universal Spirit of Islam:*
*From the Koran and Hadith,*
edited by Judith Fitzgerald and Michael Oren Fitzgerald, 2006